Beginning Web Programming using VB.NET & Visual Studio .NET

Craig Bowes

Daniel Cazzulino

Mike Clark

Chris Hart

Neil Raybould

Tobin Titus

Wrox Press Ltd. ®

Beginning Web Programming
using VB.NET & Visual Studio .NET

First printed September 2002

Published by Wrox Press Ltd,
Arden House, 1102 Warwick Road, Acocks Green,
Birmingham, B27 6BH, UK
Printed in the USA
ISBN 1-86100-736-1

Trademark Acknowledgments

Credits

Authors
Craig Bowes
Daniel Cazzulino
Mike Clark
Chris Hart
Neil Raybould
Tobin Titus

Additional Material
Elma Alvarez

Project Manager
Claire Robinson

Commisioning Editor
Paul Jeffcoat

Technical Editors
Ewan Buckingham
Mankee Cheng
Richard Deeson
Michelle Everitt
Chris Hart
Jon Hill

Managing Editor
Laurent Lafon

Technical Reviewers
Carl Burnham
Robin Dewson
Don Lee
Scott Robertson
Ken Slovak
David Schultz
Tobin Titus

Author Agent
Nicola Phillips

Production Coordinator
Neil Lote

Illustrations
Neil Lote

Proof Reader
Chris Smith

Cover
Natalie O'Donnell

Indexers
Martin Brooks
John Collin
Andrew Criddle

About the Authors

Craig Bowes

Craig Bowes lives in Fort Worth, Texas with his wife and son, and works for an electronics distributor doing web programming for its online catalog and intranet web sites. He started his interest in computers in 4th grade where he learned to program in BASIC on the Commodore PET and later on with the Commodore 64, a gift from his parents. After a long stretch without owning or using a computer outside of school, he rekindled his interest when he took a required English course on web development at the University of Texas at Arlington. He began his IT career teaching training classes in software applications, web design, and HTML. Since then, he has worked professionally in web development for 6 years and has programmed in Basic, Pascal, Java, JavaScript, ASP, ColdFusion, SQL, Visual Basic, and C#. He enjoys reading and writing science fiction, fantasy, and poetry as well as cooking Italian food. Craig also enjoys drinking too much coffee!

> *I would like to thank Ryan O'Keefe for introducing me to Wrox and .NET, my friend Ashe Richards for getting me turned on to web programming, and my wife Tricia for putting up with my long nights in front of the computer.*

Daniel Cazzulino

Daniel Cazzulino is a senior developer who discovered C# and the .NET Framework early in the Beta process, although this is a Visual Basic .NET book :o). He has been working for many years in distributed solutions based on Windows DNA, COM/COM+, and VB, and is now dedicated full time to the new platform. He runs his own company in Buenos Aires, *DEVerest*, specializing in .NET technologies, and is a regular contributor to Wrox publications and sites.

He is a big fan of computers, the W3C, and everything related to XML and the Internet (for work, learning, and fun). When he is not coding furiously, he is thinking of innovative techniques to rediscover the wheel and eventually some day will come up with a fairly original idea. The Open Source movement caught his interest too, and he actually manages a SourceForge project called *NMatrix*, which also honors the best movie he has seen (countless times) in his entire life (Reloaded and Revolutions aren't out yet ;o)). He might seem crazy, but his hobby is... COMPUTERS! From time to time, he tortures his friends playing paddle, bowling, pool, paintball, and even chess with them!

You can reach Daniel at dcazzulino@hotmail.com, or though his company's web site, www.devrest.com.ar.

> *To my wife, to whom I owe everything I am, who believed, encouraged, and supported me always, even through the toughest decisions. To my family, who gave me the best advice and all the love I hope to be able to give myself. Last, but definitely not least, to my father, who has been the greatest model to follow in my life; I hope to become half the man he is some day.*

Mike Clark

Mike Clark, who can be reached at mikec@lucin.com, currently works with *Lucin*, a research and development company that dedicates itself to web services and Visual Studio .NET technologies. Mike is responsible for www.salcentral.com, www.uddiregistrar.com, and several other web services web sites, each of which is starting to enjoy some considerable success in respect to subscribers and industry recognition.

Chris Hart

Chris is currently an editor and part-time in-house author at Wrox. She lives in Birmingham (that's UK, not Alabama), in a house full of computers. After gaining a BEng (Hons) in Mechanical Engineering at university, she moved into network administration and end-user training for a while. Moving to Wrox re-awakened her love of programming, and in the three years since joining, Chris has been working for the most part with ASP and ASP.NET and associated technologies. In her spare time, Chris can either be found down at the gym, playing with code, or looking for obscure cabling at computer fairs. Chris authored chapters in *Beginning ASP.NET 1.0* under her maiden name, Chris Goode. She recently married Java and Visual Basic .NET author James Hart.

Thanks to James for all his support and for reminding me that there is more to life than computers.

Neil Raybould

Neil Raybould is working as a software developer for *Development Dimensions International*, just south of Pittsburgh, Pennsylvania. He has given several presentations on ASP- and ASP.NET-related topics in the Pittsburgh area. Neil received a BS from Virginia Tech, an MBA from Duquesne University, and holds MCSD and MCDBA certifications.

To My Savior, the Lord Jesus Christ. Thank you for the abilities You have given me and the opportunities to use them. May You always be pleased with their results.

To my wife, Vicky. You are such a joy to me. Thank you so much for your encouragement.

To my daughter, Abby. We are incredibly thankful to have you as part of our family.

Tobin Titus

Tobin is currently working as a contractor/consultant in the Charlotte area. As an MCSD, Tobin finds his specialty in web application development and Microsoft solutions. He got his first taste of programming in 5th grade writing mostly in BASIC on an Atari-800XL computer. In the few years since then, Tobin has authored and reviewed publications for *Wrox Press* and has been invited to speak at several events. In his spare time, Tobin enjoys motorcycles, art, and shooting guns.

Special thanks to the geeks and crew in Response.Riders – Aaron "The General" Brown, Jason "QVC" Irvin , and James "Captain Colgate" Kinninger. Life at AIMCO wouldn't have been as fun without you. Thanks to comedian, Christopher Titus, for having that TV show – now all the telemarketers know how to pronounce "Titus". Thanks to the kind folks at Wrox – Cil, Paul, Claire, and Nicola for inviting me in on this project.

Solut...
BM   Refer...   System...
                  System.Dat...
                  System.Drawing
                  System.Web
                  System.XML
            AssemblyInfo.vb
      Assembly...
      BM.vsdisco
      Global.asax
      Styles.css
      Web.config
      WebForm1.aspx

WebForm1.aspx*   WebForm1.aspx.v

ebForm1.aspx*

Table of Contents

Table of Contents

Table of Contents

Table of Contents

Solut...
BM
Reference
System...
System.Dat...
System.Drawing
System.Web
System.XML
AssemblyInfo.vb
Assembly
BM.vsdisco
Global.asax
Styles.css
Web.config
WebForm1.aspx
WebForm1.aspx.v
WebForm1.aspx* | WebForm1.aspx.v
ebForm1.aspx*

Introduction

Before the world of .NET, web programming was a job for scripters who'd create ASP pages using a script language (mostly VBScript) to add any server-side code. VB6 coders would either be restricted to writing COM components that the ASP guys could make use of, or they'd be developing Windows software. With .NET, Visual Basic developers can transfer their skills to the Web with ease, because developing a web application is now very similar to developing a Windows application.

The class libraries in the .NET Framework are structured so that whether we develop desktop applications or web applications, the methodology we use is the same. ASP.NET, the .NET web development technology, is really just a series of classes in the .NET Framework, in exactly the same way as the Windows Forms classes. From this perspective, web development shouldn't be too much of a leap.

Yet there are some major differences that we need to consider when we develop for the Web. We are no longer talking about applications running on individual machines, we're talking about hosting an application on a central server, ready to be accessed by hundreds or thousands of clients every hour. The problem domain is now quite different, as we are more concerned with performance and scalability issues to ensure that the end-user experience is as smooth as possible.

Getting our heads around the issues involved in web development is a core part of learning how to develop applications for the web, but with these principles clear in our minds, we can then consider how to actually build our applications.

Who Is this Book For?

If you are a developer with experience of writing desktop applications in Visual Basic .NET who's thinking of moving into web development, then this book is for you. This book assumes you know Visual Basic syntax and coding techniques, and will apply those skills to creating fully-functional web applications. We'll walk you through examples that will highlight the differences and similarities between web applications and desktop applications, and give you the knowledge you need to get started with programming web applications. You don't even need to have extensive knowledge of HTML, because the Visual Studio .NET IDE will give you the ability to create applications by using the same drag-and-drop functionality you'll have encountered when writing Windows Form applications.

What Does this Book Cover?

This book is designed such that at the end of each chapter you will feel confident with a different aspect of web programming in .NET. The chapters in this book can be summarized as follows:

Chapter 1 – *Web Programming and ASP.NET:* This chapter introduces the technologies that lie behind the Web, how server-side web applications work, and how ASP.NET fits into the picture. We'll walk you through a simple ASP.NET application and look at some of the core features of ASP.NET applications. We'll also walk through the installation of MSDE, the Microsoft SQL Server Desktop Engine, which contains some sample databases that we'll work with later in the book.

Chapter2 – *Web Forms:* We move on from the theoretical approach and take a look at how we can create basic ASP.NET web forms using Visual Studio .NET, taking you through the creation of your first ASP.NET application. We'll also look at how web forms are processed and the life cycle of a page.

Chapter 3 – *User Interfaces and Server Controls:* This chapter introduces the core part of any web form, the server control. These controls can be dragged and dropped onto web forms in exactly the same way as Windows Forms controls, and we can add code to our forms to interact with these controls. We'll look at how we can use server controls in our applications, how to create user controls to encapsulate common elements in our applications, and generating content dynamically.

Chapter 4 – *ADO.NET:* Almost every application, at some point, will rely on data held in some kind of data store, whether it be a full-scale database or a simple formatted text file. This chapter introduces the technology we need to use to access data from our web applications, and shows how we can display it in our applications, giving us the ability to edit, create, and delete data.

Chapter 5 – *Data Binding:* Accessing data is all very well, but we need to be able to display it on our pages in a user-friendly manner. By binding data from our data source to controls on our web forms, we can easily display data that we can work with. This chapter will also discuss how to apply templates to our web forms to alter the look and feel of our data-bound controls.

Chapter 6 – *Debugging and Error Handling in Web Applications:* Debugging and error handling are two of the least glamorous and least enjoyable aspects of programming. No one enjoys making mistakes, and fixing them is rarely fun. However, thorough testing and debugging are critical stages of the development lifecycle that should not be neglected. Fortunately, Visual Studio .NET provides the same robust and friendly tools for web programming that it does for Windows programming. We'll look at how we can use these tools to debug our applications, and how to handle errors that occur in such a way that our user will barely notice that they happened.

Chapter 7 – *ASP.NET Applications, Sessions, and State:* The web is a stateless medium and by default, we have no mechanism to keep track of which users are which, or what information has been passed to any particular user. Clearly, it is useful for our applications to retain pieces of information as our users move from page to page – who they are, what fields they have filled out so far, and so on – but in order to do that, we need to be able to store information at some global level, and identify it as belonging to one user or another. In this chapter we'll look at how we can maintain state on an application level and on a session level, as well as how we can work with global events in our code.

Chapter 8 – *XML and Web Development:* XML is becoming increasingly important, as widespread Internet connectivity becomes the norm. Applications running on separate machines can now work in tandem on related tasks, and implicit in that ability is a requirement for a universally understood and standard format for the exchange of information. XML was devised largely in answer to this need. In this chapter we'll look at how XML fits into the .NET Framework and how we can use it in our web applications.

Chapter 9 – *Web Services in Web Applications:* A web service is a very powerful tool for anyone wanting to communicate application functionality using specific standards and protocols over the Internet. What this actually means is that we can use a web service in our code as if it were a component on our system, even though it actually exists over the Internet. This chapter will describe how to consume existing services, and how to create our own web services.

Chapter 10 – *The Role of the Web Server:* Whenever we create a new web project in Visual Studio .NET, numerous files and settings are created and applied automatically, including the setting up of our web applications onto a web server. This chapter examines how the web server works, and how we can configure it beyond the defaults. We'll look at how users are authenticated on our web server, and how we can limit access to our applications depending on who our users are.

Chapter 11 – *ASP.NET Authentication, Authorization, and Security:* The role of security in an application is related to the need to restrict the ability of a user to access certain resources, or to perform certain actions. For example, a web application may offer administrative tools that must be accessed only by authorized users, or some information that's restricted to registered users. This chapter will look at the tools available to us in ASP.NET for authenticating and authorizing users of our applications.

Chapter 12 – *Performance and Scalablity:* The title of this chapter alone implies that performance and scalability go hand in hand, and indeed they do. However, it is important to note that while these two topics are often discussed together, they differ greatly in definition. This chapter will set out to give you a brief explanation of what these terms mean, how they differ from each other, and how they work together. Additionally, we'll give you a few tips and tricks to help you measure performance and design scalable web applications.

Chapter 13 – *Publishing Web Applications in .NET:* There are a number of techniques and methods for installing .NET client applications, web services, user controls, and so on. In this, the final chapter, we'll examine the architecture of web applications and web services, as they appear on our customers' machines, and we'll look at creating and customizing a Web Setup project in Visual Studio .NET. This chapter will give you a good understanding of how to get the web applications you've developed into the hands of your clients, with the minimum of fuss.

What Do I Need to Use this Book?

In order to run the samples in this book, you need to have installed IIS on a Windows 2000 or XP machine, and you need to install the .NET Framework, which comes with Visual Basic .NET Standard Edition or higher. IIS is installed on Windows 2000 and XP Professional as an optional component, and has to be installed after the operating system has finished installing. If you need to, you can install IIS via the Add/Remove Programs applet that can be found in the Windows Control Panel. IIS must be installed prior to installing Visual Studio .NET in order for ASP.NET applications to work correctly.

Conventions

We've used a number of different styles of text and layout in this book to help differentiate between the different kinds of information. Here are examples of the styles we used and an explanation of what they mean.

Code has several styles. If it's a word that we're talking about in the text – for example, when discussing a For...Next loop, it's in this font. If it's a block of code that can be typed as a program and run, then it's also in a gray box:

```
<asp:TextBox id="txtNameBox" runat="server" />
<asp:Button id="btnSubmit" onclick="btnSubmit_Click"
                    runat="server" Text="Click Here!" />
```

Sometimes we'll see code in a mixture of styles, like this:

```
Private Sub calDates_SelectionChanged(ByVal sender As System.Object, _
        ByVal e As System.EventArgs) Handles calDates.SelectionChanged
   lblMessage.Text = _
        "Current Date: " & calDates.SelectedDate.ToLongDateString()
End Sub
```

When this happens, the code with a white background is code we are already familiar with; the line highlighted in gray is a new addition to the code since we last looked at it.

Advice, hints, and background information come in this type of font.

> **Important pieces of information come in boxes like this.**

Bullets appear indented, with each new bullet marked as follows:

- ❑ **Important Words** are in a bold type font.
- ❑ Words that appear on the screen, or in menus like **File** or **Window**, are in a similar font to the one you would see on a Windows desktop.
- ❑ Keys that you press on the keyboard like *Ctrl* and *Enter*, are in italics.

Customer Support

We always value hearing from our readers, and we want to know what you think about this book: what you liked, what you didn't like, and what you think we can do better next time. You can send us your comments, either by returning the reply card in the back of the book, or by e-mail to feedback@wrox.com. Please be sure to mention the book title in your message.

How to Download the Sample Code for the Book

When you visit the Wrox site, http://www.wrox.com/, simply locate the title through our Search facility or by using one of the title lists. Click on Download in the Code column, or on Download Code on the book's detail page.

When you click to download the code for this book, you are presented with a page with three options:

❑ If you are already a member of the Wrox Developer Community (if you have already registered on ASPToday, C#Today or Wroxbase), you can log in with your usual username and password combination to receive your code.

❑ If you are not already a member, you are asked if you would like to register for free code downloads. In addition you will also be able to download several free articles from Wrox Press. Registering will allow us to keep you informed about updates and new editions of this book.

❑ The third option is to bypass registration completely and simply download the code.

Registration for code download is not mandatory for this book, but should you wish to register for your code download, your details will not be passed to any third party. For more details, you may wish to view our terms and conditions, which are linked from the download page.

Once you reach the code download section, you will find that the files that are available for download from our site have been archived using WinZip. When you have saved the files to a folder on your hard drive, you will need to extract the files using a de-compression program such as WinZip or PKUnzip. When you extract the files, the code is usually extracted into chapter folders. When you start the extraction process, ensure your software (WinZip, PKUnzip, etc.) is set to use folder names.

Errata

We've made every effort to make sure that there are no errors in the text or in the code. However, no one is perfect and mistakes do occur. If you find an error in one of our books, like a spelling mistake or a faulty piece of code, we would be very grateful for feedback. By sending in errata you may save another reader hours of frustration, and of course, you will be helping us provide even higher quality information. Simply e-mail the information to support@wrox.com, where your information will be checked and, if correct, posted to the errata page for that title, or used in subsequent editions of the book.

To find errata on the web site, go to http://www.wrox.com/, and simply locate the title through our Advanced Search or title list. Click on the Book Errata link, which is below the cover graphic on the book's detail page.

E-mail Support

If you wish to directly query a problem in the book with an expert who knows the book in detail then e-mail support@wrox.com, with the title of the book and the last four numbers of the ISBN in the subject field of the e-mail. A typical e-mail should include the following things:

- The **title of the book, last four digits of the ISBN (7361)**, and **page number** of the problem in the Subject field.

- Your **name**, **contact information**, and the **problem** in the body of the message.

We **won't** send you junk mail. We need the details to save your time and ours. When you send an e-mail message, it will go through the following chain of support:

- Customer Support – Your message is delivered to our customer support staff, who are the first people to read it. They have files on most frequently asked questions and will answer anything general about the book or the web site immediately.

- Editorial – Deeper queries are forwarded to the technical editor responsible for that book. They have experience with the programming language or particular product, and are able to answer detailed technical questions on the subject.

- The Authors – Finally, in the unlikely event that the editor cannot answer your problem, they will forward the request to the author. We do try to protect the author from any distractions to their writing; however, we are quite happy to forward specific requests to them. All Wrox authors help with the support on their books. They will e-mail the customer and the editor with their response, and again all readers should benefit.

The Wrox Support process can only offer support to issues that are directly pertinent to the content of our published title. Support for questions that fall outside the scope of normal book support is provided via the community lists of our http://p2p.wrox.com/ forum.

p2p.wrox.com

For author and peer discussion join the P2P mailing lists. Our unique system provides **programmer to programmer**™ contact on mailing lists, forums, and newsgroups, all in addition to our one-to-one e-mail support system. If you post a query to P2P, you can be confident that it is being examined by the many Wrox authors and other industry experts who are present on our mailing lists. At p2p.wrox.com you will find a number of different lists that will help you, not only while you read this book, but also as you develop your own applications. Particularly appropriate to this book are the aspx and aspx_professional lists in the .NET category of the web site.

To subscribe to a mailing list just follow these steps:

1. Go to http://p2p.wrox.com/

2. Choose the appropriate category from the left menu bar

3. Click on the mailing list you wish to join

4. Follow the instructions to subscribe and fill in your e-mail address and password

5. Reply to the confirmation e-mail you receive

6. Use the subscription manager to join more lists and set your e-mail preferences

Why this System Offers the Best Support

You can choose to join the mailing lists or you can receive them as a weekly digest. If you don't have the time, or facilities, to receive the mailing list, then you can search our online archives. Junk and spam mails are deleted, and your own e-mail address is protected by the unique Lyris system. Queries about joining or leaving lists, and any other general queries about lists, should be sent to listsupport@p2p.wrox.com.

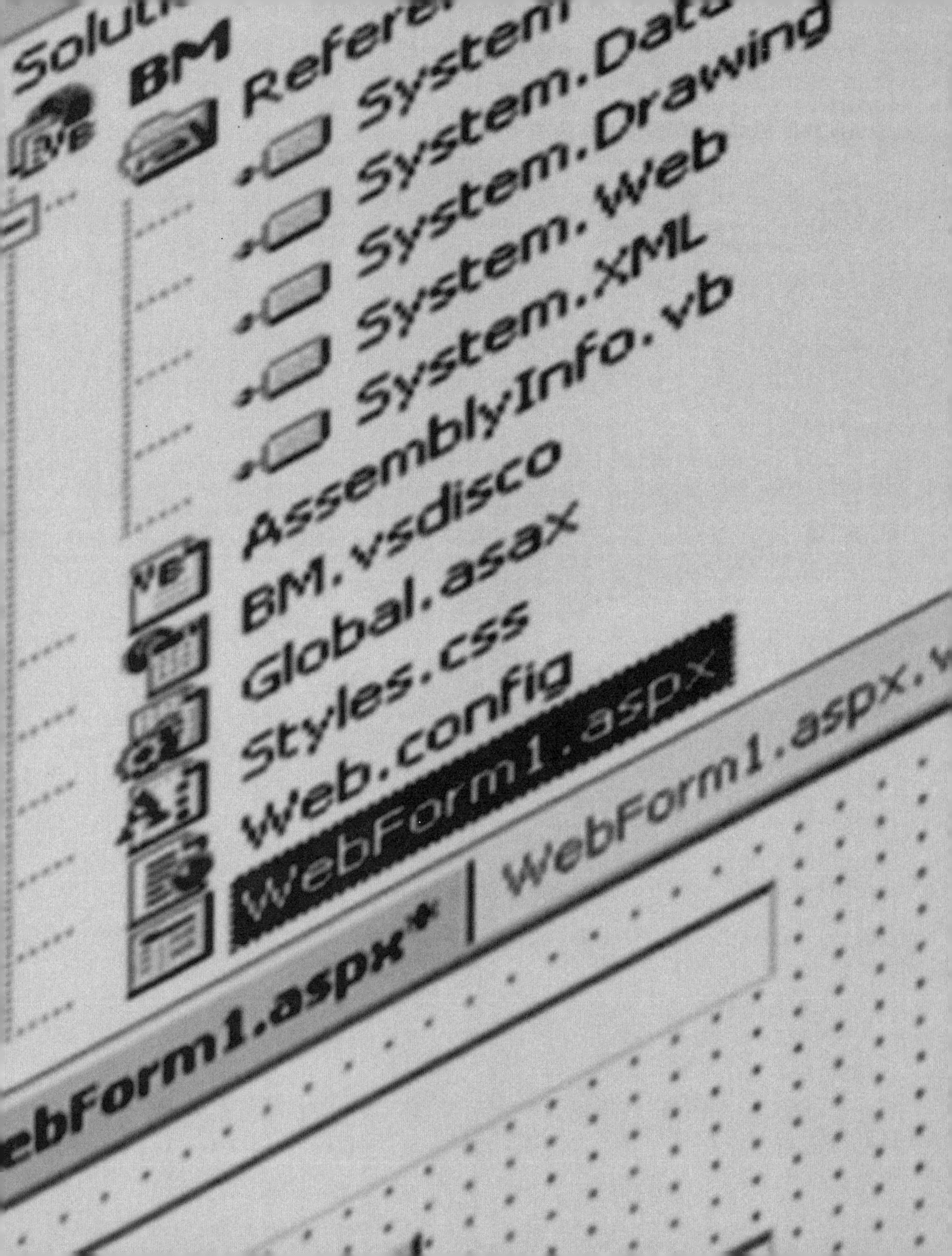

Soluti...

BM

Referen...

System...

System.Dat...

System.Drawing

System. Web

System.XML

AssemblyInfo.vb

Assembly

BM.vsdisco

Global.asax

Styles.css

Web.config

WebForm1.aspx

WebForm1.aspx.v...

WebForm1.aspx* | WebForm1.aspx.v...

ebForm1.aspx*

Web Programming and ASP.NET

With Visual Basic .NET, Visual Studio .NET, and ASP.NET, creating web applications is no more difficult than creating Windows applications. No, really; it's true. You see, when Microsoft created the .NET Framework class library, it produced two significant results. First, by bringing all manner of different functionality together under the same umbrella, it made your choice of programming language for Windows development largely irrelevant: the features of the library are available to Visual Basic, C#, C++, and so on – you knew that already. But second, the very act of creating the library forced Microsoft to rationalize the functionality it contains, so that it's available to programmers in a consistent and predictable way – and that's the key to the bold statement we were able to make above.

Of course, things are never *quite* that straightforward – this book wouldn't have much to say if they were – and there are plenty of new things that you need to learn about in order to become an effective web application programmer. But as you'll see, the development process itself is little different from the one that you employ when you're creating a Windows application.

Throughout this book, we'll be taking what you know about programming using Visual Basic .NET and Visual Studio .NET, and showing you how to apply it to creating web sites with ASP.NET. In this first chapter, we'll start by demystifying the world of web programming, and looking at how precisely how web applications work, introducing **.NET web applications** along the way. Specifically, we will cover:

- ❑ What we mean by a web application, and the roles of the client and the server

- ❑ The differences between Windows applications and web applications

- ❑ The technologies available for web development today, and how requests for pages are communicated to the server, and responses sent to the client

- ❑ .NET web applications, and how web forms development is similar to Windows forms development

- ❑ What ASP.NET is, the classes in the .NET Framework that it uses, and how it works with the web server

- ❑ The constituent parts of a .NET web application, and how we can encapsulate functionality

This chapter aims to get you up to speed with a lot of the theory behind web applications, to get you to the point where you feel comfortable with the main issues involved in .NET web development. We'll be introducing terminology that will be used throughout the book, and discussing how the web applications that you're already familiar with actually work behind the scenes – and how they could be put together using .NET. Let's get started by looking in general terms at what web applications *are*.

Web Programming Fundamentals

With the global explosion of interest in the Internet, developers all over the world are creating web sites, sharing information via e-mail or peer-to-peer applications, transferring files, and much more. With so many computers all over the world able to access the same information, giving us the ability to send an e-mail that arrives within seconds to a relative living on the other side of the world, imagining the sorts of technologies that *enable* all of this can be a bit daunting. Let's start in terms of some concepts you're familiar with, and build from there.

What are Web Applications?

We've already mentioned "web applications" a couple of times, but if the terminology sounds confusing, the reality certainly isn't. Let's consider a real-life web application: eBay, the online auction web site.

The aim of this example is to explain what actually *happens when you request a page, and how the visible output you see after requesting a page relates to the code that's used to create it. It might seem simplistic at first, but we'll soon start getting our teeth into it.*

How do we use a web application? First of all, we start up a browser window, enter the address of the site (http://www.eBay.com) into the address bar of the browser, and either click a Go button or hit *Enter*. Depending on the speed of your connection to the Internet, eventually you should see the following page:

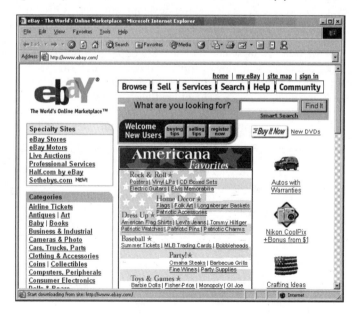

This is the front page of the eBay web site. On this page, you can see links to areas of the site that may be of interest, such as a place where we can update our user profile, and featured offers that we might be interested in purchasing. On clicking one of these links, we'll be sent to a different page, which might display information about a particular group of items, or provide a 'login' section where we can amend some information that eBay has stored about us.

Now let's look at what *exactly* has taken place over the course of this apparently simple procedure.

The Role of the Server

We might be 'browsing' the eBay site from our computer, but that's obviously not where all the information we're looking at has come from. Rather, the text, the images, and the database that holds the details about the items that eBay has for sale, all reside on the **server**. (In reality, a site like eBay is likely to involve a large number of servers in order to deal with the sheer volume of clients that visit it, but metaphorically speaking, the code and data for the site is all held "on the server".)

> *When we refer to "the server" in this chapter, we could be talking about a single web server machine, or many working together to share processing load and improve performance.*

Server-Side Code

When you look at a web page in your browser window, most of what you're looking at – the links and images, and so forth – is the browser's representation of the HTML code that has been sent to you by the server. If you select a category from the eBay site – for example, Musical Instruments – you'll see a list of the instruments that are currently available for sale. But what if an item has just been sold? How does the site stay up-to-date with information on the time left to bid on each item? The answer comes from server-side code.

When we write **server-side code**, we can specify that when someone looks for Musical Instruments, the database should be searched for relevant items. Those items, sorted by parameters specified by the user, will be retrieved from the database **dynamically**, resulting in a slightly different result each time we ask to see the page. If we were to request the same web page an hour later, some of the items that were listed previously may have been sold, and some new items may have been added. The *code* on the server remains the same, in that it issues the same query to the database, but the *results* – the HTML code that gets sent back to the browser – will vary according to what we are looking for, and when we are looking for it.

The Role of the Client

Usually, when we talk about the **client**, we're referring to the web browser that runs on our computer – for example, Internet Explorer, Netscape, Mozilla, Opera, etc. In general, these browsers simply attempt to display the HTML code that is sent to them. They don't communicate with the database on the server, so they can't access the personal details we've been talking about, or the details about a specific item. Most of the time, clients just do what they're told to do.

Web Applications vs. Windows Applications

From all that we've said so far, we can begin to form a picture of how web applications work. When we open our browser to view a web application, we're using a tool that has no knowledge at all of the application it is attempting to access. Regardless of whether server-side code is being used, or plain HTML files are being sent, no installation is required on the client before the web application can be viewed. This is the model of the Web.

Contrast this with the behavior of a typical Windows application, in which most of the code that controls what the user sees must be installed on the client, while the server – if there's a server – tends to be used as little more than a data store.

Now, in different situations, both of these solutions have merit, but our interest here lies in understanding how on earth it might be possible to use similar development techniques to create these very different-sounding application types – something that we promised was true at the beginning of the chapter. The trick, if you want to call it that, is to realize that when we're developing a Windows application with Visual Basic .NET in Visual Studio .NET, we create **Windows forms** that make up the interface of that application. When we develop an ASP.NET application with Visual Basic .NET in Visual Studio .NET, the **web forms** that we create define what the interface of the application *will* look like, when it arrives at a browser.

To put some flesh on these bones, you'll surely agree that the following screenshot contains a fairly typical example of a Windows application in development:

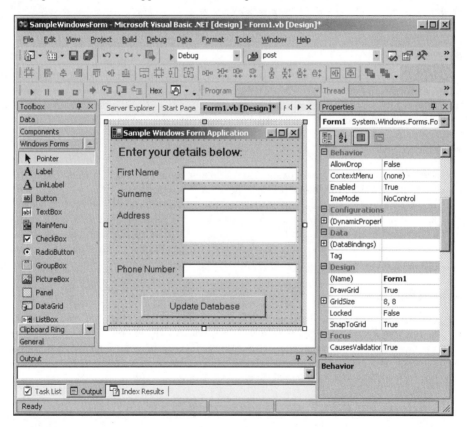

You might imagine using a form like this as part of a data-driven application, to enter or amend the details of a user in a database. But the key point here is that a similar ASP.NET application in development can look like this:

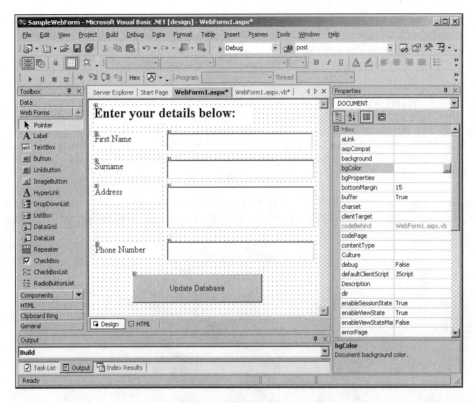

As you can see, the design-time view of this example is quite similar to that of a Windows form. We have similar controls available in our **Toolbox**, and we've arranged the controls on the form so that their position resembles the controls of the Windows form too. Furthermore, running both applications results in similar output:

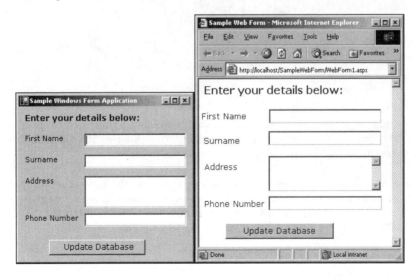

The major difference between these two applications is how they are run. For the Windows application, the code that generates the user interface resides and runs on the same machine; for the web application, that code resides and runs on the server – we just browse it on the client. However, the functionality that the user sees is very similar, as is the code that produces it, as we will see later.

Web Technology Today

Having talked a little about how web applications work, and their similarity to Windows applications in the Visual Studio .NET IDE, we now need to look in a little more detail at the processes that take place when a web application is up and running. In this way, we can start to understand what ASP.NET must be able to do, and therefore something about its nature.

We know that by entering a URL into the address bar of a browser window, we can surf and navigate among web sites, but what actually happens when we hit *Enter* or click a Go button? Let's take a quick look at the process that takes place when a web page is requested:

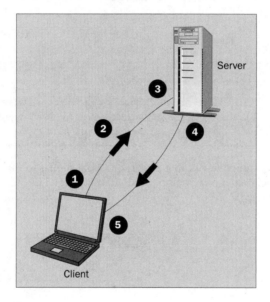

Here's what happens at each stage:

1. The end user enters a web address and initiates a request. The request is formatted as an **HTTP request**, which contains specific and important information describing the page it requires, including the type of client accessing the page.

2. The request is passed across the network until it reaches the web server that **hosts** the page that was asked for. When requesting a page over the Internet, the actual route taken by the request depends on the network conditions at the time. Two requests for the same page may take different routes along the way, due to the way the Internet works.

3. The server receives and then reads the information in the incoming HTTP request. It passes the information to the appropriate web application, which then processes the incoming data and creates a page appropriate for the client.

4. The web server sends back the appropriate page information using an **HTTP response**, which travels back across the network to the client machine.

5. The client reads the posted page and displays it on the screen. Depending on the size and complexity of the application, the posted page may take a while to load, but because the page is loaded asynchronously, the end user does not have to wait for the entire page to load before interacting with it.

Web Communication

From the descriptions above, it should be starting to become clear that the request and the response are the vital components of the communication process. From the point of view of a web application, they're critically important: it's the request that tells the application what to do, and the response is what the application must generate.

As stated above, the request is gleaned from the URL, so it's worth taking a moment to consider the different forms that a URL specifying a resource on the Web can take. The simplest kind of request that you can make is for the 'front page' of a particular site: entering http://news.bbc.co.uk into your browser, for example, will take you to the BBC News web site. Just a little more complex are the URLs that also specify a path, like this one that identifies the BBC's science and technology index page: http://news.bbc.co.uk/hi/english/sci/tech.

However, these familiar-looking URLs are not an end to the matter. We can be more specific still in the way we ask the server for a resource, by adding a **query string** to the end of a URL. This gives the server much more information about the precise resource that we want. For example, the URL http://www.google.com/search?q=ASP.NET+Programming is the location of the Google search engine's page that shows the results of an Internet search for the words ASP.NET and Programming. In this URL, everything after the ? character is the query string.

> Of course, Google doesn't have a web page already made up for every possible search query that you could ever pass into it. The results you see are created for you dynamically by the Google web application, based on the query string that you submitted, and the current Google index of web content.

HTTP GET and POST

A request for a web page is always formatted in a way that means it can be understood by all of the machines involved in routing the request, so that the machine serving the page returns exactly the information requested by the client. The standardized format for web requests is defined by the Hypertext Transport Protocol (HTTP).

Using HTTP, there are two principle kinds of request that a web client can make of a server. First, the client can ask the server to send it a resource such as a web page, a picture, or an MP3 file. This is called a GET request, because it 'gets' information from the server. Second, the client can ask the server to process a resource that it sends. This is called a POST request, because the client posts information to the server to be processed, and then awaits a response.

In day-to-day use, it's not difficult to tell these two methods apart. When we type a URL into a browser, or click on a link, we want the browser to get us a web page, and so a GET request is created. As well as a query string, the client can add further information to the request for the server to use as a way of providing the most appropriate content. For example, the browser can specify what languages its user understands, what file formats it can display, and so on. These pieces of information are placed in what are called **request headers**.

When the GET request arrives at the server, the latter processes the path information to work out which resource the client is requesting. If it's a dynamically generated resource, then it may also make use of the query string and header data, if any is supplied. The result will be a resource that can be sent back to the client. The server wraps up the resource in an HTTP response, which can contain headers that provide information about the resource, and sends it back to the client.

HTTP POST requests are used to send data from HTML forms to the server. When you fill in a form and hit Submit, the browser wraps up the form data in a POST request, addresses it to a particular resource on the server, and sends it. The server processes the request in the same way as a GET request, locating the appropriate resource, and executing any code necessary to generate a dynamic response. This time, however, the server can also make use of the additional, 'posted' data.

> *We can generate GET requests using forms as well: the front page of the Google site has a form that we can fill in to perform a search, which generates a GET request with a URL similar to the one we looked at earlier.*

So what's the difference between GET and POST? The fundamental one we gave above: GET is used to *retrieve* a resource, and POST is used to *send* one. A GET request basically just asks the server to provide the resource at a given URL. If you hit Refresh in your browser after making a GET request, the resource will be fetched again. If you copy the URL from the browser's address bar, and e-mail it to your friend, they can use it to retrieve the same resource.

A POST request is more complicated than a GET request, since it includes data outside of the URL. If we submit a form via POST, we should expect the server to process the data in the POST request, and return a resource that indicates in some way whether processing the data was successful. If you're using a web-based e-mail system, for example, hitting the Send button, causes the contents of your e-mail to be posted to the server. In response, the server will send the mail, and return a web page telling you that the mail was successfully sent.

The URL to which the mail message was posted can't be used in the same way as the GET URL: you can't mail it to a friend and expect that when they go to that page, they will see a page telling them they just successfully sent the message that you just sent. Similarly, you can't put it in your favorites and use it again later. If you hit Refresh, you will be told you can't refresh the page without re-submitting the data to the server. If you tell the browser to go ahead and refresh anyway, there's a distinct possibility that you will end up sending the same mail twice.

It wouldn't make sense for Google to use POST for its search engine. If our requests were posted to the server, we wouldn't be able to hit Refresh, we wouldn't be able to send the URL of a set of interesting results to a friend, and we wouldn't be able to store our common queries in our favorites list. For this job, GET is perfect.

Statelessness

When we request a resource from a server, using GET or POST, the server responds to our request and returns the appropriate data. Once the information has been sent back to the client, however, the server then forgets all about the client. HTTP is known as a **stateless** protocol, as state – that is, information about the connection, and who's at the other end of it – is not retained from one request to another.

If we were to accept this limitation as unavoidable, we would enormously restrict the usefulness of the web applications it's possible to create. Being able 'remember' a user is necessary in all kinds of situations, from setting the background of all the pages they see to their favorite color, to remembering what they've ordered as they make their way through an e-commerce site. To counter this problem, there are two main methods available to us:

❑   We can instruct our application to store state on the server in a variable of some type – we could store selected information about the client in a temporary location that exists for as long as the user is browsing the site. The server can then remove this temporary data when the user navigates out of scope of the application, or closes their browser.

❑   We can store selected information about the client on the client's machine, in a small file called a **cookie**. Cookies can be used to store small amounts of data, such as general preferences or login details to a site, so that each time we navigate to a page like Amazon.com, we'll have an interface personalized for us, with a link to items we might be interested in buying.

We'll have more to say about the problems of statelessness and strategies for dealing with it on several occasions later in the book, and particularly in Chapter 7.

Configuring Your System for Web Development

Before we move on to examine how all of the ideas about the Web that we've looked at here map to the world of ASP.NET programming, we'll set up the examples that we'll be looking at in the remainder of this chapter, which are available in the code download. The techniques that you'll learn here will work for installing all of the examples in the book.

Your first step is to head to www.wrox.com and download the ZIP file that contains the code for this book. Once you've extracted this archive on your system, you'll find that there's a file called index.htm in the root of the downloaded code. Double-click this file, and you'll be presented with the following interface:

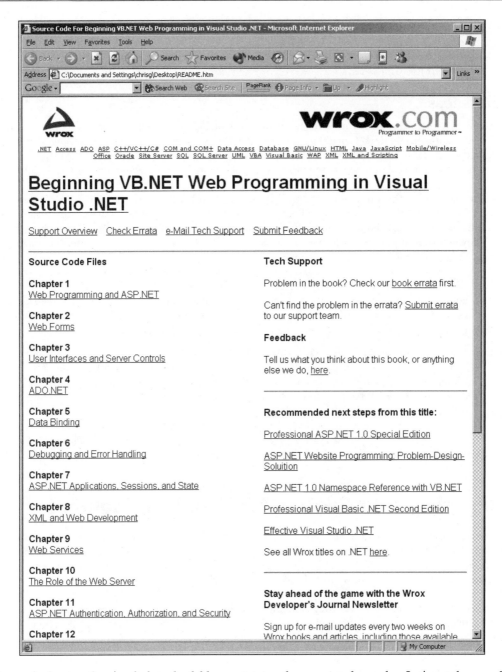

For each chapter, there's a link to the folder containing the associated samples. Let's get the sample application for Chapter 1 up and running, so that we can see some ASP.NET code in action in Visual Studio .NET.

Installing an Application from the Code Download

The process of installing the sample projects has two parts, the first of which is to place the folder containing the sample code in the following location on your system:

C:\inetpub\wwwroot*FolderName*

Once that's done, the files are in the correct location, but that's not enough. In order for these web application *projects* to be available as web *applications*, we need to tell our web server (IIS) that we intend this to be the case. What we want to do is to set up our system so that it's possible to request files in the **FolderName** folder via the web server, using the following syntax:

http://localhost/*ApplicationName*/*Page.aspx*

The 'folder' that our application appears to be in to the people that use it (**ApplicationName** in the above example) is known as a **virtual directory**.

Creating a Virtual Directory

In Windows Explorer, right-click on the application folder (the application in this chapter is called Chapter01SampleApp) and select **Properties** from the context menu:

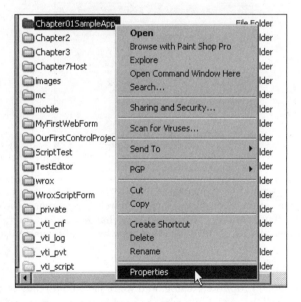

On doing so, you'll see the following dialog – or at least, you will after you've selected the **Web Sharing** tab at the top:

Select the **Share this Folder** radio button and you'll be presented with a dialog that lets you configure the options for your web application. Accept the defaults, and click OK.

> By default, the name of the virtual directory for a web application is the same as the name of the folder that contains it. It's possible to change this, but doing so is not recommended, especially for applications that have been built using Visual Studio .NET.

Click OK to close the original **Properties** dialog, and we're just about ready to start! If that's all gone a bit quickly, don't worry: we'll be examining what we've done here in more detail in Chapter 10, where we look at the role of the web server, and at how to configure IIS.

Running our Application

In order to test the web application that you just installed, we can use one of two methods. First, we can run our project straight away just by opening Internet Explorer and entering the following address into the address bar:

http://localhost/Chapter01SampleApp/VirtualPetForm.aspx

Alternatively, we can open up Visual Studio .NET and take a look inside our project. To do so, either click the **Open Project** hyperlink on the **Start Page**, or select **File | Open | Project**. Navigate to the folder on your system (located in C:\Inetpub\wwwroot\Chapter01SampleApp) and double-click the Chapter01SampleApp.vbproj file. Visual Studio .NET will now open the application.

To run the application from Visual Studio .NET, you can right-click on VirtualPetForm.aspx in the Solution Explorer and select **View in Browser**, or you can just run the project. Either way, you'll be presented with a dialog that offers to save the solution file for the application – accept the defaults here, and continue. Our sample page should look like this:

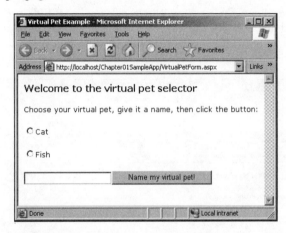

After selecting an option and naming your pet, you should see something like the following (depending on the name and the pet you selected, of course):

Over the course of the rest of this chapter, we'll look at the techniques involved in creating this simple application, and at some of the help provided by Visual Studio .NET for doing so.

Web Programming in the .NET Framework

Happily, applying the .NET Framework to the web programming concepts we've discussed so far isn't a difficult task. The technology that we use for this purpose is ASP.NET. While it's possible to create any .NET application using nothing more than Notepad, we can create ASP.NET web forms quickly and simply by using Visual Studio .NET. We can drag and drop controls from a toolbox onto a page, and all we need to do is write some code to interact with those controls.

A Control-Based Architecture

Like the controls we use when we're creating Windows forms, ASP.NET controls are self-contained units of commonly used functionality. Each control has a specific set of properties available to it that can be accessed and used programmatically. Let's take a quick look at the controls we used in our example in Visual Studio .NET's design view:

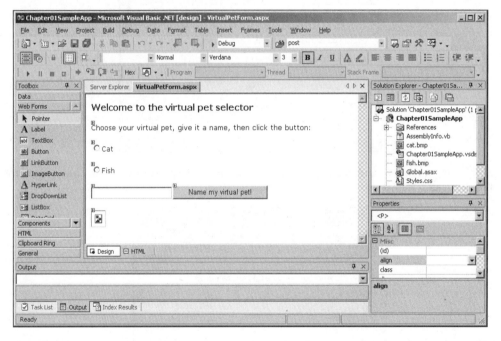

Here, you can see two radio buttons, a textbox, a button, and a placeholder for an image. We'll learn more about these controls in Chapter 3, where we'll discuss how they work, how to use them, and how to make them work for you.

Event-Driven Programming Model

Also in our example, we have a page that reacts to the clicking of a button on our web form. In exactly the same way as we'd create an event handler for a click event on a Windows form, when we work in the design view in Visual Studio .NET, we can double-click on our ASP.NET buttons and create event handlers for those buttons.

We're not just limited to reacting to button clicks. We could react to the selection of one of the options in the radio button group, or to changing focus in our application. This corresponds well to the way we work on the Web: we interact with the web pages we see, clicking links, filling in forms, and so on; so the ability to react to events raised by the controls we use in web forms development is a very intuitive programming model.

Let's take a brief look at the code used to react to the events raised by our controls:

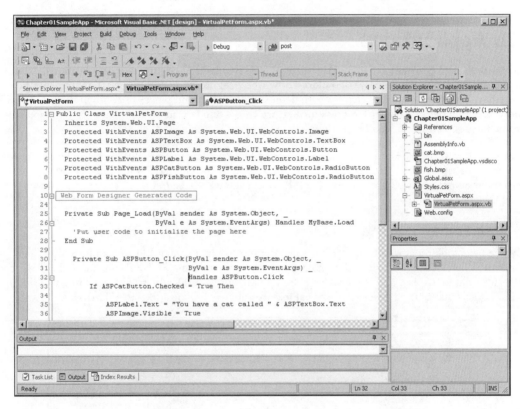

Once again, this is familiar-looking stuff, further indicating the fact that web forms are in the same league as Windows forms. We'll look at how this event-handling code actually works in general terms later in the chapter.

The System.Web Classes

All of the functionality available to ASP.NET is contained in the classes within the .NET namespaces whose names begin with System.Web. The controls that we have just been looking at, for example, reside in the System.Web.UI.HtmlControls and System.Web.UI.WebControls namespaces. The base class for all web controls is the WebControls class that resides in the System.Web.UI namespace. The properties that this class defines are therefore common to all controls, and include things like Font, ID, and Visible. You'll see much more on this subject in Chapter 3.

ASP.NET and IIS

In order to host an ASP.NET web application, the web server must have a copy of the .NET Framework installed. When that installation process takes place, the file extension .aspx is registered with IIS, so that IIS knows that if a request arrives for a file with a .aspx extension, it is to be processed by ASP.NET. We will look at this process in more detail in Chapter 10, where we'll also find out more about how ASP.NET works as a system process, and how IIS authenticates ASP.NET requests.

Web Applications

So far then, we've looked at some of the technologies involved in creating web applications, examined some simple ASP.NET pages, and explored how web programming and the .NET Framework fit together. Before we close this chapter with details of some bits and pieces of configuration that you'll need to set up before you can progress further, we've got one last question to answer: What exactly constitutes an ASP.NET web application?

Looking at this from the client's perspective, we know that whatever an ASP.NET application *is*, it must produce the web pages that are displayed in the browser. The web page is the finished article – the rendered output of a web application. In ASP.NET, each web-page-to-be has two parts: the web form, and the code-behind page.

The Web Form

We've been looking at web forms almost since the start of the chapter, but we can formalize their definition here. The web form is the ASPX page that contains the ASP.NET controls and HTML code that we want to display, and while we've been looking at it 'graphically' so far, switching to a different view reveals that barring one or two special features, it does look just like an HTML file:

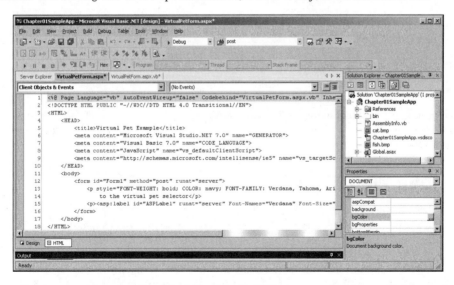

If you really want to, you can eschew the help that the IDE gives you, and just edit your web forms in HTML! We'll be discussing web forms in more detail in the next chapter.

The Code-Behind Page

When, in an ASP.NET application, we want to react to the events raised by the controls in a web form, we create event-handler code for those controls in a code-behind page. This file has the same name as the web form, but with a 'double' extension: `.aspx.vb`.

Visual Studio .NET links the `.aspx` web form and the `.aspx.vb` code-behind page by using a single line of code at the top of the former:

```
<%@ Page Language="vb" AutoEventWireup="false"
                   Codebehind="VirtualPetForm.aspx.vb"
                   Inherits="Chapter01SampleApp.VirtualPetForm" %>
```

The `Codebehind` attribute indicates the name of the file that contains the code we require, while the `Inherits` statement refers to the namespace and the class within that file that we wish to access.

Application Configuration

While we're here, there a third component of a web application that's worth mentioning. Built into ASP.NET are two methods for *configuring* our applications, at both a machine-wide and an application-specific level.

When we install ASP.NET, a file called `Machine.config` is created. This file contains basic configuration details that are common to all ASP.NET applications, and links to the most commonly used .NET assemblies. `Machine.config` can be found on any .NET system in the following location:

```
%System Root%\Microsoft.NET\Framework\V1.0.3705\CONFIG
```

Where `%System Root%` is the location of your `Windows` or `WINNT` system folder.

> Be very careful not to delete your **Machine.config** file – it is essential for ASP.NET to run smoothly! If you want to view or amend your **Machine.config**, always create a backup first!

When we create our own applications, we may want to add to or override some of this functionality, and set up some application-specific configuration. In that situation, we can use a file called `Web.config`, which is present in all Visual Studio .NET-generated ASP.NET applications. Conveniently, we only need to add entries to our `Web.config` file that alter or add to the `Machine.config`; we don't need to repeat the whole file again.

The Microsoft SQL Server Desktop Engine

As our final act in this chapter, we need to do something that will set us up for the rest of the book. One of most important ingredients of a dynamic web application is the ability to store data in and retrieve data from a database, and several of the examples in the chapters to come will involve this functionality. For that, of course, we need a database, and our choice is to use the Microsoft SQL Server Desktop Engine (MSDE), which is a specialized version of SQL Server 2000. In this section, we'll explain what it is, why we've chosen to use it, and – most important of all – how you can get hold of it and install it.

A Smaller SQL Server

The first thing to say about MSDE is that it's entirely compatible with SQL Server, which is truly an enterprise-class database server. This means that the things you learn while using MSDE will stand you in good stead when you come to use SQL Server itself – it behaves in exactly the same way. From our perspective here, though, the immediate benefits of MSDE are:

❑ It's freely distributable

❑ It's currently sitting on your Visual Basic .NET discs, just waiting for you to install it

What this means is that as well as providing the perfect system for us to learn and experiment with, a complete web application can initially be produced and distributed without incurring any costs for the database server. If the system expands at a later date, it can be ported to the commercial distribution of SQL Server with next to no effort. The only features cut down from the full version of SQL Server are that the MSDE is optimized for (but not limited to) up to five connections at a time, that the maximum database size is limited to 2GB, and that some enterprise features are absent.

> **All of the features that MSDE supports are also supported by SQL Server. The converse is not true, however; some of the richer functionality of SQL Server is not present in MSDE. However, none of this functionality is required for any of the code in this book to operate correctly.**

Obtaining and Installing MSDE

When Visual Basic .NET (or any of the various Visual Studio .NET products) is installed, an item called Microsoft .NET Framework SDK is added to your Start | Programs menu. Beneath this is an item called Samples and QuickStart Tutorials; if you select it, this is what you'll see:

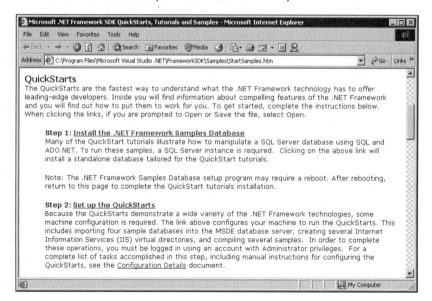

This page is self-explanatory: clicking on the first link will install the MSDE engine; clicking on the second will cause the sample databases to be created.

> *This page will only appear once, so if you (or someone else) have been here before, you won't see it. Don't worry: you'll find the* instmsde.exe *and* configsamples.exe *files that these links invoke beneath the* FrameworkSDK\Samples *folder of your Visual Studio installation.*

Ensure that you're logged on as a user with Administrator privileges on the current machine, and click on the first link (or run the executable). The following dialog will appear:

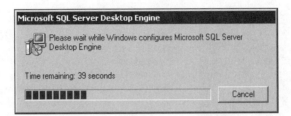

When this has finished, there's no need to restart your machine. You can go straight on to the next step, which will produce another dialog:

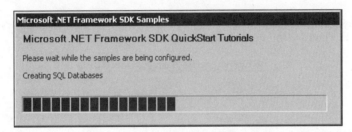

Once again, wait for this step to finish its work, and you can go on the final stage. Before you can run the database samples in this book, you need to enable **mixed-mode authentication**. By default, MSDE is set up only to use a method of authentication called Windows Integrated Security. We need to set up the database so that we can let database users that are separate from the operating system log in too.

To this end, we've provided a script that you can run on your machine to configure mixed-mode authentication. It's called MixedMode.rgs, and you'll find it in the code download for this chapter. After you've run that, you're all done... but what exactly *have* you done? The best way to understand that is to open up Visual Basic .NET, ready for the quick tour in the next section.

Try It Out – Testing MSDE

In this brief example, we'll use the Visual Studio .NET interface to make sure that our installation of MSDE has worked.

1. Open up Visual Studio .NET, and head for the Server Explorer in the IDE. Click on the button marked Connect to Database, as shown overleaf:

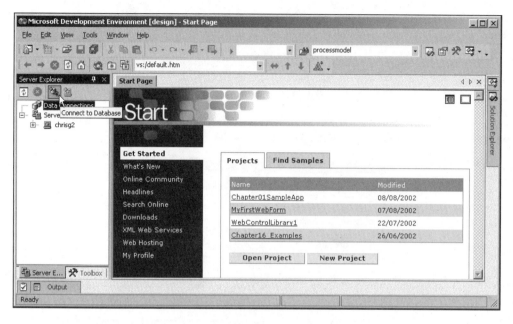

2. Fill in the dialog that appears precisely as follows, test the connection by pressing the Test Connection button, and then click OK.

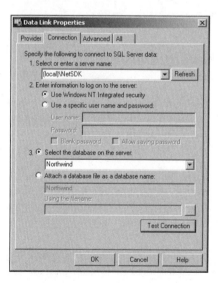

Don't worry about the precise meanings of any of these settings right now; we'll be looking at database connections and the server explorer in more detail in Chapter 4.

3. Once you've clicked OK, you are returned to the Visual Studio .NET IDE. Expand the new connection in the Server Explorer, and double-click on the Employees table in the tree to display some sample data:

How It Works

We've established a basic connection to our database, and displayed some sample data, simply by clicking some buttons in a Wizard. In the same Wizard, you can select alternative database servers on your network, different databases to connect to, and much more. As stated above, we'll discuss more about working with data in Chapter 4.

Summary

In this chapter we started by taking a walk through the fundamentals of web programming and the architecture of the Web. After that, we looked at a way of setting up web applications, and therefore how to install the sample applications in this book. Our first sample application was extremely simple, but it did show some core .NET web application concepts in detail: controls, event handling, code-behind pages, and so on. We looked at the constituent parts of .NET applications, and discussed how they related to our basic example. We'll be meeting all of these concepts again later in the book.

To recap, having finished reading through this chapter, you should now feel comfortable with:

❑ Understanding what a web application is, and how HTTP communication occurs

❑ Installing the sample applications we'll be using in this book, and running a sample .NET web application

❑ How .NET web applications are constructed, and what the different parts of the puzzle are

❑ Installing MSDE and the sample databases

In the next chapter we'll take a look at how we can create our own applications in Visual Studio .NET, and explore the differences between the web world and the Windows world in more detail.

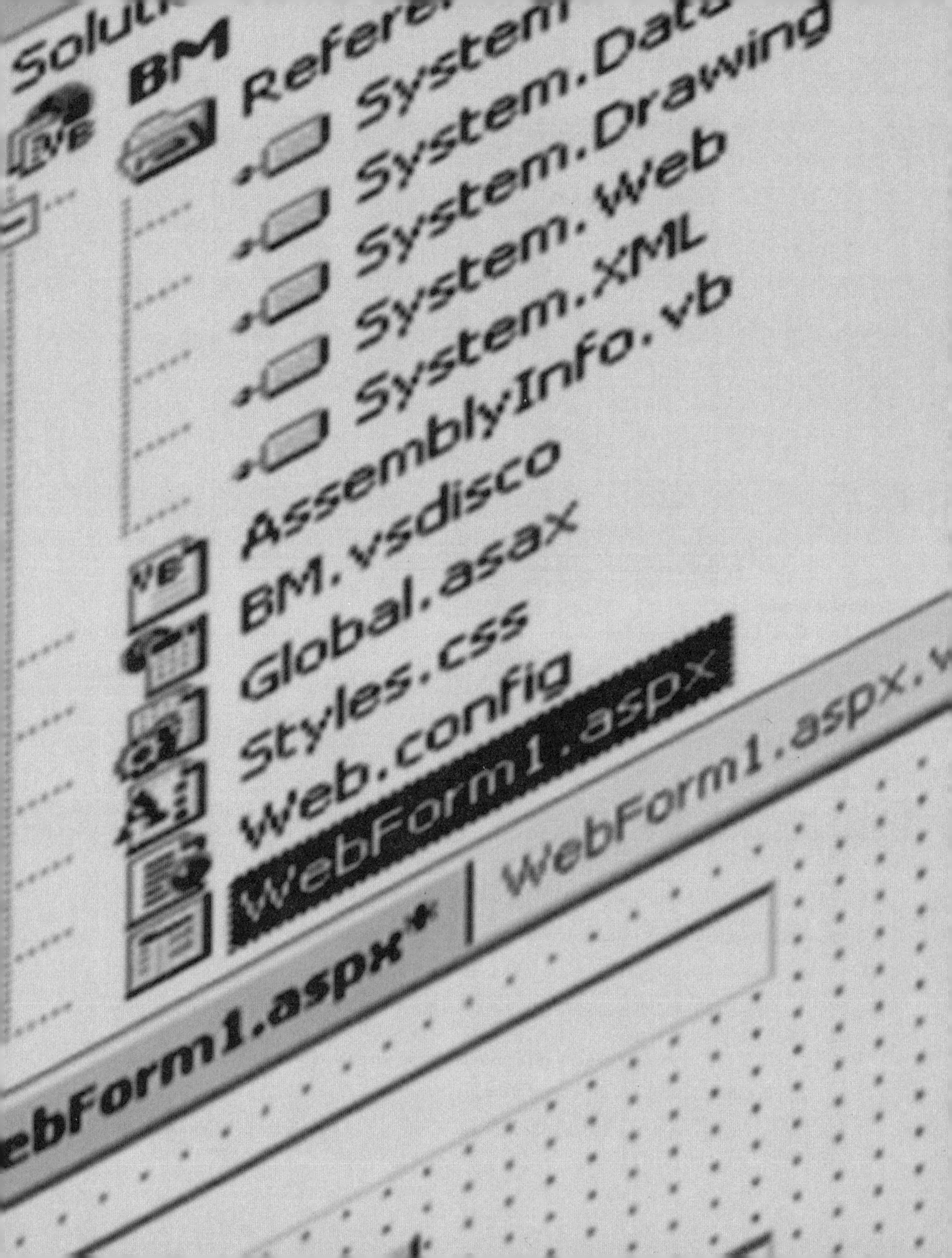

Solut...
BM
Referen...
System...
System.Dat...
System.Drawing
System.Web
System.XML
AssemblyInfo.vb
Assembl...
BM.vsdisco
Global.asax
Styles.css
Web.config
WebForm1.aspx

WebForm1.aspx* | WebForm1.aspx.v

ebForm1.aspx*

Web Forms

We've begun this book with an introduction to basic web programming concepts, a discussion of the advent of ASP.NET, and even a rapid demonstration ASP.NET web forms, in which we looked at a small web application using Visual Basic .NET. Let's now continue with a further explanation of web forms and their behavior in the context of a web application.

In this chapter, we'll start to talk about *developing* web applications using the Visual Studio .NET environment, taking advantage of the rich set of tools and options that make the experience more efficient and, quite honestly, more enjoyable. Specifically, we will delve into the following topics:

❏   Building web forms within Visual Studio .NET

❏   Examining the files of a web forms application that are automatically generated by Visual Studio .NET

❏   The processing of a web form during execution, and its lifecycle

Web Forms vs. Windows Forms

We've said on a few occasions that Visual Studio .NET makes building web forms feel like Windows forms development, but the best way to see that is simply to get our hands dirty and create an ASP.NET web application – so let's just do that!

Try It Out – Chameleon Buttons

In this example, we'll demonstrate how to add code to the event handlers that are associated with the controls on a web form. We'll create a new web application with a single page that contains three buttons. When the buttons are clicked, they'll change color.

1.   If you haven't done so already, launch Visual Studio .NET, and create a new ASP.NET web application called ChameleonButtons, as shown below:

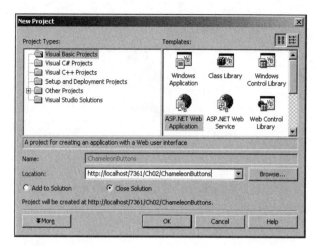

2. When the Design view for the generated `WebForm1.aspx` page becomes visible, right-click on the grid and select **Properties**. From the **Page Layout** drop-down list, select **FlowLayout**, and click on **OK**.

3. Drag three **Button** controls from **Web Forms** section the **Toolbox** onto the web form.

4. Single-click on each of the buttons, from left to right, and set the following properties in the **Properties** window:

ID	Text
btnGreen	Make Buttons Green
btnRed	Make Buttons Red
btnBlue	Make Buttons Blue

5. Now resize and rearrange your buttons so that they look like the following:

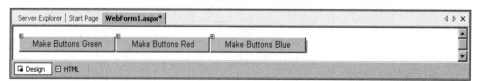

6. Double-click on `btnGreen`, and immediately you'll be presented with the following, automatically generated code:

```
Public Class WebForm1
    Inherits System.Web.UI.Page
  Protected WithEvents btnGreen As System.Web.UI.WebControls.Button
  Protected WithEvents btnRed As System.Web.UI.WebControls.Button
  Protected WithEvents btnBlue As System.Web.UI.WebControls.Button
```

```
#Region " Web Form Designer Generated Code "

    'This call is required by the Web Form Designer.
    <System.Diagnostics.DebuggerStepThrough()> Private Sub
    InitializeComponent()

End Sub

    Private Sub Page_Init(ByVal sender As System.Object, _
                        ByVal e As System.EventArgs) Handles MyBase.Init
        'CODEGEN: This method call is required by the Web Form Designer
        'Do not modify it using the code editor.
        InitializeComponent()
    End Sub

#End Region

    Private Sub Page_Load(ByVal sender As System.Object, _
                        ByVal e As System.EventArgs) Handles MyBase.Load
        'Put user code to initialize the page here
    End Sub

    Private Sub btnGreen_Click(ByVal sender As System.Object, _
                        ByVal e As System.EventArgs) _
                        Handles btnGreen.Click


    End Sub
End Class
```

7. There's quite a lot to take in here, and it certainly isn't our aim to explain everything about this code in this chapter. At the end of this class definition, however, there's a likely-looking subroutine called btnGreen_Click(). This is the event handler for clicks on the button, so add the following code:

```
    Private Sub btnGreen_Click(ByVal sender As System.Object, _
                        ByVal e As System.EventArgs) _
                        Handles btnGreen.Click
        btnGreen.BackColor = Color.Green
        btnRed.BackColor = Color.Green
        btnBlue.BackColor = Color.Green
    End Sub
```

8. Return to the **Design** view, either by clicking on the WebForm1.aspx tab above the code view, or by clicking on the **View Designer** button at the top of the Solution Explorer – the second button from the left.

9. In a similar fashion to btnGreen, double-click on btnRed and add the following code to its Click event handler:

```
    Private Sub btnRed_Click(ByVal sender As System.Object, _
                        ByVal e As System.EventArgs) _
```

```
                                    Handles btnRed.Click
    btnGreen.BackColor = Color.Red
    btnRed.BackColor = Color.Red
    btnBlue.BackColor = Color.Red
End Sub
```

10. Finally, do the same for `btnBlue` and its `Click` event:

```
Private Sub btnBlue_Click(ByVal sender As System.Object, _
                     ByVal e As System.EventArgs) _
                     Handles btnBlue.Click
    btnGreen.BackColor = Color.Blue
    btnRed.BackColor = Color.Blue
    btnBlue.BackColor = Color.Blue
End Sub
```

11. The code for this example is now complete, so press either *F5* or the **Start** button (which looks like a play button) in the top menu bar. A web browser window will appear, displaying the following web form:

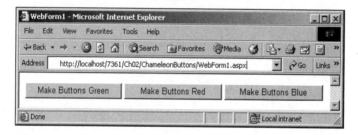

12. Click on the three different buttons, and you'll see the background colors of all three buttons change at once, as appropriate.

How It Works

The process we've just seen should have been very familiar for the most part. To begin with, we selected **ASP.NET Web Application** as our project type, and specified a location for it. Visual Studio .NET then created a virtual directory in the appropriate place, which in our case was http://localhost/7361/ch02/ChameleonButtons. After that was set up, we were greeted with the Visual Studio .NET environment, where we could begin editing our web form.

With `WebForm1.aspx` selected in the Solution Explorer, we dragged-and-dropped the three buttons that we needed to create our web form, resulting in their inclusion in the HTML file that defines the appearance of the form. We can take a look at the HTML code by selecting the **HTML** tab at the lower-left corner of the designer. Remember that Visual Studio NET generated all of this automatically – at no point were we compelled to work with HTML code.

```
<%@ Page Language="vb" AutoEventWireup="false" Codebehind="WebForm1.aspx.vb"
        Inherits="ChameleonButtons.WebForm1"%>
<!DOCTYPE HTML PUBLIC "-//W3C//DTD HTML 4.0 Transitional//EN">
```

```
<HTML>
  <HEAD>
    <title>WebForm1</title>
    <meta name="GENERATOR" content="Microsoft Visual Studio.NET 7.0">
    <meta name="CODE_LANGUAGE" content="Visual Basic 7.0">
    <meta name="vs_defaultClientScript" content="JavaScript">
    <meta name="vs_targetSchema"
        content="http://schemas.microsoft.com/intellisense/ie5">
  </HEAD>
  <body>
    <form id="Form1" method="post" runat="server">
      <asp:Button id="btnGreen" runat="server" Text="Make Buttons Green"
                Width="162px"></asp:Button>
      <asp:Button id="btnRed" runat="server" Text="Make Buttons Red"
                Width="162px"></asp:Button>
      <asp:Button id="btnBlue" runat="server" Text="Make Buttons Blue"
                Width="162px"></asp:Button>
    </form>
  </body>
</HTML>
```

At the top, we have the `Page` directive that marks out this otherwise innocuous-looking HTML file as an ASP.NET page. The first attribute to this directive, `Language`, tells the ASP.NET environment that our web form is written in Visual Basic .NET. The second, `AutoEventWireup`, indicates whether page-wide events such as `Init` and `Load` will be handled automatically.

You saw the handlers for these two events, `Page_Init()` and `Page_Load()`, when we were adding the handlers for button clicks. Broadly speaking, the `Init` event is fired while the page is being initialized but before it's displayed, while `Load` is fired when the page becomes visible for the first time. Somewhat confusingly, the default setting for `AutoEventWireup` is `True` in ASP.NET, but it's set to `False` by Visual Studio .NET, which uses an internal mechanism to control event firing.

The `Codebehind` attribute specifies the name of the file that contains our application logic for this form – that is, the file that contains our event handling code, among other things – while `Inherits` is set to the name of the class that's defined in the code-behind page.

Looking further down the HTML file, we can also see the `<form>` tag that has the attribute `runat="server"`, which is a must when using ASP.NET server-side controls. Within the form are elements representing the buttons that will be displayed on the page.

Lastly, we moved to the code-behind page by double-clicking on the `btnGreen` button. We added the following code to its event handler, which sets the `BackColor` property of all three buttons. (The `btnRed` and `btnBlue` buttons have comparable code.)

```
Private Sub btnGreen_Click(ByVal sender As System.Object, _
                    ByVal e As System.EventArgs) _
                    Handles btnGreen.Click
    btnGreen.BackColor = Color.Green
    btnRed.BackColor = Color.Green
    btnBlue.BackColor = Color.Green
End Sub
```

This event handler, like all of the handlers you'll see over the course of this book, has two parameters that are used to let the calling event pass information to it. Here, the first, sender, provides a reference to the object that raised the event, which in this case would be btnGreen itself. The second parameter, e, is an event object that's specific to the type of event being handled and contains information regarding the state of that event. Again, this is strongly analogous to the Windows mechanism that allows us to determine (say) the location of the mouse pointer on the form when the event was fired.

Web Forms Development with Visual Studio

Having managed to create our first ASP.NET application with minimal fuss, we should take a second look at Visual Studio .NET's tools for building web applications, at a slightly slower pace! In the window that you're presented with when you first create the project, you can see that the panes are very similar to those for a Visual Basic .NET Windows application project: the Toolbox is there, as are the menu bars and the Solution Explorer.

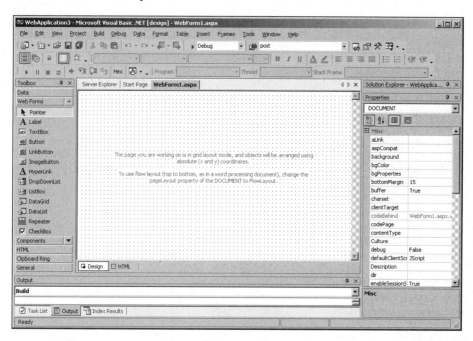

The designer, which (as you'd expect) appears in the center of the IDE, is set to "grid layout" mode by default. On a web form, dragging controls onto the design surface in this mode will place them in absolute positions (for example, 100 pixels from the left, and 200 from the top), not allowing in any way for browser resizing or varying screen resolutions – or even that some browsers don't support grid layout!

If we know our users and the browsers they're using, this doesn't matter, and we can design our form with the confidence that it will look exactly the same for all of them. More often, however, we'll change the setting to "flow layout", in which form elements are positioned from left to right and from top to bottom, remaining in their relative positions unless we provide spacing and carriage returns. At the cost of a little design flexibility, we'll produce a much more widely compatible application.

Toolbox

If the Toolbox that you can see on the left of the above screenshot does not appear, you can simply press *Ctrl-Alt-X* or select View |Toolbox from the menu bar. When an ASP.NET web application is open in the IDE, the Toolbox displays the available web forms server-side controls by default, but we can click on other categories (for example, HTML) to show those elements instead.

Over the course of the book, you'll be gaining first-hand experience of using most of the control types listed in the Toolbox, but if your curiosity simply won't wait, you can find a complete list of all of these controls in the MSDN documentation – look under .NET Framework/Reference/ Class Library/System.Web.UI.WebControls.

Solution Explorer

Next, let's explore the files that Visual Studio.NET created for our web application by examining the Solution Explorer, which for an arbitrary web application will look something like this:

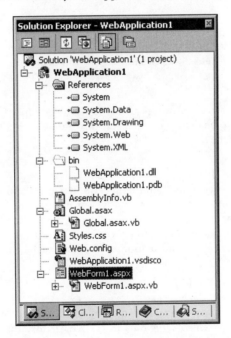

You can that there are six buttons along the top of the Solution Explorer. The first is the View Code button that takes us to the code-behind file for our web form: the .aspx.vb file. The second is the View Designer button that allows us to view the design area. (The actual window that we view on clicking this button will depend on whether we were most recently in Design or HTML mode.) The third button is the standard Refresh button that we can press to get the most up-to-date listing of files in our solution. The fourth button is the Copy Application button that will allow us to create a copy of this application on a different site. Finally, the fifth button allows us to show and hide the 'hidden' files in the solution, while the sixth allows us to see the properties of the file that's currently highlighted.

Notice the bin directory within our solution, which contains a compiled version of the project – the WebApplication1.dll file is the latest version, created by the most recent build. The second file is the project database (PDB) file, which holds debugging information for use with the Visual Studio .NET debugger. Much more interesting from our current perspective, however, are the other files in the Solution Explorer, so we'll take a look at those next.

References

The References section is a list of the namespaces that contain the .NET runtime classes required by the project under development. Although all .NET projects will have a list like this, we'll discuss the namespaces that appear above within the context of creating a Visual Basic .NET web application.

System

The System namespace is the root namespace in the .NET Framework. It includes classes that represent the basic data types used by all applications, such as String, Varchar, and Int32. Including this namespace allows us to make shortcut references to these types from within our code (for example, System.String becomes String).

System.Data

The System.Data namespace primarily contains classes that allow us to work with ADO.NET, and therefore include information from databases in our web applications, as we'll see in Chapter 4.

System.Drawing

The System.Drawing namespace provides access to GDI+ graphics functionality. GDI+ allows applications' user interfaces to be displayed on a screen without having to be concerned about the details of a particular display device.

System.Web

The System.Web namespace facilitates communication between the browser and the web server. This namespace includes the HttpRequest class that gives us information about the HTTP request, the HttpResponse class that manages HTTP output to the client, and the HttpServerUtility class that provides access to server-side utilities and processes. It also includes classes for cookie manipulation, file transfer, exception information, and output cache control. These classes are crucial for web forms development.

System.XML

The System.Xml namespace provides support for processing XML. This is useful if our web form works with XML, whether it is transforming data to HTML, performing searches against the data, or processing it for storage in a data source.

AssemblyInfo.vb

As with any .NET project, this file comes into play when our web application is compiled. AssemblyInfo.vb contains all of the metadata needed to specify the assembly's version requirements and security identity, as well as to define the scope of the assembly, and to resolve references to resources and classes.

Global.asax/Global.asax.vb

ASP.NET supports an optional, global application file for each web application, which acts as an implementation point for global event handlers, objects, and variables. The Global.asax file follows a similar format to ASP.NET pages, but the .asax extension indicates that we're dealing with an *application* file, as opposed to .as**p**x, for a *page* file.

Every ASP.NET application can contain a single Global.asax file in its root directory, which will be compiled for the first time when the web application is first requested. You can't use the Global.asax file to display content, however, and any attempt to do so will result in an error.

The code contained in Global.asax.vb constitutes part of our application. It does not contain configuration information – the Web.config file deals with that, as we'll see shortly. One of the more important sections of Global.asax.vb looks like this:

```
. . .

Sub Application_Start(ByVal sender As Object, ByVal e As EventArgs)
  ' Fires when the application is started
End Sub

Sub Session_Start(ByVal sender As Object, ByVal e As EventArgs)
  ' Fires when the session is started
End Sub

. . .
```

This code has been created by Visual Studio .NET, and you can see already that it consists of some placeholder event-handling methods that we can use for our own purposes. Each time our application starts, for example, we could create a series of public variables that would be accessible in all of our ASPX pages – and when each user initiates a new session, we could store information about them in a session-scope variable by placing appropriate code in the Session_Start() event handler.

> We'll be saying more about Global.asax in Chapter 7 in particular, and in some of the other later chapters too.

Styles.css

Stylesheets apply uniform styling to similar elements wherever they appear in your web application. Imagine, for example, that we have 30 web forms in our web application. Initially, we might decide to format all data wrapped with <H1> tags to use the Verdana font. But what if we find out later that all <H1> tags should appear in the Courier font? Without a cascading stylesheet (CSS) file, you'd be faced with making the same change to 30 pages. But with one, as we'll see in the next chapter, you can arrange to solve this problem with a change to a single line of code.

Web.config

`Web.config` is the configuration file for this particular application. It is formatted in XML and has a variety of uses, allowing you to specify the debug settings for this project, the security configuration, and a number of other things. We'll be modifying this file in most of the web applications that we create.

`Web.config` provides settings for all of the web forms pages that reside in the same directory as the configuration file. The settings are also inherited by subdirectories of that directory. Therefore, if an individual page needs special settings to function, it can be placed in a child directory with its own `Web.config` file, and any changes you make here will affect just that page, and not your whole application.

WebApplication1.vsdisco

We make use of this file if our web application contains XML web services – the VSDISCO file allows other applications to find and consume them. We will discuss web services, and how we can use them with Visual Basic .NET web forms, in Chapter 9.

WebForm1.aspx/WebForm1.aspx.vb

Now we're back on familiar ground. The `.aspx` file is the graphical portion of a web form, containing as it does the HTML that renders the form within a browser. Visual Studio .NET links this file to our code-behind page automatically. The `.aspx.vb` class file is that code-behind page, containing event-handling code and the like, as we've seen.

Lifecycle of a Web Form

The processing of a web form is fairly analogous to Windows form processing. Once we understand the sequence of events that occurs when a web form is processed, we will be able to build web applications in a more efficient way.

Web Forms Processing

As with a Windows form, web form processing causes events to fire in a certain order when it initializes and loads. After that, there are the events that occur as the user interacts with the web form (clicking on a button, entering values into textboxes, and so on). At each stage of web form processing, events may be raised, and any event handler that corresponds to the events will be run. These methods provide us with the opportunity to update the contents of the web form.

There are six basic steps that occur when a web form is processed:

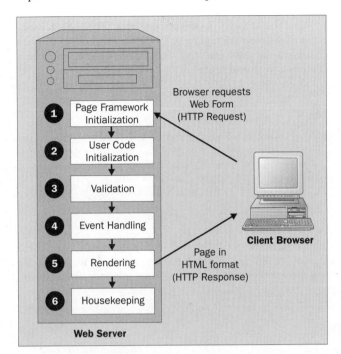

Page Framework Initialization

During initialization, Visual Studio .NET's default implementation of the Page_Init() event handler sets the page to its initial state, as described by the HTML tags within the web form. If the page is posting back (in other words, it has been previously visited, and it's sending data back to itself), Page_Init() also restores any appropriate state. If we wish, we can add customized code to this routine, such as programmatically adding controls to our web form.

User Code Initialization

At this stage, the web form's Page_Load() event handler is called. Here, if we choose to do so (and we certainly will in later examples), we can check for any previously stored values, and restore the page based on those.

Using the Page.IsPostBack property, we can determine whether this is the first time that the page has been processed. If not, we can do things like binding data to controls, or populating a text message that displays on the web form ("Welcome back!"). We can also read and update control properties – for example, we can take the text that the user has entered into a textbox, and store it in a variable for later use in the code.

Validation

Next, the `Validate()` method of any web server control that has one is executed, in order to perform validation on the content of that control (again, we'll see an example of this in the next chapter). For example, we could arrange to display a warning on the page when it's sent back to the client if the user hasn't entered any text into a 'required' textbox.

Event Handling

If the page in question was called into being in response to a form event, such as a button click, the corresponding event handler (the action that caused the page to be processed again) is called during the event-handling stage. For instance, if a button was pressed, we could perform a calculation routine and return the result to the browser.

Rendering

Penultimately, the page is rendered in the browser – in other words, the collection of HTML code and web server controls that we've put in our ASPX file is converted into a web page that the user can read and interact with. We'll discuss the process by which this miraculous transformation occurs in more depth in Chapter 3.

Housekeeping

There's one last page event that our code can handle before the page is finally disposed of: `Page_Unload()`. Since the page has already been sent to the browser, we're free to perform some cleanup: we can dispose of both the running page object, and the page itself, from server memory. Potential tasks here include closing database connections, closing files, and destroying any helper objects that we've created.

Try It Out – Dynamically Loaded Controls

To see the processing steps in action and give them a little more context, let's have another example. In this one, we'll return to our colorful theme, this time using a drop-down list to affect the appearance of three other controls.

1. Create a new ASP.NET Web Application in Visual Studio .NET and call it http://localhost/7361/Ch02/WebFormsProcessing.

2. When the design page for `WebForm1.aspx` becomes visible, right-click on it and choose **Properties**, and change the page layout to **Flow Layout**.

3. Place a DropDownList control and a PlaceHolder control from the **Toolbox** onto the form.

4. In the **Properties** window of the `DropDownList1` control, set `AutoPostBack` to `True`.

5. Double-click on DropDownList1, and in the
DropDownList1_SelectedIndexChanged() event handler on the code-behind page, add
the following code:

```
Private Sub DropDownList1_SelectedIndexChanged _
                (ByVal sender As System.Object, _
                 ByVal e As System.EventArgs) _
                 Handles DropDownList1.SelectedIndexChanged
    Select Case DropDownList1.SelectedItem.Text
      Case "Green"
        CreateColorTextBox(1, Color.Green)
      Case "Red"
        CreateColorTextBox(1, Color.Red)
      Case "Blue"
        CreateColorTextBox(1, Color.Blue)
      Case "RGB"
        CreateColorTextBox(1, Color.Red)
        CreateColorTextBox(2, Color.Green)
        CreateColorTextBox(3, Color.Blue)
      Case Else
        Dim Warning As Label = New Label()
        Warning.Text = "Please select a color"
        PlaceHolder1.Controls.Add(Warning)
    End Select
End Sub
```

6. Now add the following helper function to the end of the class:

```
Private Function CreateColorTextBox _
                    (ByVal Count As Integer, _
                     ByVal ColorName As System.Drawing.Color)
  Dim ColorTextBox As TextBox = New TextBox()
  ColorTextBox.BackColor = ColorName
  ColorTextBox.ID = Count
  PlaceHolder1.Controls.Add(ColorTextBox)
End Function
```

7. Within the Page_Load() subroutine, add the following code:

```
Private Sub Page_Load(ByVal sender As System.Object, _
                    ByVal e As System.EventArgs) Handles MyBase.Load
    If Not (Page.IsPostBack) Then
      DropDownList1.Items.Add("----")
      DropDownList1.Items.Add("Green")
      DropDownList1.Items.Add("Red")
      DropDownList1.Items.Add("Blue")
      DropDownList1.Items.Add("RGB")
    End If
End Sub
```

8. Now press *F5* to build and run the application. A browser window will appear displaying the `DropDownList` control, with no color selected by default. Select **RGB** from the list, and the browser will display the following:

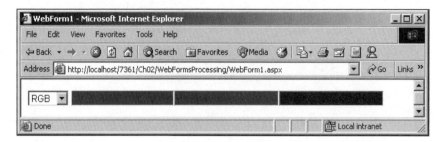

9. Repeat the process for the other options. Choosing ---- will prompt the user to select a color.

We will now modify the example slightly to show the sequence in which each routine is called as the web form is processed.

10. In the code-behind page of our web form, expand the region just above the `Page_Load()` subroutine, labeled **Web Form Designer Generated Code**.

11. Set a breakpoint at the start of the `Page_Init()` subroutine by right-clicking on the name of the routine and then selecting **Insert Breakpoint**, or by pressing *F9* when the cursor is next to it:

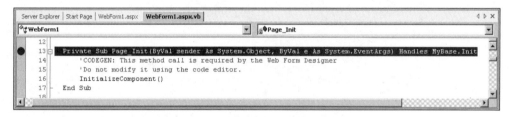

Also, set breakpoints on the `DropDownList1_SelectedIndexChanged()`, `Page_Load()`, and `CreateColorTextBox()` subroutines.

12. Press *F5* to build and run the application, which will execute in debug mode.

13. Use *F11* to progress through to the stage where the page has rendered. Once this has happened, select a color option, and continue pressing *F11* until the textboxes are displayed in the browser. Notice the order in which the routines are being called.

How It Works

There are necessarily two parts to this explanation: how the application works at all, and the *way* that it works. Taking these in order, the application has some new controls that we need to discuss. We can see the HTML that represents these controls in the shaded region:

```
<body>
  <form id="Form1" method="post" runat="server">
    <asp:DropDownList id="DropDownList1" runat="server"
                      AutoPostBack="True"></asp:DropDownList>
    <asp:PlaceHolder id="PlaceHolder1" runat="server"></asp:PlaceHolder>
  </form>
</body>
```

You'll notice that the only controls we dragged from the **Toolbox** were the `DropDownList` and a new control called a `PlaceHolder`. The latter simply serves as a region of screen real estate that can be populated with other controls, as we'll soon see.

> *With web forms, we have the ability to create controls dynamically, at run time. If you have a web form with controls whose presence in the user interface is dependent on some condition, it's a much better use of resources to instantiate only the ones that will absolutely be used. In this instance, we created one textbox for the single colors, and three for the RGB combination. Furthermore, if we select ---- from the DropDownList, a label is displayed, but no textboxes are created at all.*

Before we entered any code at all, we used the **Properties** window to set `DropDownList1`'s `AutoPostBack` property to `True`. This means that when the user makes a selection, the web form will be automatically posted back with information about the selection they made.

Then, we included the following code that will process any changes to the current selection in the `DropDownList` server-side control:

```
Private Sub DropDownList1_SelectedIndexChanged( _
              ByVal sender As System.Object, _
              ByVal e As System.EventArgs) _
    Handles DropDownList1.SelectedIndexChanged
    Select Case DropDownList1.SelectedItem.Text
      Case "Green"
        CreateColorTextBox(1, Color.Green)
      Case "Red"
        CreateColorTextBox(1, Color.Red)
      Case "Blue"
        CreateColorTextBox(1, Color.Blue)
      Case "RGB"
        CreateColorTextBox(1, Color.Red)
        CreateColorTextBox(2, Color.Green)
        CreateColorTextBox(3, Color.Blue)
      Case Else
        Dim Warning As Label = New Label()
        Warning.Text = "Please select a color"
        PlaceHolder1.Controls.Add(Warning)
    End Select
End Sub
```

We then test the selection, and call the `CreateColorTextBox()` function, using an ordinal and a `Color` object name as parameters. (In the case of `RGB`, we call the function three times, since we have three different textboxes.) In the `Else` case, we create a server-side `Label` control instead, and set its `Text` property without creating a textbox at all.

Next, let's take a look at the CreateColorTextBox() function. You can see that each time this routine is called, it instantiates a new textbox control:

```
Private Function CreateColorTextBox _
                              (ByVal Count As Integer, _
                               ByVal ColorName As System.Drawing.Color)
    Dim ColorTextBox As TextBox = New TextBox()
    ColorTextBox.BackColor = ColorName
    ColorTextBox.ID = Count
    PlaceHolder1.Controls.Add(ColorTextBox)
End Function
```

It takes the Color enumerator (Red, Green, or Blue) and uses it as the BackColor property for the new textbox. It also sets the box's ID to the value of Count. The function then places the new textbox in the PlaceHolder control.

Finally, we added the following code to the Page_Load() routine to populate the drop-down list at run time:

```
Private Sub Page_Load(ByVal sender As System.Object, _
                      ByVal e As System.EventArgs) Handles MyBase.Load
    If Not (Page.IsPostBack) Then
        DropDownList1.Items.Add("----")
        DropDownList1.Items.Add("Green")
        DropDownList1.Items.Add("Red")
        DropDownList1.Items.Add("Blue")
        DropDownList1.Items.Add("RGB")
    End If
End Sub
```

Notice that the items are only populated when the condition If Not (Page.IsPostBack) is met. The rationale here is that the Page_Load() subroutine is executed every time the form is visited, so if this condition was not present, the first visit would populate the drop-down list with five items, the second with five more, and so on. This condition is extremely useful for the initial processing of our web forms, and you'll soon be extremely familiar with it!

So, now that we've taken a look at the code involved, let's look at the execution. After pressing *F5*, the first breakpoint we reach is on Page_Init(), as in the following screenshot:

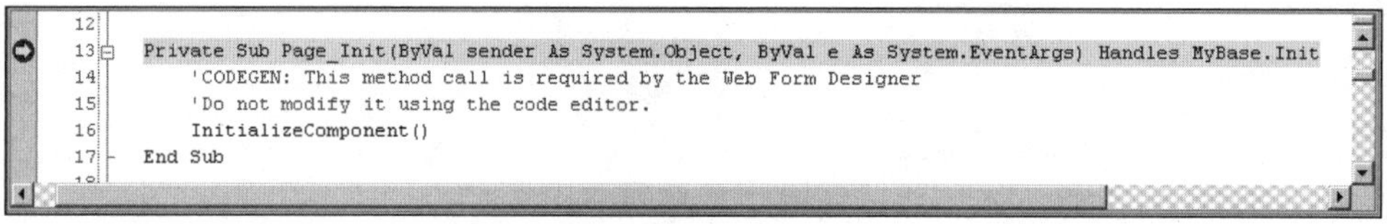

```
12
13    Private Sub Page_Init(ByVal sender As System.Object, ByVal e As System.EventArgs) Handles MyBase.Init
14        'CODEGEN: This method call is required by the Web Form Designer
15        'Do not modify it using the code editor.
16        InitializeComponent()
17    End Sub
```

This routine calls the InitializeComponent() subroutine, after which we proceed (if we continue to hit *F11*) to Page_Load(), where the DropDownList control is populated.

```
20
21        Private Sub Page_Load(ByVal sender As System.Object, _
22                          ByVal e As System.EventArgs) Handles MyBase.Load
23            If Not (Page.IsPostBack) Then
24                DropDownList1.Items.Add("----")
25                DropDownList1.Items.Add("Green")
26                DropDownList1.Items.Add("Red")
27                DropDownList1.Items.Add("Blue")
28                DropDownList1.Items.Add("RGB")
29            End If
30
31        End Sub
```

The browser then appears, as follows:

When we make a selection in the web form, Visual Studio .NET loops back through `Page_Init()` and `Page_Load()`, and then stops at the next break in the code:

```
36        Private Sub DropDownList1_SelectedIndexChanged _
37            (ByVal sender As System.Object, _
38            ByVal e As System.EventArgs) _
39            Handles DropDownList1.SelectedIndexChanged
40        Select Case DropDownList1.SelectedItem.Text
41            Case "Green"
```

As we step through the calls to `CreateColorTextBox()`, the code will break again, as shown below:

```
58        Private Function CreateColorTextBox _
59                        (ByVal Count As Integer, _
60                        ByVal ColorName As System.Drawing.Color)
61            Dim ColorTextBox As TextBox = New TextBox()
62            ColorTextBox.BackColor = ColorName
63            ColorTextBox.ID = Count
64            PlaceHolder1.Controls.Add(ColorTextBox)
65        End Function
66
```

After `DropDownList1_SelectedIndexChanged()` has completed execution, the page is rendered and sent back to the browser. At this point, all referenced objects are destroyed, and memory is released during the next garbage collection process.

Web Forms Processing at the File Level

Lastly, now that we've seen the sequence in which the routines are executed, what happens to the physical files when the web application is executed? Well, we know that a web form consists of two separate files: the .aspx file with presentation code, and the .aspx.vb file (code-behind page) with application logic. When our web application is run, they form a single entity.

The code-behind file is compiled into a .dll file that's produced when the project is built. The web form's .aspx file is also compiled, but somewhat differently. When a user browses to the web form for the first time, ASP.NET automatically generates a .NET class file that represents the page, and compiles it to a second .dll file. The generated class for the .aspx page inherits from the code-behind class that was compiled into the earlier .dll file. As subsequent visits are made to the page, the compiled .dll is used to generate the output.

If we change the .aspx file or its code-behind page, the dynamically generated DLL that represents the page will be regenerated the next time the page is requested, and will again be used by subsequent requests.

Summary

So far, we've discussed how to create web forms applications within the Visual Studio .NET environment, seen the files that Visual Studio .NET automatically creates, and considered some of the differences between web forms and Windows forms. We have seen the processing stages that a web form undergoes when a browser makes a request for it over the Internet, and we even saw the file-level processing that occurs when the web application is run.

In the next chapter, we will go into more detail about building user interfaces using the web forms controls available in Visual Studio .NET. We will also continue our investigations of event handling, leading into discussions on client-side and server-side validation, and modifying the appearance of a web form-generated application at run time.

Solut...
BM
Refer...
System.Dat...
System.Drawing
System.Web
System.XML
AssemblyInfo.vb
Assembly
BM.vsdisco
Global.asax
Styles.css
Web.config
WebForm1.aspx

WebForm1.aspx* | WebForm1.aspx. \

ebForm1.aspx*

User Interfaces and Server Controls

In the last chapter, we examined the architecture and purpose of web forms, and discussed how they improve the concept of a 'web page'. We also began to see how, in combination with the IDE provided by Visual Studio .NET, ASP.NET's **server** (server-side) **controls** can transform web page design into the drag-and-drop ballet that our colleagues in the Windows desktop programming department have enjoyed for so long. The way that server controls work is ingenious: while you're designing your web application, they behave like any other control, allowing you to position them and set their properties through the familiar Visual Basic .NET interface. At run time, however, they generate the HTML code necessary to render themselves identically in web browsers, using nothing but standard HTML elements.

Mastering ASP.NET server controls will make you a highly productive web developer, with an intuitive feel for which controls should be used when. This chapter aims to teach this proficiency by describing:

❑   How Visual Studio .NET's "HTML controls" compare with HTML elements

❑   How to react to events that take place in controls, on both the server and the client side

❑   Different ways to change the appearance of controls: attributes and stylesheets

❑   The advantages of web server controls, especially their design-time benefits

❑   How to make web-based data capture more reliable by using the validation controls

❑   The creation of user controls and custom controls that expand on built-in functionality

❑   Using the idea of dynamic content to generate user-aware web applications

Also in this chapter, we'll have our first look at a sample application that we'll be returning to on a few occasions during the course of the book. *Friends Reunion* is a simplified take on a class of web sites that's quite popular right now: they allow their users to register details of schools and colleges they've attended, or places they've worked. Then, people who were at the same place at the same time are given the opportunity to contact one another. As we progress, our application will become ever more complex, but we'll start here with some basics: a login form, a registration form, and a page for general news items. We will also work on some common header and footer components.

Server Controls

Thanks to the previous chapter, you've already had a first experience of server controls: we created some examples that used the `Button` and `DropDownList` controls. In this chapter, you'll soon discover that most of the server controls at our disposal in Visual Studio .NET are every bit as easy to place and use. While a page is being designed, they appear as controls that we can configure through the Properties window, changing their appearance, default values, and so on. At run time, ASP.NET transforms them into plain old HTML code that it sends to the browser.

Server controls offer real productivity gains over other methods of web page design, not only because of their ease of use, but also because they conform to the .NET programming model. They make the process of building a page as easy as designing a Windows Forms application. We drag controls on to our pages, tinker with their properties, and there's our user interface. There's simply no need to grapple with HTML – unless, of course, you really want to. Once you get used to the new model, you may never want to mess with HTML source code again!

> *If you've done some Visual Basic programming before the rise of .NET, it's worth pointing out that server controls are not ActiveX controls. They don't need any client-side installation, and they're not Windows-specific.*

HTML Controls

When you open a web form for editing in Visual Studio .NET, there are two areas of the Toolbox that contain user interface elements that we can place on our web pages: HTML, which contains the **HTML controls**, and Web Forms, which contains the **web controls**. We'll look at the former in this section, leaving the latter for a little later on.

The HTML controls in Visual Studio .NET correspond exactly with standard HTML elements: they have all the same properties, and they render precisely as you'd expect them to. For example, the ASP.NET Table control is equivalent to the HTML `<table>` element. If we were to drag one from the Toolbox onto an empty web form, this is how it would appear in the designer (don't worry about following along with this; we'll have a go at using some HTML controls in the next *Try It Out*):

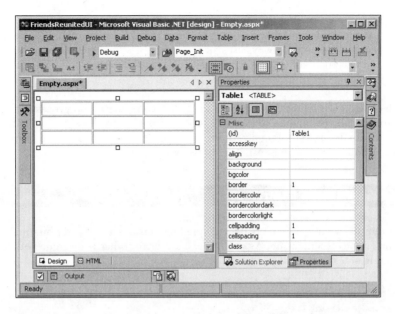

In the **Properties** window, we can change every aspect of the table, and you may recognize the names in the window (such as `border`, `cellpadding`, and `cellspacing`) as being the attributes of a traditional HTML table.

When we add a control to a web form in the Visual Studio .NET designer, HTML code for the control is generated, and we can see it (and modify it) by clicking the **HTML** button at the bottom of the designer. For the case of the table above, Visual Studio .NET would generate the following:

```
<body MS_POSITIONING="FlowLayout">
  <form id="Form1" method="post" runat="server">
    <TABLE id="Table1" style="WIDTH: 264px; HEIGHT: 75px"
    cellSpacing="1" cellPadding="1" width="264" border="1">
      <TR>
        <TD></TD>
        <TD></TD>
        <TD></TD>
      </TR>
      <TR>
        <TD></TD>
        <TD></TD>
        <TD></TD>
      </TR>
      <TR>
        <TD></TD>
        <TD></TD>
        <TD></TD>
      </TR>
    </TABLE>
  </form>
</body>
```

There's nothing strange or magical here – just plain old HTML elements. By default, Visual Studio .NET is extremely slapdash about its use of capitalization! If you wish, it's possible to change things so that Visual Studio .NET always uses all uppercase or all lowercase characters in its elements by heading for the Options item in the Tools menu. The capitalization option is under Text Editor | HTML/XML | Format.

As the HTML controls are represented by regular HTML code, there's no processing required, and ASP.NET simply passes the markup to the client browser as-is. Also, we can use all of the traditional techniques for manipulating HTML controls, such setting attributes or executing client-side script. Let's now start the ball rolling with a demonstration of using them.

Try It Out – Building a Login Form

For this first example, we're going to create a simple login form that provides minimal authentication for users of our Friends Reunion site. As you'll see, it's amazing what you can do with little more than a table and a couple of text controls!

1. Create a new ASP.NET web application in Visual Studio .NET, giving it the name `FriendsReunionUI`:

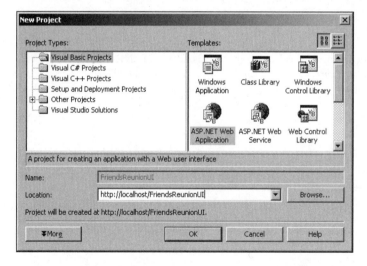

2. Later in the book, we'll be endowing the Friends Reunion application with secure login functionality, and as signal of that intent we're going to place the login page in a sub-folder of its own. Delete the default `WebForm1.aspx` web form, right-click on the project name in the Solution Explorer, and choose Add | New Folder. Call it `Secure`:

3. Right-click the newly created folder and add a new web form called `Login.aspx` to it. Use the **Properties** window to set its `pageLayout` property to `FlowLayout`, as described in Chapter 2.

4. Double-click on the **Table** control in the **HTML** tab of the toolbox to add one to the form.

5. Next, place the cursor on one of the empty cells in the third column, right-click on the same cell, and select **Delete | Columns**, so that our table now has just two columns.

6. Click the top-left cell, and type **User Name:**. In the cell below it, type **Password:**.

7. Now drag and drop a **Text Field** and a **Password Field** control respectively into the next cells along.

8. The last control to add is a **Button**, which should be placed in the first cell in the last row of the table. Using the **Properties** window, set its `value` property to `Login`, so that the page now looks like this:

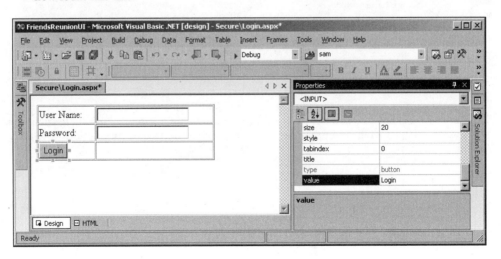

9. Finally, we can get rid of the unused cell to the right of the button. Right-click on it, this time choosing Delete | Cells from the context menu. Select the cell containing the button and set its colspan property to 2 in the Properties window. If you now switch to the HTML view, you should see something like this:

```
<%@ Page Language="vb" AutoEventWireup="false"
        Codebehind="Login.aspx.vb" Inherits="FriendsReunionUI.Login"%>
<!DOCTYPE HTML PUBLIC "-//W3C//DTD HTML 4.0 Transitional//EN">
<html>
  <head>
    <title>Login</title>
    <meta name="GENERATOR" content="Microsoft Visual Studio.NET 7.0">
    <meta name="CODE_LANGUAGE" content="Visual Basic 7.0">
    <meta name="vs_defaultClientScript" content="JavaScript">
    <meta name="vs_targetSchema"
        content="http://schemas.microsoft.com/intellisense/ie5">
  </head>
  <body ms_positioning="FlowLayout">
    <form id="Form1" method="post" runat="server">
      <table id="Table1" style="WIDTH: 264px; HEIGHT: 75px" cellspacing="1"
            cellpadding="1" width="264" border="1">
        <tr>
          <td>User Name:</td>
          <td>
            <input type="text"></td>
        </tr>
        <tr>
          <td>Password:</td>
          <td>
            <input type="password"></td>
        </tr>
        <tr>
          <td colspan="2">
            <input type="button" value="Login"></td>
        </tr>
      </table>
    </form>
  </body>
</html>
```

10. Let's add a client-side handler for the Login button being pressed. Position the cursor next to the last <input> tag, and press the space bar to view the IntelliSense options available:

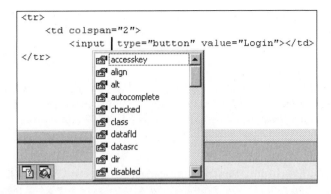

Scroll down to the `onclick` event (or just type its first few letters), and insert it (either by double-clicking, or by pressing *Tab*). Now add a small amount of code that will bring up a simple message box, as highlighted below:

```
<td colspan="2">
   <input onclick="alert('About to Login!');" type="button" value="Login">
</td>
```

11. Right-click the `Login.aspx` page in the Solution Explorer and select **Set As Start Page**. Compile and run the solution by pressing *F5*, which also saves all files.

How It Works

As we drop and set the controls' properties, the IDE automatically generates the corresponding HTML source code, as we saw when we switched to the HTML view. In this view, we also get the benefit of IntelliSense, which (among other things) lists all of the valid attributes for any HTML element.

When we view the page in a browser, the HTML code that we see in Visual Studio .NET is sent straight to the browser, which interprets it to render the controls that we placed in the designer. (In Internet Explorer, you can check this by right-clicking on the page and choosing **View Source**.) When you click the **Login** button, you should see this:

This demonstrates that we can perform client-side event handling as usual, by attaching script to the element's corresponding onxxx attribute, as we did here with onclick. If we want more sophisticated functionality, this script can call further client-side methods. Right now, however we have a more pressing concern: our login form looks pretty ugly, doesn't it? We need to add *style* to our page.

Client-side script code can perform some complex tasks, and it's a subject to which whole books are dedicated. For more information about script code, try Beginning JavaScript *(ISBN 1-86100-406-0) or* Professional JavaScript, 2nd Edition *(ISBN 1-86100-553-9), both from Wrox Press.*

Visual Styles

As we saw briefly in the last chapter, we can use **cascading stylesheets** (CSS) to define visual characteristics that we can then apply uniformly to a range of items on one page, or a range of pages. Visual Studio .NET comes with an editor that makes creating CSS stylesheets easy, and we can start it up by clicking on the ellipsis (...) button next to the style property of an HTML control in the Properties window:

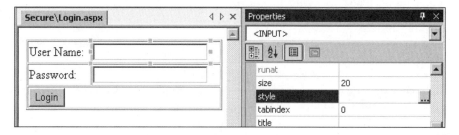

The editor is called the Style Builder, and it allows us to change every aspect of a particular control's appearance:

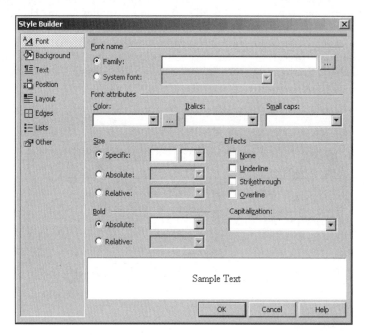

Unfortunately, adding the style for each control on the page can be tedious, and is certainly error-prone. Furthermore, if we decided at a later date to (say) change the font of all the <input> textboxes in our application, we would have some serious work to do, and it would be all too easy to miss one or two, spoiling the consistent feel. There's a better approach: still using the Style Builder, we can create a single stylesheet defining *all* the styles that we use, throughout our site. Let's see how that might work.

Try It Out – Creating a CSS Stylesheet

To create a CSS stylesheet that works across more than one web form, we can create it as a separate item that we then 'attach' to all web forms in which we want to use the definitions it contains. In this example, we'll start the process of building a stylesheet for our Friends Reunion application that we'll return to several times over the course of this chapter.

1. Continuing our desire for neatness, we'll place our stylesheet in its own sub-folder, too. Right-click on the project name in Solution Explorer, and create a new folder called Style:

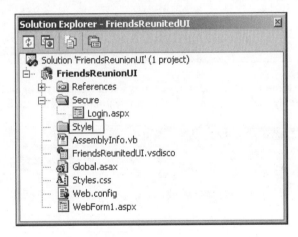

2. Right-click the new folder, and select Add | Add New Item. From the right-hand window, select Style Sheet, and name it iestyle.css. To begin with, the new file will contain just an empty body element, like this:

```
body
{
}
```

At this point, right-clicking the body element and selecting Build Style from the context menu will result in the appearance of the Style Builder we saw a moment ago. This time, however, we can use it to specify appearance characteristics that will apply to our whole application.

3. Select the Background category from the list on the left of the Style Builder, and choose a color from the Color dropdown. I chose sensible Silver, but feel free to be as garish as you like! Select OK when you're done.

4. Next, we're going to ensure that all the tables in our application have the same basic appearance. Right-click anywhere on the stylesheet, and select **Add Style Rule**. From the **Element** dropdown on the dialog that appears, select **TABLE** and click **OK**:

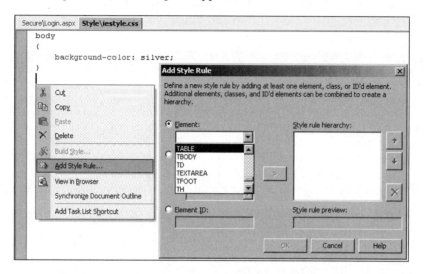

5. Now right-click the new TABLE element, and select **Build Style** again. Choose the **Tahoma** font as the **Family** value, and enter **8 pt** for the **Specific** field in the **Size** section:

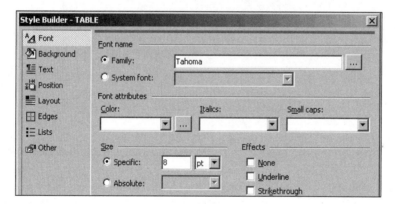

6. Click **OK**, and save the stylesheet. We can now associate the new stylesheet with the login form we built earlier by adding the following line at the top of the file's HTML code:

```
<html>
  <head>
    <title>Login</title>
    <link href="../Style/iestyle.css" rel="stylesheet" type="text/css">

    ...
```

```
</head>

. . .
```

Unfortunately, there's no drag-and-drop mechanism for adding this link – we have to do it manually.

How It Works

As described above, the CSS stylesheet groups together the layout attributes that should be applied to all instances of a particular HTML element. By linking the stylesheet with a page through the `<link>` element, the styles it contains are applied to items on the page. The path to the stylesheet is relative, based on the location of the current web form – hence the need for the `'..'` syntax to 'step back' to the application's root directory.

Once we've saved the stylesheet and linked it to our page, we can see the effect of our handiwork when we reopen the page in design view:

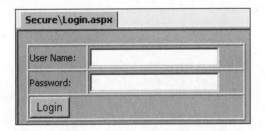

Without any further work on our part, the color we set for the `<body>` element is shown, and the text inside the table has taken on its new font. If we were to make changes to any of the values in the stylesheet, they would be automatically reflected on the page.

However, associating one style with all instances of a particular element isn't very flexible: what if we want to display some textboxes with one style, and some others with a different one? (Consider the HTML `<input>` element, which represents textboxes, buttons, password fields, checkboxes, and more!) There's another way to group styles together and associate them with elements: we can use a CSS **class**.

Try It Out – Grouping Styles by Class Name

In this example, we'll use CSS classes to provide different styles for the textboxes and buttons in our application. Both of these are facets of the `<input>` element, so it would be impossible to do this by associating style rules with the element name.

1. If necessary, reopen the `iestyle.css` stylesheet in Visual Studio .NET, and then right-click anywhere in the design view and select **Add Style Rule**.

2. This time, instead of selecting an item in the **Element** drop-down, check the **Class name** radio button, and type **TextBox** (this will also appear in the preview box in the lower right corner, preceded by a period). Click **OK**.

3. Add the following code inside the new rule's braces:

```
body
{
   background-color: silver;
}
TABLE
{
   font-size: 8pt;
   font-family: Tahoma;
}
.TextBox
{
   border-right: #c7ccdc 1px solid;
   border-top: #c7ccdc 1px solid;
   border-left: #c7ccdc 1px solid;
   border-bottom: #c7ccdc 1px solid;
   font-size: 8pt;
   font-family: Tahoma, Verdana, 'Times New Roman';
}
```

These additions should all be quite self-explanatory, but you'll notice that we've specified three fonts for the font-family value. These are in order of preference, so that if Tahoma is not available on the client machine, Verdana will be used – and failing that, Times New Roman.

4. Repeat steps 3 and 4, this time entering **Button** in the **Class name** textbox. Use the code shown below:

```
.Button
{
   background-color: gainsboro;
   border-right: darkgray 1px solid;
   border-top: darkgray 1px solid;
   border-left: darkgray 1px solid;
   border-bottom: darkgray 1px solid;
   font-size: 8pt;
   font-family: Tahoma, Verdana, 'Times New Roman';
}
```

5. Open the login page in design view, select each of the two input textboxes in turn, and set the class property of both to TextBox. Also set the button's class property to Button. You'll see the controls change as you do, reflecting the styles defined by each class.

6. Finally, select the table and set its border property to 0.

How It Works

On this occasion, we added new style rules to our stylesheet manually, but if you now open the **Build Style** dialog for any of them, it will be populated with the values we typed. Furthermore, IntelliSense is there to help us whenever we add a new line inside a rule, showing the styles currently available:

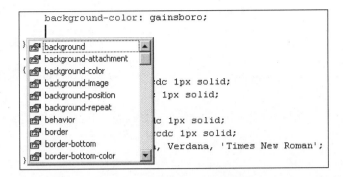

When we instruct a control to use a CSS class that we've defined in a stylesheet, Visual Studio .NET makes the association by using the HTML `class` attribute on the tag in the code that's sent to the browser. The `class` attribute is available to all HTML elements, and it's equally possible to associate controls with the styles in a stylesheet by adding it manually. If you now open the page in the browser, you'll see this:

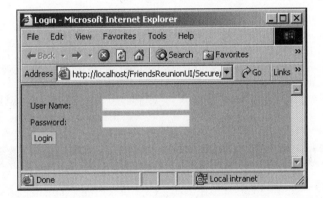

Well, that looks better! And better yet, we can now reliably and quickly apply the same style to any textbox we create, just by setting its `class` property to `TextBox`. Should we then make any further changes to the style rule, the associated controls would reflect them automatically.

> *For comprehensive information about CSS, I recommend* Cascading Style Sheets *(published by glasshaus, ISBN 1-90415-104-3). Also useful are* HTML 4.01 Programmer's Reference *(Wrox Press, ISBN 1-86100-533-4) and* Professional Style Sheets for HTML and XML *(Wrox Press, ISBN 1-86100-165-7).*

HTML Server Controls

So far, we've seen some useful features of the Visual Studio .NET IDE, but what we've ultimately produced has been good old-fashioned HTML, with a little bit of JavaScript thrown in for good measure. One of the characteristics of web 'applications' like this is that the browser does most of the work, and the principles of client-side event handling haven't changed much since the technique first began to appear several years ago. ASP.NET, however, is founded on the basis of server-side programming: events are trapped and handled on the server.

In ASP.NET, the events associated with web forms are classified into two categories: **global events**, and **page-specific events**. The first of these apply to the whole application or current user session, and is not specific to any particular page. Handlers for these events are placed in the `Global.asax` file, and we'll see more about how they work in Chapter 7. As we saw in the previous chapter, page-specific events are handled in that page's code-behind page, and it's this type that we'll be examining in more detail in the remainder of this chapter.

We can start by taking a look at the code-behind page for `Login.aspx`, by right-clicking on the page (in the Solution Explorer or the designer) and choosing **View Code**:

```
Public Class Login
  Inherits System.Web.UI.Page

  [ Web Form Designer Generated Code ]

  Private Sub Page_Load(ByVal sender As System.Object, _
                        ByVal e As System.EventArgs) Handles MyBase.Load
    ' Put user code to initialize the page here
  End Sub

End Class
```

Because we've only used plain HTML controls so far, there's no information relating to them in the code-behind page – not even in the "designer-generated code" region. Placing HTML *server* controls on the page, on the other hand, *does* result in code being placed in the code-behind file, as we'll see in the following example.

Try It Out – Converting to HTML Server Controls

Converting an HTML control to an HTML server control is simply a matter of right-clicking the control in the designer and choosing **Run As Server Control**. In this example, we'll do precisely that for the three `<input>` elements already on the login page, and we'll add a new element that provides the user with some feedback to show that their actions have had an effect.

1. Right-click on the two textboxes and the button in turn, and check **Run As Server Control**. As you do this, a small green arrow will appear in the top-left corner of each control, to indicate that it is indeed now a server control.

2. To make the ensuing Visual Basic .NET code a little clearer, use the **Properties** window to change the IDs of the controls to `txtLogin`, `txtPwd`, and `btnLogin`. Save the file.

3. Underneath the login table, add a new HTML **Label** control, and convert it to a server control as before. Then set its ID to `lblMessage`, delete its text content, and clear its `style` property.

4. Double-click on the `btnLogin` control, and add the following line of code to the event handler:

```
Public Class Login

    . . .

    Private Sub btnLogin_ServerClick(ByVal sender As Object, _
                               ByVal e As System.EventArgs) _
                               Handles btnLogin.ServerClick
        Me.lblMessage.InnerText = "Authenticated on the server!"
    End Sub

End Class
```

5. Save and test the page by pressing *F5*.

How It Works

Whenever we select **Run As Server Control** for an HTML element, a `runat="server"` attribute is added to that element's HTML declaration, and a protected class member representing that element is added to the class in the code-behind page. In the case of `Login.aspx`, the following member variables were added at the start of the code:

```
Public Class Login
    Inherits System.Web.UI.Page
    Protected WithEvents txtLogin As System.Web.UI.HtmlControls.HtmlInputText
    Protected WithEvents txtPwd As System.Web.UI.HtmlControls.HtmlInputText
    Protected WithEvents btnLogin As _
                   System.Web.UI.HtmlControls.HtmlInputButton
    Protected WithEvents lblMessage As _
                   System.Web.UI.HtmlControls.HtmlGenericControl

    . . .
```

Visual Studio .NET takes care of a lot of the necessary-but-tiresome details of writing pages, such as the skeleton code for event handlers. When we double-clicked the `btnLogin` control, the empty event handler was generated and attached to the default event of the button control, `ServerClick`, with the `Handles` keyword. (If you want to handle an event other than the default one, these handlers can also be associated manually.)

It's also worth noting that because the member variables corresponding to the server controls on our form are declared with the `WithEvents` keyword, we can access the objects from the dropdowns at the top of the code editor:

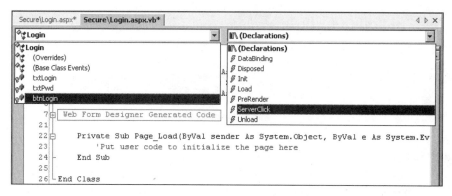

We've cheated a little here – this image is actually a collage to show both dropdowns simultaneously. The one on the right lists the methods available for the object selected in the one on the left, providing another means to create skeleton handlers for controls. We could have achieved the same result as double-clicking on the button by selecting the `ServerClick` event from the dropdown.

Inside the click handler, our code simply tells the label to display a message: we can dynamically access and modify the properties of any of the server controls in the code-behind page. (We can't access the `<table>` itself, because that *isn't* a server control.) When we test the page now, we first get the alert message from the client-side script that we added before, and then, when the form is posted to the server, the following message is returned:

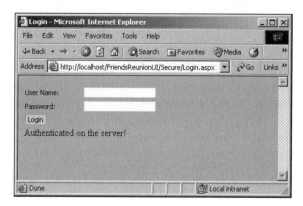

Side Note: The Postback Mechanism

At this point, a reasonable question to be asking would be: How does the server-side code know which control was clicked? In general, our form could contain any number of buttons, so how does ASP.NET determine which handler to call? To discover the answer to this, we have to look afresh at the HTML code that's generated at run time by ASP.NET. When the application is first launched, this is the code sent to the browser:

```
<body ms_positioning="FlowLayout">
  <form name="Form1" method="post" action="login.aspx" id="Form1">
    <input type="hidden" name="__EVENTTARGET" value="" />
```

```
<input type="hidden" name="__EVENTARGUMENT" value="" />
<input type="hidden" name="__VIEWSTATE"
       value="dDwtMTgxNjQwMjYyNDs7PhWazFRl2mI+06GvtWm9lpZMZTbu" />

<script language="javascript">
<!--
   function __doPostBack(eventTarget, eventArgument) {
     var theform = document.Form1;
     theform.__EVENTTARGET.value = eventTarget;
     theform.__EVENTARGUMENT.value = eventArgument;
     theform.submit();
   }
// -->
</script>

<table id="Table1" style="WIDTH: 234px; HEIGHT: 75px"
       cellspacing="1" cellpadding="1" idth="234" border="0">
  <tr>
    <td>User Name:</td>
    <td><input name="txtLogin" id="txtLogin" type="text"
        class="TextBox" style="WIDTH: 144px; HEIGHT: 17px" size="18" />
    </td>
  </tr>
  <tr>
    <td>Password:</td>
    <td><input name="txtPwd" id="txtPwd" type="password"
        class="TextBox" style="WIDTH: 144px; HEIGHT: 17px" size="18" />
    </td>
  </tr>
  <tr>
    <td colspan="2">
      <input language="javascript" name="btnLogin" id="btnLogin"
        onclick="alert('About to Login!'); __doPostBack('btnLogin','')"
        type="button" value="Login" class="Button" />
    </td>
  </tr>
</table>
<div id="lblMessage" ms_positioning="FlowLayout"></div>
</form>
</body>
```

Notice the three hidden input fields that have been added, and the new script block containing a JavaScript function called __doPostBack(). This function receives two parameters, saves them in the first two hidden fields, and then submits the form to the server.

Further down the listing, we come to the onclick handler for btnLogin. In addition to the call to alert() that we added to this attribute earlier, there is now a call to the __doPostBack() function, to which is passed the button's id attribute.

The result is that when we click the button, the function saves the id of the control that caused the postback in a hidden field, and submits the form to the server. ASP.NET receives the form and uses the hidden __EVENTTARGET value to determine the appropriate handler for the event, which in this case would be our btnLogin_ServerClick() subroutine.

The other hidden field, __VIEWSTATE, is used to retain any values that we have entered on the form. For example, if we enter a user name and a password before clicking the button, the user name is still shown after the postback. We'll be looking at this mechanism in more detail in Chapter 7.

Web Server Controls

As well as all of the HTML controls (and their server-side variants), ASP.NET offers another set of controls for the use of web form programmers. These are the **web server controls** (or just **web controls**, since they're *always* server controls), and they're located in the Web Forms tab of the toolbox. Many of these controls have direct HTML equivalents, but there are several new ones too. There are many reasons for choosing web server controls over HTML controls; here are the most important:

❑   Web server controls offer a layer of abstraction on top of HTML controls. At run time, some of them comprise a number of HTML elements, and therefore offer greater functionality with less design-time code. In a moment, we'll look at an example featuring the `Calendar` control, which demonstrates this idea quite nicely.

❑   Since web controls are independent of the markup that will render them at run time, some of them will render different HTML depending on the browser they're being viewed with, to improve compatibility. An example is the `Panel` control, which renders as a `<div>` on Internet Explorer, but as a `<table>` on Netscape browsers.

❑   Web server controls have a more consistent and logical object model than HTML elements, with some properties common to all web controls (including style-related properties such as `BackColor`, `BorderColor`, `Font`, and so on.).

❑   Web server controls have a richer event model, making it easier to write server-side code for them.

❑   Design-time support for web server controls is greatly enhanced and more flexible. Some of these controls, for example, have their own Wizards, custom property pages, and the like.

❑   Web server controls provide typed values; in HTML controls, all values are strings.

❑   Because web server controls always run at the server, they are always available from within our server-side code (in the code-behind page).

Try It Out – Creating the News Page

In this example, we'll add a 'news' page to the Friends Reunion application, which will eventually fulfill the role of notifying the user of potential new contacts. For the time being, though, we'll just use it to display a calendar that allows the user to select a date. You've got to start somewhere!

1.   We'll be using some images on our page, so create a new folder in the project, and call it `Images`. Select all the files from the `Images` directory in the code download, and drag and drop them onto the new folder in Solution Explorer.

2.   Add a new web form to the root directory of the project, and call it `News.aspx`. Set its `pageLayout` property to `FlowLayout`.

3. From the Web Forms tab of the toolbox, drop a `Panel` control onto the new page. Set the following properties for it:

Property	Value
BackColor	#336699
Font | Bold	True
Font | Name	Tahoma
Font | Size	8pt
ForeColor	White
HorizontalAlign	Right

4. Set the panel's inner text to Friends Reunion. Then, drop a new Image control inside the panel, to the right of the text:

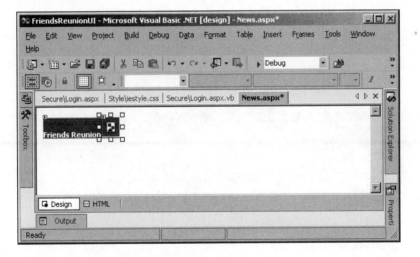

5. Set the properties of this image as follows:

Property	Value
ImageUrl	images/friends.gif
ImageAlign	Middle

6. Enter the following text below the panel, after inserting an HTML paragraph tag (<p>) by pressing the *Enter* key: "Welcome to the news for today! Here is the current calendar:"

7. Press *Enter* again after the text, and double-click on a `Calendar` control in the Web Forms tab of the toolbox. When it arrives in your application, set its ID to `calDates`.

8. Below the calendar, drop a `Label` control, and set its `Text` property to `"Selected Date: "`. The ` ` is an HTML character entity that inserts a space (strictly, a non-breaking space) after the colon.

9. For a little extra complexity, we'll add a drop-down list that allows the user to go straight to yesterday, today, or tomorrow. Next to the label, place a `DropDownList` control, and change its ID to `cbDay`. Click the ellipsis next to its `Items` property to bring up the ListItem Collection Editor. Click the **Add** button three times to add three items to the **Members** pane on the left, and set their properties as in the following table:

ListItem	Properties

0	`Selected = True`
	`Text = Today`
	`Value = 0`

1	`Selected = False`
	`Text = Tomorrow`
	`Value = 1`

2	`Selected = False`
	`Text = Yesterday`
	`Value = -1`

10. Click OK, and the page will now appear in the designer as shown below:

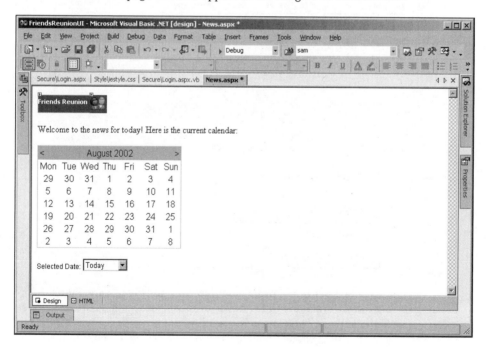

11. Set this page as the start page, and hit *F5* to run the project.

How It Works

The first thing to observe here is that, having set the `Font` property for the panel control, the calendar, the label, and the drop-down list all use the same font. This consistency derives from the fact that the controls inherit from more general controls that provide the common properties. For the controls we used on this page, the hierarchy is as follows:

Except for the `Control` class at the top, all of these classes are to be found in the `System.Web.UI.WebControls` namespace. (The root `Control` class is also the base class for the HTML controls.) The `Font` property belongs to the `WebControl` class – and all of the derived controls inherit it, providing a very consistent model. Now let's take a look at the generated output:

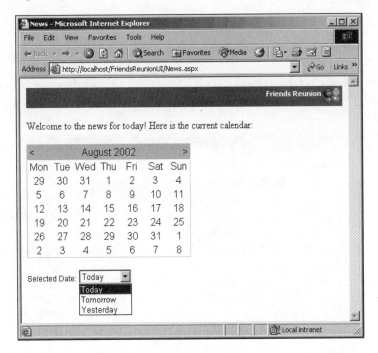

In fact, the `Calendar` is by far the most sophisticated of the web server controls. We didn't have to write a single line of code, and yet we have a full-featured calendar that automatically allows the user to select other months by using the links displayed at the top of the control, to the left and right of the month name.

71

That's not all. ASP.NET tailors the control to work optimally in different browsers. Furthermore, it is automatically localized for the culture of the user currently accessing the page (such as for Spanish users). This 'intelligent' rendering can be seen at work in the following screenshot:

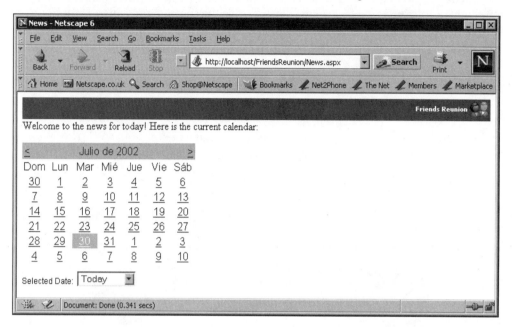

At run time, the calendar is rendered as an HTML table, with all the formatting in place. There is strong design-time support, including the Auto Format dialog, which we can use to apply a range of predefined designs. Just right-click on the calendar, and select Auto Format:

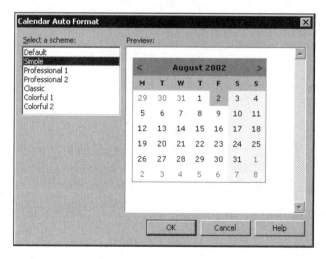

All of the more complex web controls, such as the `DataGrid` that we'll see in Chapter 5, offer easy formatting in a similar way – and we can also set these properties manually, of course. Also, just as for HTML controls, we can define CSS styles that apply to the web server controls throughout our application. To assign a style rule to a web server control, we specify its name in the control's `CssClass` property, and link the stylesheet to the page using the `<link>` element inside the `<head>` section, just as before.

Try It Out – Using CSS Styles with Web Controls

In this section, we'll do more to standardize the appearance of the controls in our application by creating some more style rules and applying them to our `News.aspx` web form.

1. First, we'll define a style that will apply fundamental formatting to any element that doesn't require something more specialized. Reopen the `iestyle.css` file and add the following style rule:

```
.Normal
{
    font-size: 8pt;
    font-family: Tahoma, Verdana, 'Times New Roman';
}
```

2. Also, we will make a change to our color scheme. Change the `body` style rule to match the following:

```
body
{
    background-color: #f0f1f6;
    font-size: 8pt;
    font-family: Tahoma, Verdana, 'Times New Roman';
}
```

3. Then, add the following element to the `<head>` section of the `News.aspx` page:

```
<html>
  <head>
    <title>News</title>
    <link href="Style/iestyle.css" rel="stylesheet" type="text/css">

    . . .

  </head>

  . . .
```

4. Set the `CssClass` property of the label that reads **Selected Date:** to `Normal`. Set the `class` property of the **Welcome to the news...** message to `Normal`, too.

5. Set the `CssClass` property of the drop-down list control to `TextBox`, and run the project.

73

How It Works

Just as HTML controls have the `class` attribute, web server controls have a `CssClass` attribute, and it has exactly the same effect – CSS styles work the same way for both types of control. Once the styles have been applied, our application looks like this:

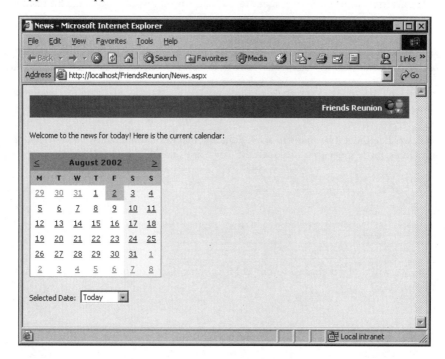

Handling events for web server controls is very similar to the process for HTML controls. Setting up a handler for a button's click event is just a matter of double-clicking on it in the Visual Studio .NET designer, and adding our code to the automatically created subroutine.

Try It Out – Handling Events for Web Server Controls

To extend our example, we'll use some server-side event handling to make the link between the calendar and the drop-down control, and to report the currently selected date to the user. We'll arrange for selections in the dropdown to change the selected date in the calendar, and for any selection change to result in the 'current' date being displayed in a label control.

1. Add a new label control at the bottom of the `News.aspx` file. Set its ID to `lblMessage`, and its `CssClass` to `Normal`. Clear its `Text` property.

2. Set the `cbDay` drop-down control's `AutoPostBack` property to `True` before double-clicking on it and adding the following code to the handler:

```
Private Sub cbDay_SelectedIndexChanged(ByVal sender As System.Object, _
                                      ByVal e As System.EventArgs) _
                                      Handles cbDay.SelectedIndexChanged
    Dim day As Integer = CInt(cbDay.SelectedItem.Value)
    calDates.SelectedDate = DateTime.Now.AddDays(day)
    lblMessage.Text = _
          "Current Date: " & calDates.SelectedDate.ToLongDateString()
End Sub
```

3. Double-click the calendar control to create the `SelectionChanged` handler, and add the following code:

```
Private Sub calDates_SelectionChanged(ByVal sender As System.Object, _
                                     ByVal e As System.EventArgs) _
                                     Handles calDates.SelectionChanged
    lblMessage.Text = _
          "Current Date: " & calDates.SelectedDate.ToLongDateString()
End Sub
```

4. Run the project.

How It Works

Visual Studio .NET makes the process of attaching an event handler to a web server control very easy. By double-clicking the control (or by selecting the control and the corresponding event from the drop-down lists at the top of the editor), we create an empty handler. Because the member variables that represent web server controls are defined with the `WithEvents` keyword, we always have easy access to the controls' properties from event handlers.

In the handler for the dropdown, we use the `SelectedItem` property to retrieve the drop-down box value (either 0, 1, or -1, as defined when we set up the list items earlier). We cast the value it contains to an integer by using the `CInt()` method, and then add this integer to the current date before setting that as the `SelectedDate` property of the calendar. This will fire the calendar's `SelectionChanged` event, which we handle by displaying the new date in the `lblMessage` label.

To ensure that the event fires as soon as a change occurs in the drop-down list, we have to set the `AutoPostBack` property to `True`. This is an important step, because unlike the button and the calendar, drop-down lists don't cause a postback by default. Here is the typical output of our page as it now stands:

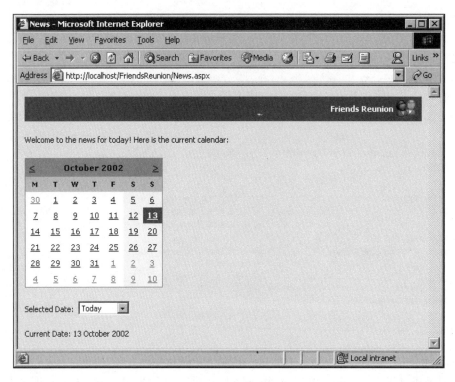

What stage have we reached? We know now that web server controls offer several features above and beyond those of the HTML controls that can make our time more productive. Their consistent object model is also beneficial, since once we've learned the set of properties that are available for one control, the chances are that we will see them again in others.

The events available for web controls are different from the HTML events that we can use in the attribute list of an HTML tag – there's no onclick, onmouseover, onkeydown, and the like. This is because web control events are exposed on the server, and so comprise only those appropriate for server-side processing. Imagine what would happen if our page caused a postback for every single mouse move operation! Even the Click event, which roughly corresponds to HTML's onclick event, is only available for those controls (such as buttons) where it makes sense.

For a complete description of all of the web server controls, and the events that each can fire, check out the information on MSDN.

Validation Controls

When you're creating a web form – especially one in which you hope to collect some data from your users – you'll often come across situations in which you need to place constraints on exactly what data they can submit. For example, you might want to mandate that a particular field must always be completed (say, a user name), or must adhere to a particular format (say, a social security number). In the past, this validation process had to be done manually, but ASP.NET comes with a set of **validation controls** that perform this task automatically.

Technically speaking, the validation controls are a subset of the web server controls, but there are enough new things to say about them that they deserve a section of their own here. Usually, they take the form of fields that are invisible most of the time, but become visible when a validation error occurs.

There are a number of validation controls available, and their names are almost self-explanatory: `RequiredFieldValidator`, `CompareValidator`, `RegularExpressionValidator`, `RangeValidator`, and `CustomValidator`. In the examples to come, you'll see the first three of these in use; `RangeValidator` doesn't apply to our example (but it's not complicated to understand), while `CustomValidator` is only used to create our own validation controls.

The ASP.NET validation controls are capable of performing validation on the server and (for IE5+ browsers) on the client, via JavaScript. To force validation to take place, we can either call the `Page.Validate()` method, or call the `Validate()` method of every validation control on the page, which has the same effect. Each validation control has an `IsValid` property that indicates whether the data it contains is currently valid. There is a similar property at the page level that indicates whether all the validation controls on the page are in a valid state.

Try It Out – Building a New User Form

In this example, we'll build a form for capturing the details of a new user, and employ the validation controls to ensure that we receive valid information in certain fields.

1. Create a new web form in the `Secure` folder, named `NewUser.aspx`. Set its `pageLayout` property to `FlowLayout`.

2. To the `<head>` section, add the `<link>` element that associates the `iestyle.css` stylesheet with this page:

```
<link href="../style/iestyle.css" type="text/css" rel="stylesheet">
```

3. Place the cursor at the top left of the page, type Fill in the fields below to register as a Friends Reunion member:, and hit *Return* when you're done.

4. Drop an HTML `Table` control onto the page, and give it ten rows with two columns each. Set the table's ID to `tbLogin`, its `cellspacing` and `cellpadding` properties to 2, and the `colspan` property of the last row to 2. Delete the rightmost cell in this row, and finally set the `border` property for the table to 0.

5. Type the text below into the left-hand column's cells, and add nine textbox web server controls to the right-hand column, setting their `CssClass` property to `TextBox`:

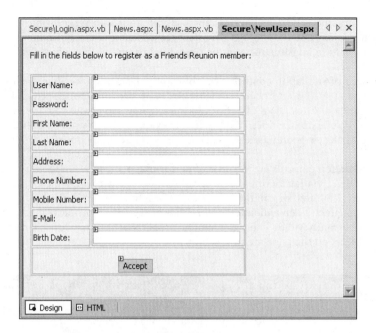

The simplest way of doing this is to place the first textbox, set its `CssClass` property, and then copy-and-paste it into the other locations.

The last row contains a centered button control (again, a web server control) with an ID of `btnAccept`, a `Text` property of `Accept`, and a `CssClass` of `Button`.

6. Give the textboxes the following IDs, in the order they are displayed: `txtLogin`, `txtPwd`, `txtFName`, `txtLName`, `txtAddress`, `txtPhone`, `txtMobile`, `txtEmail`, and `txtBirth`. Set the `TextMode` property of the `txtPwd` textbox to `Password`.

7. To narrow the **Birth Date** field, which doesn't need to be as wide as in the screenshot above, add the following style rule to the stylesheet, and set `txtBirth`'s `CssClass` property to `SmallTextBox`:

```
.SmallTextBox
{
  border-right: #c7ccdc 1px solid;
  border-top: #c7ccdc 1px solid;
  font-size: 8pt;
  border-left: #c7ccdc 1px solid;
  border-bottom: #c7ccdc 1px solid;
  font-family: Tahoma, Verdana, 'Times New Roman';
  width: 70px;
}
```

8. Drop a `RequiredFieldValidator` control next to the `txtLogin` textbox, and set its properties as in this table. In the **Properties** window, the `ControlToValidate` property is set by means of a drop-down list that contains the names of all the web server controls on the form.

Property	Value
ID	reqLogin
ControlToValidate	txtLogin
Display	None
ErrorMessage	A user name is required

9. Copy this `RequiredFieldValidator`, and paste it next to the `txtPwd` textbox. Set its properties as shown:

Property	Value
ID	reqPwd
ControlToValidate	txtPwd
ErrorMessage	A password is required

10. Carry on and paste one of these validation controls next to the `txtFName`, `txtLName`, `txtPhone`, and `txtEmail` textboxes. For each, change the ID, `ErrorMessage`, and `ControlToValidate` properties as appropriate, making particularly sure that the latter refers to the correct textbox.

11. Drop a `CompareValidator` control next to the `txtBirth` textbox, and give it these properties:

Property	Value
ID	compBirth
ControlToValidate	txtBirth
Display	Dynamic
ErrorMessage	Enter a valid birth date
Operator	DataTypeCheck
Type	Date

12. Drop a `RegularExpressionValidator` next to the `RequiredFieldValidator` for `txtPhone` (there is no problem with using these controls in tandem), and set these properties:

Property	Value
ID	regPhone
ControlToValidate	txtPhone

Table continued on following page

79

Property	Value
Display	None
ErrorMessage	Enter a valid US phone number
ValidationExpression	U. S. Phone Number (Click the ellipsis!)

13. Drop another `RegularExpressionValidator` next to the `RequiredFieldValidator` for `txtEmail`, and set these properties:

Property	Value
ID	regEmail
ControlToValidate	txtEmail
Display	None
ErrorMessage	Enter a valid e-mail address
ValidationExpression	Internet E-mail Address (Click the ellipsis!)

14. Drop a `Label` below the table, set its ID to `lblMessage` and clear its `Text` property. Set its `CssClass` property to `Normal`.

15. Drop a `ValidationSummary` control below this label, set its ID to `valErrors` and its `CssClass` to `Normal`. The form should now look something like this:

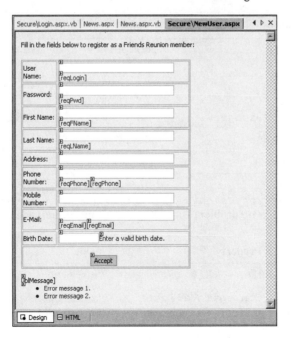

How It Works

By setting the `Display` properties of the `RequiredFieldValidator` controls to `None`, we suppress any errors they produce from appearing in the control. Instead, we'll use the `ValidationSummary` control to display errors on the page. (Had we set `Display` to `Dynamic` or `Static`, any error messages would have appeared next to the field in question.) Because the **Address** and **Mobile Number** fields are optional, we didn't use any validation controls for those.

If you now compile and run the application with `NewUser.aspx` set as the start page, and submit the page after entering an invalid birth date *and nothing more*, you'll see this screen in your browser:

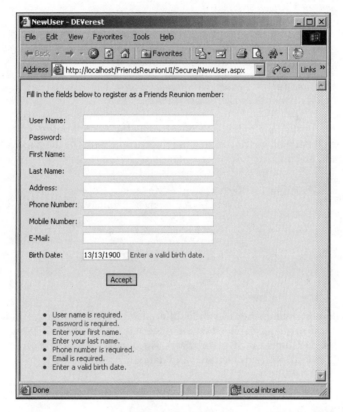

Notice how the validation errors are automatically collated in the summary control, whose format we can alter through its `DisplayMode` property. Also note that the individual validation controls don't display their error messages, just as we specified. For `compBirth`, whose `Display` property we set to `Dynamic`, the error message appears in the summary as well as the page.

The `compBirth` validation control checks that the value entered matches a `Date` data type (as a result of setting `Operator` to `DataTypeCheck` and `Type` to `Date`). When a `CompareValidator` is configured to perform this sort of check, the `ControlToCompare` and `ValueToCompare` properties are ignored. In other circumstances, we might use these properties to validate the field against another control's value, or against a constant value.

The `RegularExpressionValidator` controls for `txtEmail` and `txtPhone` contain a somewhat complicated string in the `ValidationExpression` property that we were able to set with the aid of the Visual Studio .NET IDE. As usual, it's quite possible to enter your own strings here, should you need to do so.

> *Regular expression syntax is a fairly advanced topic in its own right. You can find out more about it in* Professional JavaScript 2nd Edition *(Wrox Press, ISBN 1-86100-553-9), as it has been available in JavaScript since its early days. If you're a subscriber to ASPToday, there a number of articles related to it:*
>
> *Regular Expressions in Microsoft .NET*
> *http://www.asptoday.com/content/articles/20010309.asp*
>
> *Validating user input with the .NET RegularExpressionValidator*
> *http://www.asptoday.com/content/articles/20020528.asp*
>
> *String Manipulation and Pattern Testing with Regular Expressions*
> *http://www.asptoday.com/content/articles/19990505.asp*

To finish off this form for the time being, let's now handle the **Accept** button's `Click` event, and populate the message label with a string indicating the current status of the page. Double-click the button in the designer, and add the following code:

```
Private Sub btnAccept_Click(ByVal sender As System.Object, _
                          ByVal e As System.EventArgs) Handles btnAccept.Click
    If Page.IsValid Then
        lblMessage.Text = "Validation succeeded!"
    Else
        lblMessage.Text = "Fix the following errors and retry:"
    End If
End Sub
```

This most recent addition demonstrates a subtle difference between handling validation with client-side JavaScript code, and causing a postback when the **Accept** button is clicked. Even if there are errors, the second message will never appear in IE4+ browsers, since validation occurs on the client side. The postback will not occur until all fields contain valid data.

User Controls

In our Friends Reunion application, it would be good to have a common header and footer for every page, a common navigation bar, and so on. ASP.NET provides a straightforward reusability model for the page features that we create, in the form of the **user controls**. We create these controls in pretty much the same way as we create web forms, but they're saved with the special `.ascx` extension.

A user control doesn't contain the tags that usually start off a page, such as <html>, <head>, <body>, and so on. Also, instead of ASP.NET <%@ Page %> directives, it uses <%@ Control %> directives to customize certain features of the control. Without further ado, let's build ourselves an example, so that we can see what's going on.

Try It Out – Building a Header Control

To begin our experiments, let's build a header control that we can put to use on every single page in the Friends Reunion site. We'll make it look a little like the blue banner that currently sits at the top of the news page.

1. Create a new folder called `Controls`, right-click on it, and choose **Add | Add Web User Control** from the context menu. Call the new file `FriendsHeader.ascx`.

2. Drop a `Panel` web server control onto the page, and give it the following properties:

Property	Value
ID	pnlHeaderGlobal
CssClass	HeaderFriends

3. Set the text inside the panel to **Friends Reunion**.

4. Drop an image web server control inside the panel, to the right of the text, and set the following properties:

Property	Value
ID	imgFriends
CssClass	HeaderImage
ImageUrl	../Images/friends.gif

5. Drop another `Panel` web control next to the previous one. Clear the text inside it, and set the following properties:

Property	Value
ID	pnlHeaderLocal
CssClass	HeaderTitle

6. Drop an `Image` web server control inside this panel, and set the following properties:

Property	Value
ID	imgIcon
CssClass	HeaderImage
ImageUrl	../Images/homeconnected.gif

7. Drop a `Label` web control inside the same panel, to the right of the image, and with these properties:

Property	Value
ID	lblWelcome
Text	Welcome!

8. Save the control, which should now look like the following:

Just out of interest, switch to the HTML view to see how our control has been created. Notice the absence of any 'normal' HTML elements around the ASP.NET elements:

```
<%@ Control Language="vb" AutoEventWireup="false"
    Codebehind="FriendsHeader.ascx.vb"
    Inherits="FriendsReunionUI.FriendsHeader"
    TargetSchema="http://schemas.microsoft.com/intellisense/ie5" %>

<asp:panel id="pnlHeaderGlobal" cssclass="HeaderFriends" runat="server">
  Friends Reunion 
  <asp:image id="imgFriends" runat="server"
          cssclass="HeaderImage" imageurl="../Images/friends.gif">
  </asp:image>
</asp:panel>
<asp:panel id="pnlHeaderLocal" cssclass="HeaderTitle" runat="server">
  <asp:image id="imgIcon" runat="server"
          cssclass="HeaderImage" imageurl="../Images/homeconnected.gif">
  </asp:image>
   
  <asp:label id="lblWelcome" runat="server">Welcome!</asp:label>
</asp:panel>
```

9. As you'll have noticed, we've used some CSS styles that haven't yet been defined: `HeaderFriends`, `HeaderImage`, and `HeaderTitle`. Let's add those to the `iestyle.css` stylesheet now:

```
.HeaderFriends
{
  padding-right: 5px;
  padding-left: 5px;
```

```
    font-weight: bold;
    font-size: 8pt;
    font-family: Tahoma, Verdana, 'Times New Roman';
    width: 100%;
    color: white;
    background-color: #336699;
    text-align: right;
}
.HeaderImage
{
    vertical-align: middle;
}
.HeaderTitle
{
    padding-right: 5px;
    padding-left: 5px;
    padding-right: 10px;
    font-weight: bold;
    font-size: 8pt;
    font-family: Tahoma, Verdana, 'Times New Roman';
    width: 100%;
    color: white;
    background-color: #336699;
}
```

10. Open the `NewUser.aspx` form, and drag the `FriendsHeader.ascx` file from the Solution Explorer onto it, placing it just before the first line of text on the page. Add a new paragraph after the newly added control by pressing *Return*:

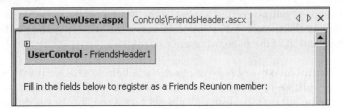

11. Save, compile, and run the application, and see what you get.

How It Works

The process of designing a new user control is just like creating a complete page – we drop controls and set their properties exactly as we have before. Apart from the lack of page-level elements, the HTML looks just like the code for a regular web form. Once created, we can place the control just as if it was a control from the toolbox. At that moment, the control is registered with the page with the `Register` directive, and the following lines are added to the page's HTML code:

```
<%@ Register TagPrefix="uc1" TagName="FriendsHeader"
             Src="../Controls/FriendsHeader.ascx" %>
<%@ Page Language="vb" AutoEventWireup="false" ... %>
<html>
```

```
...

<body ms_positioning="FlowLayout">
  <form id="frmNewUser" method="post" runat="server">
    <p><uc1:friendsheader id="FriendsHeader1" runat="server">
    </uc1:friendsheader></p>

...
```

The `Register` directive at the top of the page tells ASP.NET where to locate and load the appropriate user control: from the URL specified in the `Src` attribute. It also associates the control with a prefix that's used when we define control instances, which we can change if we want to. When we now open the `NewUser.aspx` page, we get something like this:

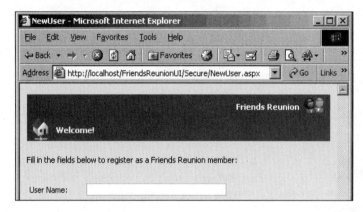

As long as you use server controls for the images in the header (in other words, don't use an HTML `Image` element without the `runat="server"` attribute), the relative paths will be properly resolved, no matter what the location of the page using the control.

Just dropping this control onto every page of our site will help to provide it with a consistent look and feel, building on the work we've already done with our stylesheets. However, always having the same icon and message on the left isn't ideal, so in a moment we'll see how to customize it for the current page. First, though, we'll deal with a problem that you may have noticed a couple of pages ago.

Side Note: Don't Believe Everything That IntelliSense Tells You

Be wary of getting too used to IntelliSense – if you do, you may find that you're missing out on something: there are some situations where IntelliSense is incomplete! If that sounds intriguing, read on; if not, wait for us at the start of the next *Try It Out* section – we'll be with you in just a moment.

Put simply, IntelliSense fails to offer some of the options that should be open to you when you're creating a CSS stylesheet. However, if you choose a legal value for a style that isn't recognized by IntelliSense, Internet Explorer *will* still render it as expected. The clearest example of this is the `vertical-align` property, which prompts the following response from IntelliSense:

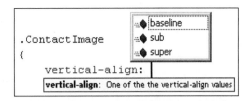

Exactly the same set of options (albeit with different names) appears in the Build Style Wizard:

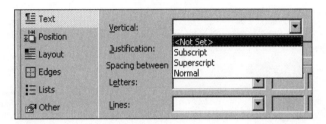

When we defined the `HeaderImage` CSS style rule, we used a `vertical-align` value of `middle`, and the Visual Studio .NET complained about it. However, if we look at W3C's CSS1 Recommendation, the legal values are given as: "`baseline | sub | super | top | text-top | middle | bottom | text-bottom | `<*percentage*>", and CSS2, a W3C Recommendation since 12 May 1998, adds "<*length*>` | inherit`" to the values defined by CSS1. (You can find these documents at **www.w3.org/Style/CSS**.)

Let's see what happens when we change this value in the `HeaderImage` style rule, and how it affects the alignment of the icon with the text next to it. As the value is set in a stylesheet, we can change it there, save the stylesheet, and see the effect by refreshing the page in Internet Explorer, without having to recompile:

baseline   sub   super   middle   text-top

As you can see, even when we use values that IntelliSense doesn't recognize, and which are marked in the editor as being invalid for that CSS property, Internet Explorer renders affected items correctly – and in this author's opinion, the last two are far better than the first three!

If the values are indeed legitimate, and Internet Explorer is happy to deal with them, surely there must be a way to convince IntelliSense that they're OK? In fact there is: the answer lies in an XML file called `cssmetadata.xml`, which (for default installations) you'll find in the folder at `C:\Program Files\Microsoft Visual Studio .NET\Common7\Packages\1033`.

```
<?xml version="1.0" encoding="utf-8" ?>
<cssmd:cssmd xmlns:cssmd="x-schema:..\CSSMetaDataSchema.xml" version="VS7">
  <cssmd:property-set>

    <!-- Font Properties -->
    <cssmd:property-def id="color" type="color"
```

```
            description="Color of an element's text"
            syntax="#RRGGBB | Named Color"
            enum="Aqua Black Blue Fuchsia Gray Green Lime Maroon
                  Navy Olive Purple Red Silver Teal White Yellow"/>

    ...

    <!-- Background Properties -->

    ...

    <cssmd:property-def id="background-position" type="composite"
            description="How the background is positioned within an element"
            syntax="[horizontal position] [vertical position]"/>

    <!-- Text Properties -->
    <cssmd:property-def id="text-align" type="enum"
            description="The horizontal alignment of an element's text"
            syntax="One of the text-align values"
            enum="center justify left right"/>
    <cssmd:property-def id="vertical-align" type="enum"
            description="The vertical alignment of an element's text"
            syntax="One of the vertical-align values"
            enum="baseline sub super"/>

    ...
```

The last element shown above contains what we're looking for: you can see the values that Visual Studio .NET will 'accept' for the vertical-align property listed in the enum attribute. To 'fix' IntelliSense, we just have to add the other valid values:

```
    <cssmd:property-def id="vertical-align" type="enum-length"
            description="The vertical alignment of an element's text"
            syntax="One of the vertical-align values or a custom unit"
            enum="baseline sub super top text-top
                  middle bottom text-bottom inherit"/>
```

We've also changed the type attribute in order to allow lengths to be assigned, and the syntax attribute to update the tool-tip help. Here's the 'new' IntelliSense:

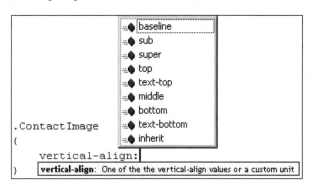

Unfortunately, the Build Style Wizard won't reflect these new values, but at least we've stopped the IDE complaining about them!

Try It Out – Adding Properties to User Controls

Returning to our Friends Reunion sample application, we were talking (before our little diversion) about providing the ability for our user control to be customized for different pages. The technique for doing this is to define some properties for it that we can set when the control is instantiated. In this example, we'll make it possible to set the image and the message on the left-hand side of our user control banner.

1. Open the code behind for the user control (right-click it and select **View Code**), and add the following code to it:

```
Public MustInherit Class FriendsHeader
    Inherits System.Web.UI.UserControl


    ...

    Private _message As String = String.Empty
    Private _imageurl As String = String.Empty


    ' Accessor methods for the Message property
    Public Property Message() As String
      Get
        Return _message
      End Get
      Set(ByVal Value As String)
        _message = Value
      End Set
    End Property


    ' Accessor methods for the IconImageUrl property
    Public Property IconImageUrl() As String
      Get
        Return _imageurl
      End Get
      Set(ByVal Value As String)
        _imageurl = Value
      End Set
    End Property


    ' Prerender will populate the controls with the property values
    Protected Overrides Sub OnPreRender(ByVal e As System.EventArgs)
      If (Message <> String.Empty) Then
        Me.lblWelcome.Text = _message
      End If
      If (IconImageUrl <> String.Empty) Then
        Me.imgIcon.ImageUrl = _imageurl
      End If
    End Sub
End Class
```

2. Open the `News.aspx` page, and delete the panel and image we added previously as a header. Drop the new user control in its place, inserting a new paragraph after it as before.

3. Switch to the HTML view and find the line containing the control's declaration:

```
<uc1:friendsheader id="FriendsHeader1" runat="server"></uc1:friendsheader>
```

Add a `Message` attribute to it, like so:

```
<uc1:friendsheader id="FriendsHeader1" runat="server"
            Message="Welcome to the news page!"></uc1:friendsheader>
```

4. Open the `NewUser.aspx` page in HTML mode, and change the control's declaration to include both a `Message` attribute and an `IconImageUrl` attribute:

```
<uc1:friendsheader id="FriendsHeader1" runat="server"
            Message="Registration form"
            IconImageUrl="../Images/securekeys.gif"></uc1:friendsheader>
```

How It Works

We can add properties to a user control, just as we can add them to any other custom class. In this example, we've implemented two properties that control the message and the icon of the second panel through a couple of private member variables:

```
Private _message As String = String.Empty
Private _imageurl As String = String.Empty
```

We initialize the variables to empty strings in order to allow us to determine whether values have been supplied. In the `OnPreRender()` override, we only change the default image and message if we have non-empty values for the properties. (This handler is called just before the HTML code is sent to the client, when the `PreRender` event takes place.) When we now open the `NewUser.aspx` page, we see something like this:

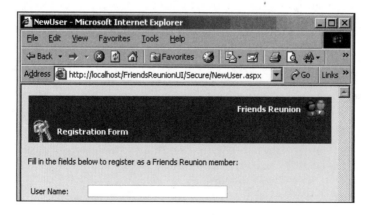

To complement the header we just created, we can build a footer called `FriendsFooter.ascx` by creating another user control with the following code:

```
<%@ Control Language="vb" AutoEventWireup="false"
    Codebehind="FriendsFooter.ascx.vb"
    Inherits="FriendsReunion.FriendsFooter"
    TargetSchema="http://schemas.microsoft.com/intellisense/ie5" %>
```

```
<asp:panel id="pnlFooterGlobal" CssClass="FooterFriends" runat="server">
   Friends Reunion Application -  Courtesy of Wrox Press
   <BR><b>Beginning Web Programming with Visual Basic .NET</b>
</asp:panel>
```

The style it uses is defined in our CSS stylesheet like this:

```
.FooterFriends
{
   font-size: 8pt;
   font-family: Tahoma, Verdana, 'Times New Roman';
   width: 100%;
   color: white;
   background-color: #336699;
   text-align: center;
}
```

Whenever we make changes to the user controls, the whole site will be instantly updated. Couple this with our extensive use of stylesheets, and we can completely renew the web application's appearance in a snap!

Custom Controls

Most of the built-in ASP.NET server controls offer great features, but the ASP.NET object model also allows us – and even encourages us – to extend them through inheritance. A control such as this that extends base functionality is called a **custom control**.

When creating a custom control, the particular base class we choose to inherit from will depend on the situation we face. We could inherit from the `TextBox` control if we wish to incorporate some custom processing into its behavior, or we might inherit from the top-level `WebControl` base class to provide customized UI rendering.

In this section, we'll start by looking at some simple custom controls, and increase their complexity by incorporating more advanced features. Our aim here is really just to raise your awareness of custom controls, which can be an invaluable addition to the ASP.NET web designer's toolbox. For a comprehensive study of this important feature, take a look at *Professional ASP.NET Server Controls – Building Custom Controls with C#* (Wrox Press, ISBN 1-86100-564-4).

Try It Out – Building the SubHeader Custom Control

In this example, we're going to create a simple custom control that displays a sub-header beneath our page header control, containing today's date and a link to the registration page.

1. Right-click the project name, and select **Add | Add Class**. Give the new class the name SubHeader.vb.

2. Add the following code to the code-behind file:

```
Imports System.IO
Imports System.Web.UI
Imports System.Web.UI.WebControls

Public Class SubHeader
  Inherits WebControl

  ' The URL to navigate to, in case the user is not registered
  Private _register As String = String.Empty

  Sub New()
    ' Initialize default values
    Me.Width = New Unit(100, UnitType.Percentage)
    Me.CssClass = "SubHeader"
  End Sub

  ' Property to allow the user to define the URL for the registration page
  Public Property RegisterUrl() As String
    Get
      Return _register
    End Get
    Set(ByVal Value As String)
      _register = Value
    End Set
  End Property

  ' This method is called when the control is being built
  Protected Overrides Sub CreateChildControls()

    ' Clear any previously loaded controls
    Me.Controls.Clear()
    Dim lbl As Label

    ' If the user is authenticated we will render his name
    If Context.User.Identity.IsAuthenticated Then
      lbl = New Label()
      lbl.Text = Context.User.Identity.Name

      ' Add the newly created label to our collection of child controls
      Me.Controls.Add(lbl)
    Else
```

```
' Otherwise, we will render a link to the registration page
Dim reg As New HyperLink()
reg.Text = "Register"

' If a URL isn't provided, use a default URL to the registration page
If _register = String.Empty Then
    reg.NavigateUrl = Context.Request.ApplicationPath & _
                  Path.AltDirectorySeparatorChar & "Secure" & _
                  Path.AltDirectorySeparatorChar & "NewUser.aspx"
Else
    reg.NavigateUrl = _register
End If

' Add the newly created link to our collection of child controls
Me.Controls.Add(reg)
End If

' Add a couple of blank spaces and a separator character
Me.Controls.Add(New LiteralControl(" - "))

' Add a label with the current date
lbl = New Label()
lbl.Text = DateTime.Now.ToLongDateString()
Me.Controls.Add(lbl)
End Sub
End Class
```

3. Add the following style to the `iestyle.css` stylesheet:

```
.SubHeader
{
  border-top: 3px groove;
  font-size: 8pt;
  color: white;
  font-family: Tahoma, Verdana, 'Times New Roman';
  background-color: #4f82b5;
  text-align: right;
}
```

4. Open the `News.aspx` page in HTML view, and add the following directive at the top of the page; it will allow us to use our new custom control:

```
<%@ Register TagPrefix="wx"
           Namespace="FriendsReunionUI" Assembly="FriendsReunionUI" %>
```

5. Right below the user control we used, add the following line:

```
<wx:subheader id="SubHeader1" runat="server" />
```

6. Set `News.aspx` as the start page, run the project, and admire our handiwork!

How It Works

Our new custom control derives from the `WebControl` base class, just like the intrinsic ASP.NET web controls. The base class provides properties for setting the control's layout, such as its `Width`, its `CssClass`, and so on, which we set at construction time. We've added a property to hold a URL, in rather similar fashion to what we did for our user control.

```
' The URL to navigate to, in case the user is not registered
Private _register As String = String.Empty

...

' Property to allow the user to define the URL for the registration page
Public Property RegisterUrl() As String
  Get
    Return _register
  End Get
  Set(ByVal Value As String)
    _register = Value
  End Set
End Property
```

The main difference is the way that the control's interface is built. For our user control, we just dropped controls onto the design surface, as we would have done for a web form. For the custom control, a special method named `CreateChildControls()` is called whenever ASP.NET needs to rebuild our control ready for display. Inside this method, we create the control hierarchy – that is, we specify the controls that make up our custom control by using the special `Me.Controls` collection. (This property comes from the `Control` base class, so any server control can be a container for any other control[s] in this model.) We have to create and configure the new controls programmatically before they are appended to that collection.

```
' If the user is authenticated we will render his name
If Context.User.Identity.IsAuthenticated Then
  lbl = New Label()
  lbl.Text = Context.User.Identity.Name

  ' Add the newly created label to our collection of child controls
  Me.Controls.Add(lbl)
Else
  ' Otherwise, we will render a link to the registration page
  Dim reg As New HyperLink()
  reg.Text = "Register"

  ' If a URL isn't provided, use a default URL to the registration page
  If _register = String.Empty Then
    reg.NavigateUrl = Context.Request.ApplicationPath & _
                      Path.AltDirectorySeparatorChar & "Secure" & _
                      Path.AltDirectorySeparatorChar & "NewUser.aspx"
  Else
    reg.NavigateUrl = _register
  End If
```

```
    ' Add the newly created link to our collection of child controls
    Me.Controls.Add(reg)
End If

    ' Add a couple of blank spaces and a separator character
    Me.Controls.Add(New LiteralControl(" - "))

    ' Add a label with the current date
    lbl = New Label()
    lbl.Text = DateTime.Now.ToLongDateString()
    Me.Controls.Add(lbl)
```

Also of note here is that we have used the `Context.User.Identity.IsAuthenticated` property to display the Register link selectively. As you'll see in Chapter 11, this property identifies an authenticated user, according to the authentication method selected. If the user is authenticated, the `Identity.Name` property will contain their user name.

When you open the `News.aspx` page, you should see something like the following:

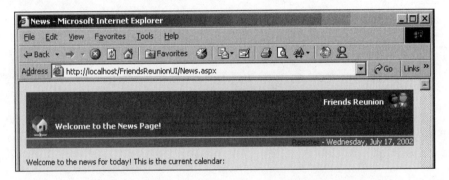

We'll learn more about security settings in Chapters 10 and 11, but for now, follow these simple steps to simulate an authenticated user:

❏ Open the IIS administration console (Start | Settings | Control Panel | Administrative Tools | Internet Services Manager). In the Default Web Site node, Right-click the FriendsReunion application, and select Properties. Select the Directory Security tab, and click the Edit button in the Anonymous access and authentication control section.

❏ Uncheck Anonymous Access, and check Integrated Windows authentication and Basic authentication:

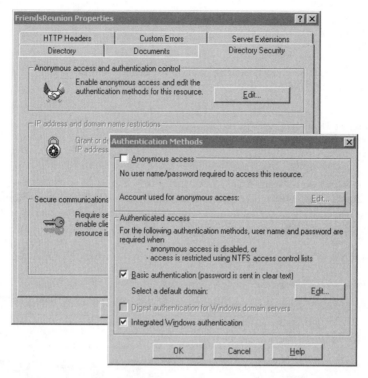

Now, we can switch from an 'authenticated' user to an 'unauthenticated' user just by changing the following setting in the application's Web.config file:

```
<authentication mode="Windows" />
```

or:

```
<authentication mode="None" />
```

The second of these will result in the Register link being shown in the sub-header. The first, which is the default, will make the currently logged-in Windows user's name visible:

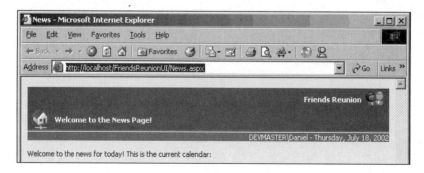

At run time, there's not much difference between this control and the user control we created for the header, but the custom control stands out at design time. With the News.aspx page in design view, we can immediately see the difference:

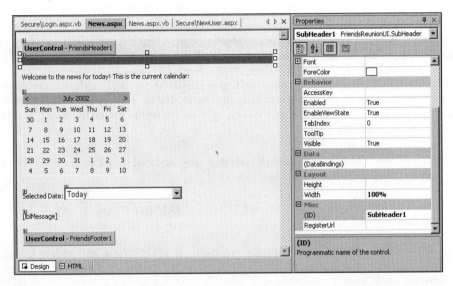

Unlike the user control, which isn't even rendered at design time, our custom control renders itself on screen, and provides the complete set of visual properties available for all web server controls through the **Properties** window. Toward the bottom of that window, we can see the RegisterUrl property that we added. This is far more intuitive than the user control approach, at the cost of just a little extra effort on the part of the control's developer.

Dynamic Content

For our next trick, we'll take a look at a subject that will become increasingly important when we look at database access in the next two chapters: dynamic content. Simply put, a dynamic application is one that's capable of altering its content or appearance at run time, depending on the identity of the user viewing the page, or the nature of some information from a database, or some other indeterminate condition. In fact, we've already seen one form of dynamic content on our news page, where we displayed either the user name or a link to the registration page, depending on whether the current user was already authenticated.

The way we achieved our dynamism was to use the custom control's Controls property to add new controls to the hierarchy. We know that this property comes from the base Control class, and as such is available to all web server controls. Perhaps surprisingly, the Page itself *also* derives from this class, and handles the controls it contains in precisely the same manner. The hierarchy is as follows:

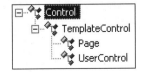

Another way to achieve dynamic content is by manipulating the `Visible` properties of the controls on the page – if we set a web server control's `Visible` property to `False`, it won't even be sent to the client browser, so it certainly won't be displayed! It's then easy to flip the property to `True` from code, with the result that controls can be displayed selectively according to certain conditions.

Try It Out – Dynamically Building Navigation Controls

As a further example of dynamic content, we will now create the `Default.aspx` entry page for our site. This will be the page that all users visit after they've logged in, and the links it offers will vary according to who they are. In it, we'll use a `PlaceHolder` control to define the location of the controls we add to the page programmatically.

1. Add a new web form to the project's root directory, and call it `Default.aspx`. Set its `pageLayout` property to `FlowLayout`.

2. Drop the `FriendsHeader.ascx` and `FriendsFooter.ascx` controls onto it. Set their IDs to `ucHeader` and `ucFooter`.

3. Add the `SubHeader` custom control by switching to HTML view, and adding a `Register` directive and a `<wx:subheader>` element, just as we did for the `News.aspx` page. This time, set its ID to `ccSubHeader`.

4. While in HTML view, add a `<link>` element for the `iestyles.css` stylesheet.

5. Below the headers, type a description for the page – something like, "Welcome to the Friends Reunion web site – the meeting place for lost friends!" Set its `class` property to `Normal`, and start a new paragraph after it.

6. Drop a `PlaceHolder` web control, and set its ID to `phNav`. This marks the location on the page where all of the controls we add will be placed.

7. Open the code-behind file, and at the top, add an `Imports` statement for the `System.Web.UI.WebControls` namespace.

8. Add the following code to the `Page_Load()` method:

```
Private Sub Page_Load(ByVal sender As System.Object, _
                      ByVal e As System.EventArgs) Handles MyBase.Load
    Dim tb As New Table()
    Dim row As TableRow
    Dim cell As TableCell
    Dim img As Image
    Dim lnk As HyperLink
```

```
If Context.User.Identity.IsAuthenticated Then

    ' Create a new blank table row
    row = New TableRow()

    ' Set up the News image
    img = New Image()
    img.ImageUrl = "Images/winbook.gif"
    img.ImageAlign = ImageAlign.Middle
    img.Width = New Unit(24, UnitType.Pixel)
    img.Height = New Unit(24, UnitType.Pixel)

    ' Create a cell and add the image
    cell = New TableCell()
    cell.Controls.Add(img)

    ' Add the new cell to the row
    row.Cells.Add(cell)

    ' Set up the News link
    lnk = New HyperLink()
    lnk.Text = "News"
    lnk.NavigateUrl = "News.aspx"

    ' Create the cell and add the link
    cell = New TableCell()
    cell.Controls.Add(lnk)

    ' Add the new cell to the row
    row.Cells.Add(cell)

    ' Add the row to the table
    tb.Rows.Add(row)
Else
    ' Code for unauthenticated users here...
End If

' Finally, add the table to the placeholder
phNav.Controls.Add(tb)
End Sub
```

9. Set `Default.aspx` as the start page, and save and run the application. Turn Anonymous **access** in IIS on and off to see how the results differ, just as before.

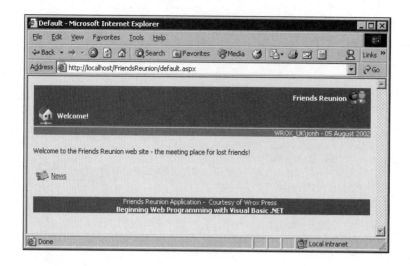

How It Works

The special `PlaceHolder` control has been designed with dynamic control loading in mind: it forms an invisible container for controls that we insert later, and positions them correctly in the hierarchy that's defined by the `Page.Controls` collection. The `PlaceHolder` doesn't render HTML to the client itself; it's only useful for this sort of scenario.

The `Page_Load()` event handler instantiates a new `Table` web control that will hold the links we add. When we finish the process of adding links, we add the table to the placeholder control. If we need to, we can add as many controls to the placeholder as we need – it's not limited to just one.

A Customized Template

At this point, we've developed a set of controls that will help us to create a consistent look and feel for the application. At the moment though, we have to add the user controls and the custom control to every new page manually. We can avoid this tedious task with a custom base page that can load user and custom controls dynamically.

Try It Out – Building a Custom Base Page

Our technique for this final example will be to create a new class that inherits from and builds upon the `System.Web.UI.Page` class. Once we've set it up with the header and footer controls we want to use, we'll inherit from the new class in all of our web forms, providing them with that functionality by default.

1. Add a new class named `FriendsBase.vb` to the project, and add the following code to it:

```
Public Class FriendsBase
    Inherits System.Web.UI.Page

    Protected HeaderMessage As String = String.Empty
```

```
    Protected HeaderIconImageUrl As String = String.Empty

    Protected Overrides Sub Render( _
                    ByVal writer As System.Web.UI.HtmlTextWriter)

        ' Get a reference to the form control
        Dim form As Control = Page.Controls(1)

        ' Create and place the page header
        Dim header As FriendsHeader
        header = CType(LoadControl( _
                    "Controls/FriendsHeader.ascx"), FriendsHeader)
        header.Message = HeaderMessage
        header.IconImageUrl = HeaderIconImageUrl
        form.Controls.AddAt(0, header)

        ' Add the SubHeader custom control
        form.Controls.AddAt(1, New SubHeader())

        ' Finally add the Page footer
        Dim footer As FriendsFooter
        footer = CType(LoadControl( _
                    "Controls/FriendsFooter.ascx"), FriendsFooter)
        form.Controls.AddAt(Page.Controls(1).Controls.Count, footer)

        ' Render as usual
        MyBase.Render(writer)
    End Sub
End Class
```

2. Add a new web form to the project called `Info.aspx`, and set it to `FlowLayout`.

3. Type some place-holding text (say, "This is an information page") on the new form, and set its `class` property to `Normal`.

4. As usual, add the `<link>` element pointing to the `iestyles.css` stylesheet.

5. Open the code-behind page, and change the class declaration to:

```
Public Class Info
    Inherits FriendsBase
```

6. Add the following lines to the `Page_Load()` subroutine:

```
Private Sub Page_Load(ByVal sender As System.Object, _
                    ByVal e As System.EventArgs) Handles MyBase.Load
    MyBase.HeaderIconImageUrl = _
                    Request.ApplicationPath & "/Images/winbook.gif"
    MyBase.HeaderMessage = "Informative Page"
End Sub
```

7. Save and run the project, with `Info.aspx` as the start page.

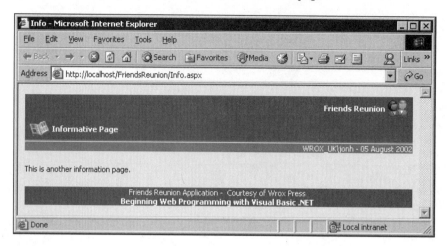

How It Works

By default, web forms inherit directly from the base `Page` class, but this is not a requirement. It's possible to inherit from any `Page`-derived class, creating a great opportunity for adding common behavior across pages. Our web application take advantage of this to insert header, sub-header, and footer controls to every page automatically, releasing the page developer from the need to drop and place these controls all the time. It's now just a case of inheriting from the new base page, as we did in Step 5, by changing the `Inherits` statement to point to the `FriendsBase.vb` class.

The base page class loads controls onto the page by two methods. For user controls, we have to use the special `LoadControl()` method, provided by the `TemplateControl` class from which both `UserControl` and `Page` derive. Once it is loaded and assigned to a variable of the correct type, we can access the properties and methods of the `UserControl`. After initializing it, we add it to the form's `Controls` collection, specifying *where* we want to add it by using the `AddAt()` method. The form itself is the control with index 1, as we saw above.

So that inheriting pages can set the message and the icon to use (these were previously set directly in every page), the base page defines two protected variables called `HeaderIconImageUrl` and `HeaderMessage`, and uses them to set the controls appropriately. The footer works in the same way as the header.

The `SubHeader` custom control, on the other hand, doesn't need any special handling, and is treated just like any other server control. We add a new instance directly, without declaring a variable.

The special processing to set up our pages has been created by overriding the `Render()` method in the base page, and before exiting the function we call `MyBase.Render()` to add the controls and let the base `Page` class perform the usual rendering of the modified control hierarchy. Any derived class that wants to override this method *must* also call `MyBase.Render()`, passing in the `writer` object that's used to create the appropriate output.

Finally, note that in the `Page_Load()` handler, we had to use the full application path to the image. For this purpose, we employed the `Request.ApplicationPath` property, which includes the virtual directory path (such as `/FriendsReunion`). The custom base page gives us exactly the same result as we achieved in the `Default.aspx` and `News.aspx` pages, but with almost no code required in `Info.aspx` at all!

Summary

During this exploratory journey into ASP.NET's brand new web forms landscape, we have uncovered a lot of new features. We looked at the various categories of server controls – HTML controls, web controls, user controls, and custom controls – and performed some of the most common tasks with them. The consistent object model makes it easy to handle all of them in a standard manner, and server-side event-driven programming raises programmer productivity to a new level.

Almost every part of the architecture is extensible, so that once you've mastered the built-in functionality, you can move on and extend it to provide powerful and reusable user controls or custom controls. This is a big leap forward for web application developers, who are no longer constrained by the limitations of the default features.

Although we've touched upon the idea of creating dynamic web sites in this chapter, we haven't yet consider the most important tools for creating them: databases. In the next chapter, we'll learn how they can be used with web forms to make great applications with minimal code.

Solut...
BM
Refere...
System...
System.Dat...
System.Drawing
System.Web
System.XML
AssemblyInfo.vb
Assembl...
BM.vsdisco
Global.asax
Styles.css
Web.config
WebForm1.aspx

WebForm1.aspx.v...

ebForm1.aspx* | WebForm1.aspx.v...

ADO.NET

In the last chapter, while we were talking about HTML controls, web controls, user controls, and custom controls, we made a number of references to the myriad of additional functionality that becomes available when data access is brought into the mix. In our nascent Friends Reunion application, for example, we could keep a permanent store of all the people who have entered their details into the form, and allow the creation of links between those records, so that users returning to the site are immediately presented with a list of the people who want to contact them. We could also let them see complete details of each other, so that they can get in touch.

To manipulate the data stored in databases, ASP.NET uses **ADO.NET**, Microsoft's new data access strategy. ADO.NET contains many classes that ease the process of building dynamic web applications, the most interesting of which we will be discussing over the course of the next two chapters. As we do so, we will be considering the following topics:

- ❑ The overall architecture of ADO.NET
- ❑ An overview of how to use ADO.NET to access different data sources, using the so-called "data providers"
- ❑ Reading data from a database, and displaying it on a form
- ❑ What datasets are, and how to use them
- ❑ How to use the Server Explorer in Visual Studio .NET to administer an MSDE database
- ❑ How to use components, which are a new feature of Visual Studio .NET

ADO.NET

Before we start coding, we'll take a brief tour of the ADO.NET architecture. If from experience you're already familiar with the terms and concepts of ADO.NET, feel free to skip the next section, and instead move directly to the *Try It Out* sections that follow it.

Architecture of ADO.NET

Before we go any further, let's get something out of the way: the name "ADO.NET" doesn't actually stand for anything at all – and before you raise a hand to point out that ADO originally stood for **ActiveX Data Objects**, just remember that Microsoft has decreed that ADO.NET is the name of a technology, and *not* an acronym! More significantly, ADO.NET is a significant technological leap forward from ADO, and has a substantially different architecture, so it's well worth taking a look at its overall design.

Whenever we want to access data in a database, the most common technique for doing so involves first connecting to the database, and then issuing a SQL statement. ADO.NET supports these two concepts, which together allow interaction between our code and a source of data. The diagram below shows a **command object**, which will usually contain a SQL statement, using a **connection object** to reach the database.

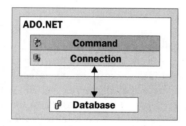

Besides direct SQL statements, a command object can also be used to execute a stored procedure that's already present in the database.

Now, depending on the query being executed, we may expect to retrieve a single value (from a SELECT COUNT(x) . . . statement, for example), a result set (from a SELECT * FROM . . . statement) or no result at all (from an INSERT or UPDATE statement). Even in the last case, however, it can be useful to know the number of table rows that were affected. For each of these options, there are different methods of the command object that we can use to execute the command:

Command method	Returns
ExecuteScalar()	An Object containing the value
ExecuteReader()	A **data reader object**, for accessing a result set
ExecuteNonQuery()	An Integer with the number of rows affected by the command

The first and last of these methods are really quite simple, and we'll see them in action shortly. The second, however, is more complex, and deserves a little more explanation here. A data reader object is a fast, read-only, forward-only, connected cursor to the data returned from the database. As such, it represents a very efficient way to display the results of a SQL statement.

Using a data reader is very similar to using the other "reader" objects in the .NET Framework, such as `StreamReader`, `XmlReader`, and so on. We get a reference to it (by calling `ExecuteReader()` in this case), we call `Read()`, and if that returns `True` (meaning that more data is available to be read), we use its methods to access data in the current position. Typically, for result sets containing multiple rows of data, we'll have a code structure like this:

```
reader = command.ExecuteReader()
While reader.Read()
  ' Process current row
End While
```

From this point, to access the values contained in the columns inside the current row, we can use any of the following approaches:

❑ The data reader object has `GetXXX()` methods for retrieving typed values. Methods such as `GetBoolean()`, `GetString()`, `GetInt32()` receive the index of the column as an argument, and return a value of the appropriate type. Inside the code block shown above, we could write:

```
Response.Write(reader.GetString(0))
```

If we know the name of a column but not its index, we can use the data reader object's `GetOrdinal()` method, which receives the column name and returns its position:

```
Dim pos As Integer = reader.GetOrdinal("CategoryID")
```

❑ The data reader object has a default `Item` property that provides direct access to the column values. We can pass either an `Integer` representing the column's position or a `String` with the column's name. The value returned is of type `Object`, so we will need to convert it to the target data type explicitly:

```
Dim id As Integer = CType(reader("UserID"), Integer)

' Or accessed by column order
Dim id As Integer = CType(reader(0), Integer)
```

❑ The data reader object has a method called `GetValues()` that fills an array with the values in the columns. This method receives an `Object` array, and fills it with the values in the current row:

```
Dim values(3) As Object
reader.GetValues(values)
```

If you wish, you can use the data reader's `FieldCount` property to initialize the array. In the code shown above, the array will be filled with the values from the first three columns of the current record.

Before you head off and try to find classes called `Connection`, `Command`, and `DataReader` in the .NET Framework, we'd better tell you that they don't actually exist as such. In ADO.NET, each different type of database has to be accessed using its own version of these objects. A particular set of these objects for a particular database is called a **data provider**. The methods we've mentioned so far are common to all data providers, but a provider may provide additional features that are unique to the database it deals with.

Data Providers

Why do we need to use data providers? Wouldn't it be less complicated to have a single set of objects for accessing any kind of database? This is an approach that's been taken in the past, but there's a problem with it: in order to have a common set of objects across disparate databases, an abstraction layer has to be implemented on top of database-specific features. This adds overhead and causes a performance impact. In ADO.NET, each database can be accessed using classes that take best advantage of its specific features. At the time of writing, the following .NET data providers exist:

- ❏ **SQL Server**. This provider is located in the `System.Data.SqlClient` namespace, and provides classes for working with SQL Server 7.0 (or later) databases. It contains the `SqlConnection`, `SqlCommand`, `SqlDataReader`, and `SqlDataAdapter` classes, and it's an integral part of ADO.NET.

- ❏ **OLE DB**. This provider is located in the `System.Data.OleDb` namespace, and provides classes for working with any data source for which an OLE DB driver exists. It contains the `OleDbConnection`, `OleDbCommand`, `OleDbDataReader`, and `OleDbDataAdapter` classes. It too is an integral part of ADO.NET.

- ❏ **ODBC**. Once installed, this provider is located in the `Microsoft.Data.Odbc` namespace, and it provides classes to work with any data source with an installed ODBC driver. It contains the `OdbcConnection`, `OdbcCommand`, `OdbcDataReader`, and `OdbcDataAdapter` classes. Installation has to be performed manually by downloading a package from http://msdn.microsoft.com/downloads/default.asp?url=/downloads/sample.asp?url=/msdn-files/027/001/668/msdncompositedoc.xml.

- ❏ **Oracle**. Once installed, this provider's classes are located in the `System.Data.OracleClient` namespace, where you'll find the `OracleConnection`, `OracleCommand`, `OracleDataReader`, and `OracleDataAdapter` classes. It has to be downloaded and installed separately from the .NET Framework, from http://msdn.microsoft.com/downloads/default.asp?URL=/downloads/sample.asp?url=/msdn-files/027/001/940/msdncompositedoc.xml.

- ❏ **MySql**. Yes, there's even a data provider for this database engine, although this time it's not from Microsoft. Instead, you can purchase and download it from Core Lab's web site, at http://crlab.com/mysqlnet.

Clearly, the different data providers will all have very different implementations as a result of the variety of database technologies they have to deal with. As stated earlier, however, they're very similar as far as we're concerned: they have common methods and properties for us to use. This means that, generally speaking, choosing a provider is a matter of performance, not of features. The product-specific providers (SQL Server and Oracle) offer superior performance for the databases they are designed to work with, compared with the generic OLE DB or ODBC providers. The SQL Server provider, for example, communicates with the database using its own proprietary format, TDS (Tabular Data Stream), resulting in significant performance gains.

For the examples in this chapter, we'll use the SQL Server data provider to connect to MSDE, which you'll remember that we configured in Chapter 1. As far as the SQL Server data provider is concerned, MSDE is indistinguishable from SQL Server, which means that the actual classes we'll be using to read data are:

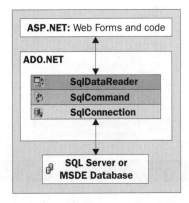

In fact, this picture is still incomplete, but we can fill in the rest of the details as we go. Specifically, there are two kinds of object left out: **data adapters**, which are components of the data providers (as mentioned in the discussion above) and the generic **DataSet** object. We will take a look at both of these in depth shortly, but first we can see some concrete uses of what you've already learned.

Programmatic Use of ADO.NET

We've started this chapter at a rapid pace, but if you're not absolutely sure that you understand how all of this works, don't worry: things will start to become clearer when we begin to look at the code. Now that you've at least begun to get a feel for how data access works in ADO.NET, let's make a start on improving our Friends Reunion application to take advantage of it.

In the previous chapter, we built a form called NewUser.aspx that accepted data from the user. Clearly though, such a form is pretty useless unless we're able save that data somewhere! That's precisely what we'll do now, and we will use a SqlCommand object to achieve it.

Adding Data to a Database

The database that we're going to save data to is called Friends, and it can be found in the code download – it consists of a detached SQL Server database that's ready to use. If you haven't attached a database to MSDE before, take a look at the first half of the section on the *Server Explorer* that appears towards the end of the chapter, which will tell you all that you need to know.

After the user has finished entering their details into the form, we will insert a new row into the User table of the Friends database. This table has the following structure:

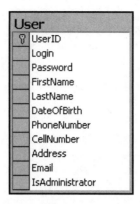

Try It Out – Adding a New User

For this first example, we're going to rewrite the handler for the `NewUser.aspx` form's **Accept** button to store the details in that form in the `Friends` database. We'll also add the improvement that we began to implement at the end of the previous chapter.

1. Open the `NewUser.aspx` page, and delete the user controls it contains.

2. Add the following imports at the top of the code-behind file, as we'll be using classes from these namespaces:

```
Imports System.Data.SqlClient
Imports System.Text
```

3. To take advantage of the common base page we created in the previous chapter, we can change the base class for our page:

```
Public Class NewUser
    Inherits FriendsBase
```

4. Just as you learned in the previous chapter, let's change the page icon and the message text in the `Page_Load()` event handler:

```
Private Sub Page_Load(ByVal sender As System.Object, _
                      ByVal e As System.EventArgs) Handles MyBase.Load
    MyBase.HeaderIconImageUrl = _
                      Request.ApplicationPath & "/images/securekeys.gif"
    MyBase.HeaderMessage = "Registration Form"
End Sub
```

5. Now we'll add the handler for the **Accept** button, which previously just tested the contents of the various textboxes for validity. In its new form, it will be responsible for building and executing the SQL `INSERT` statement that will add a new user to the database.

In this method, efficient string manipulation is achieved through the use of a
`StringBuilder` object. We also take advantage of string formatting, which makes replacing
placeholders in a string with (an array of) values a breeze.

```vb
Private Sub btnAccept_Click( _
        ByVal sender As System.Object, ByVal e As System.EventArgs)
  ' Make sure we have valid values on the page
  If Page.IsValid Then

    ' Save new user to the database
    Dim con As SqlConnection
    Dim sql As String
    Dim cmd As SqlCommand
    Dim sb As New StringBuilder()
    Dim values As New ArrayList()

    sb.Append("INSERT INTO [User] ")
    sb.Append("(UserID, Login, Password, FirstName, LastName, PhoneNumber,")
    sb.Append(" Email, IsAdministrator, Address, CellNumber, DateOfBirth)")
    sb.Append(" VALUES ('{0}','{1}','{2}','{3}','{4}','{5}','{6}','{7}',")

    ' Optional values without quotes as they can have the Null value
    sb.Append(" {8},{9},{10})")

    ' Add required values to replace
    values.Add(Guid.NewGuid().ToString())
    values.Add(txtLogin.Text)
    values.Add(txtPwd.Text)
    values.Add(txtFName.Text)
    values.Add(txtLName.Text)
    values.Add(txtPhone.Text)
    values.Add(txtEmail.Text)
    values.Add(0)

    ' Add the optional values, or Null
    If txtAddress.Text <> String.Empty Then
      values.Add("'" & txtAddress.Text & "'")
    Else
      values.Add("Null")
    End If

    If txtMobile.Text <> String.Empty Then
      values.Add("'" & txtMobile.Text & "'")
    Else
      values.Add("Null")
    End If

    If txtBirth.Text <> String.Empty Then
      values.Add("'" & txtBirth.Text & "'")
    Else
      values.Add("Null")
    End If
```

```
    ' Format the string with the array of values
    sql = String.Format(sb.ToString(), values.ToArray())

    ' Connect to the database and execute the query
    con = New SqlConnection( _
        "data source=(local)\NetSdk;initial catalog=Friends;user id=sa")
    cmd = New SqlCommand(sql, con)
    con.Open()

    Try
      cmd.ExecuteNonQuery()
      Response.Redirect("Login.aspx")
    Catch
      Me.lblMessage.Visible = True
      Me.lblMessage.Text = _
          "Insert couldn't be performed. User name may be already taken."
    Finally
      con.Close()
    End Try
  Else
    lblMessage.Text = "Fix the following errors and retry:"
  End If
End Sub
```

6. Save and run the project with `NewUser.aspx` as the start page. If you now try to create a new entry for a user that already exists, you'll see something like the following:

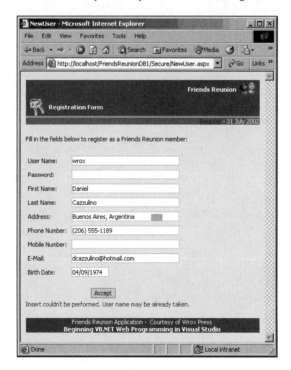

For the sake of simplicity, if the row is successfully inserted (that is, a new record is created in the database), the user will be redirected to the login page, where they will (eventually) be able to enter their user name and password for the account just created.

How It Works

As you saw in the previous chapter, the `Page.IsValid` property represents an accumulation of the validation state of all the validation controls on the page. If all of them are in a valid state, the property will return `True`.

The process of building the SQL `INSERT` statement itself isn't too complicated. We have used the `String.Format()` approach, employing a `StringBuilder` object to append the SQL statement and the list of fields. We used an `ArrayList` for the list of values to use, taking into account that optional values will be `Null` if no value is specified on the form. When we're done, we simply format the string with the values:

```
sql = String.Format(sb.ToString(), values.ToArray())
```

As far as our focus in this chapter is concerned, the database connectivity code comes next. As you know, our first order of business is to create connection and command objects, and the very next line of code achieves the first of these two tasks:

```
con = New SqlConnection( _
        "data source=(local)\NetSdk;initial catalog=Friends;user id=sa")
```

The constructor for a connection object requires you to specify a number of pieces of information, and the precise nature of this information will depend on the data store in question – consult the MSDN documentation for more information on this subject. Here, we're supplying the name of our MSDE engine (`(local)\NetSDK`), the name of the database to connect to (`Friends`), and the name of the user with rights to access that database (`sa`).

Next, we use the connection object and our SQL query string to create a new command object. With that done, we can open the connection to the database, ready for our command to be executed against it:

```
cmd = New SqlCommand(sql, con)
con.Open()
```

Any block of code that executes against an open database should (at the very least) always be placed inside a `Try...Finally` block, giving us a chance to close the connection before execution terminates unexpectedly. Inside the block, we use the command object's `ExecuteNonQuery()` method, as the `INSERT` statement doesn't return results. (We *could* optionally check the number of rows affected, but we're simply ignoring it here.) Finally, we redirect the user to the login page:

```
Try
   cmd.ExecuteNonQuery()
   Response.Redirect("Login.aspx")
Catch
   Me.lblMessage.Visible = True
   Me.lblMessage.Text = _
       "Insert couldn't be performed. User name may be already taken."
```

```
Finally
  con.Close()
End Try
```

As you can see, using `ExecuteNonQuery()` is pretty simple, but it's all you need in order to execute `INSERT`, `UPDATE`, and `DELETE` statements.

Retrieving Data from a Database

Now that we have a means of adding new users to a database, the obvious next step is to learn how to retrieve that information at a later date. In our Friends Reunion application, nowhere is the need for this ability more pressing than in the login page – when someone comes along and enters a user name and a password, we want to discover whether such a user exists, and whether the password they've supplied is correct. Once we have the ability to log a user on, we'll be able to offer them a way to view and edit their own information... but one thing at a time!

Before we look at the data access code, however, we need to make a few changes to our application's security settings. This topic will be explained in more detail in Chapter 10 and 11, but we'll run through the specifics of this particular case here.

Try It Out – Setting up Security

Simply put, we need to configure our application so that the login page is *always* the first one users see, regardless of how they try to access our application. Furthermore, we need to arrange things so that unregistered users can navigate from the login page to `NewUser.aspx`, but to no other pages. Here's how we do that.

1. Just as we did in the last chapter, use the IIS administration console (Start | Programs | Administrative Tools | Internet Services Manager) to enable Anonymous access for our application:

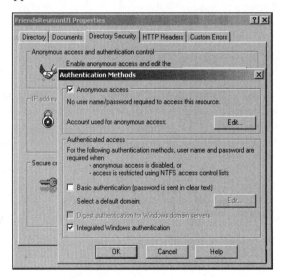

This setting means that IIS won't handle authentication, delegating that responsibility to ASP.NET and its settings. Integrated Windows authentication is enabled by default, and is needed to debug the application from Visual Studio .NET.

2. Open the `Web.config` file for the application, locate the `<authentication>` and `<authorization>` elements, and change their values to match the following:

```
<authentication mode="Forms">
  <forms loginUrl="Secure/Login.aspx" />
</authentication>
<authorization>
  <deny users="?" />
</authorization>
```

Briefly, this tells ASP.NET that we will use a form to authenticate our users, and its location. Then, we specify that anonymous users can't access any page on this application (`deny users="?"`). With this setting in effect, clients will be automatically redirected to the `Login.aspx` page whenever they try to open *any* ASP.NET page in this application.

3. Finally, anonymous users will need to access the `NewUser.aspx` form in order to register, so we have to enable anonymous access to that. Add the following code to the `Web.config` file, just above the closing `</configuration>` tag:

```
<location path="Secure/NewUser.aspx">
  <system.web>
    <authorization>
      <allow users="*" />
    </authorization>
  </system.web>
</location>
</configuration>
```

With these settings in place, we can move on and finish the `Login.aspx` form. When the form is submitted, we will receive a user name and a password, and we will need to check that those values match an existing user in our database. What we need from the database is the user ID that corresponds to the credentials passed in. This ID will be used from then on to retrieve various pieces of information for the current user.

Once we have a valid user ID, we need to tell ASP.NET that the user is authenticated, and let them see the page they originally requested. This is achieved by calling the `System.Web.Security.FormsAuthentication.RedirectFromLoginPage()` method, passing in the user ID. After this method has been called successfully, the user will be able access any resource in the application. In addition, we'll be able to retrieve the ID at any time, from any page, by reading the `Context.User.Identity.Name` property. This makes it easy to customize the content of a page according to the current user.

Try It Out – Finishing the Login Form

In this example, we'll put the things we just talked about into code. In the handler for the Login button, we'll use the ExecuteScalar() method to retrieve the ID of a user with a given login name and password.

1. Open the Login.aspx form, and then delete the header and footer controls that we added previously, leaving only the table with the textboxes and the Login button.

2. Switching to the HTML view, add a panel containing an image and a label at the bottom of the page, to hold any authentication errors that may occur:

```
    <p>
      <asp:panel id="pnlError" runat="server" visible="False">
        <img src="../images/error.gif" align="absMiddle"> 
        <asp:label id="lblError" runat="server" forecolor="Red">
        </asp:label>
      </asp:panel>
    </p>
  </form>
 </body>
</HTML>
```

3. Then, in the code-behind page, change things to match the following:

```
Imports System.Web.Security
Imports System.Data.SqlClient

Public Class Login
  Inherits FriendsBase

  ...

  Private Sub Page_Load(ByVal sender As System.Object, _
                    ByVal e As System.EventArgs) Handles MyBase.Load
    MyBase.HeaderIconImageUrl = _
                Request.ApplicationPath & "/images/securekeys.gif"
    MyBase.HeaderMessage = "Login Page"
  End Sub

  Private Sub btnLogin_ServerClick(ByVal sender As System.Object, _
                ByVal e As System.EventArgs) Handles btnLogin.ServerClick
    Dim con As SqlConnection
    Dim sql As String
    Dim cmd As SqlCommand
    Dim id As String

    con = New SqlConnection( _
        "data source=(local)\NetSdk;initial catalog=Friends;user id=sa")
    sql = "SELECT UserID FROM [User] WHERE Login='{0}' and Password='{1}'"
```

```
        ' Format the string with the values provided
        sql = String.Format(sql, txtLogin.Value, txtPwd.Value)
        cmd = New SqlCommand(sql, con)
        con.Open()

        Try
            ' Retrieve the UserID
            id = CType(cmd.ExecuteScalar(), String)
        Finally
            con.Close()
        End Try

        If Not id Is Nothing Then
            ' Set the user as authenticated and send them to the page
            ' originally requested.
            FormsAuthentication.RedirectFromLoginPage(id, False)
        Else
            Me.pnlError.Visible = True
            Me.lblError.Text = "Invalid user name or password."
        End If
    End Sub
End Class
```

4. Save all your changes, and then run the application with `Default.aspx` as the start page.
You should find that you're taken to the login page automatically:

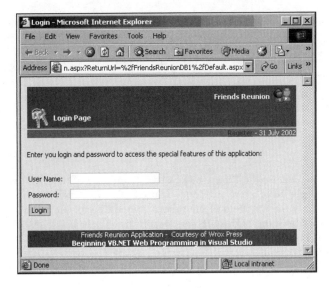

How It Works

From now on, all of the web forms that we add to this project will inherit from the `FriendsBase` class that we created in the previous chapter. We will also always use the two fields provided by the base class to set the text and the image for the current page. On this occasion, that was done in the `Page_Load()` handler:

```
Private Sub Page_Load(ByVal sender As System.Object, _
                     ByVal e As System.EventArgs) Handles MyBase.Load
   MyBase.HeaderIconImageUrl = _
                  Request.ApplicationPath & "/images/securekeys.gif"
   MyBase.HeaderMessage = "Login Page"
End Sub
```

The settings we've applied to the `Web.config` file will redirect the browser to the `Login.aspx` page when we start the project. After entering values for the user name and password and clicking the button, the code in `btnLogin_ServerClick()` is executed. The steps performed there are:

❏ Create a new `SqlConnection` object, using the same connection string as last time. After the object is created, it remains closed until we explicitly call the `Open()` method later on:

```
con = New SqlConnection( _
   "data source=(local)\NetSdk;initial catalog=Friends;user id=sa")
```

❏ Specify the SQL statement to execute against the database:

```
sql = "SELECT UserID FROM [User] WHERE Login='{0}' and Password='{1}'"
sql = String.Format(sql, txtLogin.Value, txtPwd.Value)
```

❏ Create a new `SqlCommand` object, using the query string and connection we've created:

```
cmd = New SqlCommand(sql, con)
```

❏ Open the connection:

```
con.Open()
```

❏ In the next line, we use the `ExecuteScalar()` method of the `SqlCommand` object to retrieve the single value we're selecting. (If the SQL expression returned more than one row and/or field, only the first field of the first row would be passed back to our code by this method.) As we built the SQL statement to return the user ID, that's what we'll get, after casting it to a string:

```
Try
   ' Retrieve the User ID
   id = CType(cmd.ExecuteScalar(), String)
Finally
   con.Close()
End Try
```

❑ Next, we check whether a valid user ID was returned. If it wasn't, then either the user name or the password must have been incorrect, so we show an error message. If everything is all right, we use the RedirectFromLoginPage() method to send the user to the page they requested in the first place. If you take a closer look at the URL in the above screenshot, you will notice that a **ReturnUrl** query string value has been appended to it. This is how RedirectFromLoginPage() knows where to redirect the user:

```
If Not id Is Nothing Then
    'Set the user as authenticated and send them to the
    'page originally requested.
    FormsAuthentication.RedirectFromLoginPage(id, False)
Else
    Me.pnlError.Visible = True
    Me.lblError.Text = "Invalid user name or password."
End If
```

As we said, once the user has been authenticated here, we can access their user ID from any code-behind page through the Context.User.Identity.Name property.

From now on, we will use the word wrox as both username and password in our examples – the database comes pre-loaded with some information for this user. After a successful logon, the user is presented with a welcome page, in which (if you remember our work in the last chapter) the sub-header that displays the date also includes the following code:

```
Protected Overrides Sub CreateChildControls()
    Me.Controls.Clear()

    Dim lbl As Label
    If Context.User.Identity.IsAuthenticated Then
        lbl = New Label()
        lbl.Text = Context.User.Identity.Name
        Me.Controls.Add(lbl)
    Else

    ...
```

Because of the changes we've made, the label now displays the user's ID, rather than their name – but we'll be putting that right in Chapter 11. Finally for now, Context.User.Identity.IsAuthenticated is working just as it did before – it returns True if the user has entered valid credentials in the Login.aspx form. One difference, though, is that the code after the Else statement will never be executed, because in that case (an unauthenticated user accessing the page) the browser will automatically be redirected to the login page.

Changing the Data in a Database

In general, details of the kind we've collected in our registration form do not remain the same forever, so it seems only reasonable that we should give our users the opportunity to change the data we hold about them. As the updated information is of exactly the same format as they used when they first registered, however, we can use the same form and just change some of its code. Specifically, we can discover if the user accessing NewUser.aspx is a new user seeking to register, or a registered user trying to modify their profile, by testing Context.User.Identity.IsAuthenticated.

Try It Out – Editing a User's Profile

In the case of a registered user, we will preload the form with the existing data by using the command object's ExecuteReader() method. When the time comes to save the data back to the database – that is, when the **Accept** button is clicked – we'll test the same property to determine whether an UPDATE or an INSERT is appropriate. The INSERT code is already in place, so we just need to add the UPDATE, again using the ExecuteNonQuery() method.

We'll also make a slight modification to the SubHeader.vb custom control that we built in the previous chapter, so that it shows a link to allow the user to change their profile. Since the 'register' link and the 'profile editing' link both point to the same page – NewUser.aspx – we only have to change its text.

1. Open the SubHeader.vb file, and modify the code in CreateChildControls() as follows:

```
Protected Overrides Sub CreateChildControls()
    Me.Controls.Clear()

    Dim lbl As Label
    Dim reg As New HyperLink()

    If _register = String.Empty Then
        reg.NavigateUrl = Context.Request.ApplicationPath & _
                          Path.AltDirectorySeparatorChar & "Secure" & _
                          Path.AltDirectorySeparatorChar & "NewUser.aspx"
    Else
        reg.NavigateUrl = _register
    End If

    If Context.User.Identity.IsAuthenticated Then
        reg.Text = "Edit my profile"
    Else
        reg.Text = "Register"
    End If

    Me.Controls.Add(reg)
    Me.Controls.Add(New LiteralControl(" - "))
    lbl = New Label()
    lbl.Text = DateTime.Now.ToLongDateString()
    Me.Controls.Add(lbl)
End Sub
```

2. If you recompile the project after making just these changes, and reopen the Default.aspx page (you may need to log in again), this is what you'll see:

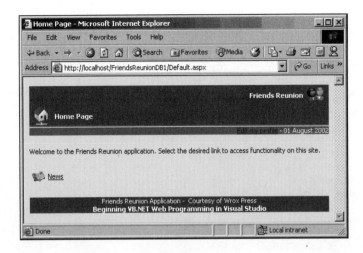

3. Let's now modify the `Page_Load()` handler in the `NewUser.aspx` page to preload the form with a registered user's data:

```
Private Sub Page_Load(ByVal sender As System.Object, _
                      ByVal e As System.EventArgs) Handles MyBase.Load
    MyBase.HeaderIconImageUrl = _
        Request.ApplicationPath & "/images/securekeys.gif"
    MyBase.HeaderMessage = "Registration Form"
```

```
    ' Postbacks can be caused by the validator controls in non-IE browsers
    If Page.IsPostBack Then Return

    ' If this is an update, preload the values
    If Context.User.Identity.IsAuthenticated Then
      ' Change the header message
      MyBase.HeaderMessage = "Update my profile"

      Dim con As SqlConnection
      Dim sql As String
      Dim cmd As SqlCommand
      Dim reader As SqlDataReader

      sql = "SELECT * FROM [User] " & _
          "WHERE UserID='" & Context.User.Identity.Name & "'"

      con = New SqlConnection( _
          "data source=(local)\NetSdk;initial catalog=Friends;user id=sa")

      cmd = New SqlCommand(sql, con)
      con.Open()
      reader = cmd.ExecuteReader(CommandBehavior.CloseConnection)

      If reader.Read() Then
        ' Retrieve a typed value using the column's ordinal position
        Dim pos As Integer
```

```
      pos = reader.GetOrdinal("Address")
      Me.txtAddress.Text = reader.GetString(pos).ToString()

      ' Avoid using the pos variable altogether, but get the typed value
      Me.txtBirth.Text = reader.GetDateTime( _
              reader.GetOrdinal("DateOfBirth")).ToShortDateString()

      ' Convert the untyped Object returned by the indexer to a string
      Me.txtEmail.Text = reader("Email").ToString()
      Me.txtFName.Text = reader("FirstName").ToString()
      Me.txtLName.Text = reader("LastName").ToString()
      Me.txtLogin.Text = reader("Login").ToString()
      Me.txtPhone.Text = reader("PhoneNumber").ToString()
      Me.txtPwd.Text = reader("Password").ToString()

      ' Use SQL Server types to have additional features
      pos = reader.GetOrdinal("CellNumber")
      Dim cel As SqlTypes.SqlString
      cel = reader.GetSqlString(pos)
      If Not cel.IsNull Then
        Me.txtMobile.Text = cel.Value
      End If
    End If
    reader.Close()
  End If
End Sub
```

4. We can test this code by compiling the project and refreshing the previous page. If you click on the **Edit my profile** link, you'll see that the values are preloaded on the form:

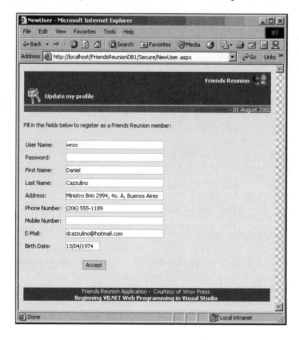

5. Next, to organize the code better, let's create a private routine called `InsertUser()`, and move the code from the `btnAccept_Click()` handler to it:

```
Private Sub InsertUser()
  If Page.IsValid Then

    . . .

  End If
End Sub
```

6. With that in place, let's create another new routine that will handle the update scenario. Inevitably, it's rather similar to the code for inserting new entries; it's called `UpdateUser()`:

```
Private Sub UpdateUser()
  If Page.IsValid Then
    ' Update the existing user
    Dim con As SqlConnection
    Dim sql As String
    Dim cmd As SqlCommand
    Dim sb As New StringBuilder()
    Dim values As New ArrayList()

    ' Build the SQL string
    sb.Append("UPDATE [User] SET ")
    sb.Append("Login='{0}', Password='{1}', FirstName='{2}', ")
    sb.Append("LastName='{3}', PhoneNumber='{4}', Email='{5}'")

    ' Add required values to replace
    values.Add(txtLogin.Text)
    values.Add(txtPwd.Text)
    values.Add(txtFName.Text)
    values.Add(txtLName.Text)
    values.Add(txtPhone.Text)
    values.Add(txtEmail.Text)

    ' Add optional values directly
    If txtAddress.Text <> String.Empty Then
      sb.Append(", Address='" & txtAddress.Text & "'")
    End If

    If txtMobile.Text <> String.Empty Then
      sb.Append(", CellNumber='" & txtMobile.Text & "'")
    End If

    If txtBirth.Text <> String.Empty Then
      sb.Append(", DateOfBirth='" & txtBirth.Text & "'")
    End If

    sb.Append(" WHERE UserID='{6}'")
```

```
                   ' Get the UserID from the context
                   values.Add(Context.User.Identity.Name)
                   sql = String.Format(sb.ToString(), values.ToArray())

                   ' Connect and execute the query
                   con = New SqlConnection( _
                       "data source=(local)\NetSdk;initial catalog=Friends;user id=sa")
                   cmd = New SqlCommand(sql, con)
                   con.Open()

                   Try
                      cmd.ExecuteNonQuery()
                      Response.Redirect("../Default.aspx")
                   Catch
                      Me.lblMessage.Visible = True
                      Me.lblMessage.Text = "Couldn't update your profile."
                   Finally
                      con.Close()
                   End Try
               End If
         End Sub
```

7. Finally, add the following code to the now empty `btnAccept_Click()` handler:

```
Private Sub btnAccept_Click(ByVal sender As System.Object, _
                            ByVal e As System.EventArgs) Handles btnAccept.Click
    If Context.User.Identity.IsAuthenticated Then
       UpdateUser()
    Else
       InsertUser()
    End If
End Sub
```

8. Save and compile the project. If you run the project again and log in to the application, you can click the new link in the subhead and not only see the form preloaded with values, but also change any of its values. It is even possible for the user to change their user name, because that's not being used as the primary key for the table – something that we can now appreciate!

How It Works

The change in the subhead control is very straightforward: we just change the text of the link according to the `IsAuthenticated` property for the current request. The interesting thing is happening in the `Page_Load()` routine, where we create the database connection and command objects as usual, but assign the result of executing the command to a variable of type `SqlDataReader`:

```
Dim reader As SqlDataReader

...

reader = cmd.ExecuteReader(CommandBehavior.CloseConnection)
```

The parameter passed to `ExecuteReader()` *indicates that we want the reader to close the connection when we close the reader later on. For all of the available values for this parameter, take a look at MSDN help.*

To read the values that form the result of our query, we start by checking that a row has actually been returned, by calling the `Read()` method:

```
If reader.Read() Then
```

After that, and partly for show, we use some of the various options that are available with the reader. First, we use the `GetOrdinal()` method to retrieve the position of a column in the reader, so that we can get a typed string using the `GetString()` method, which needs this value:

```
' Retrieve a typed value using the column's ordinal position
Dim pos As Integer
pos = reader.GetOrdinal("Address")
Me.txtAddress.Text = reader.GetString(pos).ToString()
```

The next line takes the same approach, but avoids the need for an extra variable by calling the `GetOrdinal()` method from inside the `GetDateTime()` method call:

```
' Avoid using the pos variable altogether, but get the typed value
Me.txtBirth.Text = reader.GetDateTime( _
             reader.GetOrdinal("DateOfBirth")).ToShortDateString()
```

This reduces the amount of code we need to write, at the expense of a little added complexity – note that as the value returned is a typed `DateTime` object, we can use its methods to format the date. The following lines show the most common approach, where we simply use the data reader object's indexer, which receives the column name and returns an `Object`. We can convert this object to a string very easily indeed:

```
' Convert the untyped Object returned by the indexer to a string
Me.txtEmail.Text = reader("Email").ToString()
Me.txtFName.Text = reader("FirstName").ToString()
Me.txtLName.Text = reader("LastName").ToString()
Me.txtLogin.Text = reader("Login").ToString()
Me.txtPhone.Text = reader("PhoneNumber").ToString()
Me.txtPwd.Text = reader("Password").ToString()
```

The last bit of code is a peek at the extra features we can get from a `SqlDataReader` object. Accessing the native data types of a SQL Server database can improve application performance, since by doing so we avoid the conversion between SQL Server data types and .NET's data types. However, this does make it harder to change the data provider if we decide to use a different database in the future. In this block, we use the `SqlString` type, which has (among other things) an `IsNull` property that can tell us whether a value is present:

```
' Use SQL Server types to have additional features
pos = reader.GetOrdinal("CellNumber")
Dim cel As SqlTypes.SqlString
cel = reader.GetSqlString(pos)
If Not cel.IsNull Then
  Me.txtMobile.Text = cel.Value
End If
```

Finally, we close the reader, which will also close the connection as a result of the `CommandBehavior.CloseConnection` value that we specified when we first executed the command:

```
    End If
    reader.Close()
```

When the user clicks the **Accept** button, we test the `IsAuthenticated` property, and call the update or the insert routine accordingly:

```
If Context.User.Identity.IsAuthenticated Then
  UpdateUser()
Else
  InsertUser()
End If
```

If you compare the code for the `UpdateUser()` routine with that for the insert routine that we created earlier, you will find that the two are almost identical. The only difference lies in the SQL statement building process, so we don't need to go any deeper there.

Completing the Picture – The DataSet Object

Until now, we've been looking at a **connected** model for accessing a database – that is, our code retains a connection to the database for the duration of our interactions with it. Data reader objects are very useful if we only have to move forward through the results of a query and display some values quickly, but an open connection is a valuable resource. Also, if we need to pass the retrieved data between methods, perform some processing before displaying it, or move back and forth through the results, a data reader simply doesn't cut the mustard. What we need is some way to extract data from the database on a semi-permanent basis, so that we can close the database connection for a while, and manipulate the data as we see fit. In other words, we want a way to deal with data that's **disconnected** from the data source.

An ADO.NET object that we introduced earlier but haven't examined so far is the **DataSet**. Unlike the data reader, command, and connection objects that we've been using, datasets are not data provider-dependent. `DataSet` is a class in the `System.Data` namespace, and instances of it can be used with any data source. A `DataSet` object can be thought of as an in-memory relational database, as it contains a collection of `DataTable` objects, which in turn contain collections of `DataColumn` and `DataRow` objects:

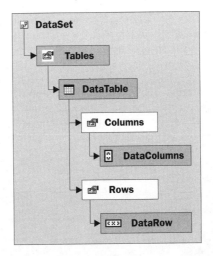

The data in a `DataSet` object can be inserted, updated, and deleted, and the object retains the details of any such modifications. However, being a generic, disconnected store for data, the dataset is completely 'unaware' of the data source, by which we mean that a dataset can be created from a database, a file, or programmatically, and it will remain always independent from the original source.

Data Adapters

Another object, which *is* data provider-specific, handles the process of filling the `DataSet` with data from a database, and posting changes back to that database. This object is a **data adapter**, and each data provider contains its own version: `SqlDataAdapter`, `OleDbDataAdapter`, `OdbcDataAdapter`, and so on. The data adapter uses command objects to retrieve data from a database, and later to post changes (inserts, updates, or deletes) back to it. In diagrammatic form, the interaction between these objects is:

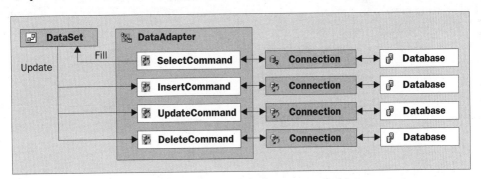

As shown in the figure, a data adapter object has two key methods: `Fill()` and `Update()`. Both of these take a `DataSet` as an argument, and use the command objects with which the data adapter is configured to interact with the database. During a `Fill()` call, the adapter executes its `SelectCommand`, and loads the data into the corresponding tables inside the `DataSet`. During an `Update()` call, the adapter inspects the data in the `DataSet`, and calls each command depending on what's happened to each row (it may have been inserted, updated or deleted). As stated above, the `DataSet` itself keeps track of all such changes.

Note that the `DataAdapter` *isn't in fact directly connected to the database(s), but through commands as shown above. Each of the commands can be configured independently to point to* **any** *database, so it is actually possible to perform the* `SELECT` *from one database and do the* `UPDATE` *on another one.*

So, let's recap: connection and command objects are used *every* time there is a need to access a database. From there, we can choose to use a connected mode, and use a data reader that's retrieved as a result of executing a command; or we can take advantage of the disconnected `DataSet` object, and use a data adapter to provide the link between it and the database. The complete picture for ADO.NET would then be:

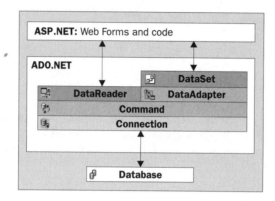

With the exception of the `DataSet`, the names of the other elements here are abstractions, since the actual class names are specific to each data provider.

Using a DataSet Object

In our Friends Reunion application, users can enter information about the places they have learned or worked at in the past, so that fellow users can contact them. This information is kept in the following tables in the database:

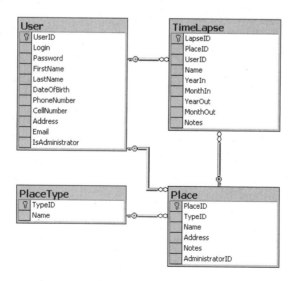

The `TimeLapse` table allows a `Name` to be specified, where the user can describe what it was they were doing in that place. For example, if the place was "Columbia University", the name of the time lapse could be "Systems Engineer", meaning that the user was in that role at that place for the period of time in question.

Try It Out – Assigning Places

For the next addition to the application, we'll build a form to allow the user to enter all of this information. We'll need to load any existing places they've registered, and allow the editing of this list, as well as the creation of new records in the `TimeLapse` table. As you've probably guessed, we'll be filling a `DataSet` object with all of the relevant information.

1. Add a new web form to the application, calling it `AssignPlaces.aspx`. Set its `Page Layout` property to `FlowLayout`.

2. Add a link to the stylesheet we've been using so far:

```
<head>

  . . .

    <link href="Style/iestyle.css" type="text/css" rel="stylesheet">
</head>
```

Change the code-behind page so that we inherit from the `FriendsBase` class, and add imports for the namespaces we'll be using too:

```
Imports System.Data
Imports System.Data.SqlClient

Public Class AssignPlaces
    Inherits FriendsBase
```

3. This form will contain a `Panel` with a `PlaceHolder`, which will be filled dynamically with a control for each time lapse record found, in much the same way that you saw in the last chapter. It will also contain an HTML table with textboxes and a combo box for the creation of a new record. Finally, there's a button for performing the insert operation:

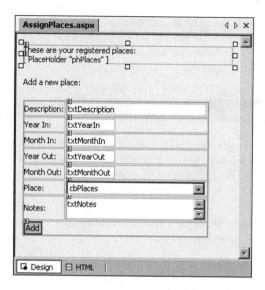

In the screenshot, the text inside each control is the ID to use for that control; the button's ID should be btnAdd. We've set CssClass to TextBox for txtDescription, cbPlaces, and txtNotes, while all of the other textboxes have the SmallTextBox value, and the button has Button.

If you wish, you could use RequiredFieldValidator controls on each of the required fields here, and you could use a CompareValidator control to ensure that the period is sensible (so that YearIn is forced to be equal to or less than YearOut, for example). In this example, we'll focus on the data access aspects.

4. Add the following code to the Page_Load() routine; it really just sets the agenda for the work to come.

```
Private Sub Page_Load(ByVal sender As System.Object, _
                     ByVal e As System.EventArgs) Handles MyBase.Load
  MyBase.HeaderMessage = "Assign Places"

  LoadDataSet()
  InitPlaces()
  InitForm()
End Sub
```

5. The first method, LoadDataSet(), will load a DataSet with all of the information needed by this page, and will necessarily be available as a class-level variable. Once we finish loading the data, the other two methods will initialize the interface. Let's see the loading process:

```
Private ds As DataSet

Private Sub LoadDataSet()
  Dim con As SqlConnection
  Dim sql As String
```

```
        Dim adExisting As SqlDataAdapter
        Dim adPlaces As SqlDataAdapter
        Dim adPlaceTypes As SqlDataAdapter

        con = New SqlConnection( _
            "data source=(local)\NetSdk;initial catalog=Friends;user id=sa")

        ' Select the place's timelapse records, descriptions, and type
        sql = "SELECT TimeLapse.*, Place.Name AS Place, "
        sql &= "PlaceType.Name AS Type FROM TimeLapse, Place, PlaceType "
        sql &= "WHERE TimeLapse.PlaceID = Place.PlaceID "
        sql &= "AND Place.TypeID = PlaceType.TypeID "
        sql &= "AND TimeLapse.UserID = '" & Context.User.Identity.Name & "'"

        ' Initialize the adapters
        adExisting = New SqlDataAdapter(sql, con)
        adPlaces = New SqlDataAdapter( _
            "SELECT * FROM Place ORDER BY TypeID", con)
        adPlaceTypes = New SqlDataAdapter("SELECT * FROM PlaceType", con)

        con.Open()
        ds = New DataSet()

        Try
            ' Proceed to fill the dataset
            adExisting.Fill(ds, "Existing")
            adPlaces.Fill(ds, "Places")
            adPlaceTypes.Fill(ds, "Types")
        Catch
            ' Just pass the exception up
            Throw
        Finally
            con.Close()
        End Try
    End Sub
```

6. The `InitPlaces()` method uses the `DataSet` we just filled to add items to the panel at the top of the page: a summary of each existing place, and a link to allow the user to delete it. We saw how to create dynamic content in the last chapter, but now we use data from the `DataSet` to drive the process:

```
    Private Sub InitPlaces()
        Dim row As DataRow
        Dim lbl As LiteralControl
        Dim msg As String
        Dim btn As LinkButton

        phPlaces.Controls.Clear()
        msg = "Type: {0}, Place: {1} From {2}/{3} to {4}/{5}. Description: {6}."

        For Each row In ds.Tables("Existing").Rows
            lbl = New LiteralControl()
```

```
      ' Format the msg variable with values in the row
      lbl.Text = String.Format(msg, row("Type"), row("Place"), _
                        row("MonthIn"), row("YearIn"), _
                        row("MonthOut"), row("YearOut"), row("Name"))

      btn = New LinkButton()

      ' Assign a unique id to the control
      btn.ID = row("LapseID").ToString().Replace("-", String.Empty)
      btn.Text = "Delete"

      ' Pass the LapseID when the link is clicked
      btn.CommandArgument = row("LapseID").ToString()

      ' Attach the handler to the event
      AddHandler(btn.Command, _
              New CommandEventHandler(AddressOf(OnDeletePlace))

      ' Add the controls to the place holder
      phPlaces.Controls.Add(lbl)
      phPlaces.Controls.Add(btn)
      phPlaces.Controls.Add(New LiteralControl("<br>"))
   Next

   ' Hide the panel if there are no rows
   If ds.Tables("Existing").Rows.Count > 0 Then
      pnlExisting.Visible = True
   Else
      pnlExisting.Visible = False
   End If
End Sub
```

7. In the previous method, we attached the same handler to all of the link buttons, but because each of them has a different `CommandArgument`, we can use that value to determine which row to delete. The code to perform the delete is little different from the database access code we've seen so far: it builds the SQL statement, creates the connection and command, and executes the command:

```
Private Sub OnDeletePlace(ByVal sender As Object, _
                      ByVal e As CommandEventArgs)

   ' e.CommandArgument receives the LapseID to delete
   Dim con As SqlConnection
   Dim cmd As SqlCommand

   ' Connect and execute the query
   con = New SqlConnection( _
        "data source=(local)\NetSdk;initial catalog=Friends;user id=sa")
   cmd = New SqlCommand("DELETE FROM TimeLapse " & _
        "WHERE LapseID='" & e.CommandArgument.ToString() & "'", con)
   con.Open()
```

```
      Try
         cmd.ExecuteNonQuery()
      Catch
         ' Just pass the exception up
         Throw
      Finally
         con.Close()
      End Try

      LoadDataSet()
      InitPlaces()
   End Sub
```

8. The `InitForm()` method initializes the form fields. It blanks any previous content, and it loads the combo box with the available places – but it only does these things if the page is being accessed for the first time:

```
Private Sub InitForm()
   If Not IsPostBack Then
      ' Clear existing values
      txtDescription.Text = String.Empty
      txtMonthIn.Text = String.Empty
      txtMonthOut.Text = String.Empty
      txtNotes.Text = String.Empty
      txtYearIn.Text = String.Empty
      txtYearOut.Text = String.Empty
      cbPlace.Items.Clear()

      ' Initialize combo box
      Dim i As Integer
      Dim item As ListItem
      Dim row As DataRow
      Dim types() As DataRow

      ' Access the table by index
      For Each row In ds.Tables(1).Rows
         ' Find the related row in Types data table
         types = ds.Tables("Types").Select( _
                 "TypeID='" & row("TypeID").ToString() & "'")

         item = New ListItem()

         ' Explicitly use the Item default property
         item.Text = types(0).Item("Name").ToString()
         item.Text &= ": " & row("Name").ToString()

         ' We can access the row's column by index too
         item.Value = row(0).ToString()
         cbPlace.Items.Add(item)
      Next
   End If
End Sub
```

9. For brevity, we will omit the code for the btnAdd's Click event handler, as that's just a simple INSERT statement that creates a new row for the TimeLapse table. We've already seen how those work, and you can download the full version of this code from the Wrox web site.

10. Compile and run the project with AssignPlaces.aspx as the start page. After logging on as the wrox user, you should see something like this:

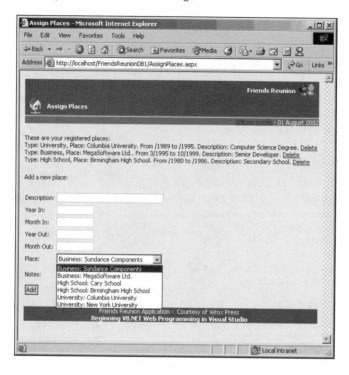

How it Works

Of the three methods that deal with what the user sees on the screen, the only one that interacts directly with the database is LoadDataSet(). Once the DataSet has been filled with data by this procedure, we don't need to refer to the database in InitPlaces() or InitForm(). This is a direct result of the disconnected nature of DataSet objects.

The data adapter class has a constructor that receives a SQL statement that's used to initialize its SelectCommand property. This has the same effect as setting this property to an existing command later on. To the same constructor, we also pass the SqlConnection that the command should use. In our code, you can see three adapters being created – one to retrieve full details, one that's just for places, and one that's just for type names.

```
'Initialize the adapters
adExisting = New SqlDataAdapter(sql, con)
adPlaces = New SqlDataAdapter( _
      "SELECT * FROM Place ORDER BY TypeID", con)
adPlaceTypes = New SqlDataAdapter("SELECT * FROM PlaceType", con)
```

As we're only retrieving data here (as opposed to editing or updating it), we don't need to configure anything else, so can we just proceed to connect to the database and create a new `DataSet` object:

```
con.Open()
ds = New DataSet()
```

Inside the `Try` block, we just call each adapter's `Fill()` method, passing the dataset and name that we want to give to the `DataTable` that's created as a result. If we didn't specify a name here, we'd get tables called `Table1`, `Table2`, and so on:

```
Try
    ' Proceed to fill the dataset
    adExisting.Fill(ds, "Existing")
    adPlaces.Fill(ds, "Places")
    adPlaceTypes.Fill(ds, "Types")
```

Once we've filled the `DataSet`, we can access its data using various approaches. In `InitPlaces()`, which fills the placeholder at the top of the user's screen, we use a couple of different ones. First, we access the table from the `DataSet`'s `Tables` property, using the table name we used when we filled it:

```
For Each row In ds.Tables("Existing").Rows
```

Now, we can use the `For Each` construct to iterate through the rows of the table in the same way that we would iterate through any standard collection or array. The `DataRow` class contains a default `Item` property that can receive the column name (or its index), and retrieve the value in that column:

```
lbl.Text = String.Format(msg, row("Type"), row("Place"), _
                         row("MonthIn"), row("YearIn"), _
                         row("MonthOut"), row("YearOut"), row("Name"))
```

The `InitPlaces()` method is just creating a literal control and a link button that's initialized with the values of each row. The link button will pass the row's `LapseID` column value, which is the primary key of the `TimeLapse` table, to the event handler for the **Delete** button. We also use this value to be the button control's ID, after removing the '-' character:

```
    ' Assign a unique id to the control
    btn.ID = row("LapseID").ToString().Replace("-", String.Empty)
    btn.Text = "Delete"

    ' Pass the LapseID when the link is clicked
    btn.CommandArgument = row("LapseID").ToString()

    ' Attach the handler to the event
    AddHandler(btn.Command, _
               New CommandEventHandler(AddressOf(OnDeletePlace)))
```

This way, the handler we attached to all the buttons will know which record to delete, as this value is used to build the DELETE SQL statement:

```
Private Sub OnDeletePlace(ByVal sender As Object, _
                         ByVal e As CommandEventArgs)
    ' e.CommandArgument receives the LapseID to delete
    Dim con As SqlConnection
    Dim cmd As SqlCommand

    ' Connect and execute the query
    con = New SqlConnection( _
          "data source=(local)\NetSdk;initial catalog=Friends;user id=sa")
    cmd = New SqlCommand("DELETE FROM TimeLapse " & _
          "WHERE LapseID='" & e.CommandArgument.ToString() & "'", con)
```

Finally, in `InitForm()`, which sets up the values in the combo box, we use some of the other choices offered by a `DataSet`. The most interesting one is that while we iterate through the records in the `Places` table, we perform a `Select` in the `Types` table to find the row corresponding to the current `TypeID`:

```
types = ds.Tables("Types").Select( _
        "TypeID='" & row("TypeID").ToString() & "'")
```

The `Select()` method receives an expression that's equivalent to a SQL `WHERE` expression, and retrieves an array of `DataRow` objects matching the criteria. In our case, we know there will only be one row returned. Next, we use the row's `Item` property explicitly to add the place type to our list:

```
' Explicitly use the Item default property
item.Text = types(0).Item("Name").ToString()
```

Then, we finish building the item's text, and add it to the items available in the combo box:

```
item.Text &= ": " & row("Name").ToString()

' We can access the row's column by index too
item.Value = row(0).ToString()
cbPlace.Items.Add(item)
```

For a more complete discussion of ADO.NET, you could read either Beginning Visual Basic .NET Databases *(ISBN 186100-555-5), or* Beginning ASP.NET Databases using VB.NET *(ISBN: 186100-619-5), both published by Wrox Press.*

Server Explorer

Now that we've started to work with data, it's not inconceivable that you might want to check what's going on in the database tables, or edit the data they contain, without having to do it through ADO.NET. For that purpose, we can use the Server Explorer tool that comes with Visual Studio .NET. If you already feel comfortable with this tool, or you'll be using SQL Server's Enterprise Manager to administer the database, feel free to skip the following section. If not, choose the View | Server Explorer menu item and take a look at the Server Explorer window, which will look something like this:

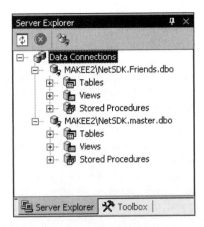

If the Server Explorer hasn't been used before, there may be nothing at all underneath the Data Connections root node. We'll address that right away.

The **Data Connections** node maintains a list of configured database connections, to which we can add new connections as we see fit. To see how it works, we'll add a connection to the database for the Friends Reunion application that we've been working with in this chapter.

In the code that you've downloaded for this book, you'll find a file called `FriendsDB.zip`, which contains a detached SQL Server database in a file called `Friends_Data.mdf`. You should extract the latter file to a folder somewhere on your local drive. To attach this file to your MSDE server, right-click on the Server Explorer's **Data Connections** node and select **Add Connection**, whereupon you will see the following dialog:

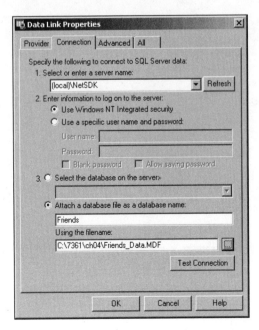

Here, Visual Studio .NET has assumed that you want to make a connection to a SQL Server database (if you need to, you can change this by clicking on the **Provider** tab). As for the specific settings you can see entered in the screenshot, (local)\NetSDK is the name of the MSDE server on your machine, and we are using **Windows NT Integrated security** to log on, which means that we don't need to enter a separate user name or password for the database. Furthermore, we have chosen to attach the Friends database that's contained in Friends_Data.mdf to MSDE, which means that we'll be able to manipulate it from the Visual Studio .NET IDE.

In the Professional and Enterprise versions of Visual Studio .NET, the Server Explorer allows us to connect to just about any database we could ever want to manipulate. Once a connection has been established, its node can be expanded, and the features of the database then appear as child nodes. In the version that comes with the Standard Edition of Visual Basic .NET, our options are more limited – we can only connect to MSDE and Access databases – but more than adequate for our needs here. Let's take a look at how we can use it to edit the data contained in a table.

Try It Out – Changing Data and Performing Queries

In this quick example, we'll use the Server Explorer to take a look at the Friends database that we just connected to, and perform some simple operations on it through the interface that Visual Studio .NET provides.

1. In the Server Explorer, go to the **Friends** connection, and open up the **Tables** node.

2. Right-click on the **User** table, and select **Retrieve Data from Table**. You should find that the main window displays something like the following, while a new tool bar – the Query tool bar – has appeared at the top left of the screen.

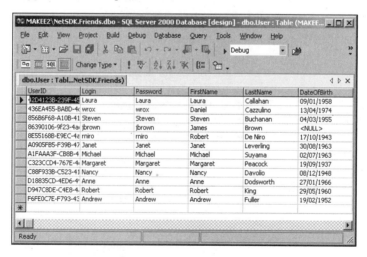

3. At this stage, any change you make to the data will be sent to the database as soon as you move the cursor to another row, just as if you were working in MS Access. For example, locate **James Brown** in the grid, and set his birth date to May 3, 1933. Move the cursor to the next row, and the change will be applied.

4. With the cursor positioned anywhere inside the table, click on the Show SQL Pane button to display the SQL code that was executed in order to produce the data you can see.

5. In the new panel, you can write any valid SQL statement, and click the Run Query button to show the results. You can also check the validity of the statements you enter by clicking the Verify SQL Syntax button.

As well as allowing us to examine and change the information in a database, setting up connections in the Server Explorer window serves another purpose that we'll start to look at in the very next section. In short, pre-configuring connections in this way allows Visual Studio .NET's Wizards to interact with databases though the use of components.

Components

Having come this far in the chapter, you may be starting to wonder what happened to the "Visual" part of Visual Studio and Visual Basic – we've been writing code as if we had nothing better than Notepad! Thankfully, Visual Studio .NET does come with some great productivity enhancements, including Wizards and designers that can make most data-related work a breeze. Now that you know the basics of ADO.NET, however, you'll have a better understanding of what's going on behind the scenes.

The fundamental concept that supports these features of the Visual Studio .NET IDE is the **component**. Putting out of your mind for a moment the various other meanings that have been ascribed to this word over the years, a component in Visual Studio .NET is a class that (directly or indirectly) implements the `System.ComponentModel.IComponent` interface. Most of the time, such a class will inherit from `System.ComponentModel.Component`.

A Visual Studio .NET component closely interacts with the IDE, and can be dropped onto a designer (like the web forms designer), appearing as an item in a section below the user interface elements. All of the ADO.NET classes we've seen are components, and as such they also cooperate with and use services provided by the designer. For example, this is what a `SqlConnection` component that's been dropped from the Toolbox's Data tab onto an empty page looks like:

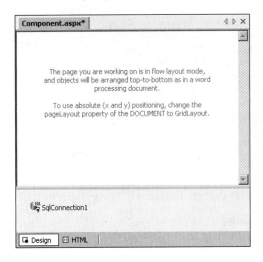

When a component is placed on a designer, it starts interacting with it, providing properties and Wizards that the developer can use to configure the component. Behind the scenes, the designer works together with the component to generate source code representing the actions we perform. As always, the best way to understand what's going on is to build an example.

Try It Out – Configuring a Connection Component

In this very short demonstration, we'll see what happens when we place a database component onto a form in a Visual Studio .NET design screen.

1. To our Friends Reunion project, add a (temporary) new web form called `Components.aspx`.

2. In the Toolbox, locate the **Data** tab, and drop a `SqlConnection` component onto the form. Use the **Properties** window to change its `Name` to `sqlCon`.

3. In the same window, from the drop-down list next to the `ConnectionString` property, you can either select **<New Connection...>** and use the **Data Link** dialog to configure a new connection, or you can use the **Friends** connection that we created before. This is another advantage of creating those connections with the Server Explorer!

4. Switch to the code view, and take a look at the code that has been generated for us.

How It Works

Components don't have a UI, so they appear in a separate section at the bottom of the page. In this example, we used the component to build the value for the `ConnectionString` property. After the steps we performed, the code-behind page contains the following:

```
Public Class Components
    Inherits FriendsBase
    Protected WithEvents sqlCon As System.Data.SqlClient.SqlConnection

#Region " Web Form Designer Generated Code "

    'This call is required by the Web Form Designer.
    <System.Diagnostics.DebuggerStepThrough()> _
    Private Sub InitializeComponent()
        Me.sqlCon = New System.Data.SqlClient.SqlConnection()
        '
        'sqlCon
        '
        Me.sqlCon.ConnectionString = [YOUR_CONNECTION_STRING]

    End Sub

    Private Sub Page_Init(ByVal sender As System.Object, _
                          ByVal e As System.EventArgs) Handles MyBase.Init
        'CODEGEN: This method call is required by the Web Form Designer
        'Do not modify it using the code editor.
```

```
      InitializeComponent()
   End Sub

#End Region

   Private Sub Page_Load(ByVal sender As System.Object, _
                     ByVal e As System.EventArgs) Handles MyBase.Load
      'Put user code to initialize the page here
   End Sub

End Class
```

The web form designer generated the code in the #Region section automatically. It also defined a protected variable, sqlCon, for the connection we added. The InitializeComponent() method creates the connection and sets the ConnectionString that we set through the **Properties** window. This method is called when the page is initialized, in the Page_Init() event handler. There is no magic here; just plain old variables and initialization code that we could have written ourselves.

In truth, the component that we've chosen to add here offers only limited advantages over manual coding, but in the next chapter we'll see how other components, such as the SqlDataAdapter, can perform some quite complex tasks on our behalf.

Dynamic Properties

Another advantage of components is the availability of **dynamic properties**, which can be configured to load their values from the application configuration file, Web.config. In Visual Studio .NET, dynamic properties live in a special section under the **Configurations** heading in the **Properties** window. Once again, the designer works together with the component to generate the appropriate code, this time for retrieving data from Web.config. Let's see how that happens.

Try It Out – Configuring a Dynamic ConnectionString

In this example, we will now modify the SqlConnection component we just added to use a dynamic property for the connection string. This is a significant improvement over the approach we've been using so far, which involved hard-coding the value everywhere we needed access to the database.

1. Open the Components.aspx web form in design view, and select the sqlCon component. In the **Properties** window, expand the (DynamicProperties) element. Click the ellipsis button next to ConnectionString, check the **Map...** box, and accept the dialog:

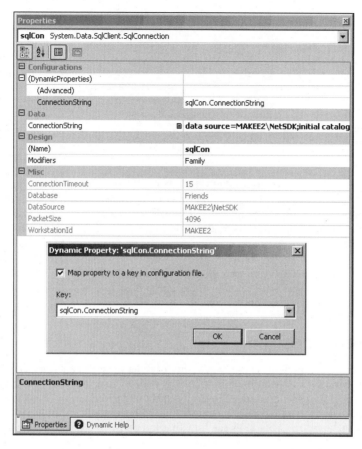

Note that a small icon has appeared next to the `ConnectionString` property under the Data category, indicating that this is now a dynamic property.

How It Works

The (DynamicProperties) section in the **Properties** window works in conjunction with components, showing only the properties that can be dynamically configured. If we now take a look at the `Web.config` file, we will see that the following element has been added:

```
<configuration>
  <appSettings>
    <!--   User application and configured property settings go here.-->
    <!--   Example: <add key="settingName" value="settingValue"/> -->
    <add key="sqlCon.ConnectionString"
         value="data source=(local)\NetSDK;initial
         catalog=Friends;integrated security=SSPI;persist security
         info=False;workstation id=MAKEE2;packet size=4096" />
  </appSettings>
</configuration>
```

  ...

142

The `integrated security=SSPI` value in the connection string denotes that we used integrated Windows security for the connection. If you now look again at the code-behind page, you'll see that there's been a change there, too:

```
...

<System.Diagnostics.DebuggerStepThrough()> _
Private Sub InitializeComponent()
    Dim configurationAppSettings As _
        System.Configuration.AppSettingsReader = _
            New System.Configuration.AppSettingsReader()
    Me.sqlCon = New System.Data.SqlClient.SqlConnection()
    '
    'sqlCon
    '
    Me.sqlCon.ConnectionString = _
        CType(configurationAppSettings.GetValue(_
            "sqlCon.ConnectionString", GetType(System.String)), String)

End Sub

...
```

The new `configurationAppSettings` variable is an instance of the `AppSettingsReader` class, which allows access to the values in the `Web.config` file. The property's value is retrieved with this object, using the key that was built by the dynamic property, and cast explicitly to a string. Whenever we change the setting in the configuration file, this page will automatically use the new value.

There's actually another way of getting hold of the values that we store in `Web.config`. We can modify the code that we've been using to create connection objects so far to use the following syntax:

```
con = New SqlConnection( _
                ConfigurationSettings.AppSettings("sqlCon.ConnectionString")
```

In fact, we can use the `Web.config` file to store pretty much anything we want, and retrieve it with this syntax. This way, this central repository can be used both for the components we use through the IDE, and from our custom code, significantly improving maintenance.

The advantage of this shortcut over an `AppSettingsReader` object is that it requires less code, but the object can offer better performance if we have to retrieve several settings at once – it caches the `<appSettings>` section as we read it, and performs physical access to the file only once. If the `Web.config` file is fairly big, using `AppSettingsReader` can be more suitable.

> The `ConfigurationSettings` class is located in the `System.Configuration` namespace, so we can either add an `Imports` statement or use the fully qualified class name.

With the database concepts you've learned so far, we're ready to build some useful data-aware applications, but the introduction to components has been just a peek into the possibilities that are available in Visual Studio .NET. In the next chapter, we'll take a much closer look at them. We'll see how they reduce the amount of code we have to type, and how they can provide advanced functionality for our applications with hardly any effort.

Summary

Data access is essential for all but the most trivial web application. We have learned the basis of ADO.NET, Microsoft's new strategy for data access, and we have seen how the various pieces fit in the whole picture of web application development.

We started to add some data-aware pages to our application, which allowed us to leverage the power of data-driven pages. We discussed how to programmatically access a database and handle its data. We were able to display that data in web forms, taking advantage of the knowledge we got from previous chapters, and we have started to use some of the features available in Visual Studio .NET, such as the Server Explorer.

Up to now, however, we have been typing a lot of code manually. Visual Studio .NET goes much further in programmer productivity, introducing the key concept of components. We got an introduction to what they are and how they work in conjunction with the IDE to perform some coding tasks for us. In the next chapter, we will dig into some exciting new features introduced by Visual Studio .NET to simplify web forms and data interaction through the concept of **data binding**. We will also learn how to use the more advanced wizards provided by components, and how to leverage web server controls to display and edit data in highly customizable ways though the use of another new concept, **templates**.

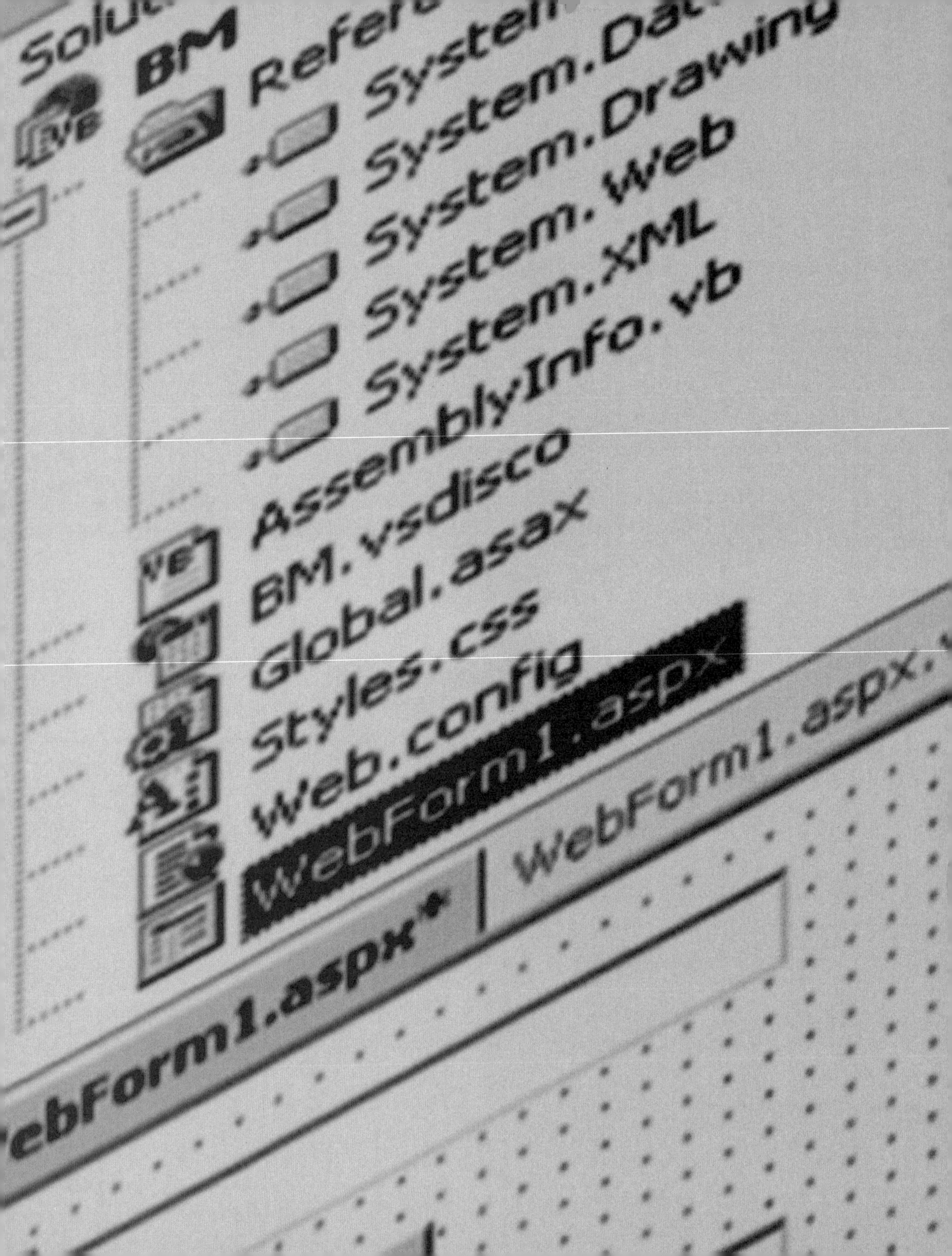

Solu...
BM Refere... System...
System.Dat...
System.Drawing
System.Web
System.XML
AssemblyInfo.vb
Assembly
BM.vsdisco
Global.asax
Styles.css
Web.config
WebForm1.aspx

WebForm1.aspx* | WebForm1.aspx.

ebForm1.aspx*

Data Binding

In the last chapter, after learning how to interact with a database using the ADO.NET classes, we took a sneak peek at Visual Studio .NET's new component architecture. This opens the door to the automatic generation of data access code, and we'll be discussing it in greater depth in this chapter. We'll also take a tour of the new data binding capabilities provided by ASP.NET, which allow us to write less code and let the platform do the heavy work of transferring data from ADO.NET objects to our web forms. From this point, we'll be able to take full advantage of another technique that relates closely to data binding: **templates** will allow us to customize the look and feel of the controls in which our data is displayed, all from the IDE and with full drag-and-drop support.

During this chapter, we will:

❑ Learn how to use simple data binding to show data on a form

❑ Make use of more complex binding that involves sets of data and presents it in tabular fashion, automatically

❑ Use the interaction between .NET components and the IDE to let Visual Studio .NET generate code on our behalf

❑ Take advantage of typed datasets, which improve the experience of data binding at design time, and offer some other improvements to our code

❑ Take a look at templates, and apply them to customize the display of complex sets of data

❑ Find out how to enable the editing of data through our web pages

Data Binding

From the last chapter, you may recall our work with the NewUser.aspx page. When we added the capability to pre-load the form with information from the database (for the current user, to allow them to edit their profile), we used code in the code-behind page to set the values to be displayed in the various controls. The code looked like this:

```
Me.txtEmail.Text = reader("Email").ToString()
Me.txtFName.Text = reader("FirstName").ToString()
Me.txtLName.Text = reader("LastName").ToString()
Me.txtLogin.Text = reader("Login").ToString()
Me.txtPhone.Text = reader("PhoneNumber").ToString()
Me.txtPwd.Text = reader("Password").ToString()
```

The need to display data from a data source – in this case, a `DataReader` object – is a situation that crops up time and time again. For this reason, ASP.NET supports the concept of **data binding**, which frees us from writing code like that shown above. The idea behind data binding is that the link between the data source and the controls that will display it is known at design time, and will rarely (if ever) change at run time.

To use data binding, we provide each control property that will display data at run time with a **binding expression** that represents that data at design time. At run time, we resolve the binding expression to its actual value, and assign that to the control property instead.

Before we discuss the precise format and run-time behavior of binding expressions, let's see where and how can we use them. A binding expression can be specified in HTML source code, in place of any web server control's property value, such as:

```
<asp:Label id="lblPending" runat="server" Text='<%# EXPRESSION %>' />
```

Here, we see a binding expression (`<%# EXPRESSION %>`) replacing the `Text` property value of a `Label` web server control. This is probably the most common use, but there's nothing to stop you from using data binding for the label's `BackColor` property, if that's what you want to do. This use of data binding is called **simple binding**, because resolution of the expression results in a single value.

To get the expression evaluated and have the results placed in the control's property, we have to call the control's `DataBind()` method. This method is inherited from the `Control` base class, and as such, it is available to all controls – even the page itself. Its effects propagate to all child controls too, so a call at the page level will cause all of the data binding expressions on a page to be evaluated, and the results to be placed in the corresponding properties.

Binding Expressions

A binding expression is evaluated in the context defined by the code-behind page – that is, all of the page-level variables, methods, and properties that are available in the code-behind page can be used as binding expressions. For example, we could have a method called `GetPending()` that performs a database query and then returns a string to be bound. We might use that as follows:

```
<asp:Label id="lblPending" runat="server" Text='<%# GetPending() %>' />
```

Similarly, if we had a page-level variable called `userID`, we could bind that to any control we wanted with the following code (for a label in this case):

```
<asp:Label id="lblPending" runat="server" Text='<%# userID %>' />
```

Just as easily, we could refer to a dataset variable defined in the code-behind page to show the count of the rows in a table, for example:

```
<asp:Label id="lblPending" runat="server"
                    Text='<%# dsUser.Tables(0).Rows.Count %>' />
```

As you can see, the mechanism is very flexible – it just leaves us to perform the appropriate variable initialization or method coding. If we're intending to use data binding, though, we have to do a little forward planning. Typically, we'll define a page-level variable to hold the data (say, a DataSet), fill it using a DataAdapter as you saw in the previous chapter, and finally call DataBind() in the page itself. This will cause all the controls that have binding expressions to be populated with the values from the newly filled DataSet.

> **The important thing to remember is that the code-behind members to be used in binding expressions must be either Public or Protected in order to be accessible at the moment binding occurs.**

The DataBinder Class

If we need to format a string prior to displaying it, we can use a helper class that's provided in the System.Web.UI namespace, called DataBinder. This class contains a static method called Eval(), which receives an object, an expression, and (optionally) a format string. The object is used as the context in which to evaluate the expression, and the result of the evaluation is formatted with the last parameter if specified.

If we wanted to apply special formatting to a user's birth date, for example, we could use this:

```
<asp:label id=lblBirth runat="server"
           text='<%# DataBinder.Eval(dsUser.Tables(0).Rows(0),
           "(DateOfBirth)", "{0:MMMM dd, yyyy}") %>'>
</asp:label>
```

Here, the first parameter to Eval() – the row we want to display the value from – is used as the context in which the second parameter is evaluated. Finally, the format string is applied.

It's worth spending a little more time learning the inner working of the Eval() method, as we'll be using it a lot from this point on – especially when we start to use the IDE to generate code for us. To illustrate the forthcoming discussion, we'll use the following expression, which displays the count of rows in a dataset's table, padded with zeros to six digits:

```
<%# DataBinder.Eval(dsUser, "Tables(0).Rows.Count", "{0:D6}") %>
```

149

Here, we've passed the dataset as the first argument, which will be the context for the expression. Now, in order for the `Count` to be retrieved, each 'step' in the expression has to be evaluated separately and used as the starting point for the next. To evaluate this expression, `Eval()` first evaluates `dsUser.Tables(0)`, then uses the result of that to evaluate `Rows`, and uses this last result in turn to evaluate `Count`. When it encounters an indexer expression start symbol, which can be either (or [(for C# users), it evaluates it as a whole, up to the closing symbol, again either) or].

The important consequence of this way of working is that two consecutive indexer accesses won't be properly evaluated. For example, look at what happens if we rewrite the earlier expression for displaying the user's birth date:

```
<asp:label id=lblBirth runat="server"
        text='<%# DataBinder.Eval(dsUser,
        "Tables(0).Rows(0)(""DateOfBirth"")", "{0:MMMM dd, yyyy}") %>'>
</asp:label>
```

This is perfectly valid Visual Basic .NET code for accessing the `DateOfBirth` column in the first row of the table, but if you tried it here you'd actually get the string `System.Data.DataRow` displayed! `Eval()` splits the expression into `Tables(0)` and `Rows(0)(""DateOfBirth"")`, according to the dot separating them. It then looks for the starting parenthesis, and evaluates it up to the closing one. This means that, first it will retrieve the first table in the `Tables` collection, and then it will only evaluate `Rows(0)`, silently ignoring the second indexer accessor.

If we add a dot between the two accessors, as follows, both of them will be properly evaluated:

```
<asp:label id=lblBirth runat="server"
        text='<%# DataBinder.Eval(dsUser,
        "Tables(0).Rows(0).(""DateOfBirth"")", "{0:MMMM dd, yyyy}") %>'>
</asp:label>
```

Of course, this is not valid Visual Basic .NET code, but in this context it's the only way to have things work as they should.

Adding Data Binding to our Application

After all of that, let's start using these new ideas to get some new functionality for our application. The way that Friends Reunion is intended to work is that when users make requests for fellow users to get in touch with them, a record will be placed in the `Contact` table. This table has the following structure:

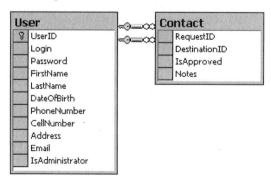

At first, a new record in the `Contact` table will have its `IsApproved` flag set to 0, indicating that this is a request waiting to be approved. In our application, a requesting user must be approved by the target user in order for the former to be able to see the latter's details. In this discussion, we will focus on the view of the target user – that is, the one specified in the `DestinationID`.

Before the target user approves a contact that has placed a request, they will surely want to see that user's details. We will now build a form that receives a `RequestID` as a query string parameter, and displays information about that user in a table. In it, we will take advantage of data binding. For the purposes of this demonstration, we will be using most of the binding expression variants you've seen; in your own applications, you'll probably use the one that best suits your needs and programming style.

In the form's code-behind page, we'll write a method that counts the number of pending requests the user has, and use data binding to display this value too. Finally, a button will allow the user to update the `IsApproved` flag whenever they want to approve the contact. Once the flag has been updated, the user will be redirected to the page they came from, which will be `News.aspx`.

Try It Out – Displaying Information about Fellow Users using Data Binding

Eventually, the page we're about to create will be arrived at as a result of navigation from `News.aspx`, in the course of which the `RequestID` will be passed as a query string. When we test this example, we'll have to simulate that by assembling the string ourselves, but don't let that put you off – we'll deal with `News.aspx` later.

1. Add a new web form called `ViewUser.aspx` to the project. Also, add the link to the usual stylesheet, and change the code-behind page to inherit from the `FriendsBase` class.

2. Add a style rule called `TableLines` to the stylesheet. This will help us to make our HTML tables look consistent across our site:

```
.TableLines
{
  border-top: #c7ccdc 1px solid;
  border-bottom: #c7ccdc 1px solid;
  border-right: #c7ccdc 1px solid;
  border-left: #c7ccdc 1px solid;
  padding-top: 5px;
  padding-bottom: 5px;
  padding-right: 5px;
  padding-left: 5px;
}
```

3. Add an HTML table with six rows and two columns. Set its `class` property to `TableLines`, `border` to 0, and `cellpadding` and `cellspacing` to 2.

4. Add `Label` web server controls to the cells on the right, except for the last row, which will contain a `HyperLink` control. Below the table, add some text and a label to reflect the following form layout:

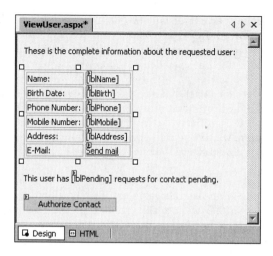

5. Add a web server `Button` control, set its `CssClass` to `Button`, and its `Text` property to `Authorize Contact`.

6. Switch to the HTML view, and make the following changes to add data binding expressions to the controls:

```
...
<body ms_positioning="FlowLayout">
  <form id="Form1" method="post" runat="server">
    <p>This is the complete information about the requested user:</p>
    <table class="TableLines" id="tbLogin" cellspacing="2"
           cellpadding="2" border="0">
      <tr>
        <td>Name:</td>
        <td><asp:label id=lblName runat="server"
               Text='<%# dsUser.Tables(0).Rows(0)("FirstName") + ", " +
                         dsUser.Tables(0).Rows(0).Item("LastName") %>'>
            </asp:label></td>
      </tr>
      <tr>
        <td>Birth Date:</td>
        <td><asp:label id=lblBirth runat="server"
               Text='<%# DataBinder.Eval(dsUser.Tables(0).Rows(0),
                         "(DateOfBirth)", "{0:MMMM dd, yyyy}") %>'>
            </asp:label></td>
      </tr>
      <tr>
        <td>Phone Number:</td>
        <td><asp:label id=lblPhone runat="server"
               Text='<%# dsUser.Tables("User").Rows(0)("PhoneNumber") %>'>
            </asp:label></td>
      </tr>
```

```
        <tr>
          <td>Mobile Number:</td>
          <td><asp:label id=lblMobile runat="server"
                Text='<%# DataBinder.Eval(dsUser,
                          "Tables(User).Rows(0).(CellNumber)") %>'>
            </asp:label></td>
        </tr>
        <tr>
          <td>Address:</td>
          <td><asp:label id=lblAddress runat="server"
                Text='<%# DataBinder.Eval(dsUser.Tables("User").Rows(0),
                          "(Address)") %>'>
            </asp:label></td>
        </tr>
        <tr>
          <td>E-Mail:</td>
          <td><asp:hyperlink id=lnkEmail runat="server"
                navigateurl='<%# DataBinder.Eval(dsUser.Tables,
                "(""User"").Rows(0).(""Email"")", "mailto:{0}") %>'>
                Send mail</asp:hyperlink></td>
        </tr>
      </table>
      <p>
        This user has
        <asp:label id=lblPending runat="server" Text="<%# GetPending() %>">
        </asp:label> requests for contact pending.
      </p>
      <p>
        <asp:button id="btnAuthorize" runat="server"
          text="Authorize Contact" cssclass="Button"></asp:button></p>
    </form>
  </body>
</html>
```

7. Next, open the code-behind page, where we need to add the DataSet as a public variable, and perform the database access in the Page_Load() event handler:

```
Public dsUser As DataSet

Private Sub Page_Load(ByVal sender As System.Object, _
                      ByVal e As System.EventArgs) Handles MyBase.Load

  Dim userID As String = Request.QueryString("RequestID")

  ' Ensure we received an ID
  If userID = Nothing Then
   Throw New ArgumentException("This page expects a RequestID parameter.")
  End If

  ' Create the connection and data adapter
  Dim cnFriends As New SqlConnection( _
      ConfigurationSettings.AppSettings("cnFriends.ConnectionString"))
```

```
Dim adUser As New SqlDataAdapter( _
     "SELECT * FROM [User] WHERE UserID='" & userID & "'", cnFriends)

  ' Initialize the dataset and fill it with data
  dsUser = New DataSet()
  adUser.Fill(dsUser, "User")

  ' Finally, bind all the controls on the page
  Page.DataBind()
End Sub
```

8. The next method, GetPending(), will return the value that's used in the lblPending label to show the number of pending requests for this user:

```
Public Function GetPending() As String
  Dim userID As String = Request.QueryString("RequestID")

  ' Ensure we received an ID
  If userID = Nothing Then
    Throw New ArgumentException("This page expects a RequestID parameter.")
  End If

  ' Create the connection and command to execute
  Dim cnFriends As New SqlConnection( _
       ConfigurationSettings.AppSettings("cnFriends.ConnectionString"))
  Dim cmd As New SqlCommand("SELECT COUNT(*) FROM Contact " & _
                            "WHERE IsApproved=0 AND " & _
                            "DestinationID='" & userID & "'", cnFriends)
  cnFriends.Open()

  ' Ensure the connection is closed after execution
  Try
    Return CType(cmd.ExecuteScalar(), String)
  Catch
    ' Just pass the exception up
    Throw
  Finally
    cnFriends.Close()
  End Try
End Function
```

9. The last piece of code that we need to add here is the handler for the **Authorize** button. This will just perform an update of the IsApproved flag:

```
Private Sub btnAuthorize_Click(ByVal sender As System.Object, _
                               ByVal e As System.EventArgs) _
                               Handles btnAuthorize.Click
  Dim userID As String
  Dim sql As String
  Dim cmd As SqlCommand
```

```
      userID = Request.QueryString.Item("RequestID")
      sql = "UPDATE Contact SET IsApproved=1 " & _
            "WHERE RequestID='{0}' AND DestinationID='{1}'"
      sql = String.Format(sql, userID, Page.User.Identity.Name)

      ' Create the connection and command to execute
      Dim cnFriends As New SqlConnection( _
            ConfigurationSettings.AppSettings("cnFriends.ConnectionString"))
      cmd = New SqlCommand(sql, cnFriends)
      cnFriends.Open()

      'Ensure the connection is closed after execution
      Try
        cmd.ExecuteNonQuery()
      Catch
        ' Just pass the exception up
        Throw
      Finally
        cnFriends.Close()
      End Try

      ' Return to the news page
      Response.Redirect("News.aspx")
   End Sub
```

10. Finally, save and compile the project. Open a browser window, and point it to the newly created page with the following parameter appended to the URL: ViewUser.aspx?RequestID=436EA455-BABD-4ca2-9D30-7B4F4608A068. After you log in to the application (again, with `wrox` as the user name and password), you should see the following page:

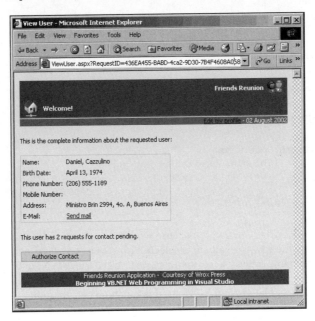

How It Works

The code in `Page_Load()` starts by checking for the existence of the `RequestID` parameter, and then creates a connection and a data adapter to perform the query. We are no longer hard-coding the connection string, as we did at the end of the last chapter. Instead, we are using the value stored in the configuration file:

```
Dim cnFriends As New SqlConnection( _
    ConfigurationSettings.AppSettings("cnFriends.ConnectionString"))
Dim adUser As New SqlDataAdapter( _
    "SELECT * FROM [User] WHERE UserID='" & userID & "'", cnFriends)
```

After we have the objects configured, we create and fill the dataset that we defined at the class level as a public variable:

```
dsUser = New DataSet()
adUser.Fill(dsUser, "User")
```

Now, instead of manually assigning each property to the corresponding value in the dataset, we let the data binding mechanism do its work and evaluate the expressions we used in the page's HTML source. We do this by explicitly calling `DataBind()` at the page level, so that every control on the page gets evaluated:

```
Page.DataBind()
```

To see exactly what's going on, though, we need to take a look at the different binding expressions we used, starting with the first one:

```
<td><asp:label id=lblName runat="server"
        Text='<%# dsUser.Tables(0).Rows(0)("FirstName") + ", " +
                  dsUser.Tables(0).Rows(0).Item("LastName") %>'>
    </asp:label></td>
```

Here, we directly specify the values from the dataset variable that we defined in the code-behind page, first accessing the value using the default property, and then doing it explicitly using the `Item` property. Notice that we can also perform simple string concatenation inside the expression.

```
<td>Birth Date:</td>
<td><asp:label id=lblBirth runat="server"
        Text='<%# DataBinder.Eval(dsUser.Tables(0).Rows(0),
              "(DateOfBirth)", "{0:MMMM dd, yyyy}") %>'>
    </asp:label></td>
```

This time, we use `DataBinder.Eval()`, because we want to give the date a special format. We split the expression just after the row to evaluate is selected (`dsUser.Tables(0).Rows(0)`), and let the method resolve the indexer property access with `"(DateOfBirth)"`. Note the relaxed syntax here – the default `Item` property actually receives a string, so the 'correct' value to pass to `Eval()` should be `"(""DateOfBirth"")"`. The version we've used is much neater, though!

```
<td>Phone Number:</td>
<td><asp:label id=lblPhone runat="server"
     Text='<%# dsUser.Tables("User").Rows(0)("PhoneNumber") %>'>
   </asp:label></td>
```

This is just to show that if we don't use `DataBinder.Eval()`, we have to code the expression as valid Visual Basic .NET code. In this case, that means passing the proper string to access the column value.

```
<td>Mobile Number:</td>
<td><asp:label id=lblMobile runat="server"
     Text='<%# DataBinder.Eval(dsUser,
                "Tables(User).Rows(0).(CellNumber)") %>'>
   </asp:label></td>
```

Getting hold of the mobile number reprises a couple of the earlier themes, but you can see that in the last part of the expression – the actual column value retrieval – we had to add a dot between the two default property accessors. Without it, you'll get the string `"System.Data.DataRow"` in the form, because that's the string representation of the row object itself, rather than the column value.

```
<td><asp:hyperlink id=lnkEmail runat="server"
     navigateurl='<%# DataBinder.Eval(dsUser.Tables,
     "(""User"").Rows(0).(""Email"")", "mailto:{0}") %>'>
     Send mail</asp:hyperlink></td>
```

Last, we provide a third argument to the `Eval()` function, as a result of which the formatting is applied just as if the following were called directly in our code:

```
String.Format("mailto:{0}", dsUser.Tables("User").Rows(0)("Email"))
```

At the bottom of the page, we have a rather simpler data binding expression, where we bind the `lblPending` label to the `GetPending()` method we created in the code-behind page:

```
This user has
<asp:label id=lblPending runat="server" Text="<%# GetPending() %>">
</asp:label> requests for contact pending.
```

The `GetPending()` method itself simply returns the count of pending requests for the current user in the `Contact` table:

```
Dim cmd As New SqlCommand("SELECT COUNT(*) FROM Contact " & _
                "WHERE IsApproved=0 AND " & _
                "DestinationID='" & userID & "'", cnFriends)
```

The `btnAuthorize` handler just performs an update and redirects the user to the `News.aspx` page. To use the command, we call `ExecuteNonQuery()`, as we don't expect a result to be returned.

Binding to Sets of Data

Up to now, we have been binding to single items of data – each of our binding expressions has selected just one value from the database. In order to generate the table on the `ViewUser.aspx` page, we had to write a different expression for each cell. There is an easier way: to display *sets* of data, we can use some of the controls provided with ASP.NET that support binding to multiple items.

ASP.NET comes with several controls for displaying sets of data, such as `DataGrid`, `DataList`, and `Repeater`. These controls provide a `DataSource` property that can be set to point to the data we want to display. When this type of binding is used, the control itself is in charge of iterating through the data source and formatting the data for display, in a fashion that's configured using the control's properties.

The concept of a "data source" is fairly wide here, and is by no means a synonym for `DataSet`. These controls can be bound to *any* set of data, provided that the object containing the data implements the `IEnumerable` interface. This definition certainly includes the `DataSet`, but also encompasses the `ArrayList`, a collection, and so on.

In our application, we want to display the current user's list of pending requests for contact. This information can be easily displayed in tabular format, so we will use a `DataGrid` control.

Try It Out – Displaying Pending Contacts in a DataGrid

The process we'll follow here involves filling a `DataSet` with the data, setting it to be the data source for the grid, and calling the grid's `DataBind()` method. In addition, the control will be placed inside a panel, so we can later hide it if there turn out to be no pending requests.

1. As our starting point, we'll use the `News.aspx` page that we created in Chapter 3. However, its existing controls aren't of much use any more (it had a calendar, a combo box, the user controls, and so on). You'll recall that the header and footer controls were moved to the `FriendsBase` base class, so we should make this page inherit from that one. Once we've tidied up a little, the page source should look like the following:

```
<%@ Page Language="vb" AutoEventWireup="false"
        Codebehind="News.aspx.vb" Inherits="FriendsReunionDB.News" %>
<!DOCTYPE HTML PUBLIC "-//W3C//DTD HTML 4.0 Transitional//EN">
<html>
  <head>
    <title>News</title>
    <meta> tags ...
    <link href="Style/iestyle.css" type="text/css" rel="stylesheet">
  </head>
  <body ms_positioning="FlowLayout">
    <form id="Form1" method="post" runat="server">
    </form>
  </body>
</html>
```

2. In the design view for the `News.aspx` file, drop a `Panel` web control onto the form and set its ID to `pnlPending`.

3. Change the text inside the panel to something meaningful – such as "These are your approved contacts:" – and add a carriage return.

4. Drop a `DataGrid` web control inside the panel, and set its ID to `grdPending`.

5. Add the following namespace imports:

```
Imports System.Data
Imports System.Data.SqlClient
```

6. Switch to the code-behind page, and change the `Page_Load()` handler as follows:

```
Private Sub Page_Load(ByVal sender As System.Object, _
                     ByVal e As System.EventArgs) Handles MyBase.Load
    ' Configure the icon and message
    MyBase.HeaderIconImageUrl = _
        Request.ApplicationPath & "/images/winbook.gif"
    MyBase.HeaderMessage = "News Page"

    Dim sql As String
    sql = "SELECT [User].FirstName, [User].LastName, Contact.Notes, "
    sql &= "[User].UserID FROM [User], Contact WHERE "
    sql &= "DestinationID='" & Context.User.Identity.Name & "' AND "
    sql &= " IsApproved=0 AND [User].UserID=Contact.RequestID"

    ' Create the connection, data adapter and dataset
    Dim cnFriends As New SqlConnection( _
        ConfigurationSettings.AppSettings("cnFriends.ConnectionString"))
    Dim adUser As New SqlDataAdapter(sql, cnFriends)
    Dim dsPending As New DataSet()

    ' Fill dataset and bind to the datagrid
    adUser.Fill(dsPending, "Pending")
    grdPending.DataSource = dsPending
    grdPending.DataBind()
End Sub
```

7. Save and run the page, and after the usual `wrox` login, you'll see a list of users who have asked to contact you, as well as their user IDs on the far right of the table.

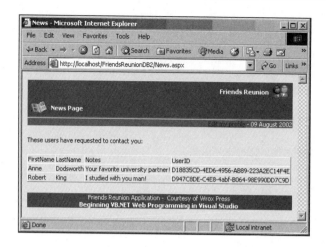

8. Once you're satisfied that everything works as described, go back to News.aspx, right-click on the data grid, and select **Auto Format**. Play with the different styles, which will surely remind you of Excel's auto-format feature. Look at how the page source changes when you modify the look and feel of the grid, and how these settings are also available for modification in the **Style** section of the **Properties** window for the data grid.

How It Works

Once again, we perform the data binding programmatically, at page loading time. To do so, we first query the database for records in the Contact table that have the IsApproved flag set to 0 and for which the DestinationID matches the current user:

```
sql = "SELECT [User].FirstName, [User].LastName, Contact.Notes, "
sql &= "[User].UserID FROM [User], Contact WHERE "
sql &= "DestinationID='" & Context.User.Identity.Name & "' AND "
sql &= " IsApproved=0 AND [User].UserID=Contact.RequestID"
```

We then create the connection and the data adapter as usual, and fill a new DataSet. Finally, we set this DataSet to be the data source for the grid, and call the grid's DataBind() method:

```
grdPending.DataSource = dsPending
grdPending.DataBind()
```

When this method is called, the DataGrid control will iterate through the DataSet and add a row to the table for each record it contains. If any of the available style properties are set, such as when we've used the **Auto Format** option, the grid uses them to format the rows. By default, the DataGrid creates a column in the table for each column in the dataset.

We could also have chosen to declare the DataSet variable at the class level, and used the following binding expression on the grid:

```
<asp:dataGrid id="grdPending" runat="server" DataSource="<%# dsPending %>">
</asp:dataGrid>
```

Doing so would allow us to avoid assigning that property directly in our code, so we could safely delete the following line:

```
grdPending.DataSource = dsPending
```

So far, so good, but we can't be happy with the way things stand: the column names at the top of the table are awful, and it certainly isn't good to display the `UserID` column at all. Let's see what we can do about that.

Try It Out – Customizing DataGrid Columns

To improve matters, we're going to change the headers, and use the `UserID` column to provide a link to the `ViewUser.aspx` page that we built earlier. This way, whenever the user sees a new request, they can ask for additional details – and, optionally, authorize that request using the button provided in the corresponding form. Operationally speaking, we need to override the automatic column generation feature, and provide our own definitions instead.

1. Click back to the design view of `News.aspx`, right-click on the data grid, and select **Property Builder**. Notice how the user interface looks very similar to that of the **Style Builder** we saw in Chapter 3.

2. Select the **Columns** category, and uncheck the checkbox at the top of the form.

3. From the **Available columns** listbox, select **Bound Column** and click the > button three times, to add the first three columns. Select each of the new columns from the list and set the following property values for them:

Header Text	Data Field
First Name	FirstName
Last Name	LastName
Notes	Notes

4. Next, from the same listbox, select **HyperLink Column** and click the > button again. Set its properties as follows:

Form Field	Value
Header text	Details
Text	View
URL Field	UserID
URL format string	ViewUser.aspx?RequestID={0}

5. If you wish, feel free to play with the various formatting options that are available under the Format and Borders sections. When you've finished, you should be faced with something like this:

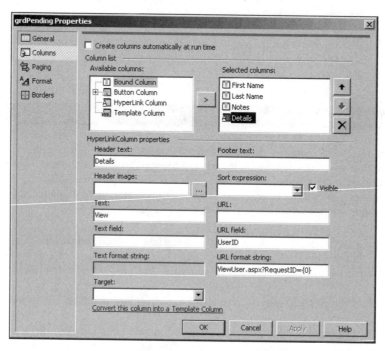

6. When you save the changes and run the application again, you should find that the appearance of the application has improved significantly:

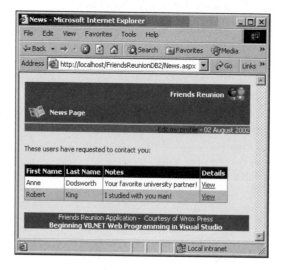

How It Works

To make this discussion a little easier, we've taken all of the styling information out of the code being presented here. If you have applied some automatic formatting, you can remove it by selecting the Remove Auto Format scheme from the Auto Format dialog. The code generated for the grid should then look something like this:

```
<form id="Form1" method="post" runat="server">
  <asp:panel id="pnlPending" runat="server">
    <P>These users have requested to contact you:</P>
    <asp:DataGrid id="grdPending" runat="server"
                  AutoGenerateColumns="False">
      <Columns>
        <asp:BoundColumn DataField="FirstName"
                         HeaderText="First Name"></asp:BoundColumn>
        <asp:BoundColumn DataField="LastName"
                         HeaderText="Last Name"></asp:BoundColumn>
        <asp:BoundColumn DataField="Notes"
                         HeaderText="Notes"></asp:BoundColumn>
        <asp:HyperLinkColumn Text="View" DataNavigateUrlField="UserID"
              DataNavigateUrlFormatString="ViewUser.aspx?RequestID={0}"
              HeaderText="Details"></asp:HyperLinkColumn>
      </Columns>
    </asp:datagrid>
  </asp:panel>
</form>
```

Our `DataGrid` control now has a child element called `<Columns>`, which contains four new controls that correspond to the four columns we set up above. The first three of these are `BoundColumn` controls, and you can see how their `DataField` and `HeaderText` attributes correspond with the columns in our `DataSet` and the labels in the `DataGrid` respectively. The fourth column in the table is implemented with a `HyperLinkColumn` control, in which the `DataNavigateUrlFormatString` attribute provides a skeleton within which to perform string formatting, using the `DataNavigateUrlField` as the first argument.

This apparent complexity simply renders the appropriate link to the `ViewUser.aspx` file, with the expected `RequestID` parameter being added according to each row in turn. The data grid is performing most of the binding work itself, using the properties that we set, rather than our having to provide binding expressions directly.

Working Visually with Data

Leaving aside the help we just received from the `DataGrid`, we find ourselves in a situation that's not dissimilar to the one we faced in the last chapter: so far, the Visual Studio .NET IDE hasn't provided us much help with our data-related tasks. We've done all of the data binding manually, and we've been accessing the database directly from our code, just as we did before. In fact, the IDE provides a number of facilities to make our coding easier, and we'll take a look at those features in this section, and indeed the rest of the chapter.

The Visual Studio .NET IDE can help us out by generating code automatically (both HTML source, and the code-behind page), based on settings we specify through the **Properties** window or in dedicated Wizards. To get the best out of it, however, we need to introduce some new concepts that are fundamental to these improved features.

Data Components

In our previous chapter, we saw how a `SqlConnection` component can be dropped from the **Toolbox** onto a web form, resulting in the automatic generation of some code on our behalf. However, we noted at the time that the benefits of using that particular component weren't exactly compelling. A better example of potential benefits is provided by the `SqlDataAdapter` component, which we've used frequently in our programs so far. In Visual Studio .NET, we can visually configure this component, including all its internal `Command` objects for `SELECT`, `INSERT`, `UPDATE`, and `DELETE` statements. In fact, provided that the `SELECT` is reasonably straightforward, Visual Studio .NET can even create the `INSERT`, `UPDATE`, and `DELETE` statements on our behalf!

When you drop a `SqlDataAdapter` component onto a web form, you're presented with a Wizard. (If you close the Wizard, you can reopen it by right-clicking on the component and choosing **Configure Data Adapter**.) The Wizard is very complete, allowing not only the creation of SQL statements, but also the creation of new stored procedures (or the reuse of existing ones). Here's a screenshot of the **Query Builder** that it makes available for this purpose:

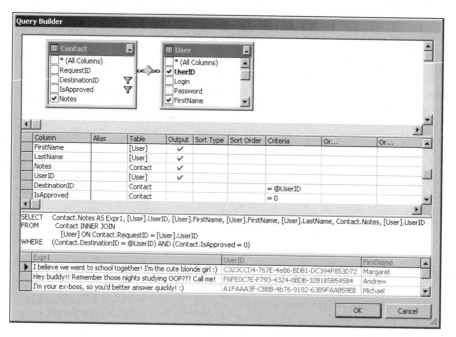

What you can see here is the result of building exactly the same query we used previously to fill the grid of pending requests for contact, except that we now use a parameter (`@UserID`) to filter the results. (A parameter is like a placeholder to be filled when the query is executed; we'll see how to set a parameter's value in a later example.)

To see how the data adapter is being 'magically' configured, you only have to look at the `InitializeComponent()` method in the code-behind page, which will contain the code that corresponds to the settings you've made through the Wizard. The `TableMappings` property that appears in the **Properties** window and the initialization code tells the adapter what tables and fields in the `SelectCommand` map to what tables and columns in the `DataSet`. This means that the names of neither the columns nor the tables in the `DataSet` have to match those in the source database.

It's also possible to use the **Properties** window to set the property of one data component to point to another one that's present on the same page. For example, we can set a `SqlDataAdapter`'s `SelectCommand` property to point to an existing `SqlCommand` component in the page, and set the latter's `Connection` property to point to a `SqlConnection` component in turn. This makes it very easy to share a common connection object, for example, between multiple data adapters.

Typed DataSets

To complete the discussion of the help that Visual Studio .NET provides with data retrieval, we can use a special type of `DataSet` – a **typed dataset** – to gain some additional benefits, both for the visual design of our applications, and for own code. You'll recall that when we discussed how to access the tables, rows, and column values in a `DataSet`, you saw that we could do so using the string name of the element:

```
dsUser.Tables("User").Rows(0)("FirstName")
```

or using its index:

```
dsUser.Tables(0).Rows(0)(0)
```

The code is simple in both cases, but it shows a drawback of the `DataSet` object: a typo in the name of a table or a field won't be trapped at compile time. Instead, it will produce a run-time exception. The alternative, which is to access the values with indexes, introduces a dependency on the SQL statement that's used to acquire the data – if we happen to change the fields returned (or even just their order), the code will not work as expected.

ADO.NET introduces the concept of a **typed dataset**, which is an automatically generated class that inherits from the generic `DataSet` class, but adds properties and classes to reflect the tables and rows in a type-safe manner. Once instantiated, a typed dataset is an object like any other, and we can use it to write code like this:

```
Dim ds As UserData()
Dim ur As UserData.UserRow
Dim value As String

ur = CType(ds.User.Rows(0), UserData.UserRow)
value = ur.UserID
```

We can now access the tables as direct properties of the dataset (as in `ds.User.Rows(0)`), and after a straightforward cast to the specific row type, we can access the fields as properties of the row itself (as in `ur.UserID`). This feature improves our productivity, as we don't have to worry about getting the names and indexes of tables and fields right – if we get them wrong, IntelliSense will tell us about it! Furthermore, the values in the columns of a typed dataset also have properly assigned types, making it impossible to (say) assign a string to a column that's expecting an integer.

A typed dataset can be generated from a data adapter component that's been placed on a web form. Provided that it has a valid `SelectCommand` assigned, we can right-click on it and choose the **Generate Dataset** option, and a typed dataset will be created based on the structure of the information that's retrieved by the command. We can give the new dataset a name and choose to add an instance of it to the current form, in order to use it right away.

Going through this process creates a **schema** for the dataset that contains a definition of its structure (such as tables, columns, and their types) in a file that has a `.xsd` extension. This file is a special type of XML document, which we will look at more closely in Chapter 8. It can be opened inside the IDE, where the designer will show the various pieces that make up the dataset's structure.

As so often, a lot of these ideas will become clearer with an example. In the next section, we will improve the features of our `News.aspx` still further, to display a list of approved contacts as well as the 'pending' ones. The query will be very similar to the one we used last time, except that we'll be looking for the `IsApproved` flag to be set to 1. The new list will appear above the existing one, and since the users on the list have already been approved, we'll show the logged on user more complete data about them, and provide a link to send them e-mail. We will also provide a link to another page showing their complete information – this will be the `ViewUser.aspx` form, with a slight change to hide the **Authorize Contact** button, as that won't be needed in this case.

Try It Out – Retrieving Contacts from the Database

In this example, as well as implementing the features described above, we'll see how using a typed dataset results in improvements to the support that's available through the IDE for configuring the way data is bound to the grid.

1. Open the `News.aspx` page, and add a carriage return before the panel where we show the pending requests. Add a new `Panel` web server control, set its ID to `pnlApproved` and change the text inside it to "These are your approved contacts:"

2. Drop a `DataGrid` inside the panel, next to the text, and set its ID to `grdApproved`. Add a carriage return to separate it from the text.

3. Now let's configure the data components. First, drop a `SqlConnection` object onto the form, set its `(Name)` property to `cnFriends`, and use the `ConnectionString` property under the `DynamicProperties` category to map this value to the suggested value, `cnFriends.ConnectionString`. As the value will be already present in the `Web.config` file (we put it there in the previous chapter), the value will be loaded and shown in the `ConnectionString` property under the **Data** category, with an icon to indicate that it's a dynamic value:

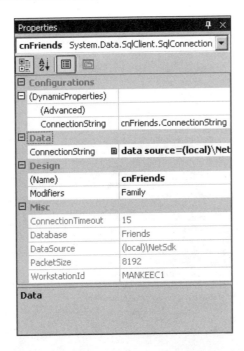

4. Drop a `SqlDataAdapter` component from the **Toolbox**'s **Data** tab onto the web form designer, and a Wizard will appear. Choose **Next**, and select the **Friends** data connection from the drop-down list. (The list is populated from the connections in the Server Explorer that point to a SQL Server database.)

5. In the next step, the Wizard offers the option to use SQL statements or stored procedures to access the database. Select the first option, and move on. The next step allows you to set various advanced options, use the **Query Builder** or directly type the SQL statement to use. Whichever method you choose, the final SQL statement should be:

```
SELECT [User].FirstName, [User].LastName,
       [User].PhoneNumber, [User].Address,
       [User].Email, [User].UserID
FROM [User]
INNER JOIN Contact ON [User].UserID = Contact.RequestID
WHERE (Contact.DestinationID = @UserID) AND (Contact.IsApproved = 1)
```

You can also uncheck the **Generate Insert...** checkbox in **Advanced Options**, as we won't be making changes to the dataset's data, and those additional commands won't be needed.

6. Change the data adapter's (Name) to `adApproved`. Optionally, expand the `SelectCommand` property and set its (Name) to `cmApproved`. Notice how the Wizard automatically detected that an existing `SqlConnection` on the page was already pointing to the same SQL Server connection, and used it for the command's `Connection` property.

167

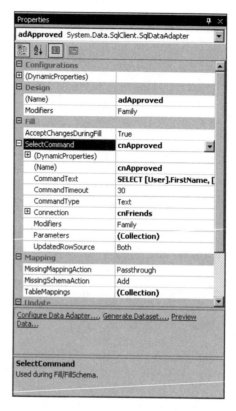

If you like, you can take a look at the `SelectCommand`'s `Parameters` collection, and see that the `@UserID` parameter we used is already configured with the appropriate type. We will fill this parameter with the current user's ID before we fill the dataset, so that we only get the contacts for the current user.

7. Let us now generate a typed dataset to be filled by this data adapter. Click the **Generate Dataset...** link that appears in the **Properties** browser, or right-click the data adapter and select the similarly named menu option. In the dialog that appears, type `ContactsData` as the new dataset name – this will be the name of the generated `DataSet`-inheriting class. The checkbox near the bottom of this dialog specifies that we want to add an instance of this dataset to the current web form designer. Accept the dialog.

8. Change the newly added dataset component's `(Name)` to `dsApproved`.

9. Set the data grid's `DataSource` property to point to `dsApproved`. Now you should see the real column names displayed in the grid, instead of the dummy columns we saw before.

10. Open the **Property Builder** for the data grid. In the **Columns** pane, see how the list of fields is now shown in the **Available columns** listbox. This makes it much easier to choose which columns to display. Add all of them except for `Email` and `UserID`, and remember to uncheck the box at the top of the pane (**Create automatic columns...**).

11. Finally, we'll add two hyperlink columns, to allow the sending of mails and the viewing of user details. We've already seen how columns like this work, so we'll just list the values we have to use. This is the first hyperlink column:

Form Field	Value
Header text	Contact
Text	Send mail
URL Field	Email
URL format string	mailto:{0}

and this is the second one:

Form Field	Value
Header text	Details
Text	View
URL Field	UserID
URL format string	ViewUser.aspx?UserID={0}

Notice that **URL Field** is now a combo box that shows the list of columns in the typed dataset. We're passing a different query string parameter to `ViewUser.aspx`, so that it knows we're not asking for the details of a pending request for contact (it receives a `RequestID` in that case).

12. Now for the 'hard' part in the code-behind page. Below the existing code in `Page_Load()`, add the following to complete the command, fill the dataset, and bind to the data grid:

```
Private Sub Page_Load(ByVal sender As System.Object, _
                      ByVal e As System.EventArgs) Handles MyBase.Load

    ...

    adApproved.SelectCommand.Parameters("@UserID").Value = _
                               Context.User.Identity.Name
    adApproved.Fill(dsApproved)
    grdApproved.DataBind()
End Sub
```

That is really *all* we need to code! To finish things off, though, let's add two lines at the end to hide the panels if there is no data to show:

```
    ...

    If dsPending.Tables(0).Rows.Count = 0 Then pnlPending.Visible = False
    If dsApproved.User.Rows.Count = 0 Then pnlApproved.Visible = False
End Sub
```

13. Save and run the project, with this page set as the start page. After the usual login process, and assuming that you've applied some cute auto-formatting to both data grids on this page, you might get something like this:

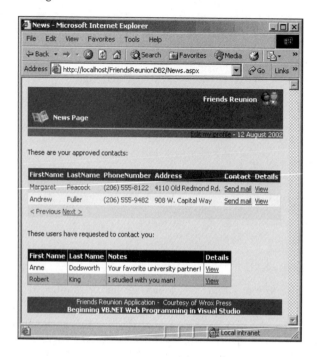

How It Works

The data components we dropped on the page, the Wizards, and the settings we specified are all reflected in the code-behind page by variable declarations at the class level:

```
Public Class News
    Inherits FriendsBase
    ... web server controls here ...
    Protected WithEvents cnFriends As System.Data.SqlClient.SqlConnection
    Protected WithEvents adApproved As System.Data.SqlClient.SqlDataAdapter
    Protected WithEvents cmApproved As System.Data.SqlClient.SqlCommand
    Protected WithEvents dsApproved As FriendsReunionDB.ContactsData
```

Each component has its own variable, and the last one – the dataset – is the most interesting. It's not defined as a generic `DataSet`, but rather as our custom `FriendsReunionDB.ContactsData` class. This is the class that was generated by the adapter when we asked it to do so. The variables for the components, just like their server controls counterparts, are initialized inside the `InitializeComponent()` method, which is placed inside the **Web Form Designer Generated Code** region.

The key point to bear in mind about this demonstration is that the code we wrote to load the list of pending requests in the last section, which performs exactly the same task as the code here, took 12 lines to achieve the same results as 3 lines here! That's four times less code – certainly *not* a minor detail. The code has been greatly simplified because all of the variable initialization code is generated automatically. We only have to pass the adapter the value for the current user ID, fill the dataset, and call DataBind() on the grid:

```
' Fill approved contacts
adApproved.SelectCommand.Parameters("@UserID").Value = _
                                Context.User.Identity.Name

adApproved.Fill(dsApproved)
grdApproved.DataBind()
```

Just in case you're concerned with the database connection, it is opened by the data adapter, and closed as soon as the data adapter doesn't need it anymore.

Finally, note that when we checked for the existence of rows in the two datasets, we could use the new property in our typed dataset that points to the right table:

```
If dsApproved.User.Rows.Count = 0 Then pnlApproved.Visible = False
```

instead of the following syntax, which we had to use for the generic dataset:

```
If dsPending.Tables(0).Rows.Count = 0 Then pnlPending.Visible = False
```

Last of all, let's make a slight modification to the ViewUser.aspx page, to take account of the fact that it can now receive a user ID query string parameter. If that happens, it has to hide the **Authorize Contact** button. Change the If statement that checks for the ID in its Page_Load() event handler to match this:

```
' Ensure we received an ID
If userID = Nothing Then
  userID = Request.QueryString("UserID")
  If userID = Nothing Then
    Throw New ArgumentException( _
      "This page expects a RequestID or UserID parameter.")
  Else
    btnAuthorize.Visible = False
  End If
End If
```

Here, we just hide the button if we receive a UserID parameter instead of a RequestID. Otherwise, we throw an exception. Remember that you'll need to make the same change in the GetPending() method.

Advanced Data Binding

Sometimes, there is a need for more flexibility over the rendering of data than a table with simple row and cell values. ASP.NET supports better customization of output through the use of **templates**. A template is a piece of ASP.NET/HTML code that can contain binding expressions, and is used inside a data grid column (for example) as a skeleton for each row/cell's representation. The web forms designer offers great integration with this concept, and makes designing templates a breeze.

Controls that support templates include DataGrid, DataList, *and* Repeater. *Third-party controls may also support them.*

Try It Out – Using a Templated Column in a DataGrid

In this example, we'll use templates to display four items in a cell: two small images, and the user's phone number and address. This will replace the columns that we previously used for this purpose. To do so, we'll need to create a template for that cell, and then take advantage of what you learned earlier about simple data binding to link values to the labels inside it.

1. Open the News.aspx page, right-click on the grdApproved data grid, and select Property Builder.

2. In the Columns pane, remove the PhoneNumber and Address columns. Next, select the Template Column element from the Available columns listbox, and add it to the list of Selected columns. Using the arrows at the right of the listbox, move the column up and position it above the Contact column:

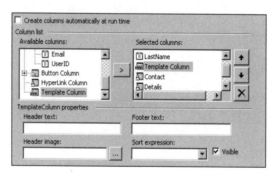

3. Set the Header text form field to Info, and click OK.

4. To add controls inside the template column, we have to start editing it. Right-click on the data grid again, and a new menu option will be available: Edit Template. Inside it, select the only item available: Columns[1] - Info. You will see that the grid layout changes, and now shows four sections named HeaderTemplate, ItemTemplate, EditItemTemplate, and FooterTemplate.

5. Drop two Image and two Label web server controls inside the ItemTemplate section. Set the ImageUrl property of the images to images/phone.gif and images/home.gif respectively; the section should then look like this:

6. Next, select the first label, and open the DataBindings dialog for it.

7. In the Simple binding listbox, locate the Container | DataItem | PhoneNumber node. Note that once again, the complete list of fields available is shown, because we're using a typed dataset.

8. Do the same for the other label, this time binding it to Container | DataItem | Address.

9. Right-click on the template, and choose the End Template Editing menu option.

10. Save everything you've done so far, make this the start page, and then run the project. You will now see something like this:

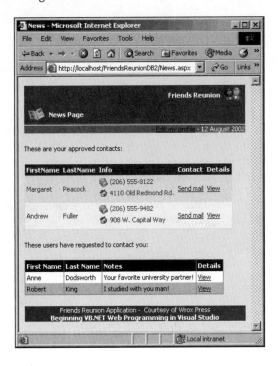

How It Works

When we add templated columns to a data grid, the **Edit Template** pop-up menu option is enabled. Inside this menu, the template design process is exactly the same as for the page itself: we drop controls on the sections we want, we set the controls' binding, and so on. As a result, the web form designer generates the following HTML code (again, we've removed the auto-formatting information to make the code more readable):

```
<asp:DataGrid id="grdApproved" runat="server" AutoGenerateColumns="False"
            DataSource="<%# dsApproved %>" >
  <Columns>
    <asp:BoundColumn DataField="FirstName" HeaderText="FirstName">
    </asp:BoundColumn>
    <asp:BoundColumn DataField="LastName" HeaderText="LastName">
    </asp:BoundColumn>
    <asp:TemplateColumn HeaderText="Info">
      <ItemTemplate>
        <asp:image id="Image1" runat="server"
                   imageurl="images/phone.gif" imagealign="Middle">
        </asp:image>
        <asp:Label id=Label1 runat="server"
          Text='<%# DataBinder.Eval(Container, "DataItem.PhoneNumber") %>'>
        </asp:Label>
        <BR>
        <asp:image id="Image2" runat="server"
                   imageurl="images/home.gif" imagealign="Middle">
        </asp:image>
        <asp:Label id=Label2 runat="server"
          Text='<%# DataBinder.Eval(Container, "DataItem.Address") %>'>
        </asp:Label>
      </ItemTemplate>
    </asp:TemplateColumn>

    ...
```

The important element inside a `<asp:TemplateColumn>` element is `<ItemTemplate>`. As you can see, it just contains ordinary server controls with binding expressions just like the ones we've seen so far. New concepts, however, are the `Container` and the `DataItem`, both of which are used in the binding expression. The first part of the binding expression evaluation, `Container.DataItem`, resolves to the current item being bound – in our case, the current row in the data table.

At run time, when the grid finds a templated column, it creates the template, performs the bindings, and adds the controls to the cell, resulting in the rich output we saw.

Paging

We've arranged for the panels to disappear if there's nothing to display, but what happens if there are a very large number of things to display? We could end up with a very long page indeed, which wouldn't be a great way to treat our users. Happily, there's something we can do about that, too.

The technique known as **paging** consists of dividing the total count of items to be displayed by the maximum number of items we want to display simultaneously, and showing only that subset of data. By also providing a means to navigate back and forth among these 'logical' pages we can allow our users to browse through the data a page at a time.

Paging is very common for applications such as the list of products for a big company, a list of expenses for the last two years, or a complete set of stock quotes. While we don't expect such a lengthy list (unless the user is really popular!), we will demonstrate its use anyway.

Try It Out – Adding Paging

The `DataGrid` control has intrinsic support for paging, and all that's required to take advantage of it is to set a couple of properties and handle a single event that's fired when the user changes the current page. We will add this functionality to our `grdApproved` grid, limiting the visible rows to only two, so that we can see paging take place.

1. Change the `grdApproved` properties as follows:

Property	Value
AllowPaging	True
PageSize	2

2. Locate the `PagerStyle` property, and set the following sub-properties:

Property	Value
NextPageText	Next >
PrevPageText	< Previous
HorizontalAlign	Left

3. To reconfigure the page when the user moves back and forth through the records, we have to handle the `PageIndexChanged` event that's fired automatically by the data grid:

```
Private Sub grdPending_PageIndexChanged( _
        ByVal source As Object, _
        ByVal e As System.Web.UI.WebControls.DataGridPageChangedEventArgs) _
        Handles grdPending.PageIndexChanged

    ' Set the new index
    grdApproved.CurrentPageIndex = e.NewPageIndex

    ' Fill approved contacts
    adApproved.SelectCommand.Parameters("@UserID").Value = _
                                Context.User.Identity.Name
```

```
      adApproved.Fill(dsApproved)
      grdApproved.DataBind()
   End Sub
```

4. Save and run the page, and voilà; we have paging:

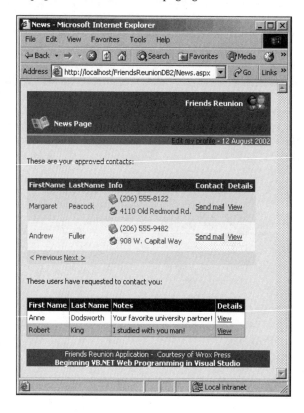

How It Works

We start the process by setting two properties that enable the paging mechanism in the grid:
`AllowPaging` and `PageSize`. The pager style is set next, where we set the text the links will have, as
well as their placement in the footer. Once the pager links are in place, they raise the
`PageIndexChanged` event when the user clicks on them, which we handle in the code-behind page:

```
   Private Sub grdPending_PageIndexChanged(
         ByVal source As Object,
         ByVal e As System.Web.UI.WebControls.DataGridPageChangedEventArgs) _
         Handles grdPending.PageIndexChanged

      ' Set the new index
      grdApproved.CurrentPageIndex = e.NewPageIndex
```

```
      ' Fill approved contacts
      adApproved.SelectCommand.Parameters("@UserID").Value = _
                                        Context.User.Identity.Name
      adApproved.Fill(dsApproved)
      grdApproved.DataBind()
   End Sub
```

The code sets the new index it receives as the second argument to the event to the
CurrentPageIndex property of the grid, and performs the binding again. As a result, the data grid
will automatically skip the rows that don't fit in the current page, according to the page size we set.

Freestyle Data Binding and Editing – The Data List

With all of the features we've seen for the DataGrid, it is quite a challenge to find a control that's more
suitable to our data displaying needs. Sometimes, though, we need even more control over presentation
than the data grid will allow us. For example, if we want to display rows in some arbitrary, non-tabular
format, a data grid doesn't seem like a good fit. Sure, we could use a complex template and a single cell,
but ASP.NET comes with another control that is better suited to this task – the DataList. With regard
to the data binding process and the design of templates, this control is very similar to the data grid, but
it has no concept of columns.

As a template-only control, the data list is highly flexible, but crucially it also supports the concepts of
selecting, editing, updating, or canceling the editing of an item. We can use different templates for each
of those actions, and react to events fired by the control to perform the actual work against the database.
The events fired by the data list are, not surprisingly, SelectedIndexChanged, EditCommand,
UpdateCommand, and CancelCommand. But how does the control know when any of these actions has
taken place?

To cause these events to be fired, we have to place a Button, LinkButton, or ImageButton control
in a template, and set its CommandName property to one of the following values, according to the event
we want to cause: Select, Edit, Update, or Cancel.

The data list decides which template to use for each item in the data source based on some properties
that we can set. When SelectedIndex is set to a value different from -1, the corresponding item at
the specified index will be rendered using the SelectedItemTemplate. Likewise, if
EditItemIndex is set to a value other than -1, the EditItemTemplate will be used for that item.
ItemTemplate and AlternatingItemTemplate are used to render the remaining items that are
neither selected nor being edited.

In our handlers for the events mentioned, we will update the SelectedIndex or EditItemIndex to
reflect the user's action, and to get the item rendered accordingly.

Adding a DataList to our Application

In our application, users create records in the TimeLapse table to reflect the places they have been
to – we created a web form for that purpose in the previous chapter. The record reflects that a user has
been in a certain place for a certain period of time – the place can be a high school, a college, or even a
company they've worked for. The different categories of places are defined in the PlaceType table.

In the `Place` table, each place has an associated `AdministratorID` field, which is the ID of the user authorized to modify its data. A user should be able to look at the places our application works with, and in the case that they are also the administrator for a place, they should be able to modify its data, such as its address or notes.

We'll take advantage of the `DataList`'s flexibility to allow this new functionality on our application. The process involves configuring data components (as we did before), designing templates for the data list, and then binding the data when necessary. We can edit the various templates available in the data list by right-clicking on it and selecting the appropriate menu option under **Edit Template**.

Try It Out – Showing Places in a DataList Control

In this example, we'll build a page that displays the list of places registered for the application, showing only their names and an icon to let the user select them. Once selected, complete data about the place will be displayed. The following screenshot shows what we will achieve, with one place selected after the user clicked the corresponding arrow next to it:

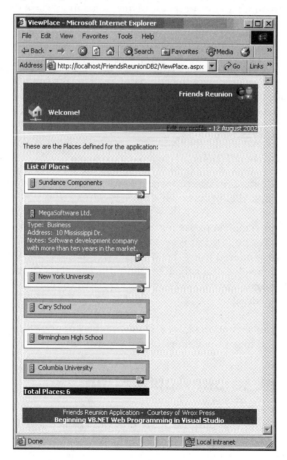

1. To our burgeoning project, add a new web form named `ViewPlace.aspx`. Add the usual stylesheet to it, and change the code-behind page to inherit from `FriendsBase`.

2. Drop a `SqlDataAdapter` component onto the form and configure it as we did before, setting the SQL statement to `SELECT * FROM Place`. Without leaving this Wizard step, click the **Advanced Options** button and leave only the first option checked. When the Wizard has finished, change the name of the adapter to `adPlaces`.

3. Change the added `SqlConnection`'s name to `cnFriends` and set its `ConnectionString` as we did before, to use the dynamic property value.

4. Set `InsertCommand` and `DeleteCommand` to None in the property browser, as we won't allow these operations. Leave `UpdateCommand` as it is, but change its name to `cmUpdate` – we'll be using updates later on.

5. As well as the details from the `Place` table, we also want to display the place type, which resides in the `PlaceType` table. Change the name of the select command to `cmSelect`. Click the ellipsis next to the `CommandText` property, add the `PlaceType` table, and add the `Name` field to the output, setting its alias to `TypeName`.

6. Select the **Generate Dataset** data adapter action, and enter `PlaceData` as the name for the new dataset. Set the new component's name to `dsPlaces`.

7. At last, having set up the database access code, we can get on to displaying the data. Drop a `DataList` control onto the page, and set the following properties:

Property	Value
ID	dlPlaces
DataSource	dsPlaces
DataMember	Place
DataKeyField	PlaceID
BorderStyle	Solid
BorderWidth	1px
Width	220px

8. In order to describe how to set up the templates, let's use screenshots. In the following steps, each control will contain its type between square brackets. If the ID of the control is important, it will appear next to the closing square bracket. If there are any special properties to be set for a control, the fact will be noted in the text below the screenshot.

Text in the controls themselves, such as labels, will not be shown, as it can easily be configured by looking at the target design we showed above.

9. Let's start with Header and Footer Templates, which just contains panels and labels:

Label:
```
Text='<%# DataBinder.Eval(dsPlaces, "Tables[Place].Rows.Count") %>'
```

10. Next is the Item Templates group. First up is the required ItemTemplate:

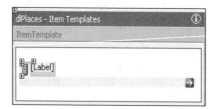

Label:
```
Text='<%# DataBinder.Eval(Container, "DataItem.Name") %>'
```

ImageButton:
```
id='cmdSelectItem', ImageAlign='Right', CommandName='Select'
```

11. Followed by the AlternatingItemTemplate:

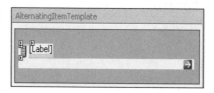

Label:
```
Text='<%# DataBinder.Eval(Container, "DataItem.Name") %>'
```

ImageButton:
```
id='cmdSelectItem', ImageAlign='Right', CommandName='Select'
```

12. And finally the SelectedItemTemplate:

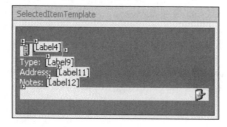

Label1:
```
Text='<%# DataBinder.Eval(Container, "DataItem.Name") %>'
```

Label2:
```
Text='<%# DataBinder.Eval(Container, "DataItem.TypeName") %>'
```

Label3:
```
Text='<%# DataBinder.Eval(Container, "DataItem.Address") %>'
```

Label4:
```
Text='<%# DataBinder.Eval(Container, "DataItem.Notes") %>'
```

ImageButton:
```
id='cmdEdit', ImageAlign='Right', CommandName='Edit', Visible='False'
```

lblAdministratorID:
```
Text='<%# DataBinder.Eval(Container, "DataItem.AdministratorID") %>'
CssClass='Hidden'
```

The `Hidden` style rule needs to be added to the stylesheet, and is as follows:

```
.Hidden { visibility: hidden; display: none; }
```

13. Reopen the code-behind page, and add the following code that prevents the data list from being displayed if there are no places to display:

```
Private Sub Page_Load(ByVal sender As System.Object, _
                    ByVal e As System.EventArgs) Handles MyBase.Load
   ' Put user code to initialize the page here
   If Not Page.IsPostBack Then
     BindPlaces()
   End If
End Sub

Private Sub BindPlaces()
   adPlaces.Fill(dsPlaces)
   If dsPlaces.Place.Rows.Count = 0 Then
     dlPlaces.Visible = False
   Else
     dlPlaces.DataBind()
   End If
End Sub

Private Sub dlPlaces_SelectedIndexChanged(ByVal sender As Object, _
       ByVal e As System.EventArgs) Handles dlPlaces.SelectedIndexChanged
   BindPlaces()
End Sub
```

14. Save and run the page. Test the selection mechanism, and see how the template is applied to the selected item to show the complete details.

How It Works

The DataList has three template groups available to edit:

- ❏ Header and footer templates
- ❏ Item templates
- ❏ Separator templates

Data binding works just as we saw for the data grid – at run time, the template is instantiated, binding expressions are evaluated, and controls are added to the output for each element in the data source.

The important controls in these templates are the ImageButtons that we've placed at the bottom right of each. The values that we've assigned to the CommandName properties of these buttons – Select and Edit – have special meanings: the data list uses them to raise the events we discussed above. We'll take care of editing in a moment, but right now let's see what happens when the user clicks on the Select button on an item (or an alternating item).

In this case, the data list detects the Select command name, and raises the SelectedIndexChanged event. Inside this event handler, we just re-bind the data:

```
Private Sub dlPlaces_SelectedIndexChanged(ByVal sender As Object, _
                                ByVal e As System.EventArgs) _
                                Handles dlPlaces.SelectedIndexChanged

   BindPlaces()
End Sub
```

The data list automatically tracks the currently selected element, and as you can see, this rather simple procedure can have a powerful impact.

An interesting point to note here is that we didn't bother to set our own IDs for the controls. This would usually be considered to be bad practice, but the process that's in play results in several controls being created from the same template, making it impossible to predict the ID of a run-time control. (If this didn't happen, there would be naming collisions.) If you can't predict the ID of a control at run time, there is little point in setting it to anything special at design time.

The final step that we need to make in order to complete this discussion of data binding is to allow the user to edit an item. To enable this feature, we'll add a handler to the code-behind page to receive the EditCommand event, which will be fired when the cmdEdit button defined earlier is clicked. Just as we stated above though, we will need to hide this button if the current user doesn't match the place's administrator.

Try It Out – Enabling Editing Capabilities

We will create an editing template that uses data binding to load the editable fields. If the user accepts the changes, we will post the changes back to the database, using the configured data adapter. The template we will build has the following layout:

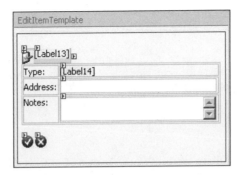

1. Set the following properties on the controls in the template:

Control	Attributes
lblPlaceID	Text='<%# DataBinder.Eval(Container, "DataItem.PlaceID") %>' CssClass='Hidden'
Label1	Text='<%# DataBinder.Eval(Container, "DataItem.Name") %>'
Label2	Text='<%# DataBinder.Eval(Container, "DataItem.TypeName") %>'
txtAddress	Text='<%# DataBinder.Eval(Container, "DataItem.Address") %>' CssClass='TextBox'
txtNotes	Text='<%# DataBinder.Eval(Container, "DataItem.Notes") %>' CssClass='TextBox', Rows='2', TextMode='MultiLine'
OK	id='cmdUpdate', commandname='Update' alternatetext='Save', imageurl='images/ok.gif'
Cancel	id='cmdCancel', commandname='Cancel' alternatetext='Cancel', imageurl='images/cancel.gif'

2. Now we will add the appropriate event handlers to the code-behind page. First, we'll deal with the `ItemDataBound` event, which is fired when an item is being bound to the template. We receive the current item in the argument to the event, and we want to hide the Edit button for users whose ID doesn't match the current place's `AdministratorID`:

```
Public Class ViewPlace

    ...

    ' Intercept the moment an item is being bound to data
    ' and set the visible property of the Edit button
    Private Sub dlPlaces_ItemDataBound( _
            ByVal sender As Object, _
            ByVal e As System.Web.UI.WebControls.DataListItemEventArgs) _
            Handles dlPlaces.ItemDataBound

        ' Is the item selected?
        If e.Item.ItemType = ListItemType.SelectedItem Then
            Dim admin As Label
```

```
      ' Locate the hidden Label containing the AdministratorID
      admin = CType(e.Item.FindControl("lblAdministratorID"), Label)

      ' If it matches the current user, show the Edit button
      If admin.Text = Page.User.Identity.Name Then
        e.Item.FindControl("cmdEdit").Visible = True
      End If
    End If
End Sub
```

3. In all of the event handlers, we call `BindPlaces()` at the end, to re-create the controls in the data list according to the last changes made. Whenever the **Edit** button is clicked, we will also need to update the data list's `EditItemIndex`, and set it to the `ItemIndex` of the item passed with the arguments to the event:

```
Private Sub dlPlaces_EditCommand( _
        ByVal source As Object, _
        ByVal e As System.Web.UI.WebControls.DataListCommandEventArgs) _
        Handles dlPlaces.EditCommand

    ' Save the edit index
    dlPlaces.EditItemIndex = e.Item.ItemIndex
    BindPlaces()
End Sub
```

4. Of course, the user could (as users are wont to do) just change their mind and directly select another item without either canceling or accepting the current's item edit session. In this case, we only have to reset the `EditItemIndex`:

```
Private Sub dlPlaces_SelectedIndexChanged(ByVal sender As Object, _
                                ByVal e As System.EventArgs) _
                                Handles dlPlaces.SelectedIndexChanged

    ' Remove the edit index just in case we were editing
    dlPlaces.EditItemIndex = -1
    BindPlaces()
End Sub
```

5. Once editing is started, the user can cancel it, which resets the `EditItemIndex` property. We also set the `SelectedIndex` property to leave the user positioned on the item they were editing:

```
Private Sub dlPlaces_CancelCommand( _
        ByVal source As Object, _
        ByVal e As System.Web.UI.WebControls.DataListCommandEventArgs) _
        Handles dlPlaces.CancelCommand

    ' Reset the edit index
    dlPlaces.EditItemIndex = -1
```

```
        ' Set the selected item to the currently editing item
        dlPlaces.SelectedIndex = e.Item.ItemIndex
        BindPlaces()
    End Sub
```

6. Another option is for the user to click the **OK** button to perform an update. At this time, we reload the dataset, locate the row corresponding to the current `PlaceID`, and issue an `Update` through the data adapter. Finally, we reset the indexes as we did for `CancelCommand`:

```
    Private Sub dlPlaces_UpdateCommand( _
            ByVal source As Object, _
            ByVal e As System.Web.UI.WebControls.DataListCommandEventArgs) _
            Handles dlPlaces.UpdateCommand

        ' Find the updated controls
        Dim addr As TextBox = CType(e.Item.FindControl("txtAddress"), TextBox)
        Dim notes As TextBox = CType(e.Item.FindControl("txtNotes"), TextBox)
        Dim place As Label = CType(e.Item.FindControl("lblPlaceID"), Label)

        ' Reload the dataset and locate the relevant row
        adPlaces.Fill(dsPlaces)
        Dim sql As String = "PlaceID = '" & place.Text & "'"
        Dim row As PlaceData.PlaceRow = _
                CType(dsPlaces.Place.Select(sql)(0), PlaceData.PlaceRow)

        ' Set the values using the typed properties
        row.Address = addr.Text
        row.Notes = notes.Text

        ' Update the row in the database
        adPlaces.Update(New DataRow() {row})

        ' Reset datalist state and bind
        dlPlaces.EditItemIndex = -1
        dlPlaces.SelectedIndex = e.Item.ItemIndex
        dlPlaces.DataBind()
    End Sub
```

7. Save and run the page, and edit the MegaSoftware Ltd. place, adding or changing its comment, for example.

How It Works

Let's start from the beginning. When `BindPlaces()` is first called, the first time the page is run, the `DataList` iterates through the data source and binds the corresponding template with each row. At this time, the `ItemDataBound` event is raised. In the handler for that event, we react only to items of type `ListItemType.SelectedItem`, as they are the only ones that have the **Edit** button we want to show, if it is appropriate to do so.

Note that even when we have given the control an ID, we have to use the FindControl() method (inherited from the base Control class) to access the label that contains the AdministratorID field value. To understand this, we have to recall that the controls in the corresponding template are created *once for each row*. The e argument passed to this event handler (and to the others too) has an Item property that contains the collection of controls created for the current item. We call FindControl() on this collection to retrieve the label.

If the current user ID matches the administrator ID, we set the Visible property of cmdEdit to True. With the button visible, the user can start editing the item by clicking it, which causes the EditCommand event to be fired. In this handler, similar to what we did for the SelectedIndexChanged event, we save the index received in the data list's EditItemIndex property, and re-bind the data. At this stage, the data list will render the following interface:

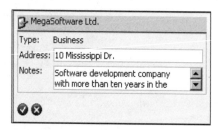

Now, the user can stop editing simply by navigating to another item. This is handled in the SelectedIndexChanged event handler, which resets any previous EditItemIndex value to -1, and calls DataBind() to refresh the display.

On the other hand, the user can click the **Save** or the **Cancel** button. If they choose the latter, the CancelCommand event is raised, in response to which we reset the EditItemIndex, and set the SelectedIndex to the current element. The user will then be positioned in the element they were just editing.

Finally, if they click the **Save** button, the UpdateCommand event is raised. The handler for this event performs the following steps:

❑ Locate the control with the data to be used for the update, as in:

```
Dim addr As TextBox = CType(e.Item.FindControl("txtAddress"), TextBox)
```

❑ Get a reference to the original row. To achieve this, we first reload the dataset:

```
adPlaces.Fill(dsPlaces)
```

Then we build a filtering expression with the PlaceID found in the corresponding (hidden) label:

```
Dim sql As String = "PlaceID = '" & place.Text & "'"
```

Then we define a row variable using the corresponding typed dataset class, Places.PlaceRow:

```
Dim row As Places.PlaceRow = _
        CType(dsPlaces.Place.Select(sql)(0), Places.PlaceRow)
```

Note that we use the `Select()` method of the `Place` table, which receives a SQL expression and returns an array of `DataRow` objects that match the request. We take the first element in the resulting array (`dsPlaces.Place.Select(sql)(0)`) and perform a type conversion to assign the value to the `row` variable.

❑ Set the new values on the row:

```
row.Address = addr.Text
row.Notes = notes.Text
```

❑ Submit changes to the adapter:

```
adPlaces.Update(New DataRow() {row})
```

Here, we use the overload of the `Update()` method that receives an array of `DataRow` objects. We initialize the array in the same method call with the single row edited. As the adapter has a configured `UpdateCommand`, it will know how to submit changes in the row we passed to it to the database.

❑ Reset the data list state, and re-bind:

```
dlPlaces.EditItemIndex = -1
dlPlaces.SelectedIndex = e.Item.ItemIndex
dlPlaces.DataBind()
```

We don't call `BindPlaces()` here, because we've already loaded the dataset – and we know that we have at least one row, because we've just edited it!

Summary

Data access is essential for all but the most trivial web application. However, the data access code itself should not hinder a programmer's productivity. Easy and intuitive data facilities are crucial in a good development environment, and Visual Studio .NET together with ADO.NET fulfils both requirements. In this chapter, we have examined what ADO.NET is about, and looked at its components and how they interact. We also saw that Visual Studio .NET includes some powerful wizards and design-time advantages that have not previously been seen in a Microsoft product.

Components and data binding make the process of displaying and editing data a breeze. We learned how it works with simple controls, and with the more advanced **DataGrid** and **DataList** controls. We saw the incredibly versatile templates, and used them to achieve some real-world goals. Our Friends Reunion sample application became much more useful, and is a good example of the possibilities of the new platform.

In the next chapter, we will learn how to protect our application from run-time errors, and how to handle them properly when they do occur. This is a very important step in making our web applications more robust, and in foreseeing the problems that may arise when building a complex application that accesses databases.

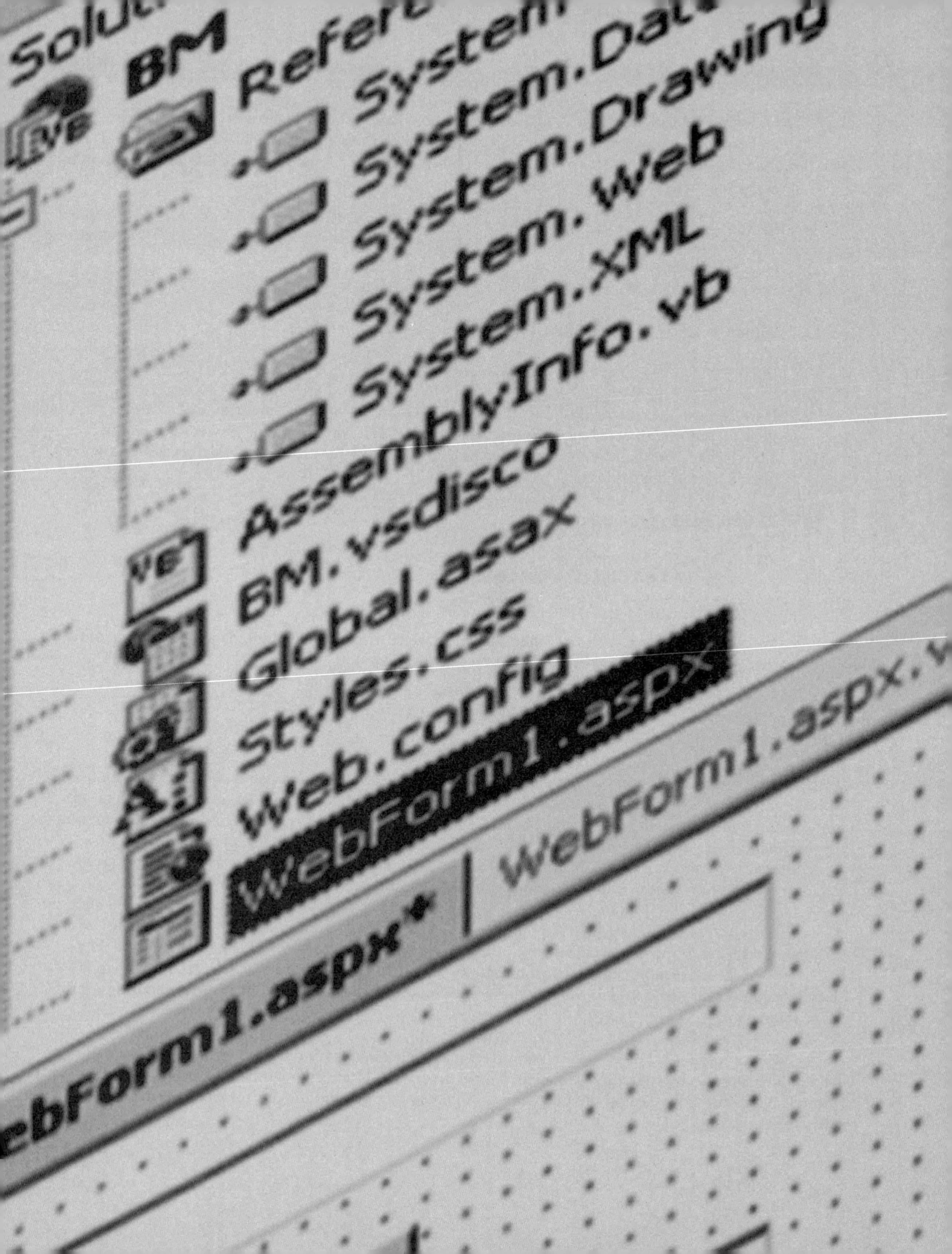

Solut
BM Refere System.Dat
System.Drawing
System.Web
System.XML
AssemblyInfo.vb
Assembly
BM.vsdisco
Global.asax
Styles.css
Web.config
WebForm1.aspx
WebForm1.aspx* WebForm1.aspx.v
ebForm1.aspx*

Debugging and Error Handling in Web Applications

Debugging and error handling are two of the least glamorous and least enjoyable aspects of programming. No one enjoys making mistakes, and fixing them is rarely fun. However, thorough testing and debugging are critical stages of the development life cycle that should not be neglected.

Fortunately, Visual Studio .NET provides the same robust and friendly tools for web programming that it does for Windows programming. If you're familiar with Visual Basic .NET and Visual Studio .NET, these tools will already be known to you, but there are also many enhancements that ASP.NET itself offers to make debugging web applications – and handling any errors that occur – simpler and easier. Our approach will be to cover facilities of both types, and you should dip in to learn about anything that's new to you.

It may be useful here to expand on the terms "debugging" and "error handling". They are closely related, but they are by no means the same. "Debugging" refers to the process of eliminating errors during development. These are usually errors with syntax or the construction of the application that will cause it to fail to compile or run correctly. However, there are some errors that are impossible to eliminate through debugging, often because they occur due to user input, or some external system. "Error handling" techniques allow these errors to be captured through programming, so that their effects on your target audience are eliminated, or at least minimized. If you get it right, the end user may not even see an error message at all.

In this chapter, you will learn about:

❑ The standard Visual Studio .NET debugging features for ASP.NET pages, such as breakpoints and debugging windows.

❑ How to attach Visual Studio. NET to already running ASP.NET pages, in order to debug them without recompiling.

❑ How to use Try...Catch...Finally statements in ASP.NET code to catch errors, and the best practices for handling them.

❑ Use of the `Throw` statement to create custom error messages when needed in an application.

❑ How to debug client-side scripts in ASP.NET pages.

❑ How to add trace statements and directives to ASP.NET code to output useful information to your web browser for debugging purposes.

❑ How to alter the `Web.config` XML file to alter trace settings for an entire web application.

❑ How to use the `Global.asax` file to implement site-wide error handling in an application.

Common Considerations for Testing and Debugging Web Applications

Microsoft has made a lot of progress in developing ASP.NET and Visual Studio .NET so that programming in a web environment is very similar to programming for a desktop environment. However, they are still different in many ways, and you need to be aware of where these discrepancies lie, so that you can plan and code your applications accordingly. Also, in the situations where ASP.NET technology 'simulates' programming a Windows application to make development easier, it can be useful to know what's going on behind the scenes.

In Windows development using Visual Basic .NET, the appearance and behavior of the forms and objects you create generally stays the same from development through to deployment. You might have to think about the size and resolution of your users' monitors, but you're not usually concerned about whether a common element – a button, say, or a drop-down list – will actually be displayed. In web development, things are not so straightforward. Everything you place on a web form will be rendered as a combination of scripts HTML, JavaScript, and Cascading Style Sheets (CSS). These in are interpreted by the browser, which in turn displays them to the user.

Browser interpretation is one of the most vexing challenges for web developers. Different brands and versions of browsers can and will alter the appearance of your pages. It may be acceptable for a page to display some things a little differently from one browser to the next (font sizes and control styles, for example), but it's unlikely to be acceptable if a major component of a form doesn't show up at all! Under Netscape 4.x, putting two submit buttons in the same table cell could sometimes cause one of the buttons to overlap the other, making it impossible to click.

In addition to this, the user of your web application has a lot of control over the behavior of the browser, and therefore the interpretation of client-side code. Users can turn on and off features such as JavaScript, applets, plug-ins, and cookies, and they can change settings that will override stylesheets. In the Opera browser, it's even possible for the user to have the browser pose as IE or Netscape by sending tailored HTTP header information to the server. In this case, even detecting the browser may not be enough to ensure that your code works correctly.

For a web developer, the ideal situation is only to be required to code for one version of one browser – but in reality, that's extremely rare. Most web development firms will choose to target several different browsers, and develop for a minimum version of each one. Eventually, you'll have the task of testing on each browser and each version for appearance and functionality. While it may be time consuming, the safest route is to test each piece of code under each browser *during development*, rather then developing entirely in one browser and then testing all the others at the end.

Standard Visual Studio .NET Debugging Features

As stated at the start of the chapter, Visual Studio .NET uses the same debugging tools for ASP.NET web applications as for desktop applications. These features include the use of breakpoints, stepping through code, and output and debugging windows. In addition, there are facilities that are specific to developing and debugging web applications under ASP.NET, such as `Trace` directives. Having a familiarity with all of these capabilities will enable you to fix and complete your applications more quickly.

Breakpoints

The first thing we'll look at is the use of **breakpoints**. Just as in Visual Basic .NET Windows Forms projects, breakpoints can be set on any executable line of code within a function or subroutine. On arriving at the line where the breakpoint is set, a running application will halt, and we are then free to view and modify variables. When we're done, we can continue to run through the code line by line, choosing to "step into", "step over", or "step out of" the current code line. Visual Studio .NET also has an array of debugging windows for viewing various details of our application, from variable names and values, to call stack information and raw memory dumps.

Try It Out – Placing Breakpoints in a Code-behind Page

In this example, we'll put together a very simple ASP.NET web application, and examine its behavior in the Visual Studio .NET debugger.

1. Create a new Visual Basic .NET ASP.NET project called `Breakpoints`. Add a `TextBox`, a `Button`, and a `Label` web server control from the **Toolbox** to the default `WebForm1.aspx` page, positioning them as in the screenshot below.

2. Clear the `Text` property of the label, and set the `Text` property for the button to **Repeat**, and you should be facing something that looks like this:

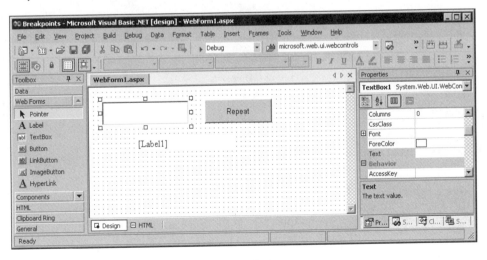

3. Double-click on the button (its default name should be `Button1`) to add the following trivial code for the `Button1_Click()` event handler:

```
Private Sub Button1_Click(ByVal sender As System.Object, _
                          ByVal e As System.EventArgs) Handles Button1.Click
    ' Set up variables
    Dim ValueEntered As Integer
    Dim count As Integer
    Label1.Text = ""

    ' Store the value entered in the textbox
    ValueEntered = TextBox1.Text
    For count = 1 To ValueEntered
      WriteTheNumber(count)
    Next
End Sub
```

4. Then add the subroutine called `WriteTheNumber()`

```
Private Sub WriteTheNumber(ByVal num As Integer)
    Label1.Text &= "Line #" & num & "<br>"
End Sub
```

5. Set a breakpoint by clicking in the gray margin to the left of the line of code that starts "`ValueEntered...`"

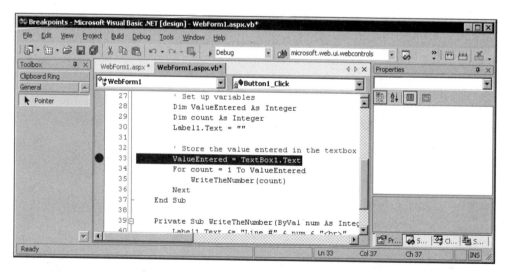

This screenshot shows line numbering, which can be handy when you're debugging. Go to **Tools | Options**, and select **Text Editor | Basic | General** in the tree view in the left-hand pane. Then click on **Line numbers**, which is under **Display**.

6. Run the application in debug mode by using the **Start** button on the standard toolbar, or by hitting the *F5* key. This will open our application in Internet Explorer (or the default web browser, if that's different on your machine – this can be altered through **File | Browse With...**).

7. Type **8** in the textbox.

8. Our breakpoint is in the `Button1_Click()` event handler, and will therefore be reached when we click the **Repeat** button, so do that now. Visual Studio .NET will automatically come to the foreground, highlighting the currently active line with a yellow arrow:

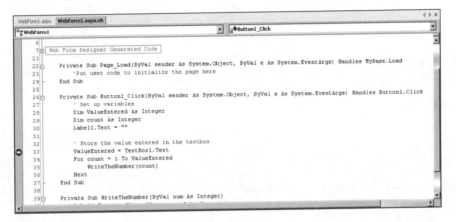

9. When in break mode (as indicated by [break] in the Visual Studio .NET title bar), the **Debug** toolbar appears in the IDE:

From left to right, the first four buttons let us start and stop the application: **Continue**, to continue normal execution from the current line; **Break All**, to enter [break] mode when running; **Stop Debugging**, to end the program and return to design mode; and **Restart**, which stops and restarts the program.

The next group of buttons allows us to continue execution on a line-by-line basis. The yellow arrow, **Show Next Statement**, simply moves the cursor back to the code line currently highlighted in yellow. Then we have **Step Into**, which moves to the next item to process, which may be inside a routine called by the current line, **Step Over**, which executes the current line, without stepping into any routines called, and **Step Out**, which completes the current routine and re-enters break mode on the line that made the call. The **Hex** button toggles between showing variables in hexadecimal and in decimal, and the last button opens the **Breakpoints** window.

While in [break] mode, we can hover the cursor over the name of a variable in the code editor to see its value in a tooltip. If you do this for the `ValueEntered` variable, you'll see that it's currently set to zero.

10. Click the Step Into button, or press *F11*, and the yellow highlighting will move to the next line of code. If you hover the mouse pointer over the `ValueEntered` variable again, you'll see that it has now been set to the value entered in the textbox.

11. Keep clicking the Step Into button, and watch as the highlighted line moves through the `Button1_Click()` handler. When it gets to the call to `WriteTheNumber()`, it jumps to the start of that subroutine, and then advances through it.

12. When execution gets back to the click handler, click Step Into again to move to the `Next` statement, and then again to return to the line that calls `WriteTheNumber()`. This time, click Step Over, and now the highlighted line doesn't enter the `WriteTheNumber()` routine, but jumps straight to the `Next` statement at the end of the `For` loop.

13. Click the Continue button to restart normal execution. Internet Explorer will pop up showing the output produced by the `WriteTheNumber()` subroutine.

How It Works

Visual Studio .NET halts the flow of control immediately on encountering a breakpoint, allowing us then to proceed through the code line-by-line. The Step Into button is so named because it will 'step into' any procedures that are called, while the Step Over button executes any calls subroutines and functions without stepping through them. This allows us to concentrate on one area of code without getting sidetracked by code in the other routines that are called, especially when we know that the called routines work properly.

You may have noticed that the output displayed in Internet Explorer did not change as we stepped through each iteration of the loop. This is because ASP.NET completes the processing of the request before the response is sent as a single lump to the browser, rather than sending output piecemeal each time the label's `Text` property is modified.

Debugging Windows

Visual Studio .NET provides many ways of inspecting the contents of variables while an application is in break mode. We've already seen one way, which is to hover the mouse over them in the code view. In the next example, we're going to use some of the other standard Visual Studio .NET features. As we hit our breakpoints, we'll look at the debugging information provided in the Locals and other windows.

Try It Out – Using Standard Visual Studio .NET Debugging Windows

In the following example, we'll revisit the application we built in the last demonstration, and see how to use Visual Studio .NET's Locals, Autos, Me, and Watch windows for debugging purposes.

1. If you haven't already closed Internet Explorer, switch to Visual Studio .NET and click the Restart button to set the application running again.

2. After Internet Explorer has re-launched, set a breakpoint on the line that says `WriteTheNumber(count)`, and remove the previous breakpoint by clicking on the red dot in the margin.

3. Switch back to the browser window, type in 4 into the textbox, and click the Repeat button. Your breakpoint will now pause execution at the call to the `WriteTheNumber()` function.

4. At the bottom of the screen, you should be able to see the Locals window. If not, you can force it to appear by selecting Debug | Windows | Locals.

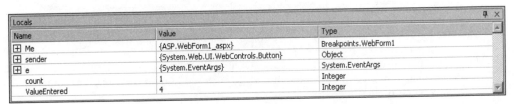

The Locals window acts as an overview of the variables and objects that are present in the current local context of your application. Variables that are not currently being used will not show up in this window. If you click on the + symbol next to objects such as Me or sender in the Name column, the object will expand to show the different values of the members of that object. Primitive variables such as count and ValueEntered here just show their values and types.

5. This window is useful for testing your application with different variable values. Double-click on the 1 in the count variable's Value column, and then type in 0, and hit *Return*. This will change the value of the count variable.

6. Click on the Step Out button twice; you will see the count variable increment to one again, and then to two.

7. Now select Debug | Windows | Autos to display the Autos window in place of the Locals window. This presents a narrower vision of the currently running application – it will only show the variables that are being used within a few lines of our breakpoint. Other than that, it's nearly identical to the Locals window.

8. Next, we will look at the Me window, so select Debug | Windows | Me. When the window appears, click on the + symbol next to the row labeled TextBox1 to expand our view of the members of this object.

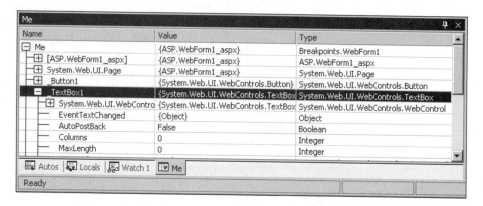

9. Scroll down until you can see the `Text` variable in the **Name** column, and you should find that the **Value** column contains the number "4" enclosed in quotes. This is the value that we originally entered into the textbox on our web form.

The **Me** window is similar to the **Locals** window, except that rather than showing only the variables in use, it shows all the data members of the current page. This is useful if you need to run through values that are shared by the entire web form, but are not specific to any one function or variables near the current breakpoint.

10. Let's try another window. Select **Debug | Windows | Watch | Watch 1**, and you'll see the **Watch 1** window appear in the usual place. Notice there aren't any variables in it yet! To fix this, click in the row directly beneath the **Name** column, and type `count`.

11. Click below this row to create a new row, type `TextBox1`, and then hit *Return*. You'll see a + symbol appear next to `TextBox1` in the **Name** column.

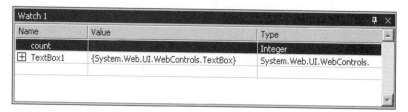

This is the most flexible of the debugging windows, as it allows us to add whatever variables we see fit, and view or change their values. If necessary, you can create a separate watch window with **Debug | Windows | Watch 2**. It's possible to create four watch windows in all.

How It Works

If you do any programming over a period of time, one of the most effective ways of debugging is simply to display the values of the variables and objects you're currently using, and make sure that they're what you expect them to be. Changing the values of variables within the debugging windows means that you don't have to change or re-run your application in order to see what happens under all manner of different circumstances.

Assertions and the Output Window

In Visual Basic 6, there was a class called Debug that had two methods: Print() and Assert(). This class still survives in Visual Basic .NET, although it has changed considerably. Where the windows we've looked at so far allow you to set variables' values, so that you know they're what you want them to be, the methods of the System.Diagnostics.Debug class provide a way to verify variables' values programmatically – and to let you know very clearly when something's wrong.

Try It Out – Using the System.Diagnostics.Debug Class

In this exercise, we'll add some code to our running example that checks the value that's been entered in the textbox, and lets us know about it if something is different from how we expected it to be!

1. Stop the debugger and return to the code-behind page for WebForm1.aspx.

2. Add the highlighted code to the Button1_Click() event handler:

```
Private Sub Button1_Click(ByVal sender As System.Object, _
                          ByVal e As System.EventArgs) Handles Button1.Click
   Dim ValueEntered As Integer
   Dim count As Integer
   System.Diagnostics.Debug.Assert(TextBox1.Text > 3, _
                                   "Input should be greater than 3.")
```

3. If you still have the breakpoint set on the call to WriteTheNumber(), turn it off by clicking the red spot in the leftmost gray margin.

4. Start the debugger, type 2 into the textbox, and click the **Repeat** button. Switch back to Visual Studio .NET and take a look at the **Output** window. (If you can't see the **Output** window, you can activate it with **View | Other Windows | Output**.)

5. In order to see what Visual Studio .NET is doing with the Debug class, you'll need to scroll up some way in the **Output** window. Eventually, you should see something like this. When you get here, stop the debugger.

How It Works

With the Debug class, we created an **assertion** – we are *asserting* that the value that gets entered in the text box will be greater than 3. The action of writing the warning message only happens if the assertion *fails*. (This is different from a standard If...Then statement, where the condition must evaluate to True for any action to take place.)

> To reiterate the behavior of the **Debug.Assert()** method, you are asserting that some condition is **True**, so the warning will only appear in the **Output** window if the assertion condition is **False**.

You can use assertions to fill the Output window with messages or values if some condition fails. This becomes useful during development as your code becomes dependent on certain values being in place. The other benefit is that assertions do not affect production code. Failed assertions will *not* fire under a production build, and nor will you incur a processing overhead by having them in your source code. This is far preferable to adding MsgBox()- or Print()-type statements that *do* persist in source code.

The Debug class can also be used to send values to the Output window without using an assertion, through the Write() method.

Attaching to Existing Processes

At some point during the development process, you'll move the ASP.NET web application that you've developed to a remote server, so that you can test it in more realistic conditions. If you come across undesirable behavior at this stage, you've got a problem. The page that you now want to debug is open in your web browser, but the server is elsewhere, and you probably didn't even launch the application from Visual Studio .NET! Is there anything at all you can do to find out what's going wrong?

For such situations, the Visual Studio .NET debugger can be attached to existing processes, enabling all of the debugging features we've seen so far: we can set breakpoints, view the Locals window, and step through code. The debugger can even be attached remotely, to debug web applications on remote machines, as long as you're a member of the Debugger Users group on the remote machine, and the machine in question has the .NET Framework installed.

Try It Out – Attaching to Processes Remotely

Using the same code that we've been experimenting with so far, we'll take this opportunity to see how to debug a web application that wasn't initiated by Visual Studio .NET.

1. Launch Internet Explorer *outside* of the Visual Studio .NET IDE, and type in the URL of our debugging project's web page. Alternatively, you can launch another web browser, to test the application with that instead of IE.

2. Switch to Visual Studio .NET, and set a breakpoint by clicking in the gray margin as before:

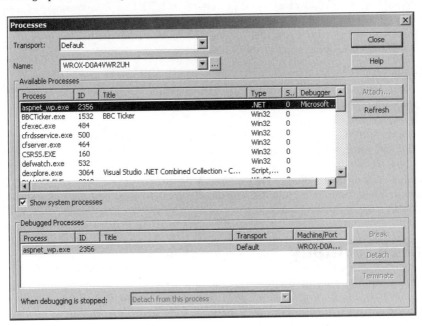

```
WebForm1.aspx *   WebForm1.aspx.vb*
WebForm1                                              Button1_Click
  24        End Sub
  25
  26   Private Sub Button1_Click(ByVal sender As System.Object, ByVal e As System.EventArgs) Handles Button1.Click
  27        ' Set up variables
  28        Dim ValueEntered As Integer
  29        Dim count As Integer
  30        Label1.Text = ""
  31
  32        ' Store the value entered in the textbox
  33        ValueEntered = TextBox1.Text
  34        For count = 1 To ValueEntered
  35            WriteTheNumber(count)
  36        Next
  37   End Sub
  38
  39   Private Sub WriteTheNumber(ByVal num As Integer)
  40        Label1.Text &= "Line #" & num & "<br>"
  41   End Sub
  42  End Class
  43
```

3. Go back to the web browser, type 3 in the textbox and click the Repeat button. Perhaps unsurprisingly, the application will execute without stopping at the breakpoint. This is because we started the browser independently of Visual Studio .NET and so our application is not linked to the debugger.

4. Let's see what we can do about that. In Visual Studio .NET, choose Tools | Debug Processes to bring up the following screen:

Make sure that the Name dropdown in this dialog shows the name of the server on which the ASP.NET web application is running.

5. Select Show system processes. Then, in the Available Processes pane, select the process named `aspnet_wp.exe`, and click the Attach button:

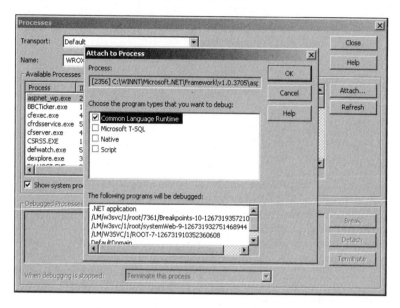

`aspnet_wp.exe` is the engine that powers all ASP.NET applications, and is known as the **worker process** (hence the `wp` on the end of its name). We want to attach the .NET debugger to this process, so ensure that the Common Language Runtime box is checked, as shown above, and click OK. Also click the Close button on the Processes dialog.

6. Switch back to Internet Explorer, and click the Repeat button again (there's no need to re-enter a number). This time, we *do* stop at the breakpoint, and flip to the Visual Studio .NET code editor, just as if we'd started the page from the IDE.

7. Click the Step Out button to exit the `Button1_Click()` procedure and return to Internet Explorer, which shows the expected output.

8. Switch back to Visual Studio .NET and click the Stop button on the debug toolbar to end debugging. If you now try out the web page in Internet Explorer, you'll see that it completes without stopping at the breakpoint.

Try...Catch...Finally

The Step Into/Over/Out buttons are useful for examining the flow of an application, and they can be very helpful for checking that variables are set as we intend them to be, and that the correct procedures are called in the correct sequence. However, there are some errors that can occur at run-time even if the application logic is correct. In earlier chapters, for example, we've been wary of the potential for a fault on a database server to disrupt the smooth running of our application, and wrapped code in `Try...Catch...Finally` blocks to insulate the users from such problems. In this section, we'll be examining that mechanism a little more closely.

The kinds of errors that `Try` blocks deal with are called **exceptions** because they are, in a sense, an exception to what Visual Basic .NET was expecting. There are many different types of exception, to the extent that in .NET, exceptions have a base class of their own: `System.Exception`. In the examples you've seen so far, we've used a simple, generic `Catch` statement that will trap any type of exception. However, it's quite possible to specify multiple `Catch` blocks for catching different exceptions.

Try It Out – Catching Specific Exceptions

Let's make a few changes to our simple web application to give it some elementary error handling, courtesy of a `Try` block with *two* associated `Catch` blocks.

1. Modify the `Button1_Click()` event handler as follows:

```
Private Sub Button1_Click(ByVal sender As System.Object, _
                          ByVal e As System.EventArgs) Handles Button1.Click
    ' Set up variables
    Dim ValueEntered As Integer
    Dim count As Integer
    Label1.Text = ""

    Try
        ' Store the value entered in the textbox
        ValueEntered = TextBox1.Text
        For count = 1 To ValueEntered
            WriteTheNumber(count)
        Next
    Catch exBadCast As InvalidCastException
        Label1.Text = "<br>You have to enter a number!"
    Catch exUnknown As Exception
        Label1.Text = "<br>Unexpected error: " & exUnknown.ToString()
    Finally
        Label1.Text += "<br>Finished!"
    End Try
End Sub
```

2. Hit the Start button to run our application, and try entering some text rather than a number into the textbox. When you press the Repeat button, you'll see a message pointing out that you ought to have entered a number instead. This message is due to the first of the two `Catch` statements.

3. Now, try entering a very large number (say, 999999999999) in the textbox, and click Repeat. This time, the resulting exception is caught by the second `Catch` statement, which displays an error message detailing the nature of the exception. In this case, it's an exception of type `System.OverflowException`:

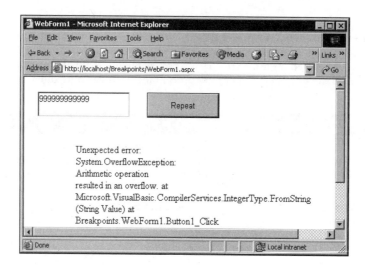

How It Works

When there are multiple `Catch` statements following a `Try` block, they are checked in the order that they appear in the code. The first one to be encountered that matches the type of the thrown exception will be executed. The first `Catch` statement in our code declares `exBadCast` as a particular type of exception, namely an `InvalidCastException`. This statement will catch any exceptions that were thrown because of an invalid cast, such as trying to convert a string containing characters to an integer – which is exactly what we tried to do here. Details of the exception are encapsulated by the `exBadCast` object, although we don't use it in this example.

The second `Catch` statement catches *any* exception, and because `Catch` statements are matched against in the order in which they appear, the code in this block will run if there is any error other than an `InvalidCastException`. The problem with entering a very large number wasn't that it couldn't be cast to an integer – theoretically. When we entered a very large number in the textbox, the problem wasn't about casting, but that it was simply too large to be stored in an `Integer` variable. The `OverflowException` that resulted was dealt with by the second `Catch` statement, which would have dealt with any exception not already caught. Here, we used the exception object's `ToString()` method to output the error details to the page as a string. It's always worth adding a final 'catch-all' `Catch` statement to handle any unexpected exceptions.

Throwing Exceptions

Having looked at catching exceptions of different kinds, let's see now how to throw our own exceptions that can be handled using `Catch` statements. Why would we deliberately cause an exception? In some situations, such as when we want to consolidate our error-handling code in a single location, we actually *want* a particular kind of error to occur, so that we can stop processing and handle it elsewhere.

As a simple illustration, let's imagine that we want to prevent users of our page from entering numbers greater than 10 in the textbox. In fact, this particular requirement would be better handled by ASP.NET's validation controls, but it makes for a good demonstration of the mechanism. We will throw an exception if the user enters any number greater than 10.

Try It Out – Throwing a Custom Exception

Throwing custom exceptions can be an effective error-handling technique – if you structure it correctly, you can arrange for several related errors to be handled by the same `Catch` block. In this example, we'll have a look at the syntax that enables it.

1. Modify the `Button1_Click()` event handler as follows:

```
Private Sub Button1_Click(ByVal sender As System.Object, _
                          ByVal e As System.EventArgs) Handles Button1.Click
    ' Set up variables
    Dim ValueEntered As Integer
    Dim count As Integer
    Label1.Text = ""

    Try
        ' Store the value entered in the textbox
        ValueEntered = TextBox1.Text
        If ValueEntered > 10 Then
          Throw New Exception("Values above 10 are not permitted here!")
        End If
        For count = 1 To ValueEntered
          WriteTheNumber(count)
        Next
    Catch exBadCast As InvalidCastException
        Label1.Text = "<br>You have to enter a number!"
    Catch exUnknown As Exception
        Label1.Text = "<br>Unexpected error: " & excUnknown.ToString()
    Finally
        Label1.Text += "<br>Finished!"
    End Try
End Sub
```

2. Launch the application by pressing *F5*, type 11 in the textbox, and click the Repeat button. You should see the following error message:

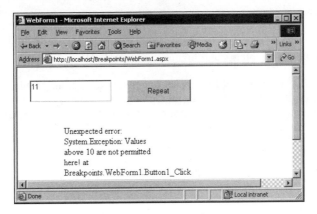

How It Works

In this example, we used a `Throw` statement in which we created a new `Exception` object with the error message provided in the constructor. The exception was caught by the second `Catch` statement, which displays the error message and other useful debug information using the `ToString()` method. To extend this example, you could imagine having a `Try` block containing several `Throw` statements, all of which could be handled neatly by a single `Catch`.

Debugging Client-side Script

ASP.NET is built to minimize the work required by the developer to create consistent effects across browsers. Almost all output is rendered in HTML 3.2, thus maximizing browser compatibility. Many server controls automatically tailor themselves according to the capabilities of the browser detected by ASP.NET, and render themselves using the most appropriate mix of server-side and client-side code for the particular browser in use.

However, there will be times when you need (or want) to write or use your own client-side script. For example, if you wanted to customize a control so that its appearance changes when the user's mouse rolls over it, you'd need to write something in JavaScript or VBScript code. ASP.NET server-side code cannot detect a mouse-over event, as this doesn't usually cause a postback to the server.

Try It Out – Debugging Client-side Script

When the ASP.NET runtime encounters client script on a page, it simply ignores the code and returns it to the browser as is. The browser then interprets and runs the script line by line. However, ASP.NET's ambivalence doesn't mean that Visual Studio .NET has no role to play in debugging client-side script, as we'll see in the following example.

1. Open `WebForm1.aspx` in the Visual Studio .NET designer, and switch to the HTML view.

2. Add an `onsubmit` attribute to the opening `<form>` tag in the `<body>` element, as shown:

```
<form id="Form1" method="post" runat="server" onsubmit="window.alert(hey)">
```

Here, we're using `alert()`, a method of the `window` object that allows to us manipulate the browser window, its toolbars and menus, and the HTML objects it is displaying.

3. Next, check that Internet Explorer is set to activate the debugger when a client-side script error occurs. Select the **Tools | Internet Options** menu item, click the **Advanced** tab, and make sure that the **Disable Script Debugging** option is *not* checked. Click **OK**, and close Internet Explorer.

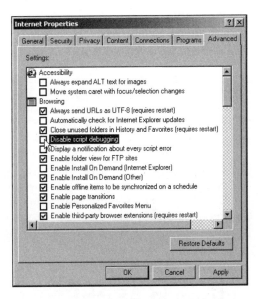

4. Switch to Visual Studio .NET, and start the application with *F5*. Type a number in the text box, and click **Repeat**. In response, Visual Studio .NET will pop up with an error message:

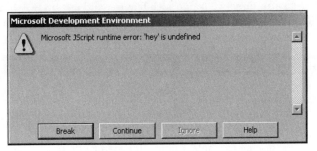

5. Click **Break**, and you'll see that Visual Studio .NET has highlighted in yellow the code that caused the error:

```
<!DOCTYPE HTML PUBLIC "-//W3C//DTD HTML 4.0 Transitional//EN">
<html>
    <head>
        <title>WebForm1</title>
        <meta content="Microsoft Visual Studio.NET 7.0" name="GENERATOR">
        <meta content="Visual Basic 7.0" name="CODE_LANGUAGE">
        <meta content="JavaScript" name="vs_defaultClientScript">
        <meta content="http://schemas.microsoft.com/intellisense/ie5" name="vs_targetSchema">
    </head>
    <body MS_POSITIONING="GridLayout">
        <form name="Form1" method="post" action="WebForm1.aspx" id="Form1" onsubmit="window.alert(hey)">
<input type="hidden" name="__VIEWSTATE" value="dDw2MzQ5MDczOTU7Oz54WzIAAjAxwYN5PG8eNB1QE6p15Q==" />

            <input name="TextBox1" type="text" id="TextBox1" style="Z-INDEX: 101; LEFT: 8px; POSITION: absolute;
            <span id="Label1" style="Z-INDEX: 103; LEFT: 9px; POSITION: absolute; TOP: 42px"></span><input type="
    </body>
</html>
```

205

The problem here is that we haven't included quotes around the message that we want to display in the alert box. The JavaScript interpreter in IE has therefore concluded that `hey` is the name of a variable, and reports an error because no such variable has been defined.

6. Click the Stop Debugging button to close IE and return to design mode in Visual Studio .NET, and change the attribute to include quotes, like so: `onsubmit="window.alert('hey')"`. If you now run the application again, the message will pop up when the Repeat button is pressed.

How It Works

By omitting the quotes around the message, we deliberately introduced an error so that we could see Visual Studio .NET's response. Note, though, that we were unable to edit the code at this point, because the IDE was showing a read-only version of the code that was sent to the browser to produce our page. Even with this restriction, however, it can be extremely useful to be able to examine client-side code in this way while you're debugging – sometimes, there's no substitute for seeing *exactly* what the browser receives.

Using Trace Directives in ASP.NET

ASP.NET has some very powerful features for examining the configuration of the server when you're debugging a page. The `Trace` directive is one such feature, and just by switching it on we can view some important information about the context in which our web applications are being executed.

Try It Out – Displaying Trace Information on a Single Page

Our objective for this example is simply to demonstrate how easy ASP.NET makes it to find out what's going on at the server while our applications are executing. It's as easy as setting an attribute!

1. Continuing with the same example, remove the client-side JavaScript that we added to the `<form>` tag. Then, add `Trace="True"` to the list of attributes in the `Page` directive at the top of the page:

```
<%@ Page Trace="True" Language="vb" AutoEventWireup="false"
    Codebehind="WebForm1.aspx.vb" Inherits="WroxDebugging1.WebForm1"%>
```

2. Press *F5* to launch the page in Internet Explorer, and scroll down. You'll find that a good deal of information has been dumped at the bottom of this page, including our server variables, the user's session ID cookie, and the HTTP header values.

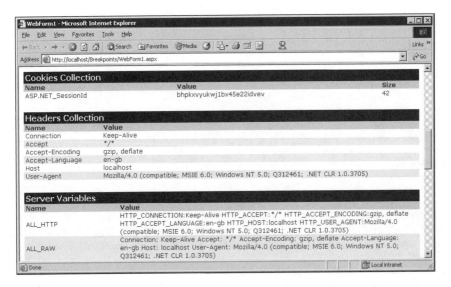

How It Works

Trace information isn't always useful, but every now and then it can help you to find and eliminate problems. Being able to see the value of a cookie, for example, can be extremely useful when you're debugging an application that relies on them. The server variables contain information about the web and application server, such as the remote IP address, the physical path on the server to the web page being displayed, or whether the HTTPS protocol is turned on. If your application is relying on the values of any of these variables, it may be useful to display them.

Adding your own Trace Statements

In addition to the trace information we just enabled, it's also possible to add your own data to the list by using the `Trace` class that resides in the `System.Diagnostics` namespace. Better still, the output you create will appear alongside the output of the other processes in the page. Since these processes are sorted by time, you can see exactly when and where events in your code happen in relation to the other events, procedures, and functions listed in the trace output.

Try It Out – Adding Trace Statements to our Code

To see exactly what the implications of adding our own trace statements are, we'll use a couple of methods of the `Trace` class to create three of them in our simple application.

1. Open the code-behind page for `WebForm1.aspx` and make sure that you have unset any breakpoints.

2. Modify the `Page_Load()` event handler procedure to look like the following:

```
Private Sub Page_Load(ByVal sender As System.Object, _
                ByVal e As System.EventArgs) Handles MyBase.Load
```

```
          ' Put user code to initialize the page here
      Trace.Write("Page_Load", "This page is beginning the Page_Load event")
   End Sub
```

3. Next, let's add some code to the `Button1_Click()` event handler:

```
   Private Sub Button1_Click(ByVal sender As System.Object, _
                             ByVal e As System.EventArgs) Handles Button1.Click
      Trace.Write("Button1_Click", "The Button1_Click procedure has started.")
      Dim ValueEntered As Integer
      Dim count As Integer
      Try
        ValueEntered = TextBox1.Text
        If ValueEntered > 10 Then
          Trace.Warn("Button1_Click", _
                     "Warning! The Button1_Click handler threw an exception.")
          Throw New Exception("Values above 10 are not permitted here!")
        End If
        For count = 1 to ValueEntered
          WriteTheNumber(count)
        Next
      Catch exBadCast As InvalidCastException
        Label1.Text = "<br>You have to enter a number!"
      Catch exUnknown As Exception
        Label1.Text = "<br>Unexpected error: " & exUnknown.ToString()
      Finally
        Label1.Text += "<br>Finished!"
      End Try
      Trace.Write("Button1_Click", "The Button1_Click procedure has finished.")
   End Sub
```

4. Now we'll take a look at what we've done. Start the debugging process by clicking the Start button or typing *F5*. If you scroll down a little, you'll see our first trace statement being displayed alongside the rest of the trace information:

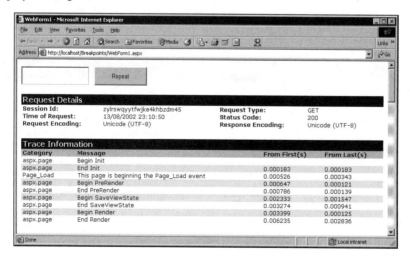

5. Next, type 4 into the textbox and click the **Repeat** button. This should invoke the `Button1_Click()` event handler. Again, scroll down to see the new trace information that was added. You'll see two rows that have `Button1_Click` as their category, and these display our text that marks the start and end of the `Button1_Click()` event handler:

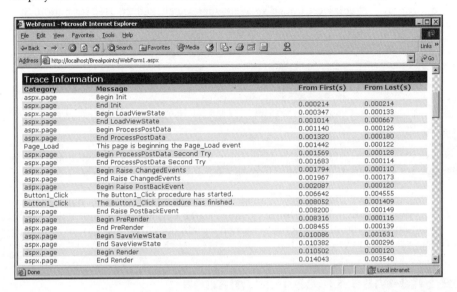

6. Finally, scroll back up and enter 22 into the textbox, and again hit the **Repeat** button. This will throw the exception that we created earlier, but if you scroll down through the trace block, you can see the addition we made:

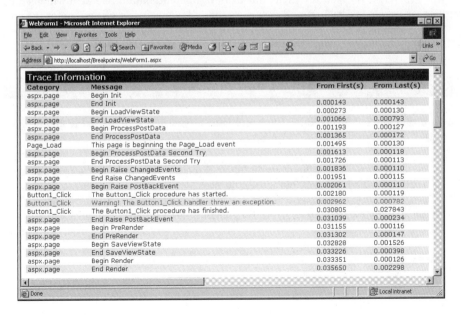

How It Works

We used two static methods of the `Trace` class. First, the `Trace.Write()` statements simply displayed the category and text that we passed as arguments in separate columns of the trace table on our page. The `Page_Load` messages appeared every time we hit the page, while the trace messages that we labeled `Button1_Click` were only displayed when we clicked the **Repeat** button. Second, we added a `Trace.Warn()` call right before the line of code that throws an exception if a number greater than 10 is entered:

```
If ValueEntered > 10 Then
    Trace.Warn("Button1_Click", _
              "Warning! The Button1_Click handler threw an exception.")
    Throw New Exception("Values above 10 are not permitted here!")
End If
```

Quite clearly, `Trace.Warn()` is nearly identical to `Trace.Write()`, except that it displays its text in red, like an error message. It made sense here to place it before the exception.

As you can see, the `Trace` class is aptly named. We can use it to track down bugs, or trace the flow of events and method calls in our code. Since the trace statements are listed in order of execution, it's possible to output information in order to see when certain code is running, or even to find out what values certain variables have at each line.

Adding Site-wide Trace Information

Sometimes, it would be useful to view trace information for every page in a web site. In such a case, we don't have to add the `Trace` directive to every single page – rather, we can simply alter the `Web.config` file. This is especially useful during development, but on release it will need to be removed for security, performance, and design reasons. Having `Trace` turned on for the entire site also means that we can add `Trace.Write()` and `Trace.Warn()` method calls to our code for debugging purposes without having to change the page directive.

Try It Out – Enabling Site-Wide Trace Information

Enabling site-wide trace information really couldn't be any easier. It involves the addition of a single line to the `Web.config` file:

1. Remove the `Trace` attribute from the `Page` directive of `WebForm1.aspx`, and open up the `Web.config` file from the Solution Explorer.

2. At the level below the `<system.web>` element, there may already be a `<trace>` element. If so, alter it to the following:

```
<trace enabled="true" requestLimit="10" pageOutput="true"
       traceMode="SortByTime" localOnly="true" />
```

If there's not one already there, just add a new one with this form.

3. Restart the application. You will again see the trace information in the browser, just as you would for any page in the project.

How It Works

ASP.NET uses the settings specified by the `<trace>` element in `Web.config` as the default for all pages in the application. Note though that the `Trace` attribute of the `Page` directive overrides the setting in `Web.config`, so if we set it to `False`, we wouldn't see the trace information for that page.

Trace information, whether site-wide or enabled on a page-by-page basis, is stored for reference, and can be accessed by navigating to a page called `Trace.axd`:

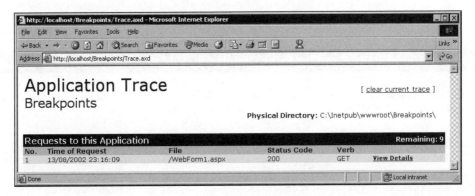

You can click the **View Details** link for a particular request to see the trace information that it produced. This is the same information that we saw overlaid on the page in Internet Explorer when the request was originally made:

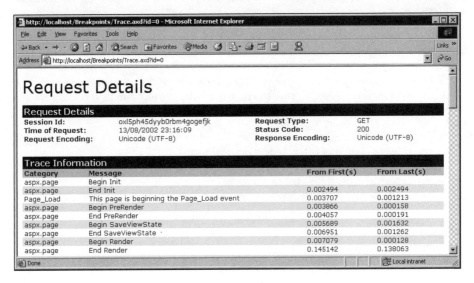

If you were to go back to our application and run it a few more times, the `Trace.axd` page would change to list each request.

Global.asax and Site-Wide Error Handling

If we lived in a perfect world, there would always be plenty of time for testing and debugging all of your projects, and you could guarantee them to be error-free at deployment time. In the real world, however, we often find ourselves having to deploy web applications before we feel they are truly 100% ready. Even if you *do* feel that an application is complete, you'll soon find that web users have a remarkable ability to find ways of producing errors.

Awareness is the key to fixing these errors quickly and efficiently, and an excellent way to stay in touch with an application's status is to be e-mailed whenever an error occurs. Sending error messages by e-mail is a good 'quick-and-dirty' notification system, although if you have vast numbers of users and the site falls over, you might find yourself inundated!

Try It Out – Automatically Sending Error Reports by E-Mail

For our final example in this chapter, we'll add e-mail error notification to our sample application by adding some code to the global error-handling subroutine, Application_Error().

1. Right-click on Global.asax in the Solution Explorer, and select **View Code**. Scroll down to find the empty Application_Error() event handler, and add the code shown below:

```
Sub Application_Error(ByVal sender As Object, ByVal e As EventArgs)
    ' Fires when an error occurs
    Dim errormessage As String

    errormessage = Server.GetLastError.ToString()
    System.Web.Mail.SmtpMail.SmtpServer = "mail.myserver.com"
    System.Web.Mail.SmtpMail.Send( _
            "from@myserver.com", "tome@myserver.com", "Error e-mail", errormessage)
End Sub
```

Don't forget to change this to specify your own e-mail address in the from and to parameters of the Send method. Also, be sure to enter the URL of your e-mail server in the SmtpServer property that's set just before the call.

2. Now open WebForm1.aspx.vb, and we'll modify it to produce an error by commenting out the two lines of code that catch general exceptions:

```
Catch exBadCast As InvalidCastException
   Label1.Text = "<br>You have to enter a number!"
' Catch exUnknown As Exception
   ' Label1.Text = "<br>Unexpected error: " & exUnknown.ToString()
Finally
   Label1.Text += "<br>Finished!"
End Try
```

3. Run the application. When the page appears in Internet Explorer, enter 50 in the textbox and click the **Repeat** button. You will receive a standard error page, showing our custom error message, but that's not what we're interested in right now.

4. Close Internet Explorer. You should soon receive an e-mail with the following text in the message body (as long as your e-mail server doesn't reject the mail). If you have a server that has tight spam controls, which does not allow e-mail to be sent outside a certain IP range or without a secure login first, ASP.NET will not be able to send these messages automatically.

```
System.Web.HttpUnhandledException: Exception of type System.Web.HttpUnhandledException was
thrown. ---> System.Exception: Values above 10 are not permitted here!
   at Breakpoints.WebForm1.Button1_Click(Object sender, EventArgs e) in
c:\inetpub\wwwroot\Breakpoints\WebForm1.aspx.vb:line 35
   at System.Web.UI.WebControls.Button.OnClick(EventArgs e)
   at
System.Web.UI.WebControls.Button.System.Web.UI.IPostBackEventHandler.RaisePostBackEvent(S
tring eventArgument)
   at System.Web.UI.Page.RaisePostBackEvent(IPostBackEventHandler sourceControl, String
eventArgument)
   at System.Web.UI.Page.RaisePostBackEvent(NameValueCollection postData)
   at System.Web.UI.Page.ProcessRequestMain()
   --- End of inner exception stack trace ---
   at System.Web.UI.Page.HandleError(Exception e)
   at System.Web.UI.Page.ProcessRequestMain()
   at System.Web.UI.Page.ProcessRequest()
   at System.Web.UI.Page.ProcessRequest(HttpContext context)
   at System.Web.CallHandlerExecutionStep.Execute()
   at System.Web.HttpApplication.ExecuteStep(IExecutionStep step, Boolean&
completedSynchronously)
```

How It Works

The `Global.asax` file that's present in all ASP.NET applications makes it very simple to add site-wide error handling to web applications. We can use the `Application_Error()` event handler it contains to set up code that will automatically notify us in the event of any problems occurring on our site. We had to comment out the code that caught general exceptions because the `Application_Error()` event only fires when an *unhandled* exception occurs.

Also worthy of note is the use of `Server.GetLastError` in the `Application_Error()` event handler, which contains details of the last error encountered by the server. This bears a certain similarity to the code we placed inside the `Catch` statements in the `WebForm1.aspx` code, where we also used the `ToString()` method to get the error message.

Finally, we use the static `System.Web.Mail.SmtpMail` class to send an e-mail containing the error message. The `Send()` method of this class takes four parameters: the 'from' address, the 'to' address, the subject line, and the message body, in that order.

We could have got fancier and sent other debugging information, or forwarded the user to a more friendly page apologizing for the error – simply adding a `Response.Redirect()` call after the line that sends the e-mail would suffice. The user could then be redirected to a common error page, perhaps one that has some of the navigation or at least the company logo to make them feel they haven't got lost. The important part, though, was that we were able to detect the exception through e-mail the minute it occurred.

Summary

This chapter reviewed the standard debugging features in Visual Studio.NET as well as the specific debugging tools within ASP.NET. We discussed the basic error types: compile, run-time and logical errors and the difference between debugging which happens during development, and error handling which is used to handle unavoidable errors in released code. We also went over issues specific to testing and debugging web applications such as browser compatibility issues with cookies and JavaScript.

Next we started trying out features in the Visual Studio IDE that enabled us to find errors by outputting and viewing information in various ways throughout our application. This included the use of breakpoints, the debug class and the various Autos, Locals, Me, and Watch windows and the use of assertions to output warnings conditionally.

We also looked at how to trap unavoidable errors and the reasons for doing so using the `Try...Catch...Finally` structured error handling that has been introduced into Visual Basic.NET.

Finally we covered a lot of ground specific to debugging web applications in ASP.NET. You should know how to enable `Trace` for a page or for an entire application in the `Web.config` file and how to use the `Trace` class to add your own warnings and messages to a page. Using what we had already learned about `Try...Catch` error handling, we were able to create a site-wide error handling system that e-mailed us in the event of a page error.

Solut...
BM   Refer...   System...
                  System.Dat...
                  System.Drawing
                  System.Web
                  System.XML
                  AssemblyInfo.vb
         Assembly
         BM.vsdisco
         Global.asax
         Styles.css
         Web.config
         WebForm1.aspx

WebForm1.aspx*   WebForm1.aspx.v...

ASP.NET Applications, Sessions, and State

In Chapter 3, when we were talking about server controls, we mentioned the two kinds of events that are associated with ASP.NET: **global events**, and **page-specific events**. In going on to discuss the latter of those two, we mentioned in passing that the handlers for the former were to be found in the Global.asax file, and made a promise to return to cover global events in more detail at a later stage. This is the chapter where, among a number of other things, we make good on that promise.

Since we're tackling one issue that has been dogging us for a while, why not two? Right back in Chapter 1, and on a couple of occasions since then, we have stated that HTTP is a **stateless** protocol – that is, HTTP itself has no mechanism to keep track of which users are which, or what information has been passed to any particular user. Clearly, it is useful for our applications to retain pieces of information as our users move from page to page – who they are, what fields they have filled out so far, and so on – but in order to do that, we need to be able to store information at some global level, and identify it as belonging to one user or another.

The theme that runs through both of the above paragraphs is that of **global** availability, and it is a theme that we will return to on a few occasions as we proceed. More practically, this chapter will cover the following subjects:

- ❑ What global events it is possible to handle, and how and where to handle them

- ❑ How to store **application state** – data that's intended to be available to all of the users of your application, all of the time – in the ASP.NET Application object

- ❑ How to store **session state** – data that's intended to be available to a single user all of the time, and from any page – in the ASP.NET Session object

- ❑ How to store the data that has been entered on a given page in ViewState, a new mechanism for tracking the appearance of the user interface

- ❑ How to transfer data between pages, a mechanism that has changed dramatically since the days of classic ASP

What Does 'Global' Really Mean?

When you're writing a desktop application, it's not unusual to need to store some data at a level 'above' all of the classes that make up that application, so that it's available for use from every method you write. Using **global** data like this is quite a common practice, and it is not difficult to implement. In a web application, however, the situation is a little more complicated: there are two different global levels. First, there is the **session**, which is global as far as any *one* user of your application is concerned. Second, there is the **application** itself, which is global for *all* of your users.

In some ways, what this means for us is twice as much work – or at least, twice as much *thinking*. For example, if you decide that your application needs to store some global data, you face the further choice of deciding whether that data would be stored more appropriately at the application or the session level. Similarly, you might conclude that some tasks need to be performed as soon as the application starts up – but do you really need those to happen when the application itself comes into being, or when every new user connects to your site?

The ASP.NET Application and Session Objects

In ASP.NET, the application and session are represented by the `Application` and `Session` objects respectively. As you would hope, they provide answers to both of the problems we talked about at the start of this chapter: they fire events at various points along the lifelines of the application and the session, and they provide stores for both kinds of global data. In the sections that follow, we will take a quick look at global event handling, and then see how this works in practice as we use the handlers as a means for storing global data.

Handling Application- and Session-Level Events

It can be important to know when certain actions happen in a web application. We may need to know when the application or session is created for the first time. We may need to know when errors occur, and we may want to know when the application or the session shuts down.

For instance, if the application shuts down, we may want to store the information it was processing at the time in a database, or on the hard drive. Alternatively, when an error occurs, we may want to determine its severity and log it in the event log. As suggested earlier, the procedure for handling events such as these is fundamentally no different from handling page-specific events – you just need to know where to do it. The answer to that, as you know, is `Global.asax`.

Global.asax

Just like any other specific page of an ASP.NET application, `Global.asax` defines a class – it's just that on this occasion, the methods of the class are event handlers for events of a general nature. As initially created by the Visual Studio .NET Wizards, these event handlers do nothing at all, as the following code shows:

```
Imports System.Web
Imports System.Web.SessionState

Public Class Global
   Inherits System.Web.HttpApplication

   #Region " Component Designer Generated Code

   Sub Application_Start(ByVal sender As Object, ByVal e As EventArgs)
      ' Fires when the application is started
   End Sub

   Sub Session_Start(ByVal sender As Object, ByVal e As EventArgs)
      ' Fires when the session is started
   End Sub

   Sub Application_BeginRequest(ByVal sender As Object, ByVal e As EventArgs)
      ' Fires at the beginning of each request
   End Sub

   Sub Application_AuthenticateRequest(ByVal sender As Object, _
      ByVal e As EventArgs)
      ' Fires upon attempting to authenticate the use
   End Sub

   Sub Application_Error(ByVal sender As Object, ByVal e As EventArgs)
      ' Fires when an error occurs
   End Sub

   Sub Session_End(ByVal sender As Object, ByVal e As EventArgs)
      ' Fires when the session ends
   End Sub

   Sub Application_End(ByVal sender As Object, ByVal e As EventArgs)
      ' Fires when the application ends
   End Sub

End Class
```

The first thing to notice about this class, apart from the two Imports at the top of the page, is that it inherits from HttpApplication. In other words, it *is* the Application object, and as such, it will be available from any code in our web application. We are not about to cover these events, and the others available, in detail – you can find them listed in the MSDN documentation – but you will see a few of them being used over the course of this chapter, and elsewhere in the book. The most useful handlers tend to be Application_Start() and Session_Start(), and their corresponding _End() methods, but it really does depend on the purpose you have in mind.

Application State

Of course, the `Global.asax` file's ability to track events in an application would be useless if we couldn't also define, track, and manipulate data specific to the application. **Application state** refers to the ability of a web application to keep track of data that's common to a particular program. A popular use of application state, for example, is to store a dataset. In this section, we will look at handling some of the application-level events that we saw a moment ago, and using them as an ideal opportunity to store some data at the level of the application.

Application Variables

Application state is stored in **application variables**, but these variables are not declared with the standard syntax that you would normally use. As a matter of fact, application variables are not actually declared at all – rather, they are added to a collection. When we store data at the application level, we do so by adding key-value pairs to the `Application` object's collection of data. The syntax for this uses the `Add()` method of the `Application` object, as follows:

```
Application.Add(<variable name>, <variable value>)
```

For example, when we introduced this section, we stated that you might want to store a dataset in an application variable. You could code this as follows:

```
Application.Add("UsersOnline", myDataSet)
```

As you can see, this is not a difficult task, and any variables that you store here are available throughout the application. Whenever we need to access it, we can read this variable by using the `Application` object's `Get()` method, as follows:

```
myDataSet = Application.Get("UsersOnline")
```

Lastly, we may wish to change the value of a variable in the `Application` object's collection. We would do this by calling the `Set()` method of the `Application` object, as follows:

```
Application.Set("UsersOnline", myDataSet)
```

> Note that if you call `Set()` without first calling the `Add()` method, the Framework automatically assumes that you mean to perform an add. No errors will be generated.

Any changes to application variables will be visible to the entire application. It is important to note, therefore, that if the data you're storing is user-specific, you should not store it in application state, because all users have access to the same set of application variables. User-specific data will be covered in depth in the later section on *Session State*.

Try It Out – Storing an Application Variable

Let's take a quick look at using one of the application-level events to store a dataset in an application variable. Open up Visual Studio .NET, and create a new Visual Basic .NET ASP.NET application called `SessionAndState`. Then, follow these steps.

1. In the Solution Explorer, right-click on the `Global.asax` file, and choose **View Code**. As you know, this file already contains skeleton handlers for several of the application-level events.

2. Let's add some code to the `Application_Start()` event handler, as follows:

```
Sub Application_Start(ByVal sender As Object, ByVal e As EventArgs)
    ' Fires when the application is started
    Dim connString As String = _
        "server=(local)\NetSDK;uid=sa;pwd=;database=NorthWind"
    Dim sqlString As String = "SELECT * FROM EMPLOYEES"
    Dim ds As New DataSet()
    Dim da As New SqlClient.SqlDataAdapter(sqlString, connString)
    da.Fill(ds, "Employees")
    Application.Set("dsEmployees", ds)
End Sub
```

This code simply adds the dataset we've retrieved as an application variable.

3. Now let's view the information that we put in this variable. In the **Design** view of `WebForm1.aspx`, drag a **Label** control onto the page from the **Web Forms** section of the **Toolbox**. Then, in the **Properties** window, change the ID of the label to `lblApplication`.

4. Double-click on the page, and the code window will open up with the cursor placed inside the `Page_Load()` event handler. Change the code to look like this:

```
Private Sub Page_Load(ByVal sender As System.Object, _
                      ByVal e As System.EventArgs) Handles MyBase.Load
    ' Put user code to initialize the page here
    lblApplication.Text = ""
    Dim ds As DataSet
    ds = Application.Get("dsEmployees")
    Dim myDataColumn As System.Data.DataColumn
    For Each myDataColumn In ds.Tables(0).Columns
        lblApplication.Text &= myDataColumn.ColumnName.ToString() & "<br>"
    Next
End Sub
```

5. Run the application, and you'll see the following list of column names from the `Employees` table in the Northwind database. (This database was installed by default when you installed MSDE.)

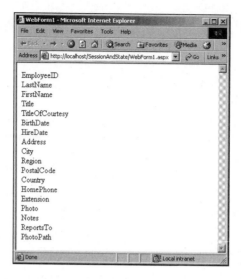

How It Works

First, you can see that we've used the `Application_Start()` event handler in the `Global.asax` file to add the dataset as an application variable:

```
Application.Set("dsEmployees", ds)
```

This line adds an item with the name `dsEmployees`, and the dataset we retrieved from the Northwind database. We can then reference this value from anywhere else in our application by using the `Get()` method. For that purpose, we use the following line of code in our `WebForm1.aspx.vb` code-behind file:

```
ds = Application.Get("dsEmployees")
```

Of course, as the `Application` object is also a .NET collection, it is possible to iterate through all of the variables it contains using a `For Each` construct, should you need to do so.

Application Locking

Having learned about storing and changing state in the `Application` object, we could go on happily changing stored data at will, *if we only had to consider one user*. However, the minute that we add another user, or five users, or hundreds of thousands of users, we have to take two new considerations into account. The first of these is **concurrency**: the potential for manipulation of the same data by more than one user at the same time. The second is the possibility of information that should be stored on a **per-user basis** (such as a user's name, or preferences).

In this section, we will look at dealing with the first of these issues: concurrent data access. This involves considering what happens when, for example, you want to implement something as simple as a hit counter on a web page. What would happen if two users accessed the same page at the same time? Both users would receive the current count, and both would increment that count. However, the count would be incorrect, because both users incremented the same value by one, and retrieved the same number. Let's look at a quick diagram of what this like:

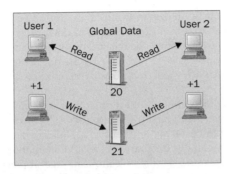

Assume that the diagram above represents two users accessing a web page, and that there are already 20 hits on the page. Both users read the current counter at 20. When executing the code that increments the counter, both users increase this count to 21. Both users then write the same value to the counter. This is obviously wrong, because the counter should now be 22.

Since this problem is so common, Microsoft has provided a mechanism for **locking** application state. When application state is locked, no updates can be made until the user who locked it in the first place unlocks it again. While this doesn't solve every possible problem automatically, it does allow us to isolate code (such as transactions) that must allow for the possibility of multiple users.

To lock an application, you simply call the Lock() method of the Application object. Once you have completed your modifications to the application state, you need to tell the application explicitly that it's OK to let others modify the Application object, by calling its Unlock() method. A typical method for changing the application state might look like this:

```
Sub ChangeApplicationState(variableName as String, variableValue as Object)
    Application.Lock()
    Application(variableName) = variableValue
    Application.UnLock()
End Function
```

Here, ChangeApplicationState() is a wrapper function that handles locking the application before changing the state. It then makes the changes using the parameters you passed in, and finally unlocks the application so that other users may now modify the application state. When the application state is locked, it means that no other user can *modify* it, but they *can* read it.

What to Store in Application State

While we've talked of what application state is, and how to store information in it, we have not really described what *kind* of information you might want to store. Generally speaking, we can say that any information that you want to make available to the entire application could be stored here – but couldn't we also store that information in a database? Why would Microsoft give us application state if we could just use SQL Server (or some other engine) instead?

The answer is pretty simple. Application state is stored and retrieved **in-process**, which means that data can be retrieved and edited quickly – it is running in the same process as the web application. Furthermore, in-process implies **in-memory**, which means no hits to the hard drive. If we were to store all of this information in SQL Server, we would have all the overhead associated with instantiating a connection, querying for the data we want, and possibly manipulating it before using it.

If all of *that* is the case though, then another question arises – why don't we store all of the information in our databases in an application variable for faster access? The answer again is quite simple. Since all of our data would then be stored in the memory of the application server, we would be tied to a single server for both our application and our database. We would need enough memory (and enough processor power) on a single server to handle this application, and pieces of our application could not be split out and placed on other servers to accommodate scalability.

Session State

We just finished a discussion of how state can be stored for an application, but application state is the same for all users of an application. What happens if we want to store some user-specific state information? For example, we wouldn't want to store a user's first name in application state – unless, that is, all of our users are called Bob. Also storing some other private information in application variables could have disastrous consequences – credit card data, addresses, phone numbers, and identification numbers should not be shared among all users. This is where sessions come to the rescue.

In ASP.NET, a **session** is created when a user first visits a web site, and generally is kept open until the information is either deleted, or a timeout on the session is reached. Any data that you store at session level is persisted from one page to the next, but not between users, and not between visits to the site. It is a bit like visiting an office block: when you arrive, you get a pass that allows you to travel freely from room to room, but you have to give it back when you leave, and you have to pick up a new one the next time you visit.

Session IDs and Cookies

Before we look at an example of storing some data in a `Session` object (the syntax is actually very similar to storing it the `Application` object), let's imagine for a moment that there are already several users (and therefore several sessions) in your web application, and all of them are storing session state. How does ASP.NET know which user is associated with which session? In fact, there are two possibilities.

The default setting in ASP.NET (it was the only setting in classic ASP) is for a new session ID to be generated for each user when they first arrive at your site. A **cookie** containing that ID is then sent to the user's browser. Each time a new page is accessed within the same web site, the cookie is read, the session is determined, and the correct user can then safely access the associated session data. This method works perfectly, *unless* a user that's unable to receive cookies comes along. In that case, another solution is required.

In ASP.NET, Microsoft has implemented an alternative solution that many developers had previously had to code for themselves. In 'cookie-less' sessions, session IDs are still assigned by the server, but they are then passed back to the browser *in the URL*. This allows users to keep their cookies turned off, but also allows the server to discover the current session ID, as before.

While this seems like something we'd want to turn on by default – we want our web applications to work for as many people as possible, right? – you need to understand that there is, once again, more overhead involved in using this option. First, the server must parse the session ID out of each page's URL. Then, it must add that session ID to any links that might exist on the page. By itself, parsing the page and adding this information is not going to bring your server to its knees, but you should be aware of this performance hit if you're trying to squeeze every ounce out of your resources.

> It's important to note that ASP.NET dynamically adds the session ID to all *relative* links, but not to fully qualified links, even if the fully qualified link points to the same application.

Configuring Cookie-less Sessions

Cookie-less sessions come as a free feature of ASP.NET, but they must be activated on a per-application basis. To turn this feature on for a single application, you simply need to modify its Web.config file. Open up the previous project, find the Web.config file, and search for an element named <sessionState>. This element has an attribute named cookieless, which is currently set to false. Simply change this value to true, and save the file:

```
<sessionState
        mode="InProc"
        stateConnectionString="tcpip=127.0.0.1:42424"
        sqlConnectionString="data source=127.0.0.1;user id=sa;password="
        cookieless="true"
        timeout="20"
    />
```

Try It Out – Testing Cookie-less Sessions

Now that you've set up the application so that sessions won't use cookies, let's test it to make sure that it's working as we anticipated.

1. Take the WebForm1.aspx file that was created when you made your new application, drag a Hyperlink control onto the form, and change the ID of the existing Label control to Label1.

2. In the Properties window for the Hyperlink control, set the NavigateUrl property to WebForm1.aspx, effectively pointing the link back at itself.

3. Double-click on the web form to display the code-behind page for this file, and change the Page_Load() event handler so that it looks like this:

```
Private Sub Page_Load(ByVal sender As System.Object, _
                      ByVal e As System.EventArgs) Handles MyBase.Load
    ' Put user code to initialize the page here
    Label1.Text = "SessionID: " & Session.SessionID & _
            "<BR>Date/Time: " & DateTime.Now().ToString()
End Sub
```

Obviously, this code will display the session ID and the current time.

4. Save this page, compile the project, and view the web form in a browser. What you will see is a page like the following, displaying the session ID, a time stamp, and a hyperlink to link back to the same page:

How It Works

When you click on the hyperlink, you are immediately redirected to a new URL that's same as the one you requested, with the addition of a session ID embedded in the request string. (Notice that this session ID matches the one that is displayed in the label control of our browser.) Also, look at the hyperlink that we added – place your cursor over it, and look at the status bar of your browser. Although we only specified that we wanted the link to send us back to our current page, the session ID is embedded in this link as well.

Session Variables

Handling session state in ASP.NET is very much like handling application state, so without any further ado we'll look at a quick example in which we're going to add some code to the `Session` object's event handlers in `Global.asax`, and then compare application and session state.

Try It Out – Session-Level Event Handling

In this little project, we are going to record the moments at which the application and the session are created, and interpret the results we find.

1. Create a new Visual Basic .NET web application called `SessionTest`.

2. In the `Global.asax` file, look for the `Application_Start()` and `Session_Start()` subroutines. This is where we will add our code for creating session and application variables respectively:

```
Sub Application_Start(ByVal sender As Object, ByVal e As EventArgs)
    ' Fires when the application is started
    Dim dateString As String = DateTime.Now.ToString()
    Application.Add("Trace", "Application Started at: " & dateString)
End Sub
Sub Session_Start(ByVal sender As Object, ByVal e As EventArgs)
    ' Fires when the session is started
```

```
    Dim dateString As String = DateTime.Now.ToString()
    Session.Add("Trace", "Session Started at: " & dateString)
End Sub
```

3. Once you've changed this code, go back to WebForm1.aspx and drag two Label controls onto the page, naming one lblApplication and the other lblSession. Double-click on the page to bring up the Page_Load() event handler again, and modify it as follows:

```
Private Sub Page_Load(ByVal sender As System.Object, _
                      ByVal e As System.EventArgs) Handles MyBase.Load
    ' Put user code to initialize the page here
    lblSession.Text = Session("Trace")
    lblApplication.Text = Application("Trace")
End Sub
```

4. Make sure that WebForm1.aspx is your startup page, and run the example. You will see something like the following:

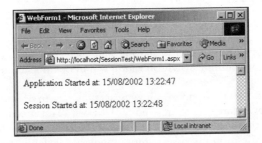

5. Once you've achieved these initial results, try closing your browser completely, opening it again, and re-accessing this web page. A new session should be created, and a new time for that session will be logged. However, when you take a look at the application time, you will find that it is still the same as the last time we accessed the page.

How It Works

These results should come as no surprise. First, the application was created just before the session, so the application time and the session time are slightly different. When we closed the browser, the session could no longer be used, so when we accessed the page again, a new session had to be created. The time for that session was set, and our web page showed us the new time accordingly. Our *application* time did not change, however, because the application didn't restart on the opening of a new browser window. It is only our session that is new, not the application.

There are some important things to note that we did not demonstrate in our application. First, the session that we left stranded on the server is still alive, even though we closed our browser. Of course, the server has no way of knowing that we closed our browser – it just continues to wait for another request with the same session ID. However, the server has a timeout period for sessions that can be configured within the Web.config file, under the same element where we configured cookie-less sessions – by default, it is 20 minutes. Each time a page is requested using the same session ID, the timer for that session is reset. If a page is not requested using the same session ID within the timeout period, the session is ended and the data for that session is lost.

227

One further piece of information that could be useful to know is that the application has *no* timeout period – it continues to run unless one of several circumstances occurs that causes the application to restart. Some of these are:

- ❑ Modifying the `Web.config` file
- ❑ Modifying the `Machine.config` file
- ❑ Modifying the `Global.asax` file
- ❑ Stopping and starting the web server
- ❑ A fatal error that causes the web server to crash

The first three items in this list are very important, since some anti-virus software can cause these files to be marked as having been modified when they are scanned. This can cause your application to restart continually, making application state useless.

Session State Modes

Now, storing data in a `Session` object on the server is all very well, but consider what happens in the case of a web farm, where there are several machines all serving the same content. Without some corrective action, the servers have no way of sharing state data with one another – each machine holds its own data, and the cost of real-time synchronization would be unbearable.

Microsoft has responded to this problem by allowing session data to be stored away from the web server process, through the use of a **state server**, or even SQL Server. This means that you can configure all of the servers in your web farm to use the same SQL server for their session data, thus allowing you to use the `Session` object that Microsoft provides without hindering scalability.

There is another benefit to using these out-of-process state servers: failover of session data is now handled automatically. When using a state server or SQL Server for session storage, web server crashes will not destroy our session data, and stopping the web service on purpose will not render all sessions dead – the remaining servers will just continue to pull the session data from the state server as normal.

If there are two out-of-process state server techniques that we can use, what makes one mode better than the other? For some, it is a purely economical decision: if you don't already have SQL Server, or you don't have the licenses to cover its use for this purpose, you will definitely want to use the state server that comes with the .NET Framework SDK. If you can afford it, SQL Server provides more stability and scalability than the state server.

Setting up a State Server

Having discussed the state server, let's look at how to configure it. We we'll try to be fairly brief here but if you need more information, you can find it at:

http://msdn.microsoft.com/library/en-us/dnaspnet/html/asp12282000.asp?frame=true

To get started, we must first prepare the environment we wish to use. Since there are two possible out-of-process types, we will cover them both here.

Preparing the Environment for State Server

If you wish to use Microsoft's state server, you must first start the ASP.NET State Service. This can be done at the Visual Studio .NET command prompt, which can be opened by going to Start | Programs | Microsoft Visual Studio .NET | Visual Studio .NET Tools | Visual Studio .NET Command Prompt. You will need to type in the following:

```
> net start aspnet_state
```

which will give you a screen like ths:

Configuring ASP.NET for State Server

Once we've prepared the state server, we need to tell ASP.NET to use it. To do that, we must manually edit the Web.config file. In our ongoing example, change the <sessionState> element so that it looks like the following:

```
<sessionState
        mode="StateServer"
        stateConnectionString="tcpip=127.0.0.1:42424"
        sqlConnectionString="data source=127.0.0.1;user id=sa;password="
        cookieless="false"
        timeout="20"
/>
```

You will notice that we have now set the mode attribute of the <sessionState> element to StateServer. This tells the application to use the state server instead of the normal in-process session module. The stateConnectionString attribute tells ASP.NET the location of the listening state server.

The question, "Can I change this to another server and another port?" may spring to mind, and the answer is that you can, although it is beyond the scope of this book to do so. For more information, please visit Microsoft's knowledge base and MSDN Library.

Preparing the Environment for SQL Server

If you would rather use SQL Server for your session data store, the process is a little more involved. First, we must prepare SQL Server to hold the data, and this means creating some tables and stored procedures. Thankfully, however, Microsoft has provided a script that does this for us. This file is named InstallSqlState.sql, and it can normally be found in your WINNT\Microsoft.NET\Framework\[version] folder. To run this script, you must type the following at a command prompt:

```
> osql -S [server name] -U [user] -P [password] < InstallSqlState.sql
```

Running this script will result in output something similar to the following:

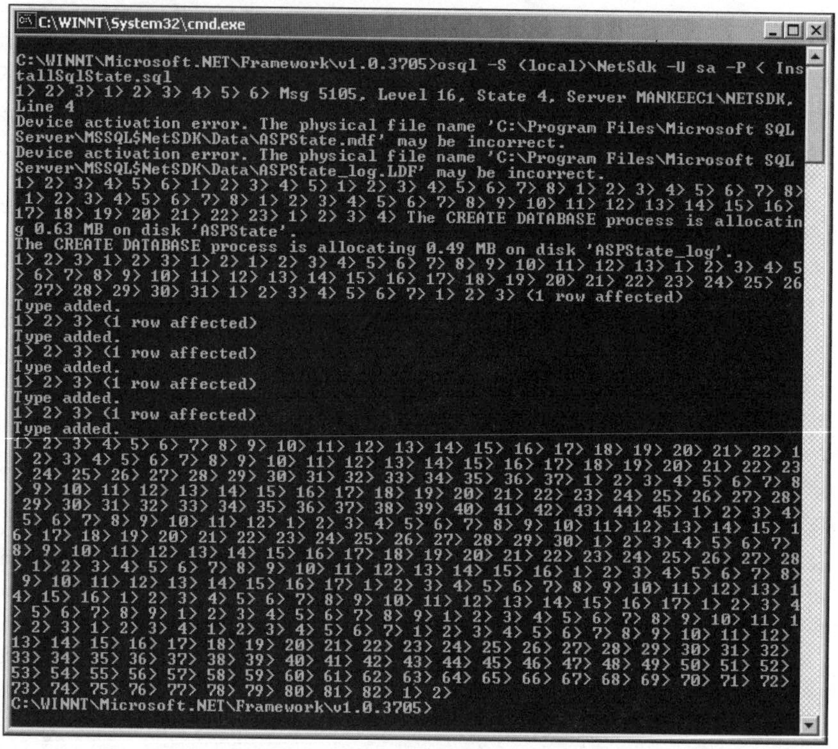

The above screenshot shows that we have successfully run the script against MSDE to create the appropriate tables and stored procedures.

Configuring ASP.NET for SQL Server

Once you have prepared SQL Server to handle the data we want to pass it, you need to tell ASP.NET to use SQL Server to handle data storage for our sessions. We do this in the same `Web.config` file that we used before, with a similar change to what you saw for the state server.

```
<sessionState
        mode="SQLServer"
        sqlConnectionString="data source=127.0.0.1;
                             user id=someUser;
                             password=somePass"
        cookieless="false"
        timeout="20"
/>
```

The main difference to note here is that we've changed the `mode` once more, this time to the obvious setting of `SQLServer`. Additionally, we have changed the `sqlConnectionString` attribute to a valid connection string that our ASP.NET application can reach – yours will obviously differ.

The connection string in our example connects to our local machine's default IP address, with `someUser` and `somePass` as our credentials. If you wish, you can connect to a remote SQL Server instead. Either way, we have successfully set up a highly scalable add-on to ASP.NET, and gained access to all the benefits, with very little work.

Using ViewState

So far, we've seen how to use session variables to keep track of user-specific state, and application variables to keep track of data applicable to *all* of our users. However, there is yet another way to keep track of state in our applications. As the title of this section suggests, that other method is called `ViewState`.

`ViewState` allows the data on the current page to be persisted when it is posted back to a server from a server-side web form. All of the properties and data on a page, as well as any controls that have `ViewState` enabled, may have their values retained by this technique. While the other methods of state management we have discussed so far have involved storing data in memory (or, in one case, SQL Server), `ViewState` is passed within the posted form data itself. Each time the page is posted back, all of the data in `ViewState` is parsed and reapplied to the controls before the page is rendered again.

The `ViewState` for all controls on the page is combined and stored in a hidden form field within the newly rendered form. This *only* happens for server-side web forms, and not for standard HTML forms or controls.

Try It Out – A Form Without ViewState

Let's take a quick look at the difference between a standard HTML form and a web form, and demonstrate how `ViewState` is retained.

1. In Visual Studio .NET, create a new ASP.NET project called `ViewState`. Add an HTML page to the project, and name it `HTMLForm.htm`. This done, go ahead and open the page up in design view.

2. In the **Properties** window for this page, change the `pageLayout` property to `FlowLayout`.

3. Click once inside the design view of the page so that it has focus. Then, choose **Insert** | **FORM**. You won't see any change right away, but if you switch to the HTML view, you should see that an empty set of opening and closing `<FORM>` tags has been added:

```
<!DOCTYPE HTML PUBLIC "-//W3C//DTD HTML 4.0 Transitional//EN">
<html>
  <head>
    <title>HTMLForm</title>
    <meta name="vs_defaultClientScript" content="JavaScript">
    <meta name="vs_targetSchema"
          content="http://schemas.microsoft.com/intellisense/ie5">
    <meta name="GENERATOR" content="Microsoft Visual Studio.NET 7.0">
    <meta name="ProgId" content="VisualStudio.HTML">
```

```
      <meta name="Originator" content="Microsoft Visual Studio.NET 7.0">
    </head>
    <body>
      <FORM>
         </FORM>
    </body>
  </html>
```

4. Clearly, this form isn't going to do much for us right now. We need to add some code to give it some structure. More specifically, we need to give the form a place to submit to, and some form elements to submit. Change this code to read as follows:

```
<body>
  <FORM action="HTMLForm.htm" method="get">
    <INPUT type="text" id="txtTest" name="txtTest">
    <INPUT type="submit" value="Submit" id="cmdSubmit" name="cmdSubmit">
  </FORM>
</body>
```

5. Save this page, and set it as the startup page. When you compile and run the project, you should see something similar to the following:

You will notice that nothing happens when you click the Submit button. Also, if you put some text in the textbox, it disappears after you submit the form – standard behavior if you're familiar with HTML forms. Finally, click in the browser's View menu, and choose Source. You'll find that – unsurprisingly – your code looks exactly like what you had in the HTML view in Visual Studio .NET.

Try It Out – A Form With ViewState

To understand ViewState, we need to look at the difference between this standard HTML form, and what goes on in an ASP.NET web form.

1. Open up WebForm1.aspx in HTML view, and you will see that not only has a set of <form> tags already been added, but also the form already has values set for the method and runat attributes: runat="server" tells ASP.NET that this is a server-side web form, and not just a plain HTML form.

2. Drag a TextBox and a Button onto the form's design surface from the Toolbox. Change the Text property of the Button to Submit. Compile and run this page, and everything should look the same.

3. Try placing a value in the textbox, and click the button again. You will notice that this time, the value persists. Moving to the source code that is returned to the browser, pay close attention to the line that looks similar to this one:

```
<input type="hidden" name="__VIEWSTATE"
    value="dDwxNDg5OTk5MzM7OZ6O0fNXn0wMF06Iuji83YCVBjhqhxw==" />
```

This line actually contains an encrypted string that holds the values of all the server-side objects on the page. Every time the form is submitted, this hidden field is submitted with it.

As well as storing the state of the controls, the values held in ViewState are used to help ASP.NET determine whether the value submitted is different from the value that was previously sent to the page. Each time the values change, the value string is changed and placed back into this hidden form field when the page is rendered again. Obviously, since the information you submit could be sensitive, it is important that this value is not in plain text form.

This is only a little of what can be achieved with ViewState. We said that ViewState is kept for each public property, form element, and data item that has ViewState enabled, but it is possible to disable it for any given element by selecting the item in design view and changing the EnableViewState property to false. When you submit the form, elements that have EnableViewState set to false will no longer persist their values.

ViewState and Variable Data

ViewState can also be used to store data that we want to persist from page to page, in much the same way that we do it with session and application variables. To store data that is unrelated to controls on the web form, the syntax is as follows:

```
ViewState(KeyName) = Value
```

So, let's say that you wanted to store a user's favorite background color. You might use the following code:

```
ViewState("FavoriteColor") = "red"
```

Of course, it wouldn't make sense to store data if you couldn't also retrieve it at some point. The syntax for retrieving information from ViewState storage is:

```
variable = CType(ViewState(KeyName), String)
```

We need to use CType() here to convert the stored value back to a string – even though we stored it as a string, the returned value will be of type Object, unless we perform an explicit conversion. To retrieve the user's favorite color, you would need to write something like this:

```
Dim favoriteColor as String
favoriteColor = CType(ViewState("FavoriteColor"), String)
```

In a real-world scenario, you might use `ViewState` to store a dataset, or an XML message string. The following code snippet extracts a dataset, and writes the results to an XML string that is then stored in a `ViewState` variable. When the page is posted back, it doesn't have to hit the database again. Instead, it grabs the value from `ViewState`, and reads the value using a `StringReader`:

```
Dim dsAllCustomers as DataSet

If Page.IsPostBack Then
  Dim dsCustomerString As String = CStr(ViewState("dsCustomers"))
  Dim stringReader As New System.IO.StringReader(dsCustomerString)
  dsAllCustomers.ReadXml(stringReader)
Else
  SqlDataAdapter.Fill(dsAllCustomers)
  Dim stringWriter As New System.IO.StringWriter()
  dsAllCustomers.WriteXml(stringWriter)
  ViewState("dsCustomers") = stringWriter.ToString()
End If
```

If we're using this in the same way as we would use a session variable, why don't we just use a session variable? The answer is that session data is stored on the server. If we want to store a large amount of data for each user, our session could potentially hog a lot of server memory. `ViewState` data, on the other hand, is stored in the user's browser. This has its advantages and disadvantages.

The main advantage we have already touched on: it conserves server resources. The disadvantage is that *all* the data we want to save must be streamed back to the user, and then posted back to the server, each time the user submits the page. This could increase your network traffic, and potentially take a larger amount of time to download your pages. While `ViewState` does give you one more option for state management, it also requires some important design decisions.

Which State Model Should You Use?

We have discussed three state models here: application, session, and `ViewState`. While reading this chapter, you may have already had the question in mind: "When should I use one state model over the other?" The question is legitimate, so let's find our answer.

As we stated before, application state is useful for storing information specific to our application, or for information that all users of our web application will need to access. For example, a communications application (secretly known as a chat site when the boss isn't around) might want to let you know who is logged in and who is not. To do that, it might use an application-scoped variable to store a dataset or an XML string of all the currently logged-in users. Each time a new user logs in, the dataset or XML string could be modified and updated. Since all of the users have access to the data in the application object, all of the users can see who is online. This would be an appropriate use of the application object.

Now, clearly, storing a list of who's online in a session variable would not work, because each user has their own session data. Simply updating a session variable when you logged in would not let others know that you were online. However, this is a good thing when we *want* to store information for each user that no one else has access to, and might be useful for code such as a shopping cart on an e-commerce site. Since each user has their own session anyway, we can use the session variable as our place to store the items a user has selected to purchase. As the user navigates from page to page, the data will be retained. We can change and modify it wherever we go throughout the site, and no one else can see what we have in our cart.

When making a decision about using session or application variables, we should ask:

❑   Does the data need to be seen by all users?

❑   Is the data exactly the same for all users of the site?

If you answered, "Yes," to both questions above, you will want to use an application variable. If you answered, "No," to either question, you should consider using a session variable instead.

Lastly, we talked about ViewState. While at first glance the ViewState looks like it could be easily interchangeable with session state, there are some major reasons to use one over the other. We have already said that ViewState is really stored in the client browser. This means that our server does not have to hold this data in memory, but it also means that our bandwidth has to cope with this additional data. Also, ViewState does not persist from page to page. If the user does not persist ViewState in some other mechanism before going to another page, the data will be lost.

When making a decision regarding ViewState versus session state, we should ask ourselves:

❑   Will my data need to be used again on the next page?

❑   Does my server have enough memory to hold this data for every user that hits this page?

If you answered, "Yes," to these questions, you will want to use session state. If you answered, "No," your data is a good candidate for ViewState.

Summary

In this chapter, we have covered an assortment of topics dealing with how to keep track of state within your web applications. More specifically, we have covered application state, session state, and ViewState. Each of these state mechanisms has its own set of advantages and disadvantages. Each also has its own appropriate and inappropriate uses.

Data that is used to keep track of the application, or data common to all users, would normally be stored in application state. Remember, however, that you should limit the amount of information you store here: the more you store, the more resources your server requires. If your data starts to look like a database table, you might consider storing this data in a database instead of the application. Ultimately, information that is small but consistently needed by your application would be a good candidate for application state.

We also discussed session variables in this chapter. Session variables are often a good place to store data that is constantly accessed and varies from one user to another. Session variables are uniquely identified by a session ID that can be stored on the user's machine as a cookie, or passed from one page to the next in the query string. Session variables should be used with caution: consider that each variable is stored once for each user. The more users your application has, the more impact a single session variable can have on the resources on your system.

ViewState was the final type of state management that we discussed in this chapter. ViewState is mostly used to track changes to controls on a web form that is posted back to itself, but it can also store pieces of information that we want to keep from one 'post' operation to the next. This second use of ViewState can be used instead of a session variable when you simply want to hold on to a variable for a form submission, instead of for the life of the user's session. The disadvantage is that using ViewState will increase your need for network resources, because the data in this state mechanism is passed back and forth in the HTTP request and response.

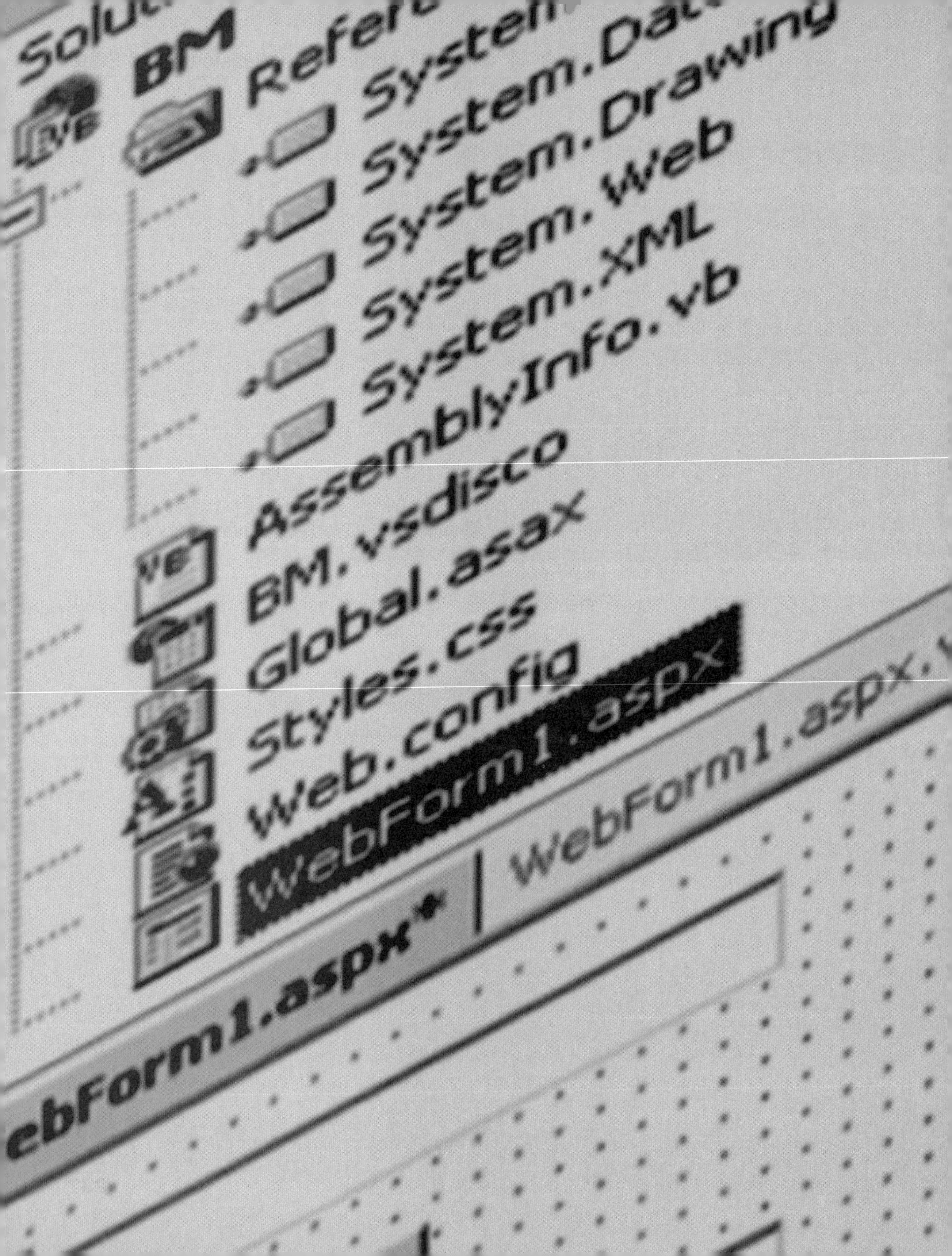

Solut...

BM

Refere...

System...

System.Dat...

System.Drawing

System.Web

System.XML

AssemblyInfo.vb

Assembly

BM.vsdisco

Global.asax

Styles.css

Web.config

WebForm1.aspx

WebForm1.aspx.v

ebForm1.aspx*   WebForm1.aspx

XML and Web Development

XML is becoming increasingly important, as widespread Internet connectivity becomes the norm. Applications running on separate machines can now work in tandem on related tasks, and implicit in that ability is a requirement for a universally understood and standard format for the exchange of information. XML was devised largely in answer to this need.

In order to introduce XML, and the .NET Framework's facilities for working with it, we're going to turn once again to our Friends Reunion web application. That project has already helped us to understand a number of major web development issues, but now we're going to start thinking about integration with external applications and partner sites – a situation in which XML can be very useful.

In this chapter, then, we will enhance our Friends Reunion application so that it can upload complete lists of users and attendees in XML format, so that large groups won't have to laboriously upload one attendee at a time. (It might be possible to export such a list directly from an existing database, as many are now able to output data in XML form.) In addition, we will examine how to read and validate the incoming XML, and how to query the document to generate statistics and reports. Also, we'll do some groundwork for the next chapter's coverage of web services, which rely heavily on XML and related specifications.

A Peek into XML

At first sight, XML is just a text-based format for the transfer or storage of data. A typical fragment of XML is:

```
<anElement anAttribute="attribute value">
  Text child
  <aChildElement>
    <aGrandChildElement />
  </aChildElement>
</anElement>
```

It is an element-based format in which the elements can be nested, forming parent-child relationships. In this respect, it is similar to HTML. Elements can contain attributes with values, text content, or other elements. XML is case sensitive, and all elements must be properly closed.

It looks pretty simple, so what's all the hype about?

The significance of XML is due to the fact that it is a standard developed by the independent W3C organization. This means that XML documents obey the same rules, regardless of platform or software vendor. Applications running on any operating system and in any programming language will produce XML in exactly the same format, and equally, are able to read XML documents irrespective of their origin. The home page for all W3C XML specs and work in progress can be found at http://www.w3.org/XML.

Part of the requirement when the W3C was developing XML was to make a format that is easily read by humans as well as machines, and it has succeeded in this aim. Consequently, XML documents are easy to author, and this is one of the reasons why XML has made so many inroads into so many areas of computing.

The Rise and Rise of XML

Since the release of version 1.0 in 1998, XML has permeated into many diverse areas of computing. The following section is not a comprehensive list of its uses, but rather is intended to illustrate the usefulness of XML, and how a good grounding in this important technology will help us in many areas.

- ❏ XML is a cornerstone of the .NET web applications model:

    - ❏ Web forms – The data contained by web controls on a page is represented by XML fragments inside HTML, and can be seen when the page is opened in HTML view. This information is used by the controls to render themselves appropriately.

    - ❏ Web services – As we'll see in the next chapter, web services are generally invoked using an XML-based language called SOAP, which is also used for returning results.

    - ❏ Configuration files – We have already seen how ASP.NET uses the `Web.config` XML file to contain settings information for web applications, and such XML files are used throughout the .NET Framework. XML's hierarchical and readable format makes it easy to locate and change configuration details.

- ❏ XML in data access provides a very suitable standard way of swapping data between applications and databases. Its inherently hierarchical nature lends itself very well to representing the structure of the data, and relations between the data:

    - ❏ Interoperability – As XML is platform- and language-neutral, it is ideal for moving data between disparate database products and operating systems.

    - ❏ ADO.NET support – The `DataSet` object, which we studied in Chapter 4, has extensive support for XML, including the ability to read and save files and streams in this format through its `ReadXml()` and `WriteXml()` methods.

    - ❏ Support from major database vendors – Most vendors now build some degree of XML support into their products. Typically, query results can be returned in XML format, and many can also natively read and process XML files or strings inside stored procedures, using functions or types added to their respective languages. For example, SQL Server, Oracle, and IBM's DB2 all offer native XML support.

- ❏ XML in e-business:

As a platform-neutral standard, XML is the perfect candidate for data representation in e-business, where business partners need their systems and applications to interact and communicate, and where systems range from the latest super-sleek setups to ancient monoliths from the time of the pharaohs. In the past, the standard for business communication was EDI (Electronic Data Interchange), which was very difficult and costly to implement. XML, in conjunction with the Internet, makes it much easier for smaller companies to implement e-commerce solutions.

Well-Formed XML

Although XML is simple to grasp, there are a number of rules that a file must satisfy in order to be useful XML – such files are said to be **well formed**. A well-formed XML document is one that conforms to the requirements of the W3C specification. The key rules are simple:

- ❑ Elements must have start and end tags, where the end tag is differentiated from the start tag by a leading / character, like this:

  ```
  <anElement>Some content</anElement>
  ```

  In the case of an element with no content, an abbreviation is possible, as you saw in the example at the start of the chapter:

  ```
  <anElement></anElement> or <anElement />
  ```

- ❑ Element names are case sensitive, so end tags must *exactly* match the start tag they belong to.

- ❑ Start tags can specify attributes for the element, where the attribute value must be enclosed in quotes (single or double).

- ❑ Elements can't overlap – that is, elements must be closed in the reverse of the order in which they were opened:

  ```
  <firstElement><secondElement></secondElement></firstElement>
  ```

- ❑ There must be one, and only one, top-level element that encloses all other elements in the document.

A XML document that meets these requirements is considered to be well formed, and can be read and used by applications that support XML. However, a document that *isn't* well formed is useless: it will generate an exception in the application that tries to read it.

How can we *guarantee* that an exception will be generated? Well, when the W3C defined the XML standard, it also specified how a 'conformant' implementation must behave in order to be considered as such. Microsoft provides this conformant implementation with the classes in the System.Xml namespace, Sun does something similar for Java programmers, and equivalent mechanisms are in place in many other programming languages.

XML Applied

So, to return to our Friends Reunion application, we will incorporate a feature whereby third parties can upload lists containing details of several people at once, in the form of an XML file. Suppose, for example, that an institution wants to upload information about its students to our web application – or maybe a social group like an old classmates society or some other club would like to add its members to our site. The webmaster, or their chosen web minion, would not be happy if we required them to add details of each user manually. A better idea would be to allow them to upload the list as an XML file.

When the XML file is received by our application, we will extract the data from it and use it to populate the `TimeLapse` and `User` tables. Let's review the structure of those tables:

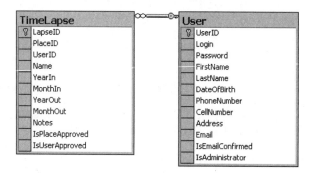

During this chapter, we will focus on the XML side of the process – we covered the issue of updating databases in Chapter 4.

`TimeLapse` describes how long a given user spent at a particular place, while `User` holds general information relating to particular users. Our XML file will contain `<User>` elements and `<Attendee>` elements, which directly map to `User` and `TimeLapse` records respectively. All of these elements will be contained by a single element, which will be called `<Friends>`. A typical document will therefore contain elements like these:

```
<?xml version="1.0" encoding="utf-8"?>
<Friends PlaceID="C9796AD1-5A7E-4d9c-9F99-0090E11E5662">
  <User>
    <UserID>E81A8BCD-47A3-4038-9F7B-2DF25C741833</UserID>
    <Login>jbrown</Login>


    ...


  </User>

  ...

  <Attendee Name="High School Complete">
    <UserID>E81A8BCD-47A3-4038-9F7B-2DF25C741833</UserID>
    <YearIn>1972</YearIn>
    <YearOut>1977</YearOut>
```

```
    ...

   </Attendee>

   ...

  </Friends>
```

This document could be created using a text editor such as Notepad, or a specialist XML editor like the one included with Visual Studio .NET. Alternatively, it could be generated by program that extracts the information from the organization's database and places into a file of this format.

Notice that there isn't a one-to-one mapping between the elements of the document and the fields in the database tables. Instead, we've tried to give the XML document a more intuitive layout, allowing us to demonstrate the full functionality of .NET's XML objects, which you'll see later on. For instance, the PlaceID field of the TimeLapse table is represented by an attribute on the root <Friends> element. The idea here is that one of these XML files will always be uploaded by a single organization, so this avoids repetition.

Valid XML

In Chapter 3, we looked at how to *validate* the fields on an ASP.NET page. Any production application must always validate every piece of data that is to be entered into a database. In the XML world, when a file is read, it is said to be **parsed**, a process that involves ensuring that the XML is well-formed. However, XML well-formedness alone doesn't guarantee that the elements required for our particular format will be present, nor that elements contain appropriate data. What we need is a **valid** XML file.

Here, the W3C again comes to the rescue, having devised a way to define the structure and the nature of the elements in an XML file, in the form of the **XML Schema Definition**, or **XSD**. An XML file that satisfies a given XML Schema is said to be **valid**. By taking the time to define a schema for our XML documents, not only do we avoid coding validation routines ourselves, but also we allow our partners to avoid that too. We simply pass them the schema that we expect files to conform to, and they use it in whichever language and platform they happen to work with.

Just as with XML, the XSD specification defines not only the structure of the file, but also how conformant implementations must behave. Microsoft provides its .NET implementation in the form of the classes in the System.Xml.Schema namespace. We will use these classes to enforce constraints on the uploaded file – to ensure that required elements are present, that the general document structure is correct, and so on. As we'll see in a moment, the .NET Framework classes will allow us to perform the validation with very few lines of code.

Before we move on to learn more about XSD and see what a schema to validate our XML documents might look like, we need to understand the sister specification of XML Namespaces.

XML Namespaces

XML namespaces are similar in principle to .NET namespaces: they provide a way to group together elements that belong to a particular context under an identifying name. In XML, the name of a namespace is just a string, but it must be a *unique* string – it would be no good if two namespaces had the same name. The recommendation is that URIs (that is, URLs or URNs) should be used to identify namespaces, because URIs must, by their nature, be unique. When companies create schemas for the data they deal with, they can place those schemas inside namespaces that are named after their own URLs. By doing so, they not only satisfy the uniqueness condition, but also identify those schemas as belonging to them.

> *When we create an XML document with the intention of validating it against a schema, the namespace of the XML elements in that document must match the namespace of the schema itself. This is necessary to indicate that the elements are defined by that particular schema, rather than by a different schema (or indeed no schema at all). We will get back to this when we return to find out more about XSD.*

We specify that an element belongs to a particular namespace by using the xmlns attribute on that element. For example, to associate a whole XML document with a namespace, we would add the xmlns attribute to the root element:

```
<?xml version="1.0" encoding="utf-8"?>
<Friends xmlns="urn:wrox-friends"
         PlaceID="C9796AD1-5A7E-4d9c-9F99-0090E11E5662">
  <User>

  . . .
```

When a namespace is added to an element, all of the latter's child elements inherit it, unless we explicitly specify another namespace for them. If we need to, we can associate a prefix with one or more of the namespaces defined for a document:

```
<?xml version="1.0" encoding="utf-8"?>
<wf:Friends xmlns:wf="urn:wrox-friends"
            PlaceID="C9796AD1-5A7E-4d9c-9F99-0090E11E5662">
  <User>

  . . .
```

This is particularly useful if we wish to use more than one namespace in a single document. If we specify a prefix for a namespace, then in order for an element to be included in that namespace, we have to precede that element's name with the prefix, as for the `<Friends>` element above. A namespace without a prefix is called the **default namespace**, and if one is defined, every element in the document without a prefix is considered to be included in that namespace.

XML Schema Definition

XSD files are in fact XML files themselves. They consist of XML elements and attributes that describe rules that XML documents must satisfy in order to be considered valid against that schema. Just as a valid XML file conforms to a defined schema, XSD schemas must themselves conform to the W3C schema that defines valid schemas!

The elements and attributes that are allowed in a valid schema are defined by a W3C Recommendation, and they belong to the `http://www.w3.org/2001/XMLSchema` namespace. Don't forget that although this has the same form as a URL, it is not a hyperlink, and there is no requirement for it to be a valid address. It simply has to be unique, to indicate unambiguously that elements that belong to it form part of an XSD definition.

Try It Out – Creating a New XML Schema

Now that we've covered the basics, the best way to get a grip on what a schema looks like is to have a go at building the schema that defines our chosen XML format. Again, there's nothing stopping us using Notepad to create a schema manually, but Visual Studio .NET has a great tool that makes the job much less painful.

1. We'll use the Friends Reunion application from the end of Chapter 5 as a starting point. Open the project, right-click on the project name in the Solution Explorer, and select Add | Add New Item. Choose the XML Schema template from the Data category, name the new file `Friends.xsd`, and click Open:

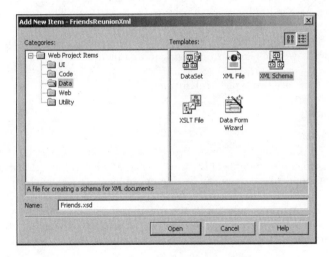

When the empty schema has been created, you'll be presented with a blank design surface onto which you can drag various items from the Toolbox in order to create your schema. This is the **XML Designer**.

2. Open the Properties window, which will be showing the options available for the root element of an XML schema, `<xs:schema>`. These options represent the attributes that may be set on this element, and will therefore apply to the schema as a whole.

Locate the `targetNamespace` property and set it to `urn:wrox-friends`. The default namespace provided by Visual Studio .NET (`http://tempuri.org`) should always be changed to your own unique name, especially when you're planning to hand the schema to third parties. This avoids conflicts that may appear if there are multiple schemas that use the same namespace and define elements with the same names.

How It Works

Just like the Visual Studio .NET form designer, the XML designer is a visual tool that generates code behind the scenes that corresponds to the drag-and-drop actions we perform. You can see the code it produces by clicking the XML button at the bottom left corner of the designer:

If you do this now, you'll see that our schema currently consists of a single, empty `<xs:schema>` element (below, which has been formatted for legibility):

```
<?xml version="1.0" encoding="utf-8" ?>
<xs:schema id="Friends" targetNamespace="urn:wrox-friends"
           elementFormDefault="qualified" xmlns="urn:wrox-friends"
           xmlns:mstns="urn:wrox-friends"
           xmlns:xs="http://www.w3.org/2001/XMLSchema">
</xs:schema>
```

You can see that it's just a regular XML file, right down to the `<?xml ?>` declaration at the start. Notice in particular how there are multiple `xmlns` attributes in the start tag. The default namespace – that is, the one defined by the `xmlns` attribute that doesn't contain a colon – is set to the value that we just set for the `targetNamespace` attribute. The effect is that any element appearing inside the schema element without a prefix will be taken as belonging to that namespace.

In an XML schema, there are two types of elements:

❑   Global elements

❑   Local elements

Elements defined as direct descendants of the top `<schema>` element are global. All other elements are local. Global elements, unlike local ones, can be referenced by other elements anywhere in the document.

The `elementFormDefault` attribute affects the way global elements are referenced, requiring use of the namespace prefix along with the element name. It can also have the value `unqualified`, which is the default if this attribute isn't specified.

> **By convention, we refer to a file conforming to a schema as an instance document of that schema. Similarly, an instance of a type in the schema is an occurrence of the corresponding element in an instance document.**

Try It Out – Adding an Element

Now that we have an empty schema, we can start to build it up by adding the definition for the root `<Friends>` element.

1. Switch back to the Schema view of the file using the button at the corner of the designer.

2. Open the Toolbox, which now offers just one tab, called XML Schema, which contains all the items used when designing a schema:

Double-click on element to drop one onto the design surface.

3. Change the new element's name from the default element1 to Friends, either through the Properties window or by clicking inside the element in the designer:

4. Drag an attribute from the Toolbox, and drop it onto the Friends element. Change its name to PlaceID, and check that string is selected in the right-hand column:

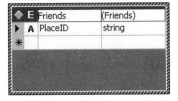

How It Works

The element we have added corresponds to the root <Friends> element of the XML format we are going to use for uploads:

```
<?xml version="1.0" encoding="utf-8"?>
<Friends xmlns="urn:wrox-friends"
         PlaceID="C9796AD1-5A7E-4d9c-9F99-0090E11E5662">

  . . .

</Friends>
```

Our schema now specifies that it must have the name Friends, and that it must have a string attribute called PlaceID. If we switch again to the XML view, we can check out the schema markup that Visual Studio .NET has generated, based on what we added in the designer:

```
<?xml version="1.0" encoding="utf-8" ?>
<xs:schema id="Friends" targetNamespace="urn:wrox-friends"
           elementFormDefault="qualified" xmlns="urn:wrox-friends"
           xmlns:mstns="urn:wrox-friends"
           xmlns:xs="http://www.w3.org/2001/XMLSchema">
  <xs:element name="Friends">
    <xs:complexType>
      <xs:sequence />
      <xs:attribute name="PlaceID" type="xs:string" />
    </xs:complexType>
  </xs:element>
</xs:schema>
```

Note that all of the new elements use the xs prefix, which is associated with the XML schema namespace. This marks these elements as XML schema elements, and they must therefore obey the rules of validity for XML schemas. That is, elements must follow the required order, and have valid values and attributes, such as the type attribute on the <xs:attribute> element.

Any XML file must have one and only one root element, and the first element within the <xs:schema> element is always an <xs:element> that describes the root element of documents that conform to this schema. The name attribute of this element defines the name that the root element must have, so here it is <Friends>.

Within any <xs:element> are further xs elements that describe the content allowed for that element in XML documents matching the schema. The first child element must always be one of the two described below:

❑ <xs:simpleType> – either a custom type, or an XSD type such as string, Boolean, or integer (the complete list is displayed in the drop-down combo box we saw above, when we made PlaceID a string type). Custom simpleTypes are modifications of the basic XSD types that will (for example) restrict numbers to a given range of values, or specify maximum and minimum lengths for string-based types. simpleType elements cannot contain attributes or child elements.

❑　　<xs:complexType> – for elements that may contain attributes, other elements, or other content. Defining a complex type is a bit like defining a new class in a project, in that we define the structure that an 'instance' of it will have in a data file. The schema that has been produced so far specifies that the <Friends> element may have an attribute called PlaceID, and this attribute's value is of type xs:string.

Definition of a Complex Type

The most useful elements that can appear in an <xs:complexType> element are <xs:sequence>, <xs:choice>, and <xs:attribute>. We've already seen <xs:attribute> in action, and the only thing to add is that its type *must* be one of the XSD simple types, because XML attributes can't contain other elements.

The <xs:sequence> element defines the elements that *must* appear in instances of the type, each defined by an <xs:element> element. Multiple instances of each element are allowed, but they *must* appear in the order given in the schema. If a document contains elements in the wrong order, it is said to be an **invalid** instance of the schema.

The <xs:choice> element, on the other hand, defines a set of elements that *may* appear in instances of the type. By default, however, only one member of the set can be present in an XML instance document. There's a third xs element for describing groups of allowed elements in an instance document: <xs:all>. This describes a set of elements that can appear in any order.

The plan that we've devised has <User> and <Attendee> elements inside the root <Friends> element. This arrangement would best be represented by <xs:sequence>, as we expect the elements to appear in a specific order, and there can be multiple instances of each element.

Try It Out – Defining the <User> Element

Let's build on the schema that we've created so far, and start to define the <User> element. This will involve two steps: first, we have to specify that we want it to be a child of the <Friends> element; second, we have to say what we want it to contain.

1. If necessary, switch to the visual designer, by pressing the **Schema** button. You may find it helpful to switch to **XML** view after each step, and see the code that has been generated – we'll explain what it all means later on.

2. Drag an **element** from the **Toolbox**, and drop it onto the **Friends** element that we added earlier, to indicate that the new element is a child of <Friends>. This relationship is shown in the designer by a solid line from the **Friends** element to the new element:

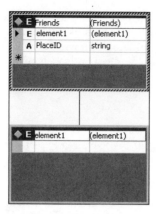

Note that the new element is represented not only by the new graphic below Friends, but also by a new row in the Friends element, currently with the default name of element1.

3. Set the name to User, by typing either in the new element, or in the new row of the Friends element.

4. Drag another element from the Toolbox, this time placing it on the new empty element that we have just added. Set its name to UserID.

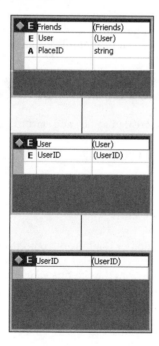

5. Using the dropdown in the right-hand column, set the type of the UserID element to string. As simple types, string elements can't contain any attributes or child content, and so the third box, representing the UserID element, disappears from the designer:

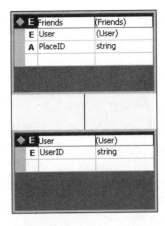

How It Works

When we add the `<User>` element in Steps 2 and 3, the code generated consists of a complex typed element with an empty `<xs:sequence>` inside it, pretty much like the code created for the `<Friends>` element:

```
<?xml version="1.0" encoding="utf-8" ?>
<xs:schema id="friends" targetNamespace="urn:wrox-friends" ... >
  <xs:element name="Friends">
    <xs:complexType>
      <xs:sequence>
        <xs:element name="User">
          <xs:complexType>
            <xs:sequence />
          </xs:complexType>
        </xs:element>
      </xs:sequence>
      <xs:attribute name="PlaceID" type="xs:string" />
    </xs:complexType>
  </xs:element>
</xs:schema>
```

The new code has been placed inside what was the empty `<xs:sequence>` child element of `<Friends>`, as the new `<User>` element will be a direct child of the root element in instance documents. A similar process takes place when we first add the `<UserID>` element in Step 4. Visual Studio .NET represents it by default as a complex type, with an empty `<xs:sequence>` element:

```
<?xml version="1.0" encoding="utf-8" ?>
<xs:schema id="friends" targetNamespace="urn:wrox-friends" ... >
  <xs:element name="Friends">
    <xs:complexType>
      <xs:sequence>
        <xs:element name="User">
          <xs:complexType>
            <xs:sequence>
```

```
            <xs:element name="UserID">

    ...

</xs:schema>
```

Once we set the type to **string** in the designer in Step 5, the code is reduced to:

```xml
<?xml version="1.0" encoding="utf-8" ?>
<xs:schema id="friends" targetNamespace="urn:wrox-friends" ... >
  <xs:element name="Friends">
    <xs:complexType>
      <xs:sequence>
        <xs:element name="User">
          <xs:complexType>
            <xs:sequence>
              <xs:element name="UserID" type="xs:string"></xs:element>
            </xs:sequence>
          </xs:complexType>
        </xs:element>
      </xs:sequence>
      <xs:attribute name="PlaceID" type="xs:string" />
    </xs:complexType>
  </xs:element>
</xs:schema>
```

This occurs because the string type is a simple type. Such elements can't contain child elements, so they don't require the extra information that the `<xs:complexType>` element specifies. Nor, therefore, is there any need to draw it as a separate element on the design surface.

Now go ahead and repeat Steps 4 to 6 to define the remaining child elements of `<User>`, one for each field in the corresponding database table, in the order and of the type given below:

E	User	(User)
E	UserID	string
E	Login	string
E	Password	string
E	FirstName	string
E	LastName	string
E	DateOfBirth	date
E	PhoneNumber	string
E	CellNumber	string
E	Address	string
E	Email	string

If you've ever used graphical database design tools such as those included with Visual Studio .NET, you may recognize the layout of schema elements on the designer, as they appear pretty much like a database table, with a row for each child element.

Try It Out – Adding an Element Directly

As well as adding new child elements by dragging and dropping from the Toolbox, we can type directly into the table to create new child elements. Let's see this in action as we create the definition of the <Attendee> element.

1. Click on the empty row at the bottom of the graphic representing the Friends element, and type in Attendee:

2. Change the default string type of Attendee to Unnamed complexType, which appears right at the top of the list. This step creates a new empty element below the Friends element, alongside the existing User element. This is where content of the Attendee element can be described.

3. Type a new element name of UserID into the Attendee element, and leave the type as string.

4. Add another row, with the name YearIn, and set its type to integer.

5. Add three more rows of type integer, with the names MonthIn, YearOut, and MonthOut.

6. Now add a final element, called Notes, which is a string.

7. We also want to specify that the <Attendee> element will have a Name attribute. Add a new row called Name, and then click the capital E that appears in the left-most column to open a drop-down list. Select attribute:

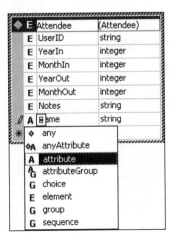

8. This is how the Attendee element should now appear in the designer:

♦	E	Attendee	(Attendee)
	E	UserID	string
	E	YearIn	integer
	E	MonthIn	integer
	E	YearOut	integer
	E	MonthOut	integer
	E	Notes	string
▶	A	Name	string
✳			

How It Works

When we create a new element by typing directly into the designer, the behavior is opposite to that of the drag-and-drop approach, where new elements are complex types by default. This time, new elements are simple types by default – namely, the string type.

> *If you're curious about the various types, what they mean, the range of valid values, and so on, take a look at the* XML Schema Part 2: Datatypes *document (www.w3.org/TR/2001/REC-xmlschema-2-20010502).*

This behavior is why we have to change the type of the <Attendee> element to Unnamed complexType. When we do this in Step 2, Visual Studio .NET produces exactly the same <complexType> definition as it generated when we were dragging and dropping from the Toolbox:

```xml
<?xml version="1.0" encoding="utf-8" ?>
<xs:schema id="friends" targetNamespace="urn:wrox-friends" ...>
  <xs:element name="Friends">
    <xs:complexType>
      <xs:sequence>
        <xs:element name="User">

          ...

        </xs:element>
        <xs:element name="Attendee">
          <xs:complexType>
            <xs:sequence />
          </xs:complexType>
        </xs:element>
      </xs:sequence>
      <xs:attribute name="PlaceID" type="xs:string" />
    </xs:complexType>
  </xs:element>
</xs:schema>
```

For the *child* elements of <Attendee> though, the default behavior is exactly what we want, as they are simple types, and mostly of the default string type too. The other default when adding new rows to an element is that the new item is itself an element. In the last step, we had to change that to attribute using the drop-down list.

Definition of a Simple Type

Usually, databases place restrictions on the allowed values for given fields. For example, the SQL Server type called `varchar` is a string with a certain maximum length, as set by the database designer. XSD schemas also let us define such restrictions, by defining **custom simple types** that modify intrinsic XSD types according to our needs. In fact, they derive a new type from a base type – once we've selected the base type, we specify the limitations we require.

Try It Out – Defining a Custom Simple Type

A suitable use of a custom simple type in our case is to restrict valid IDs to strings of exactly 36 characters, so let's see how to go about arranging that.

1. From the Toolbox, drop a new simpleType element onto a blank area of the design surface, and give it the name it KeyDef. Note that by default, the new type derives from the string type, as shown in the right-hand column on the top line.

2. On the blank row below the name and type, click on the first column of the row and turn it into a facet, indicated by the capital F. You can now open the drop-down list for the second column and select length. Tab to the next column, and enter 36:

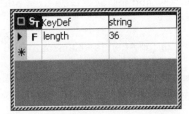

3. Then, set all of the "ID" items in our schema to the newly created simple type – specifically, the two <UserID> elements (one inside the <User> element, and the other inside <Attendee>), and the PlaceID attribute of the <Friends> element.

How It Works

Visual Studio .NET offers a variety of restrictions, which it calls **facets**, on XSD base types depending on the base type in question, and most are self-explanatory. For the KeyDef type, you may have noticed that there were options for maxLength as well as length.

> *For a complete list of base types and available facets, see the* W3C XML Schema Part 0: Primer *document at www.w3.org/TR/xmlschema-0.*

As the new type is defined as a top-level element (that is, an immediate child of the root <xs:schema> element), it is a **global type**, and is available to all other elements in the document. A global type must have a name so that other elements can reference it; it is therefore also a **named type**. It's also possible to define global *complex* types, which we can then reuse in several places in a schema, just as we did with the ID definition. Incidentally, this explains why an element such as <Attendee>, which is local to the <Friends> element, is described as an *unnamed* complex type.

Restricting Element Occurrence

By default, each element defined by a schema must appear once (and only once) in the instance document. Clearly, this is not appropriate for all cases, and in our example we want to allow multiple <Attendee> and <User> elements.

On the other hand, some of the fields in our database are optional, and they won't always have values. For instance, the MonthIn and MonthOut fields of the TimeLapse table can be null.

We can cater for requirements like these through the minOccurs and maxOccurs attributes of XSD elements.

Try It Out – Setting Minimum and Maximum Occurrences

We'll use this example to set up the rules we just described: we'll allow multiple instances of the <User> and <Attendee> elements, force the presence of the PlaceID attribute, and change the settings of a few other attributes too.

1. Select the User element in the second row of the Friends graphic in the designer.

2. Open the Properties window, and set the maxOccurs property to unbounded, and minOccurs to 0.

3. Set maxOccurs property for the Attendee element to unbounded too, and minOccurs to 0.

4. Select the PlaceID attribute, and set its use property to required, meaning that this attribute *must* be set on the <Friends> element of instance documents.

How It Works

Notice that the <Friends> element itself doesn't have minOccurs and maxOccurs properties available. This is because, as the root element, one and only one occurrence must *always* be present in any instance document, by definition.

Setting maxOccurs to unbounded means that any number of that element may be found in instance documents (as long as at least as many as specified by minOccurs are present, of course). Setting minOccurs to zero makes an element optional. We want this for the <User> element, because this could be the case should an institution not have any new users to add, but just be adding existing users as attendees of new courses.

In XML, *attributes* can either appear once or not at all. Accordingly, Visual Studio .NET gives us the choice of setting them as optional, prohibited, or required, where the first of these is the default. We want to set this property to required for the PlaceID attribute, as that must be present for us to be able to make sense of, and process, an XML file that we receive.

To complete the schema design, repeat the previous steps, setting `minOccurs` to zero for the `<User>` element's `<DateOfBirth>` and `<CellNumber>` children, and for the `<Attendee>` element's `<MonthIn>`, `<MonthOut>`, and `<Notes>` children, to reflect the database design. We can leave `MaxOccurs` at the default setting. Once this is done, save the file using *Ctrl-S*.

We have finished our schema! Maybe this seems like a lot of work before we get to write a single line of code, but we'll soon see the great benefits that this preparatory endeavor can bring. This is how our finished schema looks to the designer:

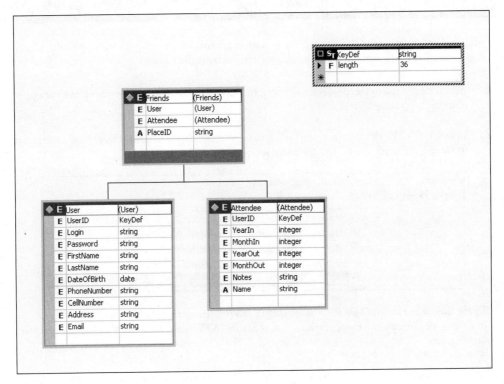

If we now switch to XML view, Visual Studio .NET lets us validate the schema to double-check that we haven't made a mistake, such as setting a invalid type for an element or attribute, or introducing an error when modifying the file manually. Select Validate Schema from the Schema menu, and any invalid content in the schema will be underlined and added to the Task List.

XML and schemas constitute an advanced topic, and there are many aspects that we have left untouched. For more in-depth information, try the following books published by Wrox Press:

- *Beginning XML, 2nd Edition* (ISBN 1-86100-559-8)

- *Professional XML for .NET Developers* (ISBN 1-86100-531-8)

- *Professional XML Schemas* (ISBN 1-86100-547-4)

Creating XML Documents Visually

With our XSD document complete, we can start to build some valid XML documents, and once again the Visual Studio .NET IDE has some very useful features to ease this process. These features are useful not only for creating small test files, but also for working with XML configuration files in custom applications, for example.

Try It Out – Creating a Valid XML Document

First off, we need a sample instance document that conforms to the schema we just built, which we can then use to test the XML upload functionality of our web application.

1. Add a new item to the project, selecting the **XML File** template from the **Data** category, and naming it `upload.xml`.

2. Below the XML declaration, start off a new `<Friends>` element. Give it an `xmlns` attribute, to set the `urn:wrox-friends` namespace as the default:

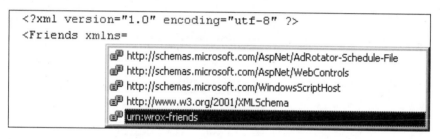

By the way, when an attribute value is selected in IntelliSense as shown above, a neat trick is to just type a double-quote character to have Visual Studio .NET insert the selected value, and wrap it inside quotes.

3. Type a right-hand angled bracket (>) to mark the end of the tag, and the closing `</Friends>` tag will automatically appear after the cursor.

4. Staying between the start and end tags, hit *Enter*, and type a left-hand angled bracket. Select **User** from the drop-down list that appears, and type the end bracket

5. Inside the `<User>` element, add the desired child elements. Start with `<UserID>`, but don't type anything for the new ID value – for that, we can use the GUID (Globally Unique Identifier) generator built into Visual Studio .NET.

6. Select **Create GUID** from the **Tools** menu. Check option 4. **Registry Format** from the dialog that appears. Click the **Copy** button, and paste the result into the XML document:

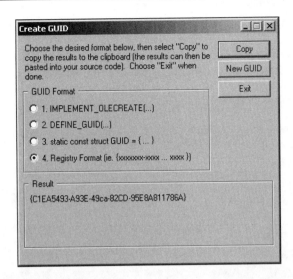

Remember to delete the surrounding braces that are automatically added. There is no need to exit the **Create GUID** dialog, and it can be left open in the background until it's needed again. Just remember to click **New GUID** each time you need a new ID.

7. Now go ahead and add the remaining child elements for <User>. Recall that DateOfBirth and CellNumber are optional elements, as we defined them with minOccurs=0.

How It Works

As soon as we type the xmlns attribute, IntelliSense starts to do its magic. Firstly, we are offered a list of available namespaces for the project, including the urn:wrox-friends namespace used by our schema. The other namespaces are added by the Visual Studio .NET IDE.

Once the namespace is specified, IntelliSense uses that schema to make suggestions as we type. Visual Studio .NET provides a list of valid elements according to the schema, and this list is context-sensitive – so we only see <Attendee> and <User> elements when we're inside <Friends>. Note, however, that the list is ordered alphabetically, which doesn't necessarily reflect the actual schema constraints, where the order of elements can be important. For instance, <Attendee> and <User> elements are suggested for children of <Friends>, but we know that if we are going to add any <User> elements, they must appear *before* any <Attendee> elements, as defined by an <xs:sequence> element in the schema.

The IDE also has an option to validate what we have entered against the schema: you just need to choose **Validate XML Data** from the **XML** menu. If there are validation errors, they will be underlined with a green wavy line in the editor, and listed in the **Task List** window.

This validation process is exactly the same as the one that we'll apply programmatically in a moment, and it demonstrates the value of namespaces. At design-time, they enable the IDE to activate IntelliSense and validation; at run-time, they allow the elements in a file to be unambiguously matched to their definition in the appropriate schema.

Creating XML Documents in Data View

There's another way to create an XML document visually when we have a schema for it: the **data view**. Click Data in the lower left corner of the designer, next to the XML button, to open a two-pane view. Here, the left pane is entitled Data Tables, while the right pane is entitled Data – and it's in the latter that we're going to add data to an XML file.

Every element that's specified as a complex type in the schema will be represented as a data table, and its simple type attributes and elements will appear as fields within it. That's why, for our document, the `<Friends>`, `<User>`, and `<Attendee>` elements are listed as 'tables' in the left pane. When a complex type element is enclosed inside another, such as the `<User>` and `<Attendee>` elements inside the `<Friends>` root element, we will be presented with a navigation link in the Data pane that lets us get inside the contained elements. Click the link, and it will expand to list the child elements:

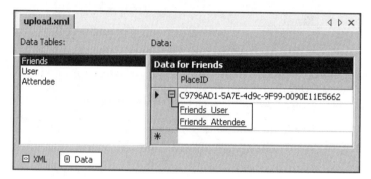

In order for elements to be put in the right place in the XML file, we have to follow the links through the elements until we get to the level where the new element must be placed. This is important, because the data view interface will let us directly select the `User` or `Attendee` 'tables', and create elements right there. However, this will cause the elements to be placed under the root element, which is not valid according to our schema.

Try It Out – Adding an Element in Data View

Let's see how the data view works in practice, as we create a new `<Attendee>` element in our `upload.xml` XML file.

1. Click on the Friends User link in the Data pane for the Friends data table (as shown in the previous screenshot).

2. Try adding a new user directly in the grid. It will look something like this:

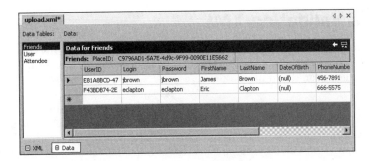

3. Switching back to the XML view reveals the new data:

```xml
<Friends xmlns="urn:wrox-friends" PlaceID="C9796AD1-5A7E-4d9c-9F99-0090E11E5662">
  <User>
    <UserID>E81A8BCD-47A3-4038-9F7B-2DF25C741833</UserID>
    <Login>jbrown</Login>
    <Password>jbrown</Password>
    <FirstName>James</FirstName>
    <LastName>Brown</LastName>
    <PhoneNumber>456-7891</PhoneNumber>
    <Address>St. John 945</Address>
    <Email>jbrown@friends.com</Email>
  </User>

  ...
```

4. Note that because we navigated inside the `Friends` element to the desired child 'table', the elements were added inside the appropriate parent element.

The tables/rows approach is suitable for most XML files, but there will be some schema designs that won't allow us to use this feature. For example, if we have child elements with the same name but different parent elements – a perfectly valid schema definition – the data view won't be available.

XML using .NET

Microsoft has made a substantial commitment to XML with the .NET platform. The Framework contains namespaces that encompass classes implementing almost every XML-related standard:

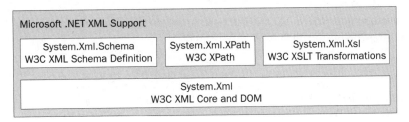

In the examples contained in the pages ahead, we will use classes in the `System.Xml` and `System.Xml.Schema` namespaces to load and validate an XML file, ready for use in our web application.

Reading and Validating XML

Reading XML files in .NET is performed in pretty much the same way as any other file type is read. As for other types, the source need not be a file as such – rather, it can be any form of **stream**, including in-memory streams, file streams, and network streams.

Throughout the .NET Framework, streams are read following the same pattern: a reader object steps from the start of the stream to the end with each successive call to the Read() method. When the end of the stream has been reached, Read() returns False. As we progress through the stream, the methods and properties provided by the specific reader implementation let us retrieve information and data for the current position in the stream. The diagram below illustrates some of the readers offered by the framework classes that are relevant to XML handling:

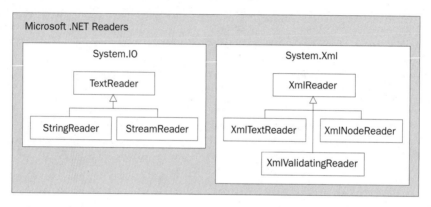

The readers in the System.IO namespace are relevant to us because we can pass them to overloaded constructors of many of the XmlReader-derived classes in order to read XML content from them. We'll see this very mechanism in action in our application later on.

Uploading an XML File

Our first step towards creating the 'upload' feature requires us to add a new web form to the application that will be used to receive a file from the client. To make the web form visually appealing, we will use an ASP.NET server control from Microsoft called TreeView. It makes displaying hierarchical information very simple, which is perfect for showing XML content. To be able to use this control, though, you must download and install the **Internet Explorer WebControls** by choosing the Automatic Install option from the drop-down list on the page at the following URL:

http://msdn.microsoft.com/downloads/default.asp?url=/downloads/samples/internet/asp_dot_net_servercontrols/webcontrols/default.asp

> *The Treeview control works in all browsers, but it will be much smoother in IE because it takes advantages of IE 'behaviors', a feature that exploits DHTML. In order to view it in the* Toolbox, *right-click on the latter, select the* Customize Toolbox *option, and add the* TreeView *control from the Microsoft.Web.UI.WebControls namespace under the .NET Framework Components tab in the list.*

We're going to build a web form that can receive an XML file posted by the user, and perform further processing on it. First, it will show the contents of the uploaded file in the `TreeView` control, so the user can see if the information they're sending is correct. We will also add links to the schema file that's used to validate the incoming file, and to a sample XML file that users can either view or load in the page for testing purposes.

Try It Out – Creating the UploadList Form

In this first section, we will build the form and review key settings in it. The code for the specific features we intend to offer will be added in later sections.

1. Add a new web form to the Friends Reunion project, and name it `UploadList.aspx`. Make the page inherit the `FriendsBase` class we built in Chapter 4, to add the site header and footer. Switch to the code view, and change the `Inherits` line to `Inherits FriendsBase`, as before.

2. Change the `pageLayout` property of the document to `FlowLayout`, and add the link to the stylesheet that we've been using so far inside the `<head>` section:

```
<link href="Style/iestyle.css" type="text/css" rel="stylesheet">
```

3. Now, add text and drop the appropriate controls on the form to give it the following layout:

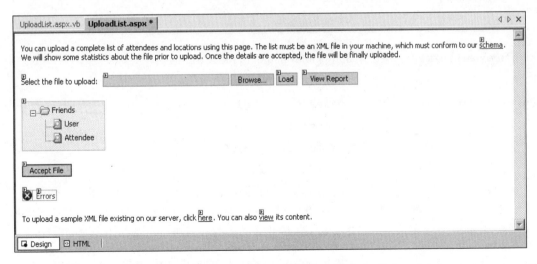

The following table contains the properties of the controls, in order of their appearance on the page, from left to right and top to bottom. The control type is specified between square brackets, followed by the control's ID and a brief description of its purpose in the form. Except for the HTML file field control, all of these are web server controls:

[HyperLink] hySchema	A link to the schema file we built, so that partners can check the validity of their files.
Text	schema
NavigateUrl	friends.xsd
Target	_blank

[HTML File Field] fldUpload	Allows the user to upload a file from their machine.
class	Button
style	WIDTH: 238px

[Button] btnLoad	Submits the file to the server.
CssClass	Button
Text	Load

[Button] btnReport	Redirects the user to a page showing statistics about the file they posted.
CssClass	Button
Text	View Report

[TreeView] tvXmlView	Shows information in the XML file.
CssClass	TreeView
ExpandedImageUrl	images/opened.gif
ImageUrl	images/findfolder.gif
SelectedImageUrl	images/selected.gif
Visible	False
Nodes	Added a root node and two children to it, with the text Friends, User, and Attendee respectively, using the editor that appears.
TreeNodeTypes	This is a collection of node type definitions, which can be used to give new nodes a default formatting. Add a new type using the editor shown, with its **Name** and **ID** set to **Normal**, and a **DefaultStyle** of font-size:8pt;font-family:Tahoma;.
ChildType	This sets the default style for new nodes. Set it to Normal, the one we created in the previous property.

[Button] btnAccept	Saves the posted file to the database.
CssClass	Button
Text	Accept File

[Panel] pnlError	Displays any errors found in the incoming file.
Visible	False

[Image]	The icon for errors. This is not a server control, so we don't need an ID.
align	absmiddle
src	images/error.gif

[Label] lblError	Contains the error messages.
ForeColor	Red
Text	Errors

[LinkButton] btnDefaultXml	Allows the user to load a sample file, already existing in our server, for testing purposes and to grasp the format they need to adhere to.
Text	Here

[HyperLink] hyXmlFile	Provides a link to the sample XML file so the user can view it in the browser or download it for testing.
Text	View
NavigateUrl	upload.xml
Target	_blank

4. Add the following style rule to the stylesheet, which is used to format the tree view control:

```
.TreeView
{
  border-right: #c7ccdc 1px solid;
  padding-right: 15px;
  border-top: #c7ccdc 1px solid;
  padding-left: 5px;
  font-size: 8pt;
  padding-bottom: 5px;
  border-left: #c7ccdc 1px solid;
  padding-top: 5px;
  border-bottom: #c7ccdc 1px solid;
  font-family: Tahoma, Verdana, 'Times New Roman';
  background-color: #f0f1f6;
}
```

5. Add the following code to the `Page_Load()` event handler to configure the header image and text (as described in Chapter 3):

```
Private Sub Page_Load(ByVal sender As System.Object, _
                      ByVal e As System.EventArgs) Handles MyBase.Load
    MyBase.HeaderIconImageUrl = _
                      Request.ApplicationPath & "/images/pctransfer.gif"
    MyBase.HeaderMessage = "Upload Attendees"
End Sub
```

6. Our page is now complete, so set it as the start page, and compile and run with *F5*. After the usual login process (using `wrox` as user name and password), this screen should appear in your browser:

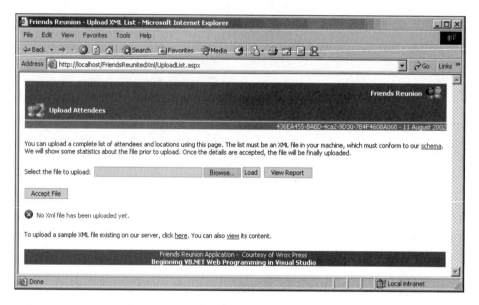

On clicking the **Browse** button, the user will be presented with the standard Windows dialog for locating files.

How It Works

As we said, the objective of this form is to allow a partner institution to submit an XML file containing all its users and attendees. In order to specify the file to upload, its representive has to click the **Browse** button. The control that makes this possible is an HTML INPUT control with its `type` attribute set to `file`. When the file is selected, however, the form isn't posted. We placed a **Load** button control on the form but in fact any postback caused by any server control will cause the file to be uploaded. For the file to be sent to the server though, the form not only has to use a `post()` method but also has to specify the `encType` attribute:

```
<form id="frmUpload" method="post" encType="multipart/form-data"
      runat="server">
```

Note that we set the file input control to run as a server control, as we learned in Chapter 4 (the little green arrow reflects that setting). We have done so in order to access the properties this control exposes at the server side, which allow us to work with the uploaded file.

The link at the top of the form pointing to the schema we created, and the last one pointing to the sample XML file, have their **Target** property set to _blank, which causes a new browser window to be opened. This will allow the user to inspect those files without leaving the current form they are working with.

When the file is uploaded, we will fill the **TreeView** control with the values in it, as we will learn in the next section. Just a couple words about this control; it is very similar to its Windows counterpart, and basically consists of a collection of `TreeNode` elements that can in turn contain other `TreeNode` elements, and so on. The server control provides several options to add style to it, such as defining the style to use to render child nodes, and so on. We used the `TreeNodeTypes` property to define a `Normal` node type, and then used it in the `ChildType`.

Finally, we provide partners access to the sample document as well as the schema file we have built, so they can get an idea of what their own files should look like according to it. We provided a link that will load this sample document so they can test the application features, and the second one will open a new window with the sample file in it.

Receiving the Uploaded File

The feature we are building will allow the user to preview the file's contents, see some statistics about it, and later decide if they actually want to post the information in the file to the database. In order to allow this, there are three areas that need to be addressed:

❑ Saving the posted file. The user should upload the file only once. If we ask them to select the file again every time a postback is performed, it could become very frustrating for them. For this reason, we will save the uploaded XML into a session variable, which we will use later when working with the file. Remember that XML is just text content, so we're actually saving a string value here.

On the other hand, as this is a testing scenario, we don't pay much attention to size limits, scalability issues, and so on. Some would say it would be better to save the file in the server's file system, while others would complain that the I/O access and security permissions involved would actually turn out to be slower and less efficient. Such topics would have to be evaluated in a production environment.

❑ Setting up the reader. Configuring an `XmlValidatingReader` object requires several steps, so we will move all that code into a private function.

❑ Using the reader. We'll create another routine in which we use the reader to add nodes to the `TreeView` control, to show the XML contents on the web page. This will help the user to preview the file they are about to post, prior to confirmation.

Try It Out – Saving the Posted XML File

Let's analyze the code for reading and saving the incoming file to the session variable that we'll use later on.

1. Add the following imports right at the top of the code-behind file:

```
Imports System.Xml
Imports System.Xml.Schema
Imports System.IO
Imports Microsoft.Web.UI.WebControls
```

The last of these points to the namespace where the TreeView control and its related classes are located. When you dropped that control onto the page, a reference to the Microsoft.Web.UI.WebControls.dll assembly was automatically added. It will come as no surprise that this is the assembly that contains the namespace we imported.

2. Add the following procedure:

```
'Save the input file if appropiate
Private Sub SaveXml()
  If Not Me.fldUpload.PostedFile Is Nothing AndAlso _
       Me.fldUpload.PostedFile.FileName <> String.Empty Then
    ' Save the uploaded stream to Session for further postbacks
    Dim stm As New StreamReader(Me.fldUpload.PostedFile.InputStream)
    Session.Item("xml") = stm.ReadToEnd()
    Session.Item("file") = Me.fldUpload.PostedFile.FileName
  End If
End Sub
```

3. Double-click the Load button, and add the following line:

```
Private Sub btnLoad_Click(ByVal sender As System.Object, _
                      ByVal e As System.EventArgs) Handles btnLoad.Click
  SaveXml()
End Sub
```

4. Set a breakpoint in this last line of code we added, so that we can test the new method. Compile and run with *F5*, and after the usual login process, select the sample XML file we built before, and click the Load button.

How It Works

When we click the button after we have selected the corresponding XML file, the corresponding handler will be called. Press *F11* to step into SaveXml(). Inside the routine, we first check that we have a valid posted file and filename:

```
If Not Me.fldUpload.PostedFile Is Nothing AndAlso _
   Me.fldUpload.PostedFile.FileName <> String.Empty Then
```

The `fldUpload` variable references the HTML `<input>` control that was used to upload the file. It has a `PostedFile` property of type `HttpPostedFile` (you can verify this by placing the cursor over that property for a while) that contains a number of useful sub-properties that describe the file being uploaded (`ContentLength`, `ContentType`, and `FileName`, for example). We use the `AndAlso` operator to avoid the error that would occur if the second test expression of this `If` statement were to be resolved when the `PostedFile` is `Nothing`.

Next, we see one of the reader implementations of the `System.IO` namespace in action – namely, the `StreamReader`:

```
Dim stm As New StreamReader(Me.fldUpload.PostedFile.InputStream)
```

Its constructor requires an object of type `Stream`, which we get from the `InputStream` property of the posted file. This `Stream` contains the uploaded content. We put all of the file content returned by the reader into a variable whose content is then further placed in a session item called `xml`, and hold the original filename in a second session variable called `file`:

```
Dim xml As String = stm.ReadToEnd()
Session.Item("xml") = xml
Session.Item("file") = Me.fldUpload.PostedFile.FileName
```

The `ReadToEnd()` method returns the whole file – that is, the XML document – as a single string. If you wish, you can check that the contents of the file are there by placing the cursor above the variable for a while.

Validating XML from a Web Application

The `XmlValidatingReader` class that we will use derives from `XmlReader`, so it shares many properties and methods with that class. It also adds a set of new properties (that is, it **extends** the class) to set options required for validation. In this text, we'll call an instance of this class a **validator**.

Once the validator is configured, we can start reading an XML file and taking values from it, just as we would with a regular `XmlReader` object. Behind the scenes though, the object ensures that the file is valid as it is read, according to the settings we have made. There are two ways that we can configure our validator to react when validation errors are found in the XML source:

❑ Throw exceptions, which is the default mode. When an error is found, processing is aborted and an `XmlSchemaException` is thrown.

❑ Fire the event handler attached to the `ValidationEventHandler` event of the `XmlValidatingReader` class. When a handler is specified for this event, the validator won't throw exceptions, but will instead call the handler when errors appear. It is up to the developer to collect information inside the handler and respond accordingly.

Clearly, the second of these allows a more complete reporting of any failures found in an XML file, and at the same time it allows us to continue through the document and process all elements.

Try It Out – Setting up Validation

We can now move on to the second part of our three-bullet list. In this example, we'll write the code to set up the `XmlValidatingReader` object.

1. Declare the following private members at class level (before the `Page_Load()` event handler). As a naming convention, we prefix class-level variables with an underscore so that we can easily differentiate them from local variables inside a method:

```
Private _errors As String = String.Empty
Private WithEvents _validator As XmlValidatingReader
```

2. Add the handler for the validation event. It needs to have exactly the signature specified here, and we'll be using it later on when we configure validation:

```
Private Sub OnValidation(ByVal sender As Object, _
                         ByVal e As ValidationEventArgs) _
                         Handles _validator.ValidationEventHandler
    _errors &= "<b>" & e.Severity.ToString() & "</b>: " & e.Message & "<br>"
End Sub
```

3. The procedure responsible for reading and displaying the XML content doesn't need to know that it's using an `XmlValidatingReader` instance – it only cares about the reading methods. We'll isolate it from our initialization code for the validator in a function that returns a generic `XmlReader` object type:

```
Private Function GetReader() As XmlReader
    Dim xmlinput As StringReader
    Dim reader As XmlTextReader
    Dim schemareader As XmlTextReader
    Dim schema As XmlSchema

    If Session.Item("xml") Is Nothing Then
      Throw New InvalidOperationException( _
        "No XML file has been uploaded yet.")
    End If

    ' Build the XmlTextReader from the in-memory string saved above
    xmlinput = New StringReader(CType(Session.Item("xml"), String))
    reader = New XmlTextReader(xmlinput)

    ' Configure the validating reader
    _validator = New XmlValidatingReader(reader)

    ' Open the schema using a URL to avoid file access security checks
    schemareader = New XmlTextReader( _
        "http://localhost/" & Request.ApplicationPath & "/friends.xsd")
    Try
      schema = XmlSchema.Read(schemareader, Nothing)
```

```
      Finally
        schemareader.Close()
      End Try

      _validator.Schemas.Add(schema)
      _validator.ValidationType = ValidationType.Schema

      Return _validator
   End Function
```

How It Works

We've set up a couple of class-level variables to handle the errors that can occur during the reading phase: one will accumulate error messages (the _error string variable, initialized to an empty string) and the other is the validator that will call our handler on encountering any errors:

```
    Private WithEvents _validator As XmlValidatingReader
```

The keyword WithEvents is the key to attaching the handler. A variable with this keyword becomes available after the Handles clause is added to an event handler. Furthermore, we can use the drop-down combo boxes at the top of the code window to create the handler by selecting the variable on the left and the event on the right, which results in the following code being added:

```
    Private Sub OnValidation(ByVal sender As Object, _
                    ByVal e As ValidationEventArgs) _
                    Handles _validator.ValidationEventHandler
```

If an error is found during the reading phase, the validator will call this procedure, passing in information about the event in the e parameter, which is of type ValidationEventArgs. This parameter supplies details about the error that we append to the string variable _errors for later use. We want to know the severity of the validation failure (which will be either an Error or a Warning) and the error message itself, with some formatting to display nicely in the page:

```
    _errors &= "<b>" & e.Severity.ToString() & "</b>: " & e.Message & "<br>"
```

Should we need it, the Exception property of the ValidationEventArgs class holds the actual exception that was caught. This property is of type XmlSchemaException, and it can be queried to obtain comprehensive information about the error, including the line number and position where the error occurred, the schema object causing the exception, and so on. For short files though, the Message property contains just about everything we need to locate the problem. For example, a UserID with a length other than the 36 characters required by the schema will generate a message string something like this:

```
The 'urn:wrox-friends:UserID' element has an invalid value according to its data
type. An error occurred at (4, 50).
```

The XML processing code, which we will build next, will call the `GetReader()` method to get the object it will use to process the XML file. Notice that we return a generic `XmlReader` object from the method:

```
Private Function GetReader() As XmlReader
```

In this way, the act of getting hold of an object for reading the file is independent of the actual `XmlReader` implementation being used to work through it. This makes it easy for us to turn validation off just by returning an `XmlTextReader` instead of an `XmlValidatingReader`.

After the variable declarations that follow, we check to see if there is actual content in the `Session` variable we saved before. The first time the page loads, or if an error on the server causes session information to be lost, we raise an exception. We use an `InvalidOperationException`, already defined in the .NET Framework, as it seems to be an appropriate exception to throw in this condition. That is, we are trying to read an XML file when none has been uploaded before:

```
If Session.Item("xml") Is Nothing Then
  Throw New InvalidOperationException( _
    "No XML file has been uploaded yet.")
End If
```

Next, we set up a `StringReader` from the `System.IO` namespace, which we will use as the source when we create our XML reader. In effect, the `StringReader` class applies a `TextReader` implementation to a simple string, which we can then pass to an `XmlTextReader` constructor:

```
' Build the XmlTextReader from the in-memory string saved above
xmlinput = New StringReader(CType(Session.Item("xml"), String))
reader = New XmlTextReader(xmlinput)
```

At this point, if we wished to disable validation, we could just add the following line:

```
Return reader
```

But instead, as we *do* want to validate, we use the `XmlTextReader` to create an instance of the `XmlValidatingReader` class:

```
_validator = New XmlValidatingReader(reader)
```

The validator needs a reference to the schema that it should validate against, through its property called `Schemas`, which is a collection of `XmlSchema` objects. We add our schema using the shared `Read()` method of the `XmlSchema` class, which loads and returns the specified schema. Once we've initialized the reader, which we do with a URL to side-step the checking of file access permissions, we pass it to `Read()`:

```
schemareader = New XmlTextReader( _
        "http://localhost/" & Request.ApplicationPath & "/friends.xsd")
Try
  schema = XmlSchema.Read(schemareader, Nothing)
Finally
```

The second parameter to the Read() method is a validation handler to deal with any errors that are found in the schema itself. In this case, we will assume the schema is valid. Once we've loaded the schema, adding it to the collection of schemas for the validator is simple:

```
_validator.Schemas.Add(schema)
```

Finally, we return the initialized XmlValidatingReader object.

Processing the Uploaded XML Data

The XmlSchema class is Microsoft's implementation of the W3C standard, and it performs validation while the XML stream is read. There is no need for a special validation method. Remember that these readers are read-only and forward-only, making them fast and light, but also meaning that we need to process the XML while we are still validating it. As we process the XML, we won't yet know that the entire file meets the requirements of our schema.

As you examine the following example, notice that the code for retrieving data from the validator (that is, the XmlValidatingReader object) always refers to **nodes** in the first instance, rather than to elements, or attributes, or text. This is due to the way that the reader perceives the XML: as it moves through the document, one by one it comes across the entities that document contains. The next 'thing' that it comes across could be an element, or an attribute of an element, or the content of an element. When each entity arrives in our code, we have to find out what it is.

Try It Out – Displaying XML Data

With that said, it's time for us to implement the steps that process the XML file. We're going to read the elements, and display them in the tree view.

1. We will place the reading and processing code in a method called BuildTreeView():

```
Private Sub BuildTreeView()
    Dim node As TreeNode
    Dim topnode As TreeNode
    Dim parentnode As TreeNode
    Dim reader As XmlReader
    Dim parent As String = String.Empty

    Me.pnlError.Visible = False

    ' Save the incoming file if appropriate
    SaveXml()

    Try
        reader = GetReader()

        ' Clear the tree view
        Me.tvXmlView.Nodes.Clear()
        topnode = New TreeNode()
```

```
    ' Add nodes to hold new users and attendees
    topnode.Text = "File: " & Session.Item("file").ToString()
    topnode.Nodes.Add(New TreeNode())
    topnode.Nodes.Add(New TreeNode())
    Me.tvXmlView.Nodes.Add(topnode)

    Do While reader.Read()
      If reader.NodeType = XmlNodeType.Element And _
         (reader.LocalName = "User" Or reader.LocalName = "Attendee") Then

         ' Add the parent User or Attendee node
         parentnode = New TreeNode()
         parentnode.Text = reader.LocalName

         ' Place the node inside the right parent node
         If reader.LocalName = "User" Then
           topnode.Nodes(0).Nodes.Add(parentnode)
         Else
           topnode.Nodes(1).Nodes.Add(parentnode)
         End If

         AddAttributes(reader, parentnode)
         parent = reader.LocalName

      ElseIf reader.NodeType = XmlNodeType.Element And _
         (parent = "User" Or parent = "Attendee") Then

         ' If it's an element node we need to add it and its attributes
         node = New TreeNode()
         node.Text = reader.Name
         AddAttributes(reader, node)
         parentnode.Nodes.Add(node)

      ElseIf reader.NodeType = XmlNodeType.Text Then
         ' If it's a text node, set the text value of the previous node
         node.Text &= ": " + reader.Value
      End If
    Loop

    ' Finally, add the count of elements to the top node values
    topnode.Nodes(0).Text = "New Users (" & _
      topnode.Nodes(0).Nodes.Count.ToString() & ")"
    topnode.Nodes(1).Text = "Attendees (" & _
      topnode.Nodes(1).Nodes.Count.ToString() & ")"
    Me.tvXmlView.Visible = True

    ' Check for errors accumulated during validation
    If _errors.Length <> 0 Then
      Throw New InvalidOperationException(_errors)
    End If

  Catch ex As Exception
    Me.lblError.Text = ex.Message
```

```
      Me.pnlError.Visible = True
   End Try
End Sub
```

2. Add the `AddAttributes()` helper method next:

```
' Helper method of BuildTreeView that adds the attributes found as
'   child nodes of the passed node, using a different icon
Private Sub AddAttributes(ByVal reader As XmlReader, _
                          ByVal node As TreeNode)
   If Not reader.HasAttributes Then Return

   Dim i As Integer
   Dim child As TreeNode
   Dim attrs As New TreeNode()

   attrs.Text = "Attributes (" & reader.AttributeCount.ToString() & ")"
   attrs.ImageUrl = "images/attributes.gif"
   attrs.ExpandedImageUrl = "images/attributes.gif"

   For i = 0 To reader.AttributeCount - 1
      child = New TreeNode()
      reader.MoveToAttribute(i)
      child.Text = reader.Name & ": " & reader.Value
      child.ImageUrl = "images/emptyfile.gif"
      attrs.Nodes.Add(child)
   Next

   node.Nodes.Add(attrs)

   ' Reposition the reader
   reader.MoveToElement()
End Sub
```

3. Now we have to change the call to `SaveXml()` in the **Load** button handler to a call to `BuildTreeView()`, as we actually want to reload the contents of this control. As you see from the code above, the call to `SaveXml()` is performed inside that method already:

```
Private Sub btnLoad_Click(ByVal sender As System.Object,
   ByVal e As System.EventArgs) Handles btnLoad.Click
   BuildTreeView()
End Sub
```

4. Save the solution and run the page. After the usual login process, load the `upload.xml` file we created, just as we did before. This time, the XML file will be represented in a tree view:

How It Works

When the user clicks the **Load** button, a postback is caused. The code in the button handler calls the `BuildTreeView()` method, where we save the incoming XML file and then use an `XmlTextReader` to create nodes and add them to the tree view. We also append any attributes that my be found by calling the helper `AddAttributes()` method. The nodes are created programmatically by initializing new variables, assigning their properties, and finally adding them to the parent node. For example, take a look at the following code, which initializes and adds the top-level nodes:

```
' Clear the treeview
Me.tvXmlView.Nodes.Clear()
topnode = New TreeNode()

' Add nodes to hold new users and attendees
topnode.Text = "File: " & Session.Item("file").ToString()
topnode.Nodes.Add(New TreeNode())
topnode.Nodes.Add(New TreeNode())
Me.tvXmlView.Nodes.Add(topnode)
```

We add different nodes to these two top-level nodes depending on the current element name – that is, either a `<User>` or an `<Attendee>` element.

If a validation error occurs while the tree view is being built, the handler we created in the previous section will be called, and the error will be appended to the _errors variable. The code will continue processing and adding nodes, until finally we check whether this variable contains any error messages, and throw an exception if appropriate:

```
'Check for errors accumulated during validation
If _errors.Length <> 0 Then
  Throw New InvalidOperationException(_errors)
End If
```

Note that this exception that we throw ourselves is handled in exactly the same as other exceptions that may happen, through a common Catch section, as we saw in Chapter 6:

```
Catch ex As Exception
  Me.lblError.Text = ex.Message
  Me.pnlError.Visible = True
End Try
```

To finish off this section, let's take a look at what happens to a file that contains some validation errors. This time, add the uploadBad.xml file that's available in the code download for this chapter, which contains an error in an ID (shorter than it should be), and an invalid <Institution> element (not expected according to the schema). After we click the Load button, the following screen should appear:

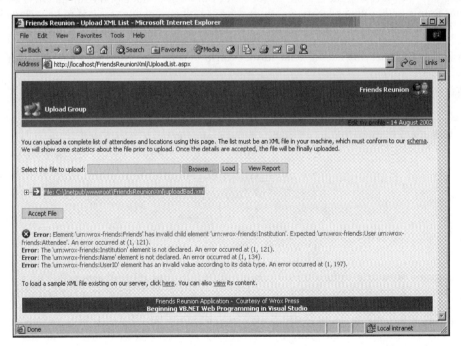

XML schema validation provides our system with a watertight seal against invalid data. As it's an external text file, we can modify our schema should our business requirements change, without necessarily recompiling or even stopping the web application.

Querying XML Documents: XPath

XML represents a powerful and increasingly popular way of storing data, so it would be a huge shortcoming if there were no way of performing queries against that data. Now, we know that the de facto standard for querying relational data stores is SQL, so why can't we just use that to extract data from our XML documents?

The answer lies in the differences between the relational model of tables and rows, and the hierarchical structure of XML documents, where elements can be arbitrarily nested to any depth. This is why the W3C came to the rescue again with **XPath**, which is, as the specification says, "A language for addressing parts of an XML document."

More information on XPath can be found at www.w3c.org/TR/xpath.

XPath will be immediately familiar if you have an understanding of the file structure of a modern PC, and particularly if you remember the days of the DOS command prompt. This is because XPath is based on the same slash-separated notation to locate items. The following XPath expression, for example, would locate all of the `<User>` elements in our sample XML document:

/Friends/User

The first slash indicates that the search should start from the root node of the document. The following elements form a path, called a **location path**, that leads to the elements we want to be included in the result. XPath expressions like this result in a collection of nodes being selected: a **node set**.

We can refine this query by adding some further constraints on the results we want returned:

/Friends/User[LastName="Brown"]

This revised expression would only return those `<User>` elements for which the `<LastName>` child element has the text value `Brown`. Let's dissect this expression:

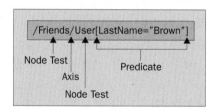

A set consisting of an axis (optional) plus a node test and an optional predicate makes up a **location step**. In the example above, we have two location steps: `/Friends`, and `/User[LastName="Brown"]`.

The **axis** determines the direction in which we move down the location path. We can move to child nodes, as we did above, with the forward slash, which means that the next step is evaluated against the children of the previously evaluated step. Other possibilities include moving to the parent node (`../`), and staying in the current node (`.`).

Other important features of XPath are numeric, string, and Boolean functions, which include `count()`, `sum()`, `string-length()`, `starts-width()`, `contains()`, and some others. You can find the complete list of functions, axes, and other features of XPath in the specification itself at www.w3.org/TR/1999/REC-xpath-19991116.html, or you might choose one of the following books:

❑ *Beginning XML, 2nd Edition* (ISBN 1-86100-559-8)

❑ *Professional XML for .NET Developers* (ISBN 1-86100-531-8)

Try It Out – Building the Reports Form

In our application, we want to provide some statistical information about the uploaded file, such as a report of new users and a count of attendees. We will achieve this using the features of XPath, without having to traverse the file laboriously.

1. Add a new web form to the application, and name it `UploadListReport.aspx`. As usual, set the `pageLayout` property to `FlowLayout`, and make the class defined in the code-behind page inherit the `FriendsBase` class:

```
Public Class UploadListReport
    Inherits FriendsBase
```

2. Link this form to our application stylesheet with the following element within the `<head>` element of the page:

```
<link href="Style/iestyle.css" type="text/css" rel="stylesheet">
```

3. Add two tables, two textboxes, two link buttons, two image controls, and three labels from the Web Forms tab in the Toolbox, and configure them as detailed in the forthcoming table, until your form looks something like this:

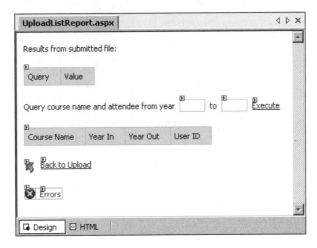

[Table] tbReport	This table will contain the statistics values we retrieve using XPath queries against the file.
CssClass	TableLines
GridLines	Both
CellPadding, CellSpacing	0
Rows	Add a new row, with its BackColor set to #D3E5FA, and the two cells shown on the page.

[TextBox] txtYearFrom	The starting year for the XPath query to filter attendees.
CssClass	SmallTextBox
MaxLength	4
Width	36px

[TextBox] txtYearTo	The ending year for the XPath query to filter attendees.
CssClass	SmallTextBox
MaxLength	4
Width	36px

[LinkButton] btnExecute	Performs the query with the range of years specified.
Text	Execute

[Table] tbDates	Holds the results from the previous query execution.
CssClass	TableLines
GridLines	Both
CellPadding, CellSpacing	0
Rows	Add a new row, with its BackColor set to #D3E5FA, and the four cells shown on the page.

[ImageButton] btnBackImg	Will redirect the user back to the upload page.
AlternateText	Back to Upload
ImageUrl	images/back.gif
ImageAlign	Middle

[LinkButton] btnBackLink	Redirects the user back to the upload page.
AlternateText	Back to Upload

[Panel] pnlError	Displays any errors found in the incoming file.
Visible	False

[Image]	The icon for errors. This is not a server control, so we don't need an ID.
align	absmiddle
src	images/error.gif

[Label] lblError	Contains the error messages.
ForeColor	Red
Text	Errors

How It Works

This form will show the statistics that we'll add in the code-behind page. The table at the top of the page will be populated with the results of some predefined queries, while the second table will execute a custom XPath query built from the values in the textboxes above it. It will allow the user to select the <Attendee> elements whose child elements' <YearIn> and <YearOut> text values match the desired range.

Before moving on to perform the queries, however, we need to introduce one last XML-related standard: the **Document Object Model** or **DOM**.

The Document Object Model (DOM)

TextReader-based objects provide forward-only access to the underlying XML data, which means that as soon as we move forward, we lose all information pertaining to the previous element. Clearly, such an approach is unsuited to querying a document, because we would end up reading the entire file for every query we perform. Even if the element we were looking for was the first one in the document, there would be no way to know that for sure, and we would have to read it in its entirety to be certain.

To perform queries effectively, we really need the complete document in memory, so that we can perform all the queries we want without the need to re-parse the file. The W3C again has the answer: the Document Object Model.

The DOM defines the way an XML document is stored in memory, and how its nodes are loaded, accessed and changed using a 'collection' approach: each node contains other nodes as children, and these in turn can contain other nodes, and so on. The DOM allows us to navigate back and forth between child and parent elements too, tinkering with them as we go – it is neither forward-only nor read-only.

DOM is built on several key building blocks. The fundamental one is the concept of the Document, which is to DOM what the Schema element is for XSD. This important object is implemented by the .NET Framework in the System.Xml.XmlDocument class.

281

Try It Out – Querying a DOM Document

With that information in mind, we're ready to build the code for performing XPath queries, as we outlined above.

1. Open the code-behind page for the `UploadListReport.aspx` web form, and add the following imports at the top of the file:

```
Imports System.IO
Imports System.Xml
Imports System.Xml.XPath
Imports System.Text
```

2. Add the `GetReader()` helper method, which will serve the same purpose as the function by the same name in the `UploadList.aspx` page:

```
Private Function GetReader() As XmlReader
   Dim reader As XmlTextReader
   Dim xmlinput As StringReader

   If Session.Item("xml") Is Nothing Then
     Throw New InvalidOperationException("No Xml file has been uploaded.")
   End If

   ' Build the XmlReader from the in-memory string saved above
   xmlinput = New StringReader(CType(Session.Item("xml"), String))
   reader = New XmlTextReader(xmlinput)
   Return reader
End Function
```

3. Locate the `Page_Load()` method, and place the following code inside it:

```
Private Sub Page_Load(ByVal sender As System.Object, _
                      ByVal e As System.EventArgs) Handles MyBase.Load
   ' Configure header
   MyBase.HeaderIconImageUrl = _
                      Request.ApplicationPath & "/images/print.gif"
   MyBase.HeaderMessage = "Upload Attendees - Report"

   Dim doc As XmlDocument
   Dim reader As XmlReader

   Dim nodes As XmlNodeList
   Dim node As XmlNode
   Dim mgr As XmlNamespaceManager

   Dim row As TableRow
   Dim cell As TableCell
   Dim sb As StringBuilder
```

```
Try
    ' Retrieve the reader object and initialize the DOM document
    reader = GetReader()
    doc = New XmlDocument()
    doc.Load(reader)

    ' Initialize the namespace manager for the document
    mgr = New XmlNamespaceManager(doc.NameTable)
    mgr.AddNamespace("wx", "urn:wrox-friends")

    ' List of new users
    nodes = doc.SelectNodes("/wx:Friends/wx:User", mgr)
    row = New TableRow()
    cell = New TableCell()
    cell.Text = "New Users: " & nodes.Count.ToString()
    row.Cells.Add(cell)

    sb = New StringBuilder()
    For Each node In nodes
        sb.Append(node("FirstName", "urn:wrox-friends").InnerText)
        sb.Append(", ")
        sb.Append(node("LastName", "urn:wrox-friends").InnerText)
        sb.Append(" (")
        sb.Append(node("Email", "urn:wrox-friends").InnerText)
        sb.Append(")")
        sb.Append("<br>")
    Next

    cell = New TableCell()
    cell.Text = sb.ToString()
    row.Cells.Add(cell)
    Me.tbReport.Rows.Add(row)

    ' Queries returning XPath intrinsic types
    Dim nav As XPathNavigator = doc.CreateNavigator()
    Dim expr As XPathExpression

    ' Total number of attendees anywhere in the document
    row = New TableRow()
    cell = New TableCell()
    expr = nav.Compile("count(//wx:Attendee)")

    expr.SetContext(mgr)
    cell.Text = _
        "Global count of new attendees: " & nav.Evaluate(expr).ToString()
    cell.ColumnSpan = 2
    row.Cells.Add(cell)
    Me.tbReport.Rows.Add(row)

    ' The last attendee in the file, in document order
    row = New TableRow()
    cell = New TableCell()
```

```
        expr = nav.Compile( _
            "string(//wx:Attendee[position() = last()]/wx:UserID)")
        expr.SetContext(mgr)
        cell.Text = _
            "Last attendee ID in file: " & nav.Evaluate(expr).ToString()
        cell.ColumnSpan = 2
        row.Cells.Add(cell)
        Me.tbReport.Rows.Add(row)

    Catch ex As Exception
        Me.lblError.Text = ex.Message
        Me.pnlError.Visible = True
    End Try


    If Me.tbReport.Rows.Count = 1 Then Me.tbReport.Visible = False
End Sub
```

4. Double-click on the `btnBackImg` and `btnBackLink` controls in the designer to create `Click` event handlers for each of these. Add the line of code below to each handler to allow the user to navigate back to the `UploadList` form:

```
Private Sub btnBackImg_Click(ByVal sender As Object, _
    ByVal e As System.Web.UI.ImageClickEventArgs) Handles btnBackImg.Click
    Response.Redirect("UploadList.aspx")
End Sub

Private Sub btnBackLink_Click(ByVal sender As Object, _
    ByVal e As System.EventArgs) Handles btnBackLink.Click
    Response.Redirect("UploadList.aspx")
End Sub
```

5. Leave this page now, and open the `UploadList.aspx` web form in the designer. Double-click the **View Report** button, and add the following code to the event handler that is created:

```
Private Sub btnReport_Click(ByVal sender As System.Object, _
                    ByVal e As System.EventArgs) Handles btnReport.Click
    SaveXml()
    Response.Redirect("UploadListReport.aspx")
End Sub
```

6. With the `UploadList.aspx` page set as the startup page, run the project with *F5*.

7. Select the sample XML file to upload, click **View Report**, and you should see a summary that looks something like this:

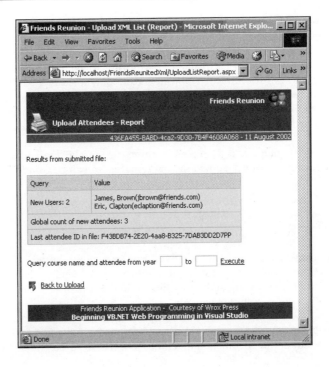

How It Works

When we click the **View Report** button in the previous page, this page takes up the XML we saved in the session variable and produces the report we see in the table at the top of the page. In order to achieve this, we load an `XmlDocument` from it, and perform the queries we need.

Loading the document involves retrieving an `XmlReader` that points to the XML string in the session variable, just as we did in the previous section, and passing it to the `Load()` method of the `XmlDocument` class:

```
' Retrieve the reader object and initialize the DOM document
reader = GetReader()
doc = New XmlDocument()
doc.Load(reader)
```

We use a class called `XmlNamespaceManager` when we perform the queries. To understand better why this class even exists, we need to understand the great effort Microsoft made to separate out functionality and make individual objects more manageable, lighter, and faster.

We saw how `XmlValidatingReader` builds upon the `XmlTextReader`. We also learned how to pass XSD schemas to it. Why was the schema a separate object and not an intrinsic part of the validating reader? The answer lies in modularization. By separating functionality that, while closely related, doesn't belong to the same classes, we achieve modularity, which allows each class to be simpler, easier to use, and more easily upgraded with new features, effectively becoming more manageable. As an example, the validating reader not only works with the new XSD schemas, but it also validates against older DTD and XDR formats.

Now, imagine that we need to perform an XPath query on a document that doesn't use namespaces – which is perfectly legal. If namespace management – that is, the resolution of XML prefixes and related operations – were built-in to the XPath classes, we would be wasting memory and making the classes more complex than required for this particular scenario. Hence, .NET 'quarantines' namespace-related operations in the XmlNamespaceManager object, and we only need to meddle with it when we need to issue queries that require namespace support. In our case, the schema design enforces the use of namespace in the XML instance files, so we need to initialize and use this object whenever a query is performed against these files.

Initializing the namespace manager is a simple operation: we simply create it and tell it to use the names found in the document, and then add the namespaces we will be using in our queries:

```
' Initialize the namespace manager for the document
mgr = New XmlNamespaceManager(doc.NameTable)
mgr.AddNamespace("wx", "urn:wrox-friends")
```

Once loaded, the document will be completely available, from top to bottom. We will focus here on the methods that the XmlDocument class provides to perform queries against data – it contains many more methods and properties to work with, and they can be found in the MSDN documentation simply by typing **XmlDocument** in the **Help Index** window.

For now, we will execute a query to retrieve the list of new users in the file – that is, all <User> elements that are present in the document, and children of the <Friends> element:

```
nodes = doc.SelectNodes("/wx:Friends/wx:User", mgr)
```

It really is that easy to get the results! Note that we need to include the namespace prefixes on both element names in the XPath expression, because our document uses a namespace. Prefixes allow us to locate elements that belong to different namespaces, and it's the namespace manager that's responsible for resolving them. Of course, we can still use documents without a namespace, and execute queries without using this class at all, but we could hardly validate a document like that.

Once we get the results, displaying them in the table is just a question of creating the appropriate TableRow and TableCell objects to contain the information. To build the result string containing all the users in the file, we use the StringBuilder class:

```
sb = New StringBuilder()
For Each node In nodes
  sb.Append(node("FirstName", "urn:wrox-friends").InnerText)
  sb.Append(", ")
  sb.Append(node("LastName", "urn:wrox-friends").InnerText)
  sb.Append(" (")
  sb.Append(node("Email", "urn:wrox-friends").InnerText)
  sb.Append(")")
  sb.Append("<br>")
Next
```

As we iterate through the nodes found, the `StringBuilder` accumulates a sort of summary about new users, containing their full name and e-mail address (between parentheses). Note that each node offers some accessors to get at its content – here, we've used the `InnerText` property to extract that content as a string value.

So far, we've loaded the first row with data about the users. The next query uses a different approach. The XPath specification defines four basic types that can result from executing expressions: node set, Boolean, number (floating-point), or string. When we use the `XmlDocument`'s `SelectNodes()` method (or for that matter, the `SelectNode()` method, which returns the first node in the results), the XPath expression issued *must* evaluate to a node set (although this might contain only one node). For example, the following query is a valid XPath expression that returns a number, representing the count of `<Attendee>` elements found in the entire document. It would fail if we used it for the `SelectNodes()` method. Note that the double slash (`//`) at the beginning of the expression means that we're looking for *all* `<Attendee>` elements *anywhere* in the document, starting from the root:

```
expr = nav.Compile("count(//wx:Attendee)")
```

If we wish to execute expressions that return simple types, instead of node sets, we need to use XPath-specific classes like these:

```
' Queries returning XPath intrinsic types
Dim nav As XPathNavigator = doc.CreateNavigator()
Dim expr As XPathExpression
```

The `XPathNavigator` is an object returned by the `XmlDocument.CreateNavigator()` method, and is optimized for XPath execution and navigation. The `XPathExpression` object is used to pre-compile commonly used queries, in a similar way to stored procedures in database systems. This can speed up execution, as we can reuse the expression and avoid repeating the string-parsing step that interprets the query. We can also find the return type of the expression dynamically, through its `ReturnType` property.

In order for the expression to resolve the namespace used, it needs an associated `XmlNamespaceManager`. This association is performed by calling the `SetContext()` method:

```
expr.SetContext(mgr)
```

Finally, we evaluate the expression and convert the result to a string:

```
cell.Text = _
    "Global count of new attendees: " & nav.Evaluate(expr).ToString()
```

After adding the corresponding row and cells to the results table, the rest of the method is almost identical to what we have already seen, except for the expression:

```
' The last attendee in the file, in document order
row = New TableRow()
cell = New TableCell()
expr = nav.Compile( _
    "string(//wx:Attendee[position() = last()]/wx:UserID)")
```

As the comment indicates, this query returns the `UserID` of the last `<Attendee>` element found in the document, for the user's verification purposes. More importantly though, this expression illustrates a number of useful XPath functions:

❑ `string()` – in this case, it converts the `UserID` node to its string value

❑ `position()` – returns the position of the context element (in our case, `<Attendee>`)

❑ `last()` – returns the position of the last element in the context node

Note that a predicate (the part of an XPath expression appearing in square brackets) can appear in any or all location steps. Here, a predicate selects the last `<Attendee>` element so that we can access its child `<UserID>` element. This element is converted to a string and shown in the results table. This query isn't particularly useful in the context of our application, but it does show the power behind XPath expressions, and the flexibility available for performing complex queries.

Dynamically Building XPath Expressions

As a final feature for our site, we are going to let the user enter a range of years, and query the uploaded file for matching nodes.

Try It Out – Querying Based on User Input

To do this, our code will build an XPath expression based on what's contained in the textboxes on the `UploadListReport` page when the **Execute** button is pressed. It will use the values to filter the matching nodes, and show them in the table below.

1. Open the `UploadListReport` page in the designer, double-click the **Execute** button (`btnExecute`), and add the following code:

```
Private Sub btnExecute_Click(ByVal sender As System.Object, _
                    ByVal e As System.EventArgs) Handles btnExecute.Click
    Dim doc As XmlDocument
    Dim reader As XmlReader

    Dim nodes As XmlNodeList
    Dim node As XmlNode
    Dim mgr As XmlNamespaceManager

    Dim row As TableRow
    Dim cell As TableCell

    Try
        ' Clear any previous state
        row = Me.tbDates.Rows(0)
        Me.tbDates.Rows.Clear()
        Me.tbDates.Rows.Add(row)
```

```
' Set up the document and namespace manager for it
doc = New XmlDocument()
reader = GetReader()

doc.Load(reader)
mgr = New XmlNamespaceManager(doc.NameTable)
mgr.AddNamespace("wx", "urn:wrox-friends")

nodes = doc.SelectNodes( _
    "/wx:Friends/wx:Attendee[wx:YearIn >= " & Me.txtYearFrom.Text & _
            " and wx:YearOut <= " & Me.txtYearTo.Text & "]", mgr)

For Each node In nodes
    row = New TableRow()
    row.Cells.Add(New TableCell())
    row.Cells.Add(New TableCell())
    row.Cells.Add(New TableCell())
    row.Cells.Add(New TableCell())

    ' Set values
    row.Cells(0).Text = node.Attributes("Name").Value
    row.Cells(1).Text = node("YearIn", "urn:wrox-friends").InnerText
    row.Cells(2).Text = node("YearOut", "urn:wrox-friends").InnerText
    row.Cells(3).Text = node("UserID", "urn:wrox-friends").InnerText
    Me.tbDates.Rows.Add(row)
Next

Me.tbDates.Visible = True

Catch ex As Exception
    Me.lblError.Text = ex.Message
    Me.pnlError.Visible = True
End Try
End Sub
```

2. Hit *F5*, leaving `UploadList.aspx` as the start page. Select the sample XML document, and click View Report.

3. Insert a range of years in the boxes on the `UploadListReport` page, and click Execute to view the results. Here is an example of the output when the years 1970 and 1990 are inserted into the textboxes:

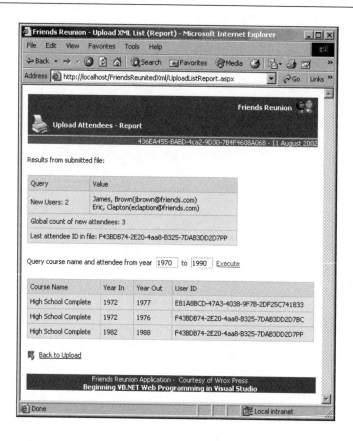

How It Works

When we click the Execute button, an expression is built with the values in the textboxes. We use this dynamically-created expression to retrieve the results in a very similar way to before, adding rows and cells to the table.

As the query can be executed multiple times, we must clear the existing rows before each new query. We have to be careful not to delete the header row, though, which we accomplish by saving it to a variable before we clear the rows, and adding it back as the new header row afterwards. The execution of the expression is straightforward:

```
nodes = doc.SelectNodes( _
    "/wx:Friends/wx:Attendee[wx:YearIn >= " & Me.txtYearFrom.Text & _
                " and wx:YearOut <= " & Me.txtYearTo.Text & "]", mgr)
```

In other words, our queries will typically be represented by strings such as this:

```
/wx:Friends/wx:Attendee[wx:YearIn >= 1970 and wx:YearOut <= 1990]
```

Once we have the results loaded in the table, we can change the values and click the Execute button again, to reload the table with the new values.

XmlDocument vs. XmlReader

So there are two basic approaches available when accessing an XML file; the XmlReader and the DOM through XmlDocument. In this section, I'd like to sum up what differentiates one from the other, to help you make the correct decision when deciding between them.

The primary difference is that the DOM caches an entire document in memory, while XmlReader and derived classes provide forward-only, read-only access to documents, with no caching.

This difference gives rise to a range of pros and cons for both. The following table analyzes key features of both techniques, and compares implementations. I have added **CON** or **PRO** as a conclusion for each case:

XmlReader	XmlDocument
Context	
The reader doesn't persist any information about the file. Once the cursor has moved on, there is no access at all to the previous element. To preserve information, we have to set up our own mechanisms and variables.	The document is completely loaded in memory when opened, and it stays there until we are done with it. This means we can move freely from the current element to its parent, siblings, and children. The complete document is available to provide any context information we may require.
CON	**PRO**
Resources consumed	
Stemming from the previous CON, the reader gets its most important PRO: it consumes minimal resources because of the fact that only the current element is held in memory. As soon as the position is changed, the previous element is discarded, and its resources are freed up.	Loading a complete document in memory can become a serious hindrance, especially for applications that work with large files. For smaller files, the impact is less noticeable, although even then, several concurrent users of a web application can quickly gobble up significant resources.
PRO	**CON**
Random Access	
These readers only provide sequential access – to find a particular element, we must start at the beginning and work our way through. This can be a real problem if we need to access elements scattered through the XML 'tree'.	Nodes can be accessed using indexes or names, even queried using XPath, as we learned. This complete random access support makes the DOM ideal for storing configuration files, or offline data files.
CON	**PRO**

Table continued on following page

XmlReader	XmlDocument
Read-write access	
As the name implies, XMLReader and family can only read. **CON**	The XmlDocument class provides complete control over elements in a file – we can add, remove, and change them. This makes it very suitable for data storage (from a form, for example) and for offline client-side functionality (where we send intermittent batch updates to the server). **PRO**
Speed	
The reader can be considerably faster, because it is so lightweight. If read-only access is suitable for a scenario, these classes are well worth consideration. **PRO**	Due to the comprehensive features it offers, DOM can take much longer to load and read a document from top to bottom than a reader. Improvements can be made through caching, but this will only increase the already high level of resources consumed. **CON**
Ease of use	
The reader has several methods, and the fact that it simultaneously represents the reader object and the current element makes the interface somewhat clumsy. For example, some methods will be useful when the current element is of some specific type, but not when it is another type. We have to work harder with readers – for instance, if we wish to retrieve the value of an element (with the Value property), we must first check the HasValue property to determine whether the current element can have a value or not! **CON**	The DOM has a more structured specification. There is an inheritance tree of classes, which starts from a general node type, and adds specialization for other node types. The base XmlNode class is very easy to master, and it is inherited by all the other disparate node types, greatly easing our learning curve. **PRO**

This list is by no means a definite comparison, but aims to provide some guidance. However, like almost everything in programming, there is no guaranteed formula for successfully choosing one technique over another, and we must weigh up the particular needs of each application.

A loaded XmlDocument object can also be used for validation. We can use its OuterXml property to get a string with the whole XML file, and handle it exactly the same way we did for the string session variable. The code would look like the following:

```
'The doc variable has been loaded elsewhere
xmlinput = New StringReader(doc.OuterXml)
reader = New XmlTextReader(xmlinput)

'Configure the validating reader
_validator = New XmlValidatingReader(reader)
```

Clearly, the advantages of an `XmlDocument` aren't so clear with regards to validation, as we are only using its string representation. It turns out to be that it is actually much more suitable for the querying scenario we have seen above.

Summary

In this chapter, we learned some important concepts about the usage of XML in web applications. We saw several standards that are regulated by the W3C and have a crucial role to play in the evolution of the web.

When we use XML files, we need to understand the difference between well-formed XML and valid XML. Looking at valid XML led us to the W3C's XML Schema Definition specification. We looked at some of the most important elements for defining the structure of XML instance documents, such as simple types, complex types, sequences, and attributes. We added occurrence constraints and learned how to restrict a base type to meet our needs. We added validation to our application using the schema we built, and it proved to be simple yet highly flexible and powerful. Storing validation logic for incoming data separate from business logic by the use of schemas helps maintenance and minimizes the coding required should our validation requirements change.

We exploited the full power of the XML support built into Visual Studio .NET, to visually create both schemas and instance documents. We saw how a schema enables IntelliSense during the creation of an XML document, and also played with the visual designers provided for drag-and-drop authoring.

A closer look at .NET's XML classes shed some light on the close relation between disparate namespaces, such as `System.IO` and `System.Xml`, as we used them in conjunction when building a useful upload feature for our application. On the way, we had a go with an add-in custom control, in this case the `TreeView` from Microsoft.

While reading XML may suffice for some applications, we usually need to perform queries against XML data. XPath is designed to fulfill this goal, and we applied it generate statistical information about the file being uploaded to our web page.

Finally, we examined the W3C's DOM standard, and its implementation in the .NET Framework: the `XmlDocument` class. We contrasted it with the `XmlReader` alternative, to determine which situations each is most suited to.

The foundation I hope that this chapter has provided will be useful as you work through the following chapter, about the very important emerging XML technology of web services.

Solut...
BM
Refere...
System.Da...
System.Drawing
System.Web
System.XML
AssemblyInfo.vb
Assembly...
BM.vsdisco
Global.asax
Styles.css
Web.config
WebForm1.aspx

WebForm1.aspx* | WebForm1.aspx.v

ebForm1.aspx*

Web Services in Web Applications

In previous chapters, we've looked at creating web applications that can connect to data sources, that present a personalized experience to end users, and that use XML for importing and exporting data. In this chapter, we'll introduce a new type of application that combines your knowledge of XML with some new ways of writing classes and methods to create a new way of coding applications.

If you're unfamiliar with **web services**, the first two things you'll want to know are what they are, and how they work. After that, you'll probably ask why you should want to use them, and why there's so much hype about them. Let's start with an example.

Imagine that you're working on an intranet site, and you want the front page to display the current stock value for your company. Further imagine that you want to have the ability to check the exchange rate of dollars to euros, because your company has offices both sides of the Atlantic. And finally imagine that your company would like to make their product catalog searchable by customers. Typically, you'd end up coding the first two of these yourself, but wouldn't it be great if you could make use of code that other people have written for these extremely common scenarios? Furthermore, what if your customers wanted to add your product searching functionality to their own sites? Both of these scenarios have a solution in web services.

There are two sides to this example. On the one hand, we're making use of services that have been written for us. These services can be made available over the Internet, for general consumption, and we can simply use them in our code as if they were components on our own machines. On the other hand is the ability to create our own services and expose *those* over the Internet, so that others can consume them.

If you like, you can think of a public web service as a (literally) globally available set of methods that we can invoke over the Internet and use in our own code. In a currency conversion example, we could pass in one parameter (the quantity in either dollars or euros), and the result would be sent back from the web service as the current equivalent in the other currency. In the stock value example, we would simply pass the same parameter to the web service each time (the identifier for our company), and the current value of our company's shares would be returned.

We can create our own web services and expose them so that others can use them in their code in exactly the same way. We define a set of methods that can be invoked, and a set of parameters that our methods accept. In the situation where a customer wants to list our product catalog on their sites, we could expose methods to return lists of stock sorted by one of two parameters: price or category. The customer could then further sort or filter this data themselves before displaying it on their site.

Importantly, since web services all adhere to a specific standard, we can consume web services written using ASP.NET running on a Windows machine, or using Java running on Linux. The key is that all web services are accessible over HTTP, and use XML to ensure compatibility. In this chapter, we'll look at both consuming and writing web services, giving you a grounding in this important new technology.

Accessing a Third Party Web Service

They best way to understand what web services are and how they work is to look at an example of using one, and happily there are already many web services that third party organizations have made available for a variety of purposes. In this section, we'll develop a Visual Basic .NET application that can access a web service, but we need to cover a little more groundwork before we do so.

When we create web applications, we can access class libraries in our code that contain methods and properties that we need to access to perform a specific task. For example, we can reference classes within the .NET Framework, like the classes contained within the `System.Web.UI.WebControls` namespace, which contains the classes behind the ASP.NET web controls, and their associated functionality. We have the ability to create our own class libraries to encapsulate commonly used functionality, and we now have the ability to use the functionality exposed in web services over the Internet in the same way.

Accessing, or **consuming**, someone else's web service is really quite straightforward – your application just needs to know the details of the methods that the service makes available. This information is contained in the web service's **WSDL** file, an XML schema file that describes the names, parameters, and return values of the methods in question. To discover what such a thing might look like, you can see an example of a WSDL file by entering http://www.soapengine.com/lucin/salcentral/ cnotes.asmx?wsdl into the address bar of Internet Explorer:

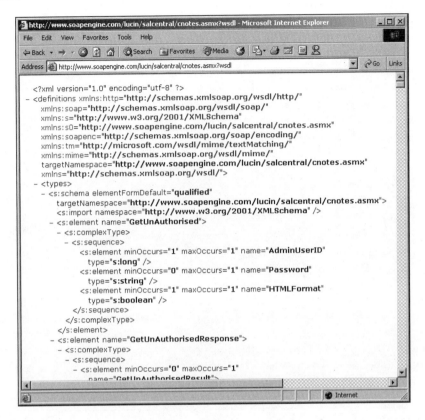

At first glance, this file appears quite complex, and it's certainly long, but once you get used to it things start to become a little clearer. The WSDL file lists:

❏ The methods available for this web service (the **web methods**)

❏ The arguments required for each method

❏ The data type of each argument

❏ Whether each web method returns a value, and the type if it does

❏ The servers that accept SOAP requests for this web service

❏ The supported ways of transferring SOAP messages (e-mail, TCP/IP, and so on)

If you search this file in your browser for the string GetMyNotes, you'll arrive at the description of the web method with this name:

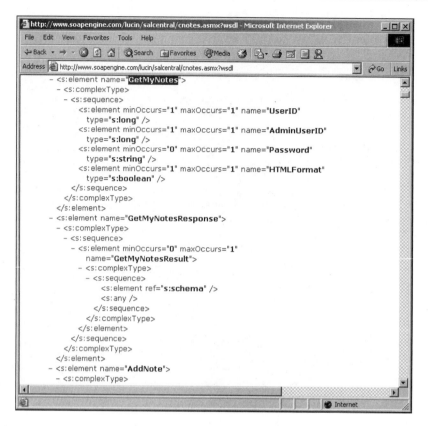

The first `<s:sequence>` element that you can see here defines the arguments that may be sent to this method. It's not too hard to see that all of the arguments are required, except for the optional `Password`, which has a `minOccurs` attribute of zero. The second `<s:sequence>` element you can see, which is the child of an element whose attribute has the value `GetMyNotesResponse`, defines the result that may be returned.

Thankfully, we don't have to trawl our way through WSDL files, trying to divine how to call the methods that they describe. WSDL is a key enabling technology of web services, and Visual Studio .NET can take a WSDL file and create a local class that offers all the methods it details. We then use this local class, called the **proxy class**, to make calls to the web service from our code.

Try It Out – Consuming a Web Service

In the following example, we'll use the web service that corresponds to the WSDL schema we just looked at from an ASP.NET web page. This service provides a store for textual notes that are stored on a by-user basis, in a way that makes your notes available from anywhere in the world with an Internet connection.

1. Start by creating a new Visual Basic ASP.NET web application named `NotesConsumer`:

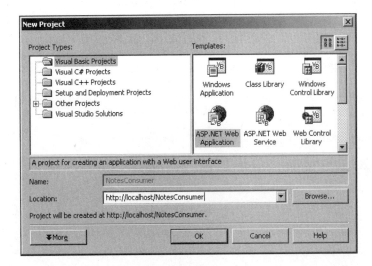

2. Drag a DataGrid control from the **Toolbox** onto the `WebForm1.aspx` designer, like so:

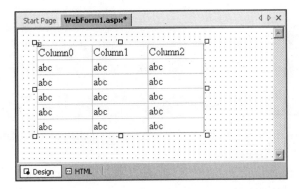

3. With the user interface sorted out(!), we need to get Visual Studio .NET to create the proxy class that will let us use the web service from our application. Right-click on References in Solution Explorer, and select **Add Web Reference**:

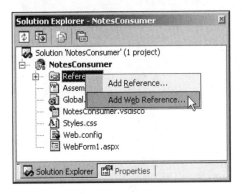

4. The main parts of the Add Web Reference dialog that appears are the Address bar along the top, an HTML browser window on the left below it, and the Available references pane on the right.

The HTML pane shows links to the main **UDDI directory**, and to the Microsoft test UDDI directory. These directories are repositories of web services that are offered by the companies and individuals who've registered them here – and there are many of them. Alternatively, we can simply enter the location of a known WSDL schema file in the address bar, and for this example we'll use the one that we've looked at already: http://www.soapengine.com/lucin/salcentral/cnotes.asmx?wsdl:

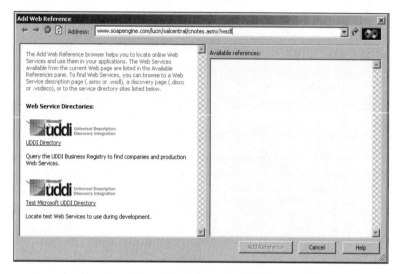

Once you've typed in the address, hit *Enter*, and then click on the Add Reference button when it becomes available.

5. The Solution Explorer will now show an entry under the Web References node that corresponds to the web service we just selected. If you click the Show All Files on the Solution Explorer tool bar, you'll see a file called Reference.vb. This file contains the proxy cnotes class that Visual Studio .NET has generated for us:

6. The new reference, com.soapengine.www, uses the inexplicable reverse-domain-naming convention that Visual Studio .NET employs by default for the remote web services referenced by a WSDL file. This will be the name of the namespace that encloses the cnotes class, so let's set it to something more readable. Right-click on the reference, select **Rename** and change the name to soapengine:

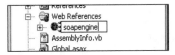

7. Now we can access the web service from our ASP.NET application. Add the following code to the Page_Load() event handler for WebForm1.aspx:

```
Private Sub Page_Load(ByVal sender As System.Object, _
                      ByVal e As System.EventArgs) Handles MyBase.Load
    Dim oNotes As New soapengine.cnotes()

    ' 123336 and 970Dog are the name and password of a registered user
    Dim oDataSet As DataSet = oNotes.GetMyNotes(123336, 0, "970Dog", False)
    DataGrid1.DataSource = oDataSet.Tables(0).DefaultView
    DataGrid1.DataBind()
End Sub
```

Notice that as you type the call to the GetMyNotes() method, IntelliSense will prompt you for each argument, and inform you of the correct data type. All of this information is extracted from the web service's WSDL file.

8. Now run the web service by selecting **Debug | Start** from the main menu, or by pressing *F5*. You should see a page similar to the following appear in your browser, showing the notes assigned to the user with ID 123336:

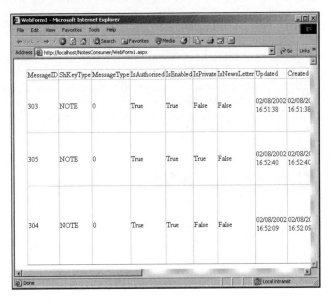

How It Works

Our web service was used to populate a simple `DataGrid` control with information returned over the Internet as a `DataSet`. First, we created an instance of the proxy class, using the name we just assigned:

```
Dim oNotes As New soapengine.cnotes()
```

Once we've got this local proxy class, all we have to do is call its methods, and the details of connecting to the web service and transferring data are all handled for us behind the scenes:

```
Dim oDataSet As DataSet = oNotes.GetMyNotes(123336, 0, "970Dog", False)
```

Note that we're calling the `GetMyNotes()` method with a user ID and password that have been created specifically for this example. To obtain a new account, navigate to http://www.soapengine.com/lucin/salcentral/cnotes.asmx, and follow the instructions there.

In the last two lines of code, we bound our newly acquired `DataSet` to our `DataGrid` to display the data, in a manner that you've seen before.

More About Web References

If you take a look at the representation of the web service in the Solution Explorer, you can see an entry for the `cnotes.wsdl` file, which is an exact copy of the WSDL file that resides on the server – it was copied to our local machine at the moment we referenced it. This might ring some alarm bells, and it's worth noting that if the remote web service changes, this file must be updated. We can do this by right-clicking on the name of the service, and selecting **Update Web Reference**.

In response, Visual Studio .NET will re-examine the remote WSDL schema file, comparing it with the one stored in the project, and updating the latter if necessary. Of course, an update could mean that some of the methods and argument have changed, resulting in the failure of your application, but any such problems will appear as syntax errors that you can easily identify and change within your code.

The `reference.map` file contains information about the location of files, including the remote web service URL, and the name of the local WSDL schema file. It too is automatically generated when a web service is referenced, but it can be changed to allow for customization. If, for example, the supplier created a new WSDL schema when creating a new version of their web service, you could change the location within the `reference.map` text file manually, and simply **Update Web Reference**, instead of having to remove the entry and re-reference it.

Creating an XML Storage Web Service

Now we've seen how we can consume an external web service, let's have a go at creating a web service of our own. In the following example, we'll demonstrate a web service that can save data in an XML file. This technique allows us to store complex data structures without using a SQL Server database, and provides a solution to a variety of data storage requirements.

Choosing the Best Design

Our web service will create, store, edit, and retrieve a simple 'hot list' of user contacts, and will actually consist of two separate web services:

❑ `HotList.asmx` – allows adding, deleting, updating, and retrieval of information in the XML file

❑ `IO.asmx` – controls the actual reading and writing of the XML file

As with any project, we need to get the design right before we start, and this is especially important for web services – if they're well designed, they can be reused time and time again in a variety of situations. Below, you can see a simple diagram that shows how our two web services employ a multi-tier approach to providing the client application with the required functionality:

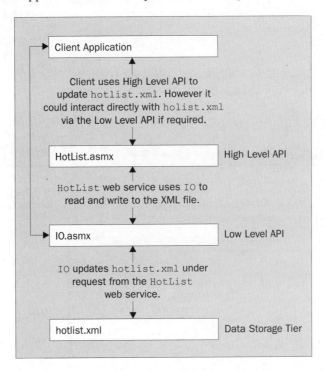

Our web service is broken up into three distinctive tiers, plus the client. Each can be developed and tested independently before moving on to the next. By splitting the web service functionality into a high-level API and a low-level API, we enhance reusability, and facilitate testing and development with a 'divide and conquer' strategy.

Try It Out – Creating a Web Service

First of all, then, we'll create a web service that does nothing more than read a dataset from, and write a dataset to, an XML file.

1. In Visual Studio .NET, create a new Visual Basic ASP.NET Web Service project called XmlStorage:

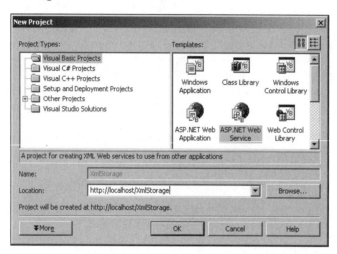

2. As usual, the Solution Explorer will now show the files that Visual Studio .NET creates for us. Service1.asmx is the default web service file, containing a skeleton code template that we'll fill in to create our web service. Rename this file to IO.asmx:

3. Open up IO.asmx, and you'll see that the name of the Public Class that's defined in this file is still Service1. It's preferable to give the class the same name as the file, so you should change that, and you should also change the Namespace from Visual Studio .NET's default (and meaningless) http://tempuri.org/ to http://wrox.com/XmlStorage/:

```
<WebService(Namespace := "http://wrox.com/XmlStorage/")> _
Public Class IO
    Inherits System.Web.Services.WebService
```

4. The body of our IO class contains a commented-out example web service (the ubiquitous "Hello World"), which can be uncommented should we ever require it for testing. Be reckless, and delete it. Insert the following code in its place:

```
' Loads XML file into a DataSet, as long as the fields passed in correspond
' to the elements in the XML data file.
<WebMethod()> Public Function LoadXML(ByVal sFileName As String, _
                       ByVal ParamArray asFields() As String) As DataSet

    Dim oDataSet As DataSet = CreateTableStruct(sFileName, asFields)
    oDataSet.ReadXml("http://localhost/XmlStorage/XML/" & sFileName & ".xml")
    Return oDataSet
End Function

' Saves data in the DataSet argument as XML with the filename supplied.
<WebMethod()> Public Function SaveXML(ByVal sFileName As String, _
                          ByVal oDataSet As DataSet) As Boolean

    Dim oFile As System.IO.FileInfo = New System.IO.FileInfo( _
                   Server.MapPath("") & "\XML\" & sFileName & ".xml")
    Dim oSW As System.IO.StreamWriter = oFile.CreateText()
    oSW.Write(oDataSet.GetXml)
    oSW.Close()
    Return True
End Function

' Function creates a DataTable within a DataSet from a list of fields
' supplied in asFields argument - does not cater for data types
Private Function CreateTableStruct(ByVal sTableName As String, _
                    ByVal ParamArray asFields() As String) As DataSet

    Dim oTable As New DataTable()
    Dim oDataSet As New DataSet()
    oTable.TableName = sTableName
    Dim asField As String

    ' Loop through fields adding to DataTable
    For Each asField In asFields
       oTable.Columns.Add(asField)
    Next

    ' Add DataTable to the DataSet
    oDataSet.Tables.Add(oTable)
    oDataSet.DataSetName = "tables"

    Return oDataSet
End Function
```

How It Works

With these three methods, we've created the first layer of our web service design. The code is designed to be as generic as possible, by permitting XML files to be saved to and read from a DataSet, using the filename passed in as an argument.

ASP.NET provides a very neat IE-based interface for testing simple web services, but unfortunately we can't use it in this example because of the complex arguments to some of the methods. (We'll see this test interface in action later on.) If we wanted to test this web service at this stage, we could do so by creating a simple client, but for now a brief overview of the workings of each method will suffice:

- ❑ LoadXML() – Loads XML data from a file situated in a subdirectory of the current project called XML, and stores it in a DataSet that we can then return from the web service.

- ❑ SaveXML() – Saves the data in a DataSet to an XML file in the XML subdirectory.

- ❑ CreateTableStruct() – Creates a table from a supplied list of field names. This table is then attached to a DataSet and can be used to store the XML.

The methods of the IO class that we wish to be accessible to consumers of the web service have been prefaced with <WebMethod()>, as you may have noticed. This is required before *every* web method of a web service. Methods without this preface are reserved for internal use by the web service, and are not available to the web service's consumers.

Web Services On Web Services

The methods exposed by the IO class fulfill the low-level requirement of directly changing the XML file, and therefore we can reasonably refer to it as our web service's "low-level API". However, the class does not perform any validation of the data being placed in the fields, or any checking of the data structures to make sure that they conform to our requirements. We'd better provide something that does.

Try It Out – Creating the User Interface

We now need to create the "high-level API", which will be implemented by a web service that's easier for our customers to interact with through its more recognizable interface – namely, add, delete, update, and get methods. This web service will act as the main 'point of contact' for client applications.

1. Right-click on the XmlStorage project name in Solution Explorer, and select Add | Add Web Service. Enter HotList in the Name box. Click Open, and open the code for the new web service.

2. Change the generated class's namespace to http://wrox.com/XmlStorage/, as before.

3. Add a web method called GetHotList() to the code. This returns a DataSet containing the data from a file named Hotlist.xml. The DataSet mirrors the data structure of that XML file:

```
' Returns a DataSet populated with data from hotlist.xml
<WebMethod()> Public Function GetHotList() As DataSet

    ' Create an instance of IO web service
    Dim oIO As New IO()
```

```
   ' Create a DataSet and load it with data from hotlist.xml
   Dim oDataSet As DataSet = oIO.LoadXML("hotlist", "name", "email")
   Return oDataSet
End Function
```

4. Below it, add the following method, which updates a specific record in the XML file. The `RowNo` used here is a unique identifier for each row in the file. Note that a `DataSet` has a zero-based index, so to change the second record in the list, we would set `RowNo` to 1.

```
' Change existing details in hotlist.xml
<WebMethod()> Public Function UpdHotList(ByVal RowNo As Long, _
                  ByVal Name As String, ByVal Email As String) As Boolean

   Dim oIO As New IO()
   Dim oDataSet As DataSet = oIO.LoadXML("hotlist", "name", "email")

   ' Add the new information
   oDataSet.Tables("hotlist").Rows(RowNo)("name") = Name
   oDataSet.Tables("hotlist").Rows(RowNo)("email") = Email

   ' Save and return
   Return oIO.SaveXML("hotlist", oDataSet)
End Function
```

5. Next, we have a method to delete a specific row from the XML file:

```
' Removes the specified row from hotlist.xml
<WebMethod()> Public Function DelHotList(ByVal RowNo As Long) As Boolean

   Dim oIO As New IO()
   Dim oDS As DataSet = oIO.LoadXML("hotlist", "name", "email")

   ' Delete row and save file, if row is in range
   If (RowNo < oDS.Tables("hotlist").Rows.Count) Then
     oDS.Tables("hotlist").Rows(RowNo).Delete()
     Return (oIO.SaveXML("hotlist", oDS))
   Else
     Throw New System.Exception("RowNo is beyond rows in dataset")
   End If
End Function
```

6. Lastly, we need a method for adding a new record to the XML file. New records will always be appended to the end of the file:

```
' Add new details to hotlist.xml
<WebMethod()> Public Function AddHotList(ByVal Name As String, _
                             ByVal Email As String) As Boolean

   Dim oIO As New IO()
   Dim oDS As DataSet = oIO.LoadXML("hotlist", "name", "email")
```

```
  ' Add new details
  Dim asValues() As String = {Name, Email}
  Dim oDataRow As DataRow = oDS.Tables("hotlist").Rows.Add(asValues)

  ' Save and return
  Return oIO.SaveXML("hotlist", oDS)
End Function
```

7. Our two web services are now all ready for testing. First though, we have to create the XML subdirectory where we'll keep the Hotlist.xml file. Right-click on the XmlStorage project in Solution Explorer, and select **Add | New Folder**. Name the new folder XML:

As well as the organizational advantage, we're using a subdirectory for our XML file because this directory will require lower security rights, and we can thus keep the main project code in the directory secure.

8. To alter the security for the XML folder, we need to locate it in Windows Explorer. One way to do this is to right-click the XmlStorage project, choose **Properties**, and then select **Web Settings** in the right-hand tree view. The **File share** box shows the directory of the project on disk:

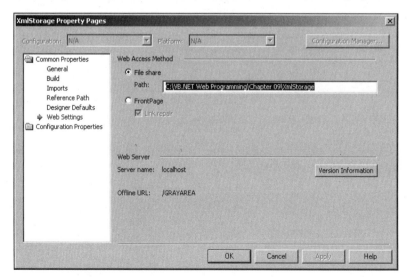

Now you can just copy this path and paste it into the Run dialog in the Windows Start menu to open the directory in Windows Explorer.

9. Next, right-click on the XML directory and select Properties. Open the Security tab, and select Everyone in the list of users at the top. Give this user Full Control in the Permissions pane below, and click OK to complete:

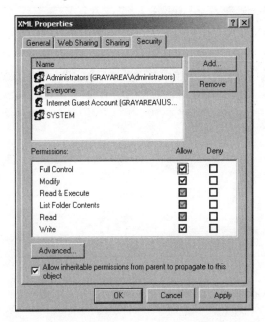

We've now given every Tom, Dick, and Harriet the ability to read and write data to this directory, so this is *not* something we would want to do for a commercial web service available to the general public. In the next two chapters, we're going to cover the topic of security in some depth, and you'll learn some techniques for preventing this kind of security hole.

10. To complete our web service, we need to return to Visual Studio .NET and create a Hotlist.xml file that gets us started. Right-click the XML folder in Solution Explorer, and select Add | Add New Item. Choose the XML File template, and call it hotlist.xml.

11. When the new file opens in the Visual Studio .NET editor, enter the following elements:

```
<tables>
  <hotlist>
    <name>Mike Clark</name>
    <email>mikec@lucin.com</email>
  </hotlist>
  <hotlist>
    <name>Joe 90</name>
    <email>joe@joey.com</email>
  </hotlist>
</tables>
```

12. We can now test our web service. Right-click `Hotlist.asmx`, select **Set as Start Page**, and press *F5* to compile and run it.

This opens the ASP.NET test interface for the `Hotlist.asmx` web service, which we mentioned earlier, in Internet Explorer:

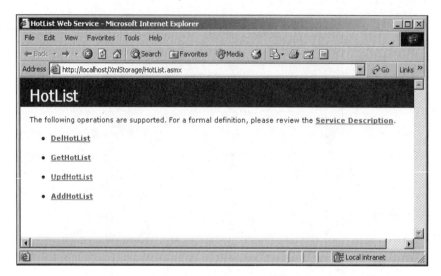

As you can see, this page lists the four web methods, or **operations**, of the `HotList` web service. The **Service Description** link displays the WSDL file that Visual Studio .NET has created to describe our web service.

13. Let's test the `GetHotList()` web method. Click on that link to go to the test page:

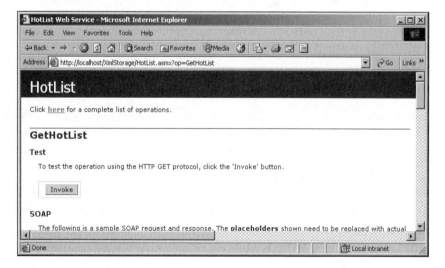

14. Press Invoke, and something like this will appear:

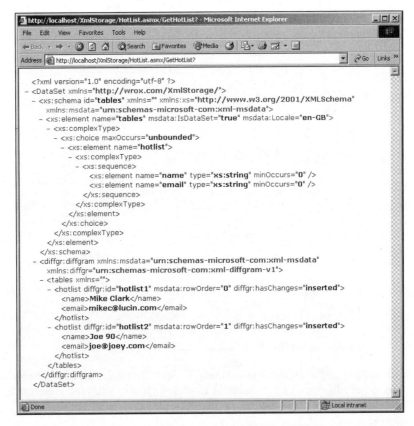

This is the `Hotlist.xml` file, returned as a dataset in XML format. Feel free to test out the update, add, and delete functionality using this interface to get a good feel for how the web service works.

Consuming Our Web Service

Now that we've created a web service, let's complete the picture and show how we could use it from a client application. As you might guess, this follows the same pattern as the first example, when we consumed a third party web service. For the sake of simplicity, we will again create our client as an ASP.NET application.

Try It Out – Consuming the XmlStorage Application

Because you've seen this process in action before, we can afford to be quite speedy here. In these steps we'll create a user interface, connect up to our web service, and try running some tests against it.

1. We can create our client within the existing `XmlStorage` solution. Call it `XmlStorageClient`.

2. `WebForm1.aspx` will open automatically in the design view, and you now need to drag the controls shown below onto the page from the **Web Forms** tab of the **Toolbox**. The following image also shows the IDs that need to be set for certain controls, and the `Text` properties for the buttons and labels also need to be set accordingly:

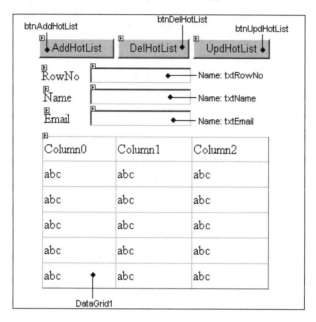

3. Now we need to add a reference to our web service. Right click on **References** under the `XmlStorageClient` project in Solution Explorer, choose **Add Web Reference**, and enter the following in the **Address** box:

http://localhost/XmlStorage/HotList.asmx

Press *Enter*, and click the **Add Reference** button. Your solution should now look like this:

4. Add the following member declaration to the top of the code-behind page for
WebForm1.aspx to instantiate a class that we can use to access our web service:

...

```
Protected WithEvents btnDelHotList As System.Web.UI.WebControls.Button
Protected WithEvents btnUpdHotList As System.Web.UI.WebControls.Button
Dim oHotList As New localhost.HotList()
```

5. Next, add the following line to the Page_Load() event handler:

```
Private Sub Page_Load(ByVal sender As System.Object, _
                         ByVal e As System.EventArgs) Handles MyBase.Load
    RefreshDisplay()
End Sub
```

6. The RefreshDisplay() subroutine that was called is created next. It will be used to fill the
DataGrid when the page first loads, and after every button click.

```
Private Sub RefreshDisplay()
    Dim oDataSet As DataSet = oHotList.GetHotList
    DataGrid1.DataSource = oDataSet
    DataGrid1.DataBind()
End Sub
```

7. Now flip back to the design view and double-click the **AddHotList** button. Add this code to the
event handler that's created:

```
Private Sub btnAddHotList_Click(ByVal sender As System.Object, _
                   ByVal e As System.EventArgs) Handles btnAddHotList.Click
    oHotList.AddHotList(txtName.Text, txtEmail.Text)
    RefreshDisplay()
End Sub
```

8. Repeat Step 7 for the DelHotList and UpdHotList buttons, adding the code
highlighted below:

```
Private Sub btnDelHotList_Click(ByVal sender As System.Object, _
                   ByVal e As System.EventArgs) Handles btnDelHotList.Click
    oHotList.DelHotList(txtRowNo.Text)
    RefreshDisplay()
End Sub

Private Sub btnUpdHotList_Click(ByVal sender As System.Object, _
                   ByVal e As System.EventArgs) Handles btnUpdHotList.Click
    oHotList.UpdHotList(txtRowNo.Text, txtName.Text, txtEmail.Text)
    RefreshDisplay()
End Sub
```

9. We're now ready to try running our client. Right-click on the `XmlStorageClient` project in Solution Explorer and select **Set as Startup Project**. Press *F5* to compile and run, and the following screen should appear in your browser:

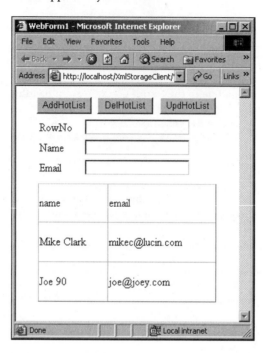

10. To test our form, try the following, in this order:

AddHotList – Enter a Name and an Email address, and press the AddHotList button.

DelHotList – Records are numbered from 0, so to delete the second record, enter a RowNo of 1, and press the DelHotList button. In this case, it doesn't matter what the Name and Email fields are set to, as they are not used.

UpdHotList – Change the Name and Email to something different, and then press the UpdHotList button to update that row.

11. Each time we perform an amendment using our client, the XML file is being changed. You can see these alterations as they happen if you open another instance of Internet Explorer, and type in the following URL:

http://localhost/XmlStorageClient/XML/hotlist.xml

Now make some changes with the client, switch back to the Internet Explorer window showing `Hotlist.xml`, and simply refresh the screen. You will see all your amendments being reflected in the XML file.

SOAP Messages

As we've mentioned, XML Web Services work by sending SOAP messages between the client and the web server hosting the web service. The web service's methods are invoked by an appropriate SOAP message, and a SOAP message is returned in response.

SOAP Message Types

There are three types of SOAP message:

- **SOAP request.** This is **sent to** a SOAP-compliant server, such as IIS, to invoke a method exposed by a web service. It contains any arguments required by the method.

- **SOAP response.** This is **returned from** a SOAP-compliant server and contains the results of processing a SOAP request.

- **SOAP fault.** This is **returned from** a SOAP-compliant server if an error occurs while processing a SOAP request.

SOAP Message Format

Each of the three types of SOAP message conforms to the following basic structure:

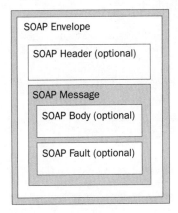

- The **SOAP envelope** contains the entire SOAP message.

- The **SOAP header** can contain information pertaining to transactions, security, logon information, the source of a request, and so on.

- The **SOAP message** contains either a SOAP fault or a SOAP body construct.

- The **SOAP body** contains the bulk of the message, including the method to call and the names and values of the arguments to use.

- The **SOAP fault** is only available if an error occurs, and it's only used during a SOAP response message. It passes an error back to the calling client.

Of course, we've never seen any of these SOAP messages in our examples, because so much of the workings of web services are hidden from view by Visual Studio .NET and the .NET Framework. Sometimes, however, it's handy to be able to see what is happening under the hood, and trapping and saving the SOAP messages that pass between our client and the web service can be useful when debugging. This is what we'll do in the following example, and it will also provide a little insight into the mechanism at work.

Try It Out – Trapping the SOAP Request

In this example, we'll add some code to the 'update' handler that interrupts the ongoing process and sends a snapshot of the SOAP message to an external XML file for our perusal at leisure.

1. Right-click on the XML folder in Solution Explorer, and select **Add | New Item**. Select the **XML File** template, and enter a name of soap.xml.

2. Add an empty <tables> element to the new soap.xml file as shown:

```
<?xml version="1.0" encoding="utf-8" ?>
<tables></tables>
```

3. Now all we have to do is change the code for the UpdHotList() method in HotList.asmx, as highlighted:

```
<WebMethod()> Public Function UpdHotList(ByVal RowNo As Long, _
                    ByVal Name As String, ByVal Email As String) As Boolean

    Dim oIO As New IO()
    Dim oDataSet As DataSet = oIO.LoadXML("hotlist", "name", "email")

    ' Add the new information
    oDataSet.Tables("hotlist").Rows(RowNo)("name") = Name
    oDataSet.Tables("hotlist").Rows(RowNo)("email") = Email

    ' Get the SOAP request from the Context application variable
    Dim sSOAPRequest As String
    Dim oStreamReader As System.IO.StreamReader
    oStreamReader = New System.IO.StreamReader(Context.Request.InputStream)
    oStreamReader.BaseStream.Seek(0, System.IO.SeekOrigin.Begin)
    sSOAPRequest = oStreamReader.ReadToEnd()

    ' Use the existing methods to save the SOAP request to an XML file
    Dim oDataSet2 As DataSet = oIO.LoadXML("soap", "type", "message")
    Dim asValues() As String = {"request", sSOAPRequest}
    Dim oDataRow As DataRow = oDataSet2.Tables("soap").Rows.Add(asValues)
    oIO.SaveXML("soap", oDataSet2)

    ' Save and return
    UpdHotList = oIO.SaveXML("hotlist", oDataSet)
End Function
```

Here, we're using the `Context` object to obtain the SOAP request. This contains data relating to the current communication with the remote client, including the full SOAP message received by the web service.

4. With `XmlStorageClient` still set as the startup project, press *F5* to start up the client. Update any of the XML records using the `WebForm1.aspx` page.

5. Open http://localhost/XmlStorage/XML/soap.xml in yet another Internet Explorer window. You should find that the SOAP request for the update you have just run now appears in this XML file, inside the `<message>` element.

Note that the request doesn't appear in the usual XML hierarchical form in Internet Explorer – the text is black in the screenshot. This is because it has been saved as escaped text (where `&lt;` is substituted for <, and so on). However, we can still see the structure of a typical SOAP request:

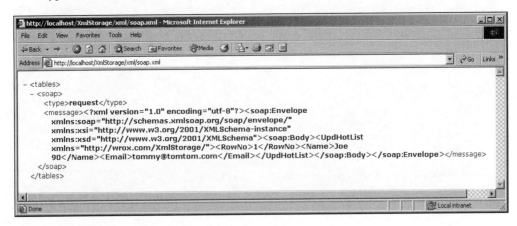

Validating and Error Trapping

One of the interesting things about web services is their ability to use functionality from other web services, perhaps provided by other companies.

For example, our `XmlStorage` web service has very little in the way of error checking and validation. Rather than go to the trouble of adding our own code to test whether an e-mail address is valid however, we could use a third party web service to do it for us!

Try It Out – Calling a Third Party Web Service From Our Own Web Service

We'll use another free web service provided by Lucin to validate e-mails in our `XmlStorage` project; this one's called `IsEmailAddress`. We'll also add some code that raises an exception that can be handled by the client in the event of an error.

1. First of all, we need a reference in our web service project to the `IsEmailAddress` web service. Right-click on the **References** node under the `XmlStorage` web service project, and select **Add Web Reference**. The URL we need to refer to is:

http://www.soapengine.com/lucin/salcentral/ccomms.asmx

2. Now open the code-behind page for `HotList.asmx`, and change the `AddHotList()` method as shown:

```
<WebMethod()> Public Function AddHotList(ByVal Name As String, _
                                        ByVal Email As String) As Boolean

    ' Instantiate web service proxy
    Dim oEmail As New com.soapengine.www.ccomms()

    ' Check validity of email address
    If oEmail.IsEmailAddress(123336, "970Dog", Email) Then

        ' Set up variables
        Dim oIO As New IO()
        Dim oDS As DataSet = oIO.LoadXML("hotlist", "name", "email")

        ' Add new details
        Dim asValues() As String = {Name, Email}
        Dim oDataRow As DataRow = oDS.Tables("hotlist").Rows.Add(asValues)

        ' Save and return
        AddHotList = oIO.SaveXML("hotlist", oDS)
    Else
        Throw New System.Exception("Invalid email address")
    End If
End Function
```

3. Run the solution by pressing F5. Enter any value you fancy for the name, but use an invalid e-mail address, such as `abcdefg`. When you now press the **AddHotList** button, the following error message will appear in your browser:

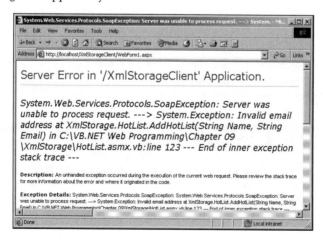

We can handle this exception from our client in fairly straightforward fashion, as we'll see in the next section.

Handling Web Service Errors

We don't really want our web application to come up with this unsightly and user-unfriendly screen whenever an invalid e-mail address is entered. Rather, we want our client to trap this error, which is created by the following line in the UpdHotList method:

```
Throw New System.Exception("Invalid email address")
```

In a web service, this line causes a SOAP fault message to be returned to the client by the server, and it's this SOAP fault that ASP.NET uses to get all the lovely information that appeared on the error page. The following diagram shows how this SOAP fault travels from the web service to the client:

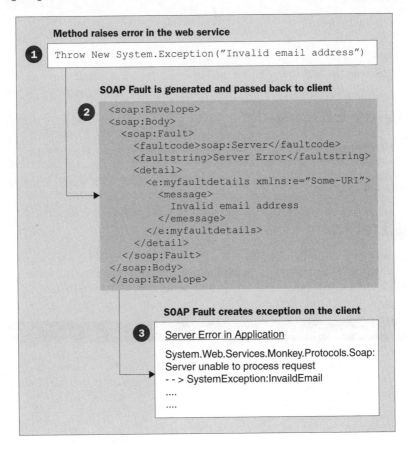

Method raises error in the web service

1 Throw New System.Exception("Invalid email address")

SOAP Fault is generated and passed back to client

2
```
<soap:Envelope>
<soap:Body>
  <soap:Fault>
    <faultcode>soap:Server</faultcode>
    <faultstring>Server Error</faultstring>
    <detail>
      <e:myfaultdetails xmlns:e="Some-URI">
        <message>
          Invalid email address
        </emessage>
      </e:myfaultdetails>
    </detail>
  </soap:Fault>
</soap:Body>
</soap:Envelope>
```

SOAP Fault creates exception on the client

3 Server Error in Application

System.Web.Services.Monkey.Protocols.Soap:
Server unable to process request
- - > SystemException:InvaildEmail
....
....

You've seen us handling exceptions in our web applications, and happily the process is no different for web services.

1. Change the code in the btnAddHotList_Click() event handler to add a Try...Catch block:

```
Private Sub btnAddHotList_Click(ByVal sender As System.Object, _
                    ByVal e As System.EventArgs) Handles btnAddHotList.Click
    Try
        oHotList.AddHotList(txtName.Text, txtEmail.Text)
        RefreshDisplay()
    Catch e1 As System.Exception
        Response.Write(e1.Message)
    End Try
End Sub
```

2. Run the project again and try to add new details, using an invalid e-mail address as in the previous example. Press the **AddHotList** button, and now our own error message appears on the page.

Web Service Efficiency

Comparatively speaking, transferring information over the Internet is a slow and expensive process, and for that reason it's always important to ensure that your applications do it no more, and no more often, than they absolutely have to. In this section, we'll look at a couple of ways that you can optimize these aspects of your web services.

Reducing Traffic

One way that we can increase the speed of our web services is to reduce the amount of data they return. For example, our GetHotList() web method returns an entire DataSet that contains the data structure (field names, data types, and so on) as well as the data itself. Surely there's a better way?

Try It Out – Streamlining Our Web Service

We can simplify our service by sending back the data alone, rather than a whole DataSet object, as long as the client knows what the data structure should be. The client can then reconstruct the data in the required format.

1. Change the GetHotList() method in the code for HotList.asmx as shown:

```
<WebMethod()> Public Function GetHotList() As String
    ' Create an instance of IO web service
    Dim oIO As New IO()
```

```
' Create a DataSet and load it with data from hotlist.xml
Dim oDataSet As DataSet = oIO.LoadXML("hotlist", "name", "email")
Return oDataSet.GetXml
End Function
```

All we've done is to return `oDataSet.GetXML`, rather than the entire `DataSet`, and changed the return type to `String`.

2. Right-click the `XmlStorage` project in Solution Explorer, and select **Set as Startup Project**. Now press *F5* to compile and run the application. Test the `GetHotList()` method, and you will see that it returns the following:

```
<?xml version="1.0" encoding="utf-8" ?>
<string xmlns="http://tempuri.org/"><tables> <hotlist> <name>Mike Clark</name>
<email>mikec@lucin.com</email> </hotlist> <hotlist> <name>Joe 90</name>
<email>joe@joey.com</email> </hotlist> </tables></string>
```

This is considerably less data than an entire `DataSet`, which also includes the data structure and data type definitions. Of course, we still need to modify our client to recreate the structure from this string, but that's not a difficult task, and it's well worth it for the performance gain.

Caching Results

ASP.NET web services have an in-built caching system that stores the result of each method call in the server's memory. The next time the same method is run with exactly the same arguments, the server can return the cached results without having to execute the web service again.

We can configure individual methods to cache their results on the server. It's worth designing web methods with caching in mind, as it can make a significant difference for processes that are called often, or that are time consuming to run.

Try It Out – Implementing Web Service Caching

Let's rewrite our 'get' handler to use caching, and see what effect this has on the operation of our web service.

1. Create a new method in the code for the `HotList.asmx` page, like so:

```
<WebMethod()> Public Function GetHotList_Cached(ByVal UID As Long) As String
   Return (GetHotList())
End Function
```

2. We can enable caching for this function by setting an attribute on the `<WebMethod()>` declaration. In this case, we need to set the `CacheDuration` attribute like so:

```
<WebMethod(CacheDuration:=600)>
```

The 600 here indicates that the server cache should hold a copy of the value returned by this method for no more than 600 seconds, at which point the web service should be invoked to refresh the cached value.

3. Press *F5* and click the `GetHotList_Cached()` link. Enter a `UID` (user ID) parameter of 1. This will return a result something like this:

```
<?xml version="1.0" encoding="utf-8" ?>
<string xmlns="http://tempuri.org/"><tables> <hotlist> <name>Mike Clark</name>
<email>mikec@lucin.com</email> </hotlist> <hotlist> <name>Joe 90</name>
<email>joe@joey.com</email> </hotlist> </tables></string>
```

As this was the first time the method was run since compilation, this result will be placed in the cache.

4. We can illustrate what's going on (and also one of the dangers of caching) by adding some new details through the test interface for the `AddHotList()` method. If we then invoke the `GetHotList_Cached()` method again, using the same `UID` of 1, we will see that the new details do not appear on the returned list.

5. Now run `GetHotList_Cached()` again, but this time using a `UID` of 2. This time, the new hot list entry *will* appear, because the argument is different from that used for the cached result.

When Not to Cache

So, the cached result for `UID` 1 will not be updated until 600 seconds have elapsed since it was last run. After that time, a subsequent call will cause the web service to be run again, and the cache will be updated with the latest results. Hence, you should only cache web methods that return results that do not have to be the very latest version, or where the result is fixed for fixed arguments.

Another factor to consider is that caching consumes memory space on the server hosting the web service, so care must be taken to avoid caching methods that will use up substantial amounts of memory. For illustration, here are two possible web service declarations:

```
<WebMethod(CacheDuration:=3600)> Public Function WhatsMyHoroscope( _
          ByVal MySign As String, ByVal CurrentDefCon as String) As String
```

```
<WebMethod(CacheDuration:=3600)> Public Function WhatsMyHoroscope( _
          ByVal MySign As String, ByVal CurrentDefCon as String, _
          Byval MyFavoriteColor As String) As String
```

Both of these will cache their output for 3600 seconds (1 hour), and the first takes a sign of the zodiac and the current DEFCON as arguments. There are twelve signs of the zodiac, and five DEFCONs, so a maximum of 12 x 5 or 60 results will ever be held in the cache. This is bearable, and could save a lot of time when the web method is called.

The second has both these arguments, but it adds a third: a string representing the person's favorite color. While it may be useful to cache results for colors such as blue, red, and so on, results for every other color requested would also be cached: aquamarine, periwinkle, flamingo pink, and on, and on. Caching such a web method would occupy much more of the cache, and be less useful in general, as fewer requests could be satisfied by previously cached results.

Web Services are Forgetful

By design, web services are **stateless**. This means that variable values and the like are forgotten as soon as one call completes, and further calls cannot make use of them. This is standard practice for all sorts of web applications, and makes for easier unit testing and enables jobs to be completed quite independently of each other.

It also reduces the drain on server resources, because if a web service maintained state – that is, remembered results of calculations from previous calls – the server would have to store information in memory for each user that called it, which would quickly become a significant problem when an application is scaled up to allow many users at once. Some operating systems would not even be physically able to maintain state, and this is another reason why it is not supported in XML Web Services.

Asynchronous Communication

Asynchronous communication refers to the ability to invoke a web service, but rather than waiting for a response, leaving it to complete processing while the client continues with other tasks. When the web service completes, the client can simply collect the results at a convenient moment.

Try It Out – Implementing Asynchronous Communication

Let's quickly demonstrate this idea by creating a new Windows client that consumes a third-party web service asynchronously. The web service we will use is supplied by www.salcentral.com, and searches for other commercial web services that are available for us to use within our applications.

1. Create a new Visual Basic .NET *Windows* application project called WebServiceSearch as a new solution.

2. Add the controls from the Windows Forms tab of the Toolbox to the Form1.vb form as shown below, and set the IDs and Text properties as indicated:

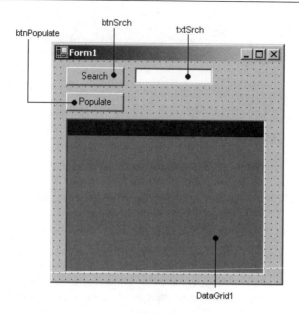

btnPopulate   btnSrch   txtSrch

DataGrid1

3. Now we need to reference the web service, and you'll be pleased to hear that referencing a web service from a Windows Forms application is exactly the same as doing it from an ASP.NET application. Right click on References, select Add Web Reference, and use the following URL for the third party web service:

http://www.soapengine.com/lucin/salcentral/csearch.asmx

4. Right click Form.vb in Solution Explorer, and choose View Code. Type in the following three methods after the Windows Form Designer generated code region:

. . .

```
Dim oDataSet As DataSet

' Invoke the search web service asynchronously
Private Sub btnSrch_Click(ByVal sender As System.Object, _
                    ByVal e As System.EventArgs) Handles btnSrch.Click

    Dim oSrch As New com.soapengine.www.csearch()
    Dim oCallBackMethod As New AsyncCallback(AddressOf ServiceCallBack)

    oSrch.BeginSearch(123336, "970Dog", txtSrch.Text, _
                "https://uddi.microsoft.com/inquire", _
                True, True, True, 30, False, oCallBackMethod, Me)
End Sub
```

```
' Populate the DataGrid with returned results
Private Sub btnPopulate_Click(ByVal sender As System.Object, _
                ByVal e As System.EventArgs) Handles btnPopulate.Click
   If (Not oDataSet Is Nothing) Then
      DataGrid1.DataSource = oDataSet.Tables(0).DefaultView
   End If
End Sub


' This will be called when the web service completes
Public Sub ServiceCallBack(ByVal oSync As System.IAsyncResult)
   Dim oSrch As New com.soapengine.www.csearch()
   oDataSet = oSrch.EndSearch(oSync)
   btnSrch.Text = "Completed"
End Sub
End Class
```

5. Start the project by pressing *F5*. Enter **sms** in the text box, and click **Search**. Our web service now starts searching for web services and businesses that contain **sms** in their title or description, a task that will take a moment or two.

Not a lot seems to be happening, but eventually the text on the **Search** button will changes to read **Completed**. If you now press the **Populate** button, data appears in the DataGrid as shown:

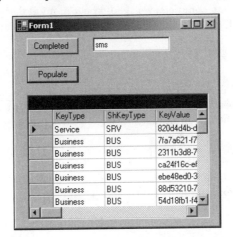

How It Works

When we click the **Search** button, the web service gets to work looking for matching web services and businesses. In the meantime, however, we're free to carry on doing the sorts of things users do, like repeatedly pressing the **Populate** button. The click handler for this button contains an If statement that won't let anything happen unless oDataSet contains any data, and so we see the button moving, even though nothing happens.

Inside the click handler for the **Search** button, notice this line:

```
Dim oCallBackMethod As New AsyncCallback(AddressOf ServiceCallBack)
```

325

This line sets up the `ServiceCallBack()` method that we added as the **callback method**, which is called when the web service completes, and returns its result. This object is then passed into `BeginSearch()`, which starts the asynchronous processing.

```
oSrch.BeginSearch(123336, "970Dog", txtSrch.Text, _
                "https://uddi.microsoft.com/inquire", _
                True, True, True, 30, False, oCallBackMethod, Me)
```

The actual web method we are calling is called `Search()`, but Visual Studio .NET automatically creates two methods for calling web methods asynchronously when we add a web reference. These methods are:

❑ `BeginSearch()` – invokes the web service without waiting for the results to be returned.

❑ `EndSearch()` – we call this method when the web service has completed in order to get the returned results.

Passing the `ServiceCallBack()` method into `BeginSearch()` as an `AsyncCallback` means that our callback method will automatically be executed as soon as the asynchronous process completes.

It's important to note that asynchronous invocation is not a part of the SOAP standard – it's just one of the extra services that ASP.NET provides. This is very nice of Microsoft, but when we design web services that take a long time to complete, we should bear in mind that not all consumers will be able to call it asynchronously, and there is in fact a danger of restricting our customer base.

Summary

This chapter has tried to cover the important aspects of web service design and implementation. Web services are a great way of providing functionality over an intranet or the Internet. They provide a very accessible interface to a variety of applications, and the advice is to get on board the bandwagon, and try them out.

Once you've created a useful web service, you can publish it on the Internet through UDDI, or another registry like www.salcentral.com. Any individual with software that understands SOAP will be able to access your web service by examining its WSDL file. Then it's just a case of waiting to see what sort of reaction you get from potential customers.

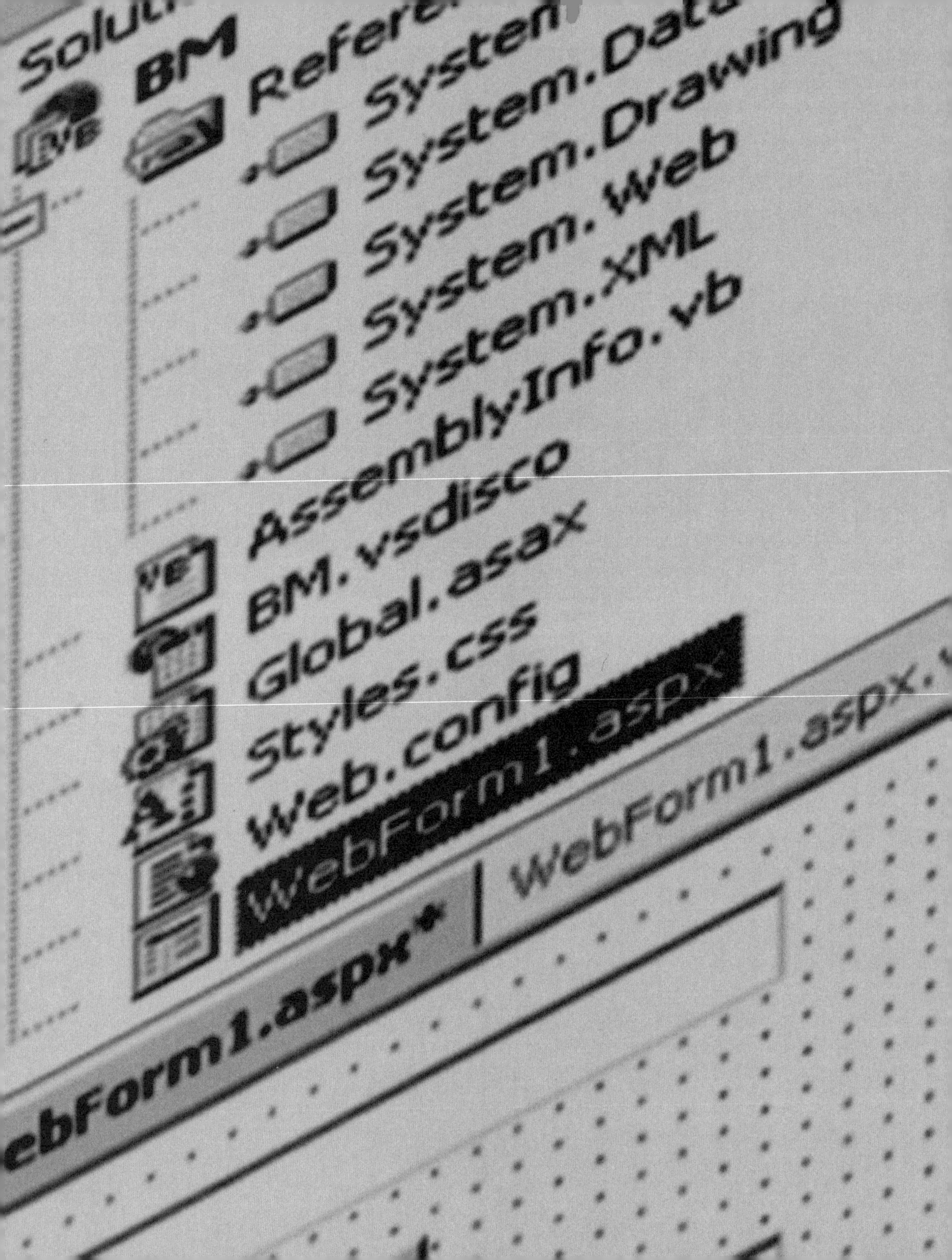

Solut...
BM Referen... System...
                System.Dat...
                System.Drawing
                System.Web
                System.XML
                AssemblyInfo.vb
        Assembly
        BM.vsdisco
        Global.asax
        Styles.css
        Web.config
        WebForm1.aspx

WebForm1.aspx

ebForm1.aspx* | WebForm1.aspx.v

The Role of the Web Server

Whenever we create a new web project in Visual Studio .NET, numerous files are created for us behind the scenes. Visual Studio .NET handles a lot of basic configuration details for us automatically, including setting up our application so that it's hosted on our web server and can be accessed by external clients. So far, we've been taking this for granted, but now we're going to look at the settings that Visual Studio .NET applies, and at how we can tweak them to suit our purposes.

In this chapter, we will look at:

- ❑ What a web server is, and what features are provided by IIS

- ❑ Configuring IIS manually, discussing exactly what a **virtual directory** is, and how to create and configure virtual directories by hand

- ❑ Locking down IIS to reduce the impact of hack attacks

- ❑ Using code in ASP.NET to take advantage of the security features of IIS that use **impersonation**

As a result of the current prerequisites for running ASP.NET, we will be concentrating mainly on discussing the web server that comes with Windows 2000 (IIS 5) and Windows XP Professional (IIS 5.1). These two versions, 5.0 and 5.1, are very similar, and can be considered as one for our purposes.

How Does a Web Server Work?

In Chapter 1, we described how the web server takes an incoming request, processes it, and sends it back to the client. When a web server is installed on a system, a TCP port is set aside so that any incoming requests for hosted pages are processed correctly. With IIS, the default TCP port is port 80.

> *TCP/IP is the default protocol for information exchange over the Internet. TCP is an abbreviation for Transmission Control Protocol; IP (Internet Protocol) is an addressing system. A TCP **port** is used for communication between two machines; and on any one machine there are up to 65,535 TCP ports.*

A TCP exchange between two machines occupies the whole of one port, so when a web page is requested, the request passes initially via port 80, then gets relayed to a different port, allocated from those available. This effectively limits the number of available connections between the server and any client to the maximum number of free ports.

Changing the default incoming port on our web server would change the address we need to use to access the server by adding the port number to the end of the request. For example, if we switched the default port to 4444, the address could be http://123.123.123.123:4444

When ASP.NET is installed on a server, IIS is set up so that it understands what to do when it receives a request for a page ending in `.aspx` – it knows that it has to process it differently from the other requests that it might receive.

Internet Information Services (IIS)

As we stated in the introduction, IIS is Microsoft's web server, and at the time of writing IIS 5 is included with Windows 2000 (all editions) and Windows XP Professional. However, IIS is more than just a web server: it can also host news services, act as an FTP server, and relay SMTP e-mail. Our interest here, though, is to look at the web server part of IIS and understand how it works.

IIS as a Web Server

In this section, we're going to start off by looking at how IIS handles page requests, and how our system must be configured in order to create or host ASP.NET applications. Later on, we will look at how we can administer IIS and use many of its features.

The Role of ISAPI

ISAPI is an acronym for **Internet Server Application Programming Interface**. It's a low-level interface that resides beneath higher-level abstractions like ASP.NET. In many ways, you can think of ASP.NET as a developer-friendly way of working with ISAPI – it's possible to work with it directly, but it's much easier if you can find an alternative approach! Every web development technology that's compatible with IIS must be able to communicate with ISAPI, which provides the ability to process page requests and send responses.

An ISAPI module, such as the ASP.NET module, is the go-between that can accept code written in a web programming language, and process it so that it's possible to send an appropriate response to the client browser. IIS has a list of acceptable file extensions that it can handle, and each file extension maps to an ISAPI module designed to handle that type of request.

Our ASP.NET pages have the extension `.aspx`, and our ASP.NET ISAPI module is `aspnet_isapi.dll`, which is located in the `%WinDir%\Microsoft.NET\Framework\v1.0.3705` folder. When a request comes in, the file extension will tell IIS which module to pass the request to for processing. This module will then pass the request on to the ASP.NET system process to be processed.

The ASP.NET System Process

The ASP.NET ISAPI module passes requests for ASP.NET pages to `aspnet_wp.exe`, which runs as a system process. The following screenshot shows this process at the bottom of the list that's produced by the Windows Task Manager:

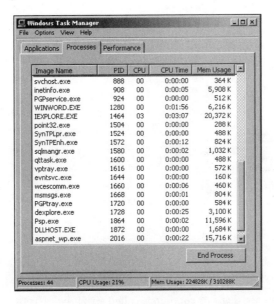

On the first request for a `.aspx` page after the server has been rebooted, this process is started automatically. (This is one reason why the first hit on a `.aspx` page can take so long.) Subsequent hits benefit from the facts that not only is there a cached, compiled version of the page stored on the server, but also this process is already active.

> *Note that there's also an entry near the top of the list called* `inetinfo.exe`. *This is the name of the process that IIS runs under, and will appear in the list whenever the web server is up and running.*

FrontPage Server Extensions

You may have heard of **FrontPage server extensions** before – when you install Visual Studio .NET, they are installed automatically, so that you can create ASP.NET web applications in the IDE. You don't need to install them on a server that just hosts applications, since they are only used during development.

The FrontPage server extensions enable certain functionality for communicating with the web server, and for uploading files to a web application from our development environment. It's a good idea *not* to install the server extensions on machines that host production web applications – they're not needed, and they can act as a security hole unless they're configured correctly.

IIS and the Management Console

It's time to take a closer look at IIS itself. Click the Start button on the desktop, and select Run... from the menu. In the box that appears, type `inetmgr` and click OK to launch the Internet Information Services Manager. Expanding some of the nodes on the left-hand side, you should see the following:

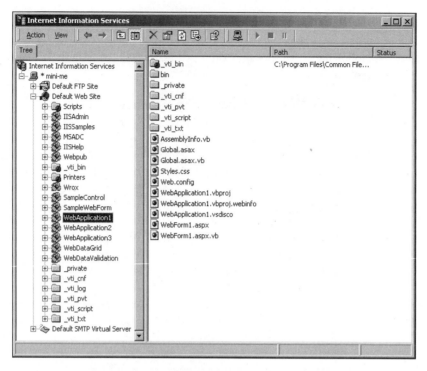

In the screenshot you can see that this computer, called mini-me, has been set up to act as a web server and an FTP server. The bottom main node is the SMTP Virtual Server node, which can be configured if you require SMTP forwarding (to relay SMTP mail to a mail server).

Underneath the Default Web Site node is a series of icons, some of which look a bit like folders, and some that look quite different. Take, for example, the currently selected icon, which refers to a web application that was created by Visual Studio .NET. The icon indicates that this is the virtual directory for the WebApplication1 application, which will correspond somehow to a physical location on our server.

Virtual Directories

When we request Internet web pages, we use URLs such as http://www.asp.net/default.aspx. For local content, we have been using things like http://localhost/applicationname/page.aspx. However, we know that applications created using Visual Studio .NET have *actually* been saved in a file system folder on our machine, and that our page.aspx file is *actually* in a location such as C:\inetpub\wwwroot\applicationname\page.aspx. The mapping between the physical location and the address that we type into an address bar is defined using **virtual directories**. Let's consider an example.

Imagine that there's a collection of web pages making up a site that resides on the local hard drive at the following location:

```
C:\My Files\My Apps\My Home Page\
```

To view this site via a web server, we can set up a virtual directory that 'points' to this path, so that we can browse the application by typing in the following into the address bar of our browser:

http://localhost/AllAboutMe/

In this case, the virtual directory is called AllAboutMe, and it acts as an alias for the local, physical path to the code. The physical path is hidden from anyone who browses to the virtual directory, and the actual address is kept simple. We can also assign web server-specific properties to this virtual directory that affect how the contents of the folder are processed on the server, including whether our web users are able to write to the folder, and whether any server-side script, such as ASP.NET pages, can be run in that directory. (Disabling this would restrict us to being able only to serve static pages, such as plain HTML files.)

Note that spaces aren't recommended in virtual directory names because they get changed to their HTML encoded equivalents when a page is requested, so requesting the following:

http://localhost/All About Me/

Would be resolved to:

http://localhost/All%20About%20Me/

Which is far less attractive and considerably more confusing.

The method we used to create a virtual directory in Chapter 1 was different from and simpler than this technique. Creating virtual directories from the IIS Management Console is more powerful, and gives us greater control over the result.

Try It Out – Creating a Virtual Directory

Let's have a go at creating our own virtual directory, and look at the settings available to us as we go along. In this example, we'll make one that points to a folder on our system, and then run the ASP.NET page that resides within it. Let's start by creating the physical directory and the sample file, and then we'll create the virtual directory and test the code.

1. Create a folder on your drive called My Code, and then create a sub-directory within this called BegVBNETWeb, producing the following path: C:\My Code\BegVBNETWeb

2. Because we want to go through this process manually, we're not going to use Visual Studio .NET here. We still need that sample file, though, so open up Notepad and enter the following code into a new file:

```
<%@ Page Language="VB" %>

<html>
  <head>
```

```
    <title>Simple test ASP.NET page</title>
  </head>
  <body>
    <form runat="server">
      <h2>A Simple ASP.NET Page</h2>
      <p>Enter your name in the box below, then click the button:</p>
      <p>
        <asp:TextBox id="txtNameBox" runat="server" />
        <asp:Button id="btnSubmit" onclick="btnSubmit_Click"
                    runat="server" Text="Click Here!" />
      </p>
      <p>
        <asp:Label id="lblMessageLabel" runat="server" />
      </p>
    </form>
  </body>
</html>

<script runat="server">
  Sub btnSubmit_Click(sender As Object, e As EventArgs)
    lblMessageLabel.Text = "Hello " & txtNameBox.Text
  End Sub
</script>
```

3. Select **Save As** from the **File** menu, navigate to the `My Code\BegVBNETWeb` directory you just created, and save the file as `HelloWorld.aspx`.

4. Open up the IIS management console (as described previously), right-click on the **Default Web Site** node, and select **New | Virtual Directory** from the context menu:

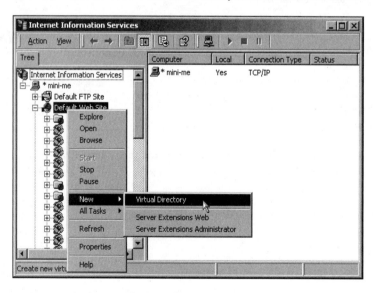

At this point, an introductory dialog will appear, but you can just click **Next** to continue.

5. In the first dialog of the Wizard proper, you'll be prompted for the name you want to give to your virtual directory. Enter 7361, which is the last 4 digits of the ISBN of this book, and click Next:

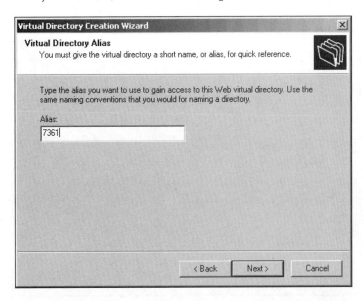

6. In the next dialog, either browse to the BegVBNETWeb directory or just enter the path into the textbox, and then click Next again:

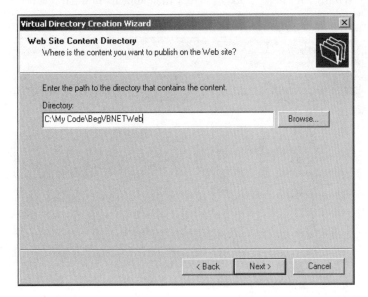

7. The penultimate dialog offers us a series of permissions that we can either enable or disable. For now, we're going to leave them with their default setting, so click on Next to continue:

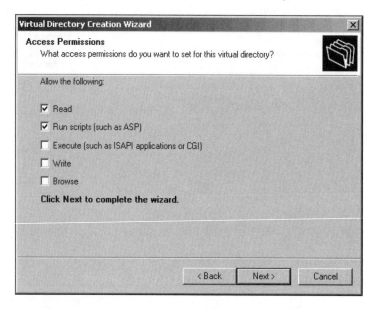

8. The last dialog confirms that our directory has been created successfully, so click Finish to close the Wizard. Our new virtual directory then appears in the directory list in the IIS console window:

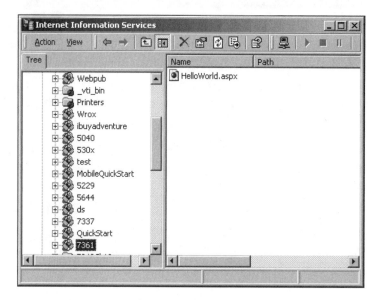

9. Open up your browser, type http://localhost/7361/HelloWorld.aspx into the address bar, and you should see the following:

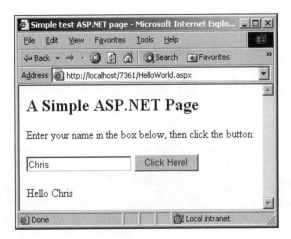

How It Works

The virtual directory that we've just created forms the name of our application, and we can refer to it as a subfolder beneath our `localhost` domain. Any ASP.NET code residing within this folder can now be hosted by the web server, and served up on demand to our clients.

If we choose to do so, we can create multiple virtual directories on our web server, each one pointing to a different physical location. If we really want to, we can even have more than one alias for the same physical directory, each with different permissions and settings.

In the sample page itself, rather than placing our code in a code-behind page, we placed our event handler in a script block on the same page as the controls. This syntax is useful for quick and simple solutions, but it doesn't make the code as easy to maintain as a code-behind page.

Configuring Server-Wide Settings

There are many different settings that we can apply to the virtual directories on our system. Server-wide settings configure the 'defaults', and we can then override or change those settings on a per-directory basis. Let's begin our analysis of them by looking at the former before moving on to the latter.

Back in the IIS management console, right-click on the name of your computer, and select Properties. You should see the following dialog box appear:

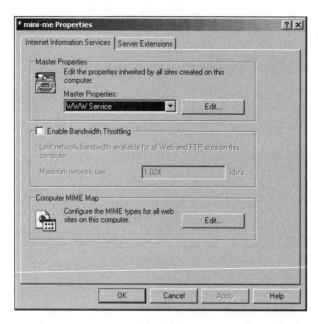

We are going to concern ourselves with the **WWW Service** on our machine, so click on the **Edit...** button to the right of the **Master Properties** section. That will produce the following:

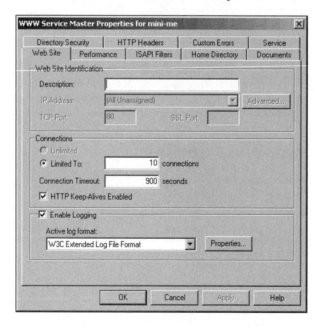

Each setting that we apply in this dialog sets the default settings for all applications on our web server. As stated above, an individual application can override the defaults, but these will always be the starting point.

Connection Settings

The maximum number of connections, and the connection timeout properties, are as good a pair of settings to begin with as any. The values you can see here are typical for a development machine, where we're unlikely to have multiple simultaneous connections, and we might want to keep a connection alive for quite a long time while we're testing.

At the other end of the spectrum, a machine serving sites with some element of personalization based on user login might use shorter values in this box, forcing users to log back in after they've been idle for a relatively short time. This could be particularly important in a banking application, for example, where an unattended computer that's left logged in to someone's on-line banking details could be a security issue.

Logging User Activity

The other item to notice on this dialog is that IIS will keep a log of all visits to the web server. By clicking on the **Properties** button to the right of the logging section, we open up a dialog in which we can customize the type of information logged, and the frequency of generation of log files:

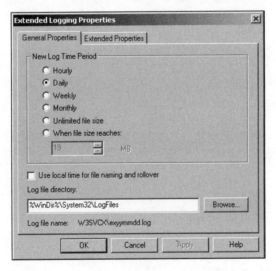

These logs are stored in the `%WinDir%\System32\LogFiles\w3svc1\` folder, and are labeled along the lines of `exyymmdd.log`. The content of such a log file might look something like this:

```
#Software: Microsoft Internet Information Services 5.0
#Version: 1.0
#Date: 2002-07-31 12:31:54
#Fields: time c-ip cs-method cs-uri-stem sc-status
12:31:54 127.0.0.1 GET /7361/helloworld.aspx 200
12:32:05 127.0.0.1 POST /7361/helloworld.aspx 200
12:33:01 192.168.202.185 GET /7361/helloworld.aspx 200
12:33:08 192.168.202.185 POST /7361/helloworld.aspx 200
12:34:50 192.168.0.121 GET /7361/helloworld.aspx 200
12:35:00 192.168.0.121 POST /7361/helloworld.aspx 200
```

Here, we can see a request for the `HelloWorld.aspx` page that we saw earlier, originating from the local machine, and then some requests for the same page from other machines on the intranet. The IP addresses of all machines are listed, along with the name of the resource that was either requested (HTTP GET) or sent back to the client (HTTP POST). The number 200 at the end of each entry indicates that the transaction was successful.

Logging hits to your web server is a great way to look out for malicious activity, and to track general usage of your site.

Increasing Performance

Moving on to the Performance tab of the main dialog produces a page with a slider that can help Windows to decide how much of its resources to allocate to IIS. Again, a development machine is unlikely to receive many hits in a day, so we've moved the slider from the default position, in the middle, to the left. That might just give us some extra juice for working with Microsoft Word!

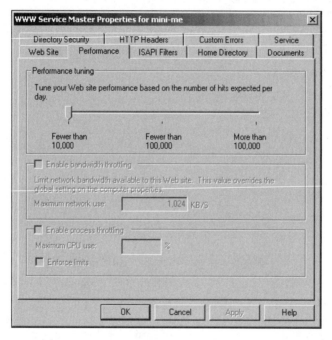

Configuring IIS for optimum performance in a production environment is obviously fairly crucial, but equally crucial and not to be forgotten is the impact on performance of the code you've used in your application. We'll examine performance issues in depth in Chapter 12.

General Security Settings

If we look now at the Directory Security tab in the Master Properties dialog, there's a section for configuring anonymous access and authentication on our web server. Here, we can click on the Edit... button to bring up a further dialog that we can use to configure access to our web server:

By default, **Anonymous** access to our web server is enabled, which is a logical choice in an Internet environment where clients can come from all over the world to view our sites. When we say "anonymous access", our users are still authenticated by the web server, but they are all authenticated under the same account. The default account used for this purpose in IIS is the IUSR_*MachineName* account, which defines the basic rights assigned to all anonymous access. We'll look at this account in more detail in just a moment.

Anonymous access is great for public web sites, but we may want to change this for an intranet scenario, or for any other restricted area in which we want to control access to our web server. In this case, we can make use of some of the other authentication options available to us. The three options available in this window are **Basic authentication**, **Digest authentication**, and **Integrated Windows authentication**.

❑ **Basic authentication.** This prompts the user for a valid user name and password, but these are transmitted to the server base64-encoded and unencrypted, which isn't a very secure technique. (Base64 encoding is a standard used for sending binary information over a network.) On the other hand, it's standards-compliant, and it's compatible with almost all browsers. If you're sure that the connection between your server and your client is secure, then basic authentication should work fine.

> *The Secure Sockets Layer (SSL), which we'll look at in more detail in just a moment, is commonly used alongside basic authentication to provide a secure method of communication.*

❑ **Digest authentication.** This works similarly to basic authentication, except that all transmitted information is encrypted using a hashing technique, making it very difficult for a malicious user to intercept the data and decrypt it. This method of authentication can pass data through firewalls and proxy servers, so it's great in an Internet scenario. However, it relies on HTTP version 1.1 in order to work, excluding some older browsers, and it's dependent on the server residing in a domain with a Windows 2000 domain controller.

❑ **Integrated Windows authentication.** Here, user details are encrypted before being transmitted to and from the server, so information exchange is a much more secure process. Users are not prompted for their details, as the current login details for the client machine are sent automatically when requested. If this process fails, the user is prompted to enter their user name and password, but the information will still be transmitted using this scheme.

Integrated Windows authentication is dependent on your users having a compatible browser, but it's great for intranet environments where the clients and server are on the same domain, making it simple for users to log in to a site and gain access to the information they require. The drawback of this method is that it can't reliably pass data through firewalls and routers, so it's best to keep it only for intranets

> **If both basic authentication and Windows authentication are selected in this dialog, then if the browser supports Windows authentication, it will attempt to use Windows authentication first.**

The Role of Secure Sockets Layer

It's also possible to configure our server to work with **SSL certificates** in order to enable secure communication between the server and the client. SSL was created by Netscape, and is designed to run between the root level of communication over the Web (TCP), and the application-level communication (HTTP). An SSL-enabled server and an SSL-enabled client can authenticate each other, and establish 128-bit encrypted connection.

You may be familiar with this process if you've ever purchased anything online – by default, your browser will warn you whenever you switch between a secure and an 'unsecure' site; and when you're in a secure area, you'll see a padlock icon somewhere in the window:

SSL uses **public key cryptography** to establish a secure connection between the client and the server. The server side of the connection must be equipped with an SSL certificate; these are available from various vendors. A good discussion of public key cryptography can be found at http://www.iplanet.com/developer/docs/articles/security/pki.html, and for more information on SSL you may want to read *Professional ASP.NET Security* (Wrox Press, ISBN: 1-86100-620-9).

Authentication Accounts

As we started to explain above, when we talk about "anonymous access", we are not actually allowing the world and its dog to log on to our web server. Anonymous requests are authenticated as the IUSR_MachineName user, a special Windows account that we can configure to be used for this purpose. In fact, this is not the only special account that you might come across when using IIS:

❑ IUSR_MachineName – Used for authenticating anonymous users requesting basic web content (not ASP.NET content) on our system. We can affect the permissions available to all anonymous users by altering the permissions available to this user on our system.

❑ IWAM_MachineName – An account used when working with older COM or COM+ components with ASP. We'll spend no more time looking at this account in this book, but you may see it mentioned in some areas of the IIS configuration tool.

❑ ASPNET – A user account that the ASP.NET worker process runs under, and the account used for anonymous access to ASP.NET applications. This account has very few permissions on the local machine, which ensures that ASP.NET code can't be used for malicious purposes on the server. We will look at this account in more detail later in this chapter.

Configuring ASP.NET Applications in IIS

Having looked at some of the options available for the server-wide configuration of IIS, let's look now at how we can specify properties that apply to each application individually. Start by right-clicking on the 7361 directory in the management console, and selecting Properties from the context menu. A dialog like this will pop up:

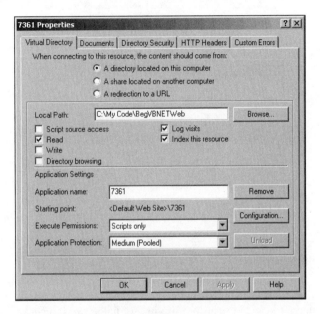

The active tab when we open this dialog, Virtual Directory, has several settings that we can alter. Let's start by looking at the section that defines the Local Path, which incorporates a series of checkboxes that determine the basic permissions for our application.

❑ Script source access – This option determines whether the client can view the source code for server-side applications. This is normally left unchecked, as it's unlikely that you'll want to allow users to view your source code, rather than the rendered page. Note that this permission can only be set if Read or Write permission is also set.

❑ Read – Enables browsers to read or download files in the virtual directory. This option should be left checked for published web applications – unchecking it will mean that clients requesting the page will see an error message.

❑ Write – Allows users to create or modify files within the directory. In most situations, this should be left turned off.

❑ Directory browsing – A useful feature to use when you're working with an application that contains many files, and you want to allow users to browse the contents of a directory. In most cases, however, it's recommended that you leave this turned off in order to hide away as much of your site as possible from prying eyes.

The other two options are related to site administration: logging user activity is a good idea when you want to track usage, while indexing your virtual directory speeds up searches on your system.

Moving on, we come to the **Application Settings** section, and we can see that our **Application Name** is set to **7361**. To the right of this box is a button marked **Configuration**. Clicking on this button brings up some options that are specific to our application, including the mappings of file extensions to the ISAPI DLLs that handle each extension. Looking through this list, you'll see several file extensions that you recognize, but many more that you'll probably never have to worry about!

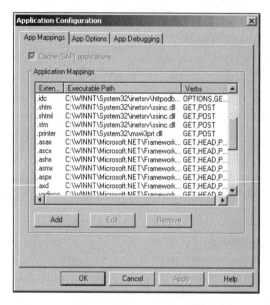

It's actually possible to remove some of these file extensions from IIS (or just from an application), and in some circumstances doing so can aid security. Also in this dialog, we can click on the **App Options** tab to configure session timeout length, which will affect any ASP.NET application that relies on session state:

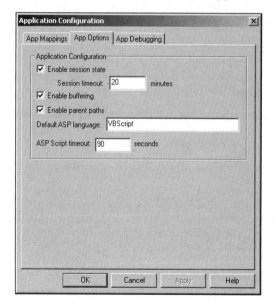

In this dialog, we're overriding the defaults that we specified in the server-wide settings, giving us the ability to work with different timeouts for each application on the server.

We are not going to look at every option available, but it is worth looking through the tabs and dialogs to see what's possible. IIS configuration is something of an art, and balancing performance configuration, security settings, and application load settings is a tricky job for system administrators.

Locking Down IIS

In general, there are a lot of things that you can do on a day-to-day basis to close down security holes on your IIS server, including turning off directory browsing on sites, enabling logging, removing IIS samples, and installing anti-virus software.

To simplify this process, Microsoft has released a very useful tool that helps to secure IIS 5 called the **IIS Lockdown Wizard**. This tool is used to turn off unnecessary features and disable some loopholes in IIS. Furthermore, you should always make sure that your IIS installation is as patched and up-to-date as possible, to prevent newly discovered holes from affecting your server.

The Lockdown Wizard is available for download from http://www.microsoft.com/Downloads/ Release.asp?ReleaseID=33961. We recommend that you read the instructions very carefully and understand each step in the process before proceeding with this tool, though, as being too enthusiastic can result in too many features being turned off.

ASP.NET and IIS

When we're hosting a web application for general consumption, we're usually quite happy to allow anonymous access to our web server, but what if we wanted to enable more functionality for certain users that would require greater permissions than the anonymous user account can provide? What if our user needed to have write permissions on a target folder on the web server, or if we wanted to write to an event log? ASP.NET can handle this situation by using a technique known as **impersonation**.

Impersonation

In any situation where we're using Windows Integrated Security (in an intranet or extranet application, for example), we can enable impersonation on our ASP.NET setup. This means that our users can be authenticated as local accounts that have more privileges than the standard ASPNET account, or the IUSR_*MachineName* account. By default, all ASP.NET applications access resources using this standard account, even if their users are currently logged on to a Windows domain – authentication occurs at application level, not operating-system level. When we turn impersonation on, we authenticate users under different local accounts, or different Windows domain accounts.

With impersonation turned off, there's an entry in the Machine.config file that determines which account is used for anonymous access. The entry is <processModel>, and the default setting is username="Machine", password="AutoGenerate". Impersonation can be turned on by adding the following to the System.Web element of either Machine.Config, or a Web.Config file:

```
<identity impersonate="true" />
```

Using this setting, our anonymous ASP.NET users are now authenticated using the
`IUSR_MachineName` account, instead of the `ASPNET` account. We can configure this further by adding
to this definition:

```
<identity impersonate="true" username="name" password="password"/>
```

Here, the username and password must relate to a valid account on the hosting server. This setting *only*
affects the account under which ASP.NET is run, and doesn't affect anonymous access to any other IIS-
based application. Implementing impersonation gives users of our application a specific set of
permissions for performing tasks that the basic `ASPNET` user account cannot perform.

Try It Out – Establishing Identity

Let's take a look at how we can use impersonation with a quick example that declares the user account
under which ASP.NET is currently authenticated.

1. Open up Visual Studio .NET, and create a new web application called
   `ImpersonationExample`.

2. Create a new web form in our application by right-clicking on the application in the Solution
   Explorer and selecting **Add | Add Web Form**. Call the new form `ImpersonateMe.aspx`.

3. Delete `WebForm1.aspx` from the project, right-click on `ImpersonateMe.aspx`, and select
   Set as Start Page from the context menu.

4. View the code-behind file for `ImpersonateMe.aspx`, and enter the following code into the
   `Page_Load()` event handler:

```
Private Sub Page_Load(ByVal sender As System.Object, _
                      ByVal e As System.EventArgs) Handles MyBase.Load
    Response.Write("I am authenticated as: " & _
                              WindowsIdentity.GetCurrent().Name)
End Sub
```

5. When you do this, you'll notice that IntelliSense complains about the `WindowsIdentity` bit.
   This is because we need to tell our web application to reference the classes in the
   `System.Security` namespace. Add the following line to the top of the code-behind page,
   before the class definition:

```
Imports System.Security.Principal

Public Class ImpersonateMe
```

6. Run the project, and view the results:

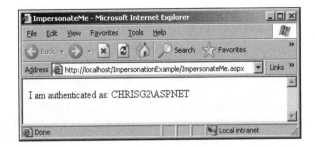

How It Works

So far, we've not done anything too complex – we've just confirmed the fact that ASP.NET pages are run under an account on the web server called ASPNET.

```
Response.Write("I am authenticated as: " & _
                              WindowsIdentity.GetCurrent().Name)
```

Here, we've output a simple line of text on our browser that gathers information from the local system, using functionality provided by the System.Security namespace.

Try It Out – Enabling Impersonation with Anonymous Access

Let's now extend the example to see how we can enable impersonation for anonymous users, and what effect this has on our application.

1. Back in our application, open up the Web.config file, and add the following line near the top:

```
<?xml version="1.0" encoding="utf-8" ?>
<configuration>

  <system.web>

    <identity impersonate="true" />


    ...
```

2. Run the application again, and you'll see something similar to the following:

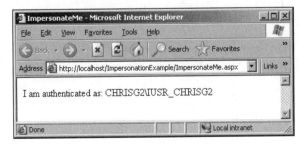

How It Works

Adding a single line to our `Web.config` file has changed the default user account for anonymous access to our ASP.NET application. We have reverted to the default user account for all IIS anonymous access, which is `IUSR_MachineName`. If we had configured IIS to use a different account for standard anonymous access, then the details of that account would be displayed instead.

To log in as a specific user in this example, we need to have a user account on our local system that we can use. Let's imagine that we've set up a temporary account called `TestUser`, with an eminently hackable password: `letmein`. Let's also imagine this account to be a member of the Power Users group on the local machine. Here's what the line in the `Web.config` file needs to look like:

```
<identity impersonate="true" userName="TestUser" password="letmein" />
```

With all of the above configured, you'd end up with the following result:

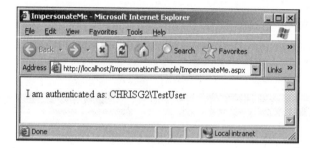

Since this user has more privileges on the local machine than the basic anonymous users, code in ASP.NET applications can now create and modify files as required.

Try It Out – Impersonation and Integrated Windows Authentication

While we've got an example for looking at impersonation and authentication, we can take a quick peek at what happens when Integrated Windows Authentication is switched on for our application.

1. Open up the IIS management console, and right-click and select **Properties** on the ImpersonationExample virtual directory.

2. In the **Directory Security** tab, click the **Edit** button to bring up the anonymous access and authentication control dialog. In here, uncheck the box for anonymous authentication, and enable only Integrated Windows Authentication, as shown:

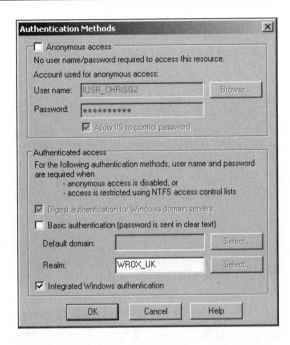

3. Remove the line that we entered in the `Web.config` file, run the application, and you'll find that ASP.NET will revert to using the `ASPNET` account for authentication.

4. Add the following line to the `Web.config` file:

```
<identity impersonate="true" />
```

5. Run the application again, and ASP.NET will attempt to use the currently-logged in user's account for authentication:

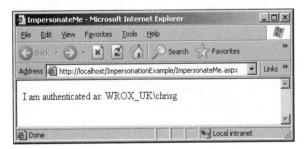

How It Works

As a result of the switch to Integrated Windows Authentication, ASP.NET pages are now running under the current Windows user's account. Access to our application is now controlled by the Access Control Lists (ACLs) maintained by the operating system, moving the authentication portion of our exchange to the underlying security settings of the system, rather than IIS.

When using impersonation, you should always consider what it is you're trying to achieve. You need to take care to restrict access to the minimum possible privileges for each user, and rarely will you need to give any user full administrative capacity on your server.

Summary

In this chapter, we have taken a brief tour around IIS 5, and discovered a few useful features that can help us to configure our server for deploying applications. In particular, we have looked at:

❑ The role of the web server in ASP.NET, and how IIS 5 works

❑ The IIS configuration tool that runs in the MMC, and how to create virtual directories using the IIS console

❑ The permissions and settings available to applications, and how to apply settings that affect the server as a whole

❑ Security features of IIS, and general lockdown areas

❑ Impersonation in ASP.NET

In the next chapter, we will concentrate on security at the ASP.NET level, covering the security options provided by ASP.NET and how to configure them. We will also be covering some familiar ground by looking again at IIS, but this time focusing on how it interacts with ASP.NET.

Solut...
BM Refere...
ve
System.Dat...
System.Drawing
System.Web
System.XML
AssemblyInfo.vb
Assembly
BM.vsdisco
Global.asax
Styles.css
Web.config
WebForm1.aspx
WebForm1.aspx.v

ebForm1.aspx* | WebForm1.aspx.

ASP.NET Authentication, Authorization, and Security

The role of **security** in an application is related to the need to restrict the ability of a user to access certain resources, or to perform certain actions. For example, a web application may offer administrative tools that must be accessed only by authorized users, or some information that's restricted to registered users. In previous chapters, we've seen this in action through our Friends Reunion application. We've also seen how different security-related settings can be applied at the web server level. Now, we will focus on ASP.NET, and see how to configure and take advantage of the security features it offers. ASP.NET works closely with IIS to provide the infrastructure available, so we will take a look at their interaction too.

During this chapter, we will discuss:

- ❑ The ASP.NET security infrastructure
- ❑ Interaction between ASP.NET, IIS, and the operating system
- ❑ Authentication and authorization – what are they and how they interact
- ❑ ASP.NET security settings
- ❑ Authentication options and how to use them

We've already seen some of these concepts in action, but we haven't said much about how they actually work. We will take a closer look at the mechanics during this chapter, and will gain a much better understanding of what is going on behind the scenes.

Overview

Security is a long-standing concept that pervades all kinds of software, including operating systems (think of the Windows NT/2000/XP login process), web servers (recall our last chapter), database servers (remember the login process to add a connection to MSDE in Chapter 4), applications (you must know several) and web sites (such as e-commerce sites, or even Hotmail). In each of them, the main purpose is to restrict unauthorized access to sensitive information, or to restrict the actions you can take. For example, you may not be able to post comments on a site unless you log in, or you may not be allowed to delete records in a table, or create a new database in a server.

With Internet connectivity available almost everywhere, this becomes increasingly important, because the information in your application is potentially exposed to the entire world. If an application isn't secure, meaning that unauthorized access is possible, users will not be willing to trust it to keep critical information. Whether you configure it carefully or not, your ASP.NET web applications will always have some kind of security in place. This is a consequence of the security architecture itself, which can be divided into three layers:

- ❑ **Operating system** – Unless you are using DOS or Windows 9x, security will always be in place. Windows NT/2000/XP uses domains to keep users' information, and to ensure that they have permission to access resources such as files and folders, printers, network shares, and so on. You always have to log in before using the system, and every action you take is first checked for the respective permission.

- ❑ **Web server** – A web server runs in the operating system, and as such, also uses the security infrastructure built in it. You have seen how to configure IIS in the previous chapter, and you have learned that even when 'anonymous' access is enabled for an application, it will actually be bound to the account specified for the anonymous user – by default, the `IUSR_MACHINENAME` account.

- ❑ **Web application** – An ASP.NET application needs IIS to run, of course, so it may come as no surprise that the security available in the previous two levels is always in effect, whether we actually decide to use it or not. At this level, we have some additional configuration options and features that ASP.NET offers.

Security Infrastructure

Before we dig into the implementation of the various security options available for our ASP.NET web applications, we will discuss some more generic concepts that are related to security in general, and to ASP.NET/IIS interaction in particular.

Essential Terms

Because they crop up so frequently in discussions about security, we can start by making absolutely sure that we know what's meant by two key terms: authentication and authorization. If we get this right now, much of what follows will become a great deal easier.

In order for a user to get access to a resource with restricted access, they have to be **authenticated**. This means that they have to provide some sort of credentials, such as a login name and a password, so that the resource knows who they are. The way these credentials are validated depends on the authentication schema we choose, and ASP.NET offers several, which we will discuss during this chapter.

Once the user has been identified, another step known as **authorization** takes place. Here, the process consists of checking whether the authenticated user has permission to access the resource they asked for. For example, an ordinary user may not be allowed to access certain administrative features of a web application.

As a side effect of authentication, an application may also provide customized content that's tailored for the current user accessing the resource. In fact, some applications will use security concepts with the sole aim of offering the user an improved experience through **personalization** – that is, by supplying content filtered according to their needs.

Authentication and Authorization

So: authentication is the process of identifying a user based on the credentials they supply. These credentials are compared to those existing in a **credential store**, where – once again – the nature of this store depends on the type of authentication. For example, Windows authentication compares the credentials against a Windows domain. Passport sites such as Hotmail, MSN, eBay, and McAfee use the Microsoft-owned Passport store, which is in charge of the authentication. The store can also be a database, an XML file, or any other media we decide to use for this purpose. We will later discuss the types of authentication we can choose for our ASP.NET applications.

In order for applications that use security to be aware that the current user has already been authenticated, a **security token** is attached to that user. This token is used to keep information about the user, and yet again its format and manner of use depends on the application. In a Windows environment, for example, this token is directly associated with the user while their session remains open. It is later used as a sort of key when they perform an action such as opening a folder or printing a document – security settings on any of these objects may bar them from accessing the resource. In a web environment, things are somewhat different, because of the disconnected and stateless nature of the HTTP protocol. We will see later how ASP.NET solves this problem.

Once the user has been authenticated, and their security token is in place, authorization happens. Once more, the association between a resource and the list of users allowed to access it depends on the specific application type or environment. For example, restrictions in access to files and folders in Windows are kept in so-called **ACLs**, or **access control lists**. These are set though the Security tab of the Properties window corresponding to the file or folder. This picture shows the security settings of a folder called 7361:

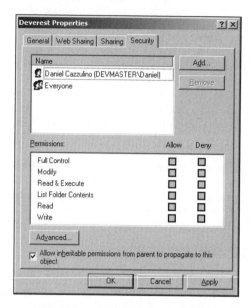

If you have used COM+ before, you may have used the Component Services MMC snap-in to assign permissions to COM+ applications. In this case, it also uses the Windows domain credentials store, just like the folder's properties window we saw above, but assigns access permissions to components based on them. The following picture, for example, shows a component that can only be accessed by managers:

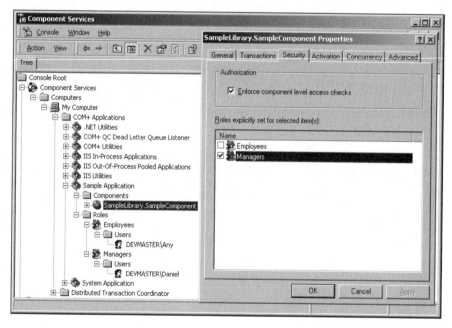

In ASP.NET applications, there are other options for assigning permissions to resources, which we will see soon.

Role-Based Security

If you take a closer look at the first of the two pictures opposite, you'll see that Everyone isn't a user at all – rather, it is a Windows **group**. The second picture shows a similar idea: that of **roles**, such as Employees and Managers. This leads us to the next key concepts.

If we focus on the process of assigning permissions to resources, we can easily imagine the administrative nightmare it would be to assign them to one user at a time, especially if we have a large number of users. What's more, each new user created would have to be manually added to all of the resources they are supposed to be able to access. To avoid this, a higher-level construct is created, where users are assigned to groups or roles according to application requirements. For example, a project administration and tracking system may define groups such as 'administrators', 'developers', 'testers', and 'users'.

This generalization allows us to apply permissions according to roles, besides (or even instead of) the permissions of individual users. New users can then be included in certain roles. The most obvious advantage to this is that once a particular permission has been given to a role, new users with that role will automatically gain access to the resource. For example, if there is a resource that allows a developer to upload the code they have developed, and which is obviously restricted to users who are included in the 'developers' role, a new programmer hired by the company will be able to access it automatically, provided they are included in the 'developers' role when the system administrator creates their account.

A user can be included in more than one role simultaneously. For example, a user may be added to the 'developers' and 'testers' roles, as they may perform both tasks simultaneously. (Some would say, with good reason, that this is not a good idea!)

Principal and Identity

In order for an application to use these security concepts, it needs a way to access them – for example, it must be able to check that the current user is included in a certain role, and act accordingly. The .NET Framework supports and exposes this scheme through the concepts of **principal** and **identity**.

A principal is an object that contains the roles associated with a user. It also contains an identity object that encloses information about that user. Together, they map onto the functionality we have shown above for Windows and COM+ security. In fact, though you may not have noticed it at the time, we have already used these objects in our Friends Reunion application, to pass around the current user's ID, and to check if they were authenticated. In Chapter 4, we had the following:

```
If Context.User.Identity.IsAuthenticated Then
    ...
```

and:

```
id = Context.User.Identity.Name
```

Context.User contains the Principal object associated with the current user for ASP.NET applications. Context is a property of the Page object, and as such is available to all of the code in our code-behind page. (It's actually a shortcut to the static HttpContext.Current property.)

If you look at the type of this property (place the cursor above User, and IntelliSense will do the rest), you'll find that it's actually an interface, IPrincipal. Likewise, the Identity property is of type IIdentity. This abstraction allows us to use the methods and properties defined in those interfaces irrespective of the concrete types of principal and identity, which depend on the type of authentication used, as we will see shortly. These two interfaces belong to the System.Security.Principal namespace, and provide a the most common properties and methods we may need when working with role-based security:

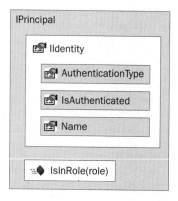

The Page object provides access to the principal through a User property too, which actually points to the same value in Context.User.

Processing and Initialization

In the previous chapter, we saw that when a request for an ASP.NET resource (such as an .aspx page) is received by IIS, it is handed to the ASP.NET ISAPI module, which continues processing the request. In order to understand how the security context is initialized, we need to take a closer look at what happens beyond that point:

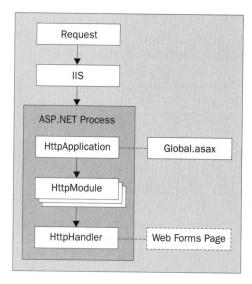

When the ASP.NET process (aspnet_wp.exe) receives the request from IIS, it hands it to the application corresponding to the page requested. The HttpApplication object is defined in the Global.asax file of your web application, hence the line in the drawing showing that relationship:

```
Public Class Global
    Inherits System.Web.HttpApplication
```

In turn the HttpApplication passes the request through any HttpModule that's configured for the application. These modules have the chance to process the request at various points, attaching to the corresponding events fired by the application, such as AuthorizeRequest, BeginRequest, and EndRequest. Of course, these events, being fired by the class defined in Global.asax, can also be handled in that class. You can see empty skeletons for those event handlers in the code-behind file:

```
Public Class Global
    Inherits System.Web.HttpApplication
    ...
    Sub Application_BeginRequest(ByVal sender As Object, ByVal e As EventArgs)
        ' Fires at the beginning of each request
    End Sub

    Sub Application_AuthenticateRequest(ByVal sender As Object, _
        ByVal e As EventArgs)
        ' Fires upon attempting to authenticate the user
    End Sub
    ...
End Class
```

The key event for security initialization is AuthenticateRequest, which is fired whenever a client requests a resource for which some kind of authorization is set. We will shortly see how we can configure this for our application.

Security-related modules subscribe to this event, and initialize the security context *before* the request is handled by the particular page the user asked for. Several modules are configured by default for all our web applications, and you can find them in the %WinDir%\Microsoft.NET\Framework\ v1.0.3705\CONFIG\machine.config file, in the <httpModules> section. Here are the ones we're interested in right now:

```
<httpModules>
    ...
    <add name="WindowsAuthentication"
        type="System.Web.Security.WindowsAuthenticationModule"/>
    <add name="FormsAuthentication"
        type="System.Web.Security.FormsAuthenticationModule"/>
    <add name="PassportAuthentication"
        type="System.Web.Security.PassportAuthenticationModule"/>
    ...
</httpModules>
```

Depending on the authentication scheme we choose for our application, which we'll discuss in the next section, the appropriate module loads and sets the current principal and identity objects. If we choose Windows authentication, the module will use the information passed by IIS (which must be configured to use the same type of authentication) to create a `WindowsIdentity` object with the user's Windows account name, such as `MYCOMPANY\Daniel`. It will then use this object, together with the list of Windows groups to which the user belongs, to initialize a `WindowsPrincipal` object. The new principal object is set then to the `Context.User` property.

If Passport authentication is used, the user will be redirected to the Microsoft Passport login page (more on this later). When the user is redirected back to our application from this page, the module will use the information passed back to create a `PassportIdentity` object. As roles can't be configured in Passport (because it is only intended to authenticate users) a `GenericPrincipal` object has to be initialized with the newly created identity. Finally, the object must be set to the `Context.User` property. All this has to be done manually for Passport, as the `PassportIdentity` object itself contains the methods to perform the checks.

Finally, if we choose Forms authentication, the module will rely on a cookie-based mechanism. Cookies are small files that can be attached to a client, and which are saved on the client's machine. Once they are set, they are passed back to the server on subsequent requests, so the application can use them to save some information about the current user. As we will see in a moment, Forms authentication settings include a `loginUrl` setting that points to a web forms page to be used for authentication purposes.

The Forms authentication module will check for the presence of an **authentication cookie** in the current request. If it finds one, it will use the information in it to create a `FormsIdentity` object. This module doesn't support roles either, so this identity object is used to create a `GenericPrincipal`, which is set to the `Context.User` property. If the cookie is *not* present, the user is redirected to the login page. A utility method that we've been using already, `FormsAuthentication.RedirectFromLoginPage()`, is used to allow the module to create the authentication cookie and save it to the client browser's cookie collection. Once this process finishes, the user is redirected to the page they asked for originally, this time with the cookie in place.

With all of this new information, we can complete the previous picture:

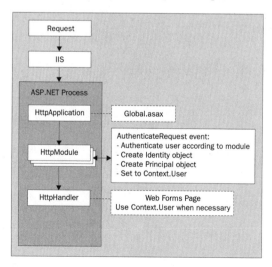

If this infrastructure is not enough for our particular security requirements, we can extend it by overriding the `AuthenticateRequest` handler in the `Global.asax` file. The .NET Framework provides us with another generic object that we can use for custom security, `GenericIdentity`, which we can use or even extend to suit our needs. Towards the end of this chapter, we will see how to do this, and discover why might we need to.

Application Security Configuration

A repeated refrain in this chapter is that the security behavior will largely depend on application configuration. As you already know, all application-wide settings are configured in a file called `Web.config` under the application root folder. We have already used some of the security settings here, but let's now take a look at all the options available.

Security-related settings are divided into three elements in the configuration file:

- ❏ `<authentication>`
- ❏ `<authorization>`
- ❏ `<location>`

The first element defines the type of authentication that will be in force, and can contain child elements like `<forms>` and `<passport>` for those two types of authentication options. The element's syntax can be found in the MSDN help:

```
<authentication mode="Windows|Forms|Passport|None">
  <forms name="name"
         loginUrl="url"
         protection="All|None|Encryption|Validation"
         timeout="30" path="/" >
    <credentials passwordFormat="Clear|SHA1|MD5">
      <user name="username" password="password" />
    </credentials>
  </forms>
  <passport redirectUrl="internal"/>
</authentication>
```

When the authentication mode is set to `Windows`, all other tags will be ignored. For `Forms` authentication, all of the `<forms>` element's attributes have pre-configured default values, which are also found in the `Machine.config` file we saw above:

```
<forms name=".ASPXAUTH"
       loginUrl="login.aspx"
       protection="All"
       timeout="30" path="/">
```

So, if we configure Forms authentication only with the following syntax:

```
<authentication mode="Forms" />
```

we will have to provide a `login.aspx` page under the application root. The other attributes and their meanings are explained in depth in the MSDN help.

So now we can fully understand the meaning of the configuration settings we have been using so far:

```
<authentication mode="Forms">
  <forms loginUrl="Secure/Login.aspx"/>
</authentication>
```

We let the default values take effect, and only override the `loginUrl` attribute to point to the location of our login form.

The `<authorization>` element is the one used in ASP.NET to assign permissions to resources. The process of creating this element and its sub-elements and attributes is therefore comparable to the process of assigning file or folder security in Windows, or to that of defining the application roles allowed in COM+, as we saw earlier. Again, the complete syntax of this element is found in the MSDN help:

```
<authorization>
  <allow users="comma-separated list of users|?|*"
         roles="comma-separated list of roles"
         verbs="comma-separated list of verbs" />

  <deny users="comma-separated list of users|?|*"
        roles="comma-separated list of roles"
        verbs="comma-separated list of verbs" />
</authorization>
```

The `?` and `*` (which don't actually appear in the documentation) represent the anonymous user (that is, an unauthenticated user) and all users, respectively. The default setting for this element in `Machine.config` is:

```
<authorization>
  <allow users="*" />
</authorization>
```

In other words, all users are allowed to access the resources, unless otherwise specified in our application configuration file. The authorization setting we've been using so far is:

```
<authorization>
  <deny users="?"/>
</authorization>
```

Which means that we don't allow unauthenticated users to access any resource in the application.

Finally, the `<location>` element can be used to specify `<authorization>` elements with regard to a certain path in the application. This is useful for setting exceptions to the rules defined for the whole application. We have used it before to explicitly allow anonymous access to the `NewUser.aspx` form, which wouldn't be available according to the authorization setting used above:

```
<location path="Secure/NewUser.aspx">
  <system.web>
    <authorization>
      <allow users="*"/>
    </authorization>
  </system.web>
</location>
```

If we didn't set this rule, unregistered users wouldn't be able to register themselves, since the NewUser.aspx page won't be available unless they were previously authenticated! The path can also be a folder instead of a specific file, so the following setting would work equally well:

```
<location path="Secure">
  <system.web>
    <authorization>
      <allow users="*"/>
    </authorization>
  </system.web>
</location>
```

In fact, using a `<location>` element with a path to a folder instead of a file, like the one shown above, is exactly equivalent to adding a `Web.config` file in that folder with the same authorization settings. So, we could achieve exactly the same as the `<location>` setting in the code shown above by adding a `Web.config` file to the `Secure` folder and adding the following elements to it:

```
<configuration>
  <system.web>
    <authorization>
      <allow users="*" />
    </authorization>
  </system.web>
</configuration>
```

It's worth noting how the process of authorization takes place here. There is another module that's registered by default to *all* web applications, called `UrlAuthorizationModule`, that performs the checks. It is called *after* the other modules have processed the request, so it uses the `Principal` that was associated to the current user by the appropriate authentication module. This way, these checks are independent of the authentication mode selected. This means that we can use authorization elements to deny or allow access to certain roles, for example, and leave the settings intact even if we later decide to change the authentication mode, as long as the role names remain the same.

The settings in a configuration file apply to the current folder and all its child folders, except for the `<location>` element, which applies only to the element specified in `path`. Application configuration files are hierarchical, meaning that we can place multiple configuration files in different folders under the root application path, overriding the appropriate elements whenever we need to.

These overrides can either broaden or tighten the settings in the parent folders, which may seem strange at first, but a second thought will reveal its usefulness: we can deny anonymous access to an application in general, just like we did for our Friends Reunion application, but make available a subfolder that contains such things as registration information or help pages.

Windows Authentication

Let's now move on and see how we can implement the three authentication modes, and examine their advantages and drawbacks. As stated above, Windows authentication works closely with IIS and Windows. In fact, ASP.NET doesn't do much more than receive what IIS passes it, and map it to .NET principal and identity objects. All of the business of exchanging credentials and authentication is handled at the IIS side, where Integrated Windows authentication (and optionally Basic authentication) should be used, with anonymous access disabled. This is most suitable for intranet and extranet scenarios, where the users are a part of your organization, and already have a Windows account in the company domain.

If you use Integrated Windows authentication, this will be the most secure method, as everything will be handled inside the Windows domain. Additionally, access to pages can be set directly using file access permissions, like the one we saw at the beginning of the chapter, which makes for the lowest impact in your pages' design with regards to security. User experience will also be improved, as users won't even need to login to the application – the security token will automatically be passed to ASP.NET whenever they open the browser and point to a page.

> *In Chapter 4, we alternated between Integrated Windows authentication and Anonymous access settings. Now we can fully understand what was going on. The* Web.config *file was left with the default authentication mode of* Windows*, so when Integrated Windows authentication was turned on, the user automatically became authenticated – the token was received by ASP.NET behind the scenes. When we turned on Anonymous access, ASP.NET no longer received the Windows user's security token, so the user became unauthenticated.*

If you select this authentication mode in ASP.NET, and set the IIS security settings to use any method other than Anonymous access, you won't see the Windows login form unless you try to access the application through the Internet from another machine. Machines on your LAN will get the effect we achieved in Chapter 4: the credentials will be passed automatically, and you become authenticated to the application without entering a single word. On the other hand, trying to access the application through the Internet will open up the following window:

This window replaces the Forms authentication redirect to the login page that we've been using so far. The information entered in this window is encoded/encrypted according to the specific setting used, as we learned in the previous chapter. This pop-up window is exactly the same as the one that appears when you try to access a network share for which you haven't been authenticated, such as a share from a computer outside your domain.

Passport Authentication

Passport is an authentication service provided by Microsoft. It is the one backing up Hotmail, MSN, and .NET Messenger, so you could say that it's a well-tested, streamlined, production quality, high volume service. However, setting it up for use in your web application is not such an easy task as with Windows or Forms authentication. It involves several steps:

1. Download and install the Microsoft .NET Passport SDK at http://msdn.microsoft.com/downloads/default.asp?url=/downloads/sample.asp?url=/msdn-files/027/001/885/msdncompositedoc.xml&frame=true.

2. Create a personal .NET Passport account for yourself (if you don't have one already).

3. Register an application with the .NET Services Manager site at https://www.netservicesmanager.com/(raxn1prpuq3xri45s01eub45)/wizard/default.aspx. You will need to provide additional information about yourself, and fill in several settings, for the new application to be created.

4. Then you get a key that must be installed in your server. After that, there are a couple more steps that are better described at http://msdn.microsoft.com/library/default.asp?url=/library/en-us/dncold/html/ssf2psprtauth.asp?frame=true.

Finally, the actual authentication process is not as 'automatic' as it is for the other modules. Here, we have to create a `PassportIdentity` object manually, and use its methods and properties to interact with the service. Perhaps the worst part is that for production systems, you will have to pay a fee.

Forms Authentication

This has been the authentication mode of choice for our web application, for two reasons. First, it is easily implemented; second, it is the most likely to be used for web applications, as it allows administration of users outside of Windows accounts, which is paramount for the Internet. However, we have already said that Windows authentication is better suited for intranet/extranet scenarios.

The processing sequence that has been taking place in our Friends Reunion application, which is a typical Forms authentication interaction, can be represented in the following diagram (numbers reflect the request's order of execution):

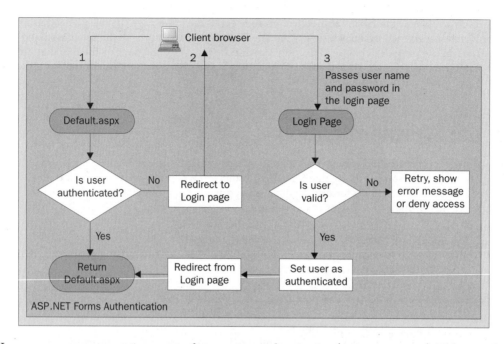

Here we see a user requesting a page that requires authentication (default.aspx). If the user hasn't been authenticated previously with the application, they are redirected to the login page. After they have entered their user name and password, if these are successfully validated, they are set as being authenticated. As we said, this involves the creation of an authentication cookie that is saved with the request, and which is later passed back to the server on every subsequent request. Using the built-in infrastructure will suffice for most types of applications, such as our own Friends Reunion.

In the next example, we'll take a look at the login form we've been using so far, and elaborate on its functionality. We will then improve it by giving the user the ability to 'persist' their login information – that is, to save the cookie so that it survives browser restarts. This will let them avoid entering the same information again when they come back to the site. Most sites offering this feature also allow the user to sign out of the application explicitly, so that any authentication cookies are removed from their machine. This is very important for users who access our application from public machines.

Try It Out – Improving the Authentication Process

Let's add the 'permanent' login and 'total' logout functionality to our application by way of some extra elements in the user interface.

1. Open the Login.aspx form and add a new row to the table that is already present (the easiest way to do this is to position the cursor in the cell with the **Login** button, and press *Ctrl+Alt+Up*). Drop in a **CheckBox** web server control named chkPersist, and set its Text property to match that of the screenshot.

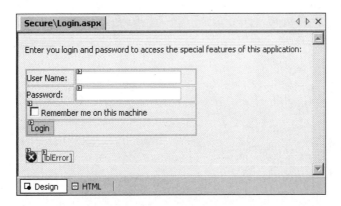

2. Now we can add the code to persist the cookie according to the user's selection in the new checkbox – a change to just one line!

```
Private Sub btnLogin_ServerClick(ByVal sender As System.Object, _
  ByVal e As System.EventArgs) Handles btnLogin.ServerClick
  ...
  If Not id Is Nothing Then
     'Set the user as authenticated and send him to the page
     'originally requested.
     FormsAuthentication.RedirectFromLoginPage(id, chkPersist.Checked)
  Else
     Me.pnlError.Visible = True
     Me.lblError.Text = "Invalid user name or password."
  End If
End Sub
```

3. Now let's add the logout feature. The natural place to put this is as a link next to Edit my profile, in the subhead control we created in Chapter 2. Open SubHeader.vb and add the code to create and add the new link next to the old one:

```
Protected Overrides Sub CreateChildControls()
  Me.Controls.Clear()

  Dim lbl As Label
  Dim reg As New HyperLink()

  If _register = String.Empty Then
     reg.NavigateUrl = Context.Request.ApplicationPath + _
     Path.AltDirectorySeparatorChar + "Secure" + _
     Path.AltDirectorySeparatorChar + "NewUser.aspx"
  Else
     reg.NavigateUrl = _register
  End If

  If Context.User.Identity.IsAuthenticated Then
     reg.Text = "Edit my profile"
     reg.ToolTip = "Modify your personal information"
```

```
      Dim out As New HyperLink()
      out.NavigateUrl = Context.Request.ApplicationPath & _
                        Path.AltDirectorySeparatorChar & "Logout.aspx"
      out.Text = "Logout"
      out.ToolTip = "Leave the application"
      Me.Controls.Add(New LiteralControl(" | "))
      Me.Controls.Add(out)
    Else
      reg.Text = "Register"
    End If

    'Add it before the logout control if it was added
    Me.Controls.AddAt(0, reg)
    Me.Controls.Add(New LiteralControl(" - "))
    lbl = New Label()
    lbl.Text = DateTime.Now.ToLongDateString()
    Me.Controls.Add(lbl)
  End Sub
```

Note that we will actually redirect the users to a confirmation page, just as Passport does.

4. Let's now create the logout confirmation page. Add a new web form called `Logout.aspx`, add the link to the usual stylesheet, and change the code-behind page to inherit the class from our `FriendsBase` class. Add an image, some text asking for confirmation, and a button to perform the actual logout operation:

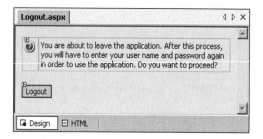

5. Add the following event handler to the **Logout** button:

```
Private Sub btnLogout_Click(ByVal sender As System.Object, _
                  ByVal e As System.EventArgs) Handles btnLogout.Click
  ' Remove the authentication ticket
  System.Web.Security.FormsAuthentication.SignOut()

  ' Redirect the user to the root application path
  Response.Redirect(Request.ApplicationPath)
End Sub
```

6. Add the following code to `Page_Load()` to set up the message and icon for the page:

```
Private Sub Page_Load(ByVal sender As System.Object, _
                  ByVal e As System.EventArgs) Handles MyBase.Load
```

```
        MyBase.HeaderMessage = "Leave the Application"
        MyBase.HeaderIconImageUrl = _
                        Request.ApplicationPath & "/images/back.gif"
    End Sub
```

7. Finally, let's recap the security-related settings the application is using:

```xml
<?xml version="1.0" encoding="utf-8" ?>
<configuration>
  ...
  <system.web>
    ...
    <authentication mode="Forms">
      <forms loginUrl="Secure/Login.aspx" />
    </authentication>
    <authorization>
      <deny users="?" />
    </authorization>
    ...
  </system.web>
  <location path="Secure/News.aspx">
    <system.web>
      <authorization>
        <allow users="*"/>
      </authorization>
    </system.web>
  </location>
</configuration>
```

8. Run the application with `Default.aspx` as the start page. After the usual login, caused by the security settings in place, the default page with the new Logout link looks like this:

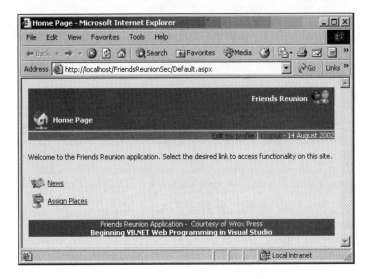

369

After the user clicks the **Logout** link, they are taken to the confirmation page:

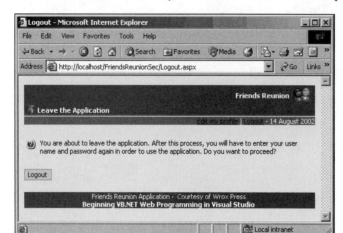

If at last they confirm the logout, they will be sent back to the application's login page.

How It Works

The login form uses the following method to set authentication:

```
FormsAuthentication.RedirectFromLoginPage(id, chkPersist.Checked)
```

As we stated above, this method takes care of creating the authentication cookie (also called a **ticket**), and saving it for subsequent requests. We pass the UserID, just as we did before, which is used to perform queries across the application. The new parameter we pass now, the Checked state of the checkbox, tells the method to create a persistent cookie that will be preserved in the client machine even across browser and machine restarts.

The other new feature is the logout link in the subhead control. The process for creating this is very similar to what we already had: we just add the link, and then add the previous link at the first position, to appear at the left of the new link:

```
Me.Controls.AddAt(0, reg)
```

As you can see, the best advantage of Forms authentication comes from its flexibility. We have been able to authenticate against a database store of credentials, using the infrastructure absolutely as-is, and achieve some very acceptable results! We were able to query the database, customize content tailored to the current user, and secure the whole application to require authentication, and we could even have used authorization on a per user basis, although it wasn't needed for our application. Not bad for a sample project!

Putting the Login and NewUser forms in a separate folder from the rest of the application makes it easier to increase security for these two especially sensitive forms. One way to do this would be to set SSL security for that folder, forcing the web server and client browser to encrypt the entire conversation between them, making it impossible for hackers to get in the middle. This is an advanced topic that's treated in greater depth in Professional ASP.NET Security *(Wrox Press, 186100-620-9).*

370

Customizing Authentication and Role-based Security

Forms authentication is great, but it doesn't make use of the role-based features we talked about at the beginning of the chapter. As we saw, it will simply create an empty `GenericPrincipal` object, containing only the initialized `FormsIdentity` object. If we were to build an administration section in our application, and we wanted to restrict access to administrator users only, we would have to deny access to everyone, and then add the administrator users one by one.

To take advantage of role-based authentication, we have to customize the process. When we looked at the role-based security infrastructure and its overall architecture, we saw that the various authentication modules actually hook into the same events that we can use, particularly `AuthenticateRequest`, a handler for which is available in our `Global.asax` file.

We also learned that the infrastructure is prepared to work with any role-based scheme, as long as it works around the concepts of `IPrincipal` and `IIdentity`. So far, however, we've let the default modules take charge. Our only intervention in Forms authentication was to check a user name and password in the login form – we didn't have to bother about the cookies, encryption/decryption (yes, it *is* encrypted), creation of the principal and identity objects, or anything else. Some things are going to have to change.

For our implementation of custom authentication, we will start by using the `GenericPrincipal` and `GenericIdentity` objects, which provide a reasonable and simple implementation for us to use. In case they are not enough, we can always inherit and extend them, or even implement `IPrincipal` and `IIdentity` directly in a custom class.

We already know the processing that takes place in order to make the default modules work. We can now apply that knowledge to build our custom authentication. As we stated, the key event to handle in the process is `AuthenticateRequest`. During the handler for this event, we can perform some actions, and then set the `Context.User` property to our custom principal and identity objects. As with any other authentication scheme, this security context will follow the user though pages, user controls, code-behind pages, and so on. We will be able to access these objects from any point in running code.

To customize authentication, we need to intercept the process at some point. In this instance, we'll leave the code as it is in the `Login.aspx` page, and let the Forms authentication module perform all the work it has been doing so far, until a certain point. Let's look again at the steps for a typical request in our application, and see where to override the default behavior:

1. `Default.aspx` – Initial request to enter the application.

2. `Application_AuthenticateRequest` – Event is fired, `IsAuthenticated=false`, so Forms module redirects to `Login.aspx`.

3. `Login.aspx?ReturnUrl=...` – This redirect causes a new request to another page, this time `Login.aspx`.

4. `Application_AuthenticateRequest` – This time the event is fired by the access to `Login.aspx`. The module realizes that this is the page for handling authentication, so it doesn't redirect to itself again.

371

5. Enter credentials and submit – posting the form to itself is actually a new request again.

6. `Application_AuthenticateRequest` – `IsAuthenticated=False`. The same as before, so the module doesn't redirect.

7. Our code checks against database; returns OK – Module saves `UserID` with the authentication cookie. Performs redirect to `ReturnUrl` (`Default.aspx`).

8. `Default.aspx` – A new request is made for this page. This time, the authentication cookie is set.

9. `Application_AuthenticateRequest` – This is the first time we get `IsAuthenticated=True`. We pick up processing from here, and rebuild customized versions of `GenericPrincipal` and `GenericIdentity`, based on the information retrieved from the database using the `UserID` attached to the authentication cookie. We replace the `Context.User` with the new complete `Principal`.

Note from the sequence above that the last `AuthenticateRequest` is the first one for which the `IsAuthenticated` property returns `True`. From now on, this is the only response that will be issued to an authenticate request, as the authorization cookie will be present, and the Forms authentication module will take care of recovering the `UserID` from it. We are actually customizing the authentication mechanism *after* the Forms authentication module has handled it.

We can refer to `Default.aspx` more generally as a "restricted page", which can be any protected resource in the application. Graphically, the interaction is as follows:

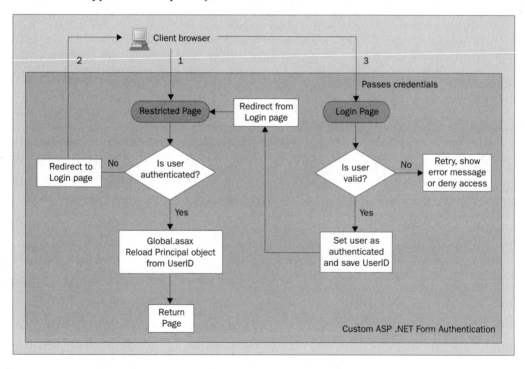

After we use the `FormsAuthentication.RedirectFromLoginPage()` method, the restricted page is actually requested again – but this time, with the security token set. At this time, we have a chance to override the default behavior implemented by Forms authentication, and we can set the `Context.User` property to an object that better represents our needs. This will be a `GenericPrincipal` that contains the roles associated with the current user.

Try It Out – Using and Replacing the Principal Object

In our database, there are only two roles: 'users' and 'administrators'. These roles aren't actually defined anywhere, but administrators are distinguished by the `IsAdministrator` flag in each record in the `User` table. This is the information we will use to create a `GenericPrincipal` containing the 'user' role, or both the 'user' and 'administrator' roles (an administrator will always be a user too).

1. Open the `Global.asax` (also called the `Global.asax.vb`) file, and add the following import statements:

```
Imports System.Data.SqlClient
Imports System.Security.Principal
```

2. Find the `Application_AuthenticateRequest()` event handler, and add the following code to it:

```
Sub Application_AuthenticateRequest(ByVal sender As Object, _
                                    ByVal e As EventArgs)
    ' Cast the sender to the application
    Dim app As HttpApplication = CType(sender, HttpApplication)

    ' Only replace the context if it has already been handled
    ' by forms authentication module (user is authenticated)
    If Not Context.User Is Nothing AndAlso _
                Context.User.Identity.IsAuthenticated Then
        Dim con As SqlConnection
        Dim sql As String
        Dim cmd As SqlCommand
        Dim reader As SqlDataReader

        Dim id As String = Context.User.Identity.Name

        con = _
            New SqlConnection(ConfigurationSettings.AppSettings("connection"))
        sql = "SELECT IsAdministrator FROM [User] WHERE UserId='{0}'"
        sql = String.Format(sql, id)
        cmd = New SqlCommand(sql, con)
        con.Open()

        ' Ensure closing of the connection
        Try
            reader = cmd.ExecuteReader( _
                    CommandBehavior.SingleRow Or CommandBehavior.CloseConnection)
```

```
      ' If we find a record, it was a valid UserID
    If reader.Read() Then
      Dim ppal As GenericPrincipal
      Dim roles As String()

      ' If IsAdministrator field is true, add both roles
      If reader.GetBoolean(0) Then
        roles = New String() {"User", "Admin"}
      Else
        roles = New String() {"User"}
      End If

      ' We reuse the identity created by Forms authentication
      ppal = New GenericPrincipal(Context.User.Identity, roles)
      Context.User = ppal
    Else
      ' If UserID was invalid, clear the context so he logs on again
      Context.User = Nothing
    End If
  Catch
    Throw
  Finally
    ' Connection may have been closed by the reader
    If con.State <> ConnectionState.Closed Then con.Close()
  End Try
  End If
End Sub
```

3. Create a new folder named `Admin`, and add a new web form called `Users.aspx`. As always, add the stylesheet reference to it, and change the code-behind page so that it inherits from the `FriendsBase` class. Drop a `DataGrid`, give it the name `grdUsers`, and set its width to 100%. Right-click on the `DataGrid`, select **Auto Format**, and select **Colorful 4**. The `Users.aspx` page ought now to look something like this:

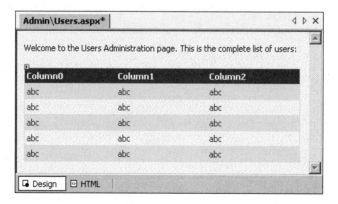

4. Drop a `SqlDataAdapter` object onto the form, and follow the same routine as we used in Chapter 4. Set the SQL statement to `SELECT * FROM [User]`, and change the name of the object to `adUsers`. Rename the connection added as `cnFriends`, and the `SelectCommand` as `cmUsers`. If you haven't unchecked the **Generate insert...** advanced option, remember to set the `UpdateCommand`, `InsertCommand`, and `DeleteCommand` properties to `None`. Finally, set the `cnFriends` connection string property to use the dynamic configuration we used before.

5. Right-click the data adapter component, and select **Generate Dataset....** Select the **New** option button, and give it the name `UserData`. Accept the dialog, and rename the new dataset component to `dsData`.

6. Bind the data grid to this new dataset. The form will look something like this by now:

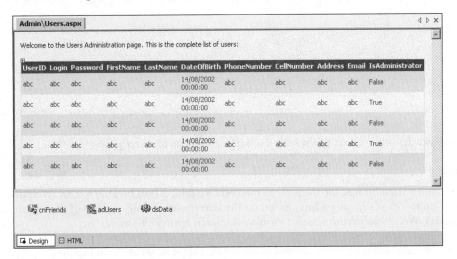

7. Let's add the code to load the dataset and bind the grid to display the data. Add the following code to the `Page_Load()` method of this page:

```
Private Sub Page_Load(ByVal sender As System.Object, _
                      ByVal e As System.EventArgs) Handles MyBase.Load
    MyBase.HeaderIconImageUrl = _
        Request.ApplicationPath & "/images/padlock.gif"
    MyBase.HeaderMessage = "Administer Users"

    If Not Page.IsPostBack Then
      Me.adUsers.Fill(Me.dsData)
      Me.grdUsers.DataBind()
    End If
End Sub
```

8. Now we will add a link to this new page in the `Default.aspx` page, so that administrators have easy access to it. Open the `Default.aspx` page, and add the following code to the bottom:

```
<form id="Form1" method="post" runat="server">
  <p>
    Welcome to the Friends Reunited application. Select the desired
    link to access functionality on this site. </p>
  <p></p>
  <p><asp:placeholder id="phNav" runat="server"></asp:placeholder></p>
  <p><asp:hyperlink id="lnkUsers" runat="server"
                    navigateurl="Admin/Users.aspx">
    Users Administration Page
  </asp:hyperlink></p>
</form>
```

9. Finally, let's make the link visible only if the current user is an administrator. Open the code-behind page for `Default.aspx`, and add the following code at the bottom of the method:

```
Private Sub Page_Load(ByVal sender As System.Object, _
                      ByVal e As System.EventArgs) Handles MyBase.Load
   ...

   ' Show the link only to administrators
   Me.lnkUsers.Visible = User.IsInRole("Admin")
End Sub
```

10. Save the project, and run it with `Default.aspx` as the start page.

How It Works

As you can see from Step 9, the purpose of the code we added is to be able to control application behavior (in this case showing a link) based on the current user's role, instead of their particular user name or ID. We discussed the benefits of this role-based approach before.

So, just as we explained before we began to build this example, we're handling the `AuthenticateRequest` event in the `Global.asax` file in order to replace the default principal that's associated by Forms authentication with a custom one. This will allow us to add roles to the current user, based on the information in the database. Note that we used the application request's `IsAuthenticated` property, instead of the `Context.User.Identity.IsAuthenticated` property we've used before:

```
If app.Request.IsAuthenticated Then
```

We had to do this because the first time the page is accessed, the `Context.User` property isn't initialized, and we would have caused an exception. To take this into account, we could have replaced the code above with the following:

```
If Not Context.User Is Nothing AndAlso _
   Context.User.Identity.IsAuthenticated Then
```

If we pass the `IsAuthenticated` check, it will mean that Forms authentication has already done its work, and the `UserID` is placed where we're used to finding it: in the `Context.User.Identity.Name` property. This is the work that's already achieved in the `Login.aspx` page, and it's what we've been doing since Chapter 4.

In the remainder of the handler, we replace the empty `GenericPrincipal` object that's created by the Forms authentication module with one containing the actual roles the user belongs to. So, in the `Application_AuthenticateRequest()` handler, we retrieve the `UserID` and use it to issue a database query to discover whether it corresponds to an administrator or not. When we execute the query, we pass a couple of flags to `ExecuteReader()` that help to improve the performance (`SingleRow`) and specify the behavior of the connection:

```
reader = cmd.ExecuteReader( _
    CommandBehavior.SingleRow Or CommandBehavior.CloseConnection)
```

The second flag means that once the reader has finished reading the row, it will close the connection automatically. If an exception is thrown, we need to check whether the connection has indeed been closed by the reader, inside the `Finally` block:

```
If con.State <> ConnectionState.Closed Then con.Close()
```

The `GenericPrincipal` constructor receives an identity and a string array containing the roles it belongs to. We reuse the identity created by Forms authentication, which is attached to the `Context.User.Identity` property we have been using, as we don't need to change anything about it:

```
ppal = New GenericPrincipal(Context.User.Identity, roles)
```

Finally, we attach the newly created principal to the `Context.User` property:

```
Context.User = ppal
```

If you go back to the picture showing the flow for these actions, you'll notice that the original page requested is processed next. So, when execution reaches our code for the page, it will have access to the new role-aware principal we attached. We use this in the `Page_Load()` method of the `Default.aspx` page to display a link to the user's administration page:

```
Me.lnkUsers.Visible = User.IsInRole("Admin")
```

`User` is a property of the `Page` object that provides a shortcut to `Context.User`, and its `IsInRole()` method allows us to check whether it pertains to a specific role. Here, we see an administrator user logged in:

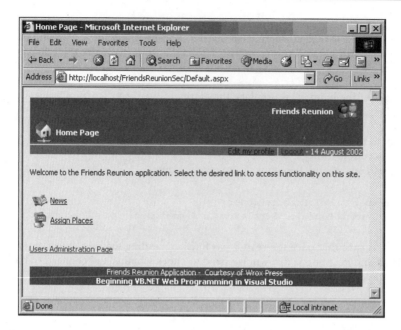

We have used our new, custom, roles-aware principal to display information on the page selectively. However, merely hiding or showing a link is not enough security: if a non-administrator user knows the administration page's location and name, they could type the address into the browser's address bar and gain access to a resource that is supposed to be restricted! To solve this, we will add a configuration file inside the Admin folder, to secure all the items in that folder.

> *If we add more administration tools later, the configuration file will automatically protect them too. Organizing an application into separate folders according to resource features makes it extremely easy to administer its security settings, and ensures that future growth won't become a maintenance nightmare.*

Try It Out – Taking Advantage of Roles for Authorization

To secure the items in our new Admin folder, we just have to provide it with a new web configuration file, as we're about to see.

1. Right-click on the Admin folder, select **Add | Add New Item**, and choose **Web Configuration File** from the **Web** folder:

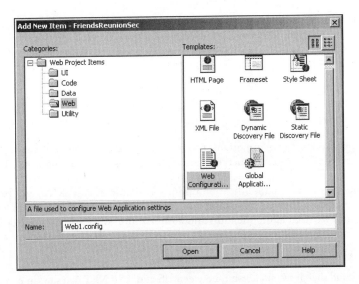

2. Remove all of this file's content, and replace it with the following:

```xml
<?xml version="1.0" encoding="utf-8" ?>
<configuration>
  <system.web>
    <authorization>
      <allow roles="Admin" />
      <deny roles="User" />
    </authorization>
  </system.web>
</configuration>
```

How It Works

Now, if a user who is not an administrator is logged in, they won't see the link to the administration page because the page's code hides it, according to the code we added in the previous example. But if the user tries to type the page's address directly into the browser's address bar, they won't be allowed to access it *either*, thanks to the configuration file we just placed in the folder. Instead, they will be redirected to the login page again, to provide appropriate credentials.

Up to now, we have been using user-related information to restrict access to resources, such as denying anonymous users, or granting all users. Now, we are taking advantage of role-based security to set permissions. This means that new administrator users registered with the application later on will automatically gain access to these resources, without any further changes to the application's configuration. If we'd used user-related information, we could have granted the wrox user access to this folder, but new administrators would have to be added manually.

Having logged on as a non-administrator user, try typing the URL directly into the browser's address bar, and see what happens. All of these checks are performed automatically, and the redirection to the login page makes sense, since a user without the required role might even be an unauthenticated user. Only a user belonging to the administrator role will be able to see the administration page we built, regardless of how they try to access it.

Now, our Friends Reunion application has become much more secure, though the use of the concepts you've learned in this chapter. However, we certainly haven't covered every possible security-related feature available in .NET, as that is a subject for a whole book. The book in question is *Professional ASP.NET Security* by Wrox Press, ISBN 186100-620-9.

Summary

Security in web applications is very important, much more so than in traditional desktop applications. During this chapter, we have looked at some general security concepts, as well as modern role-based security.

We have examined the various authentication options available in ASP.NET, and provided some guidance to choose among them. Application configuration files were discussed in the context of security settings, and we used authentication and authorization to secure an application, and custom authentication to meet application requirements, showing the level of extensibility available in the general security infrastructure.

In order to understand the close relationship between IIS and ASP.NET, we saw an overview of the modular and extensible architecture that exists to process web requests, and how the various authentication options are implemented internally, as well as their interaction with the main web application.

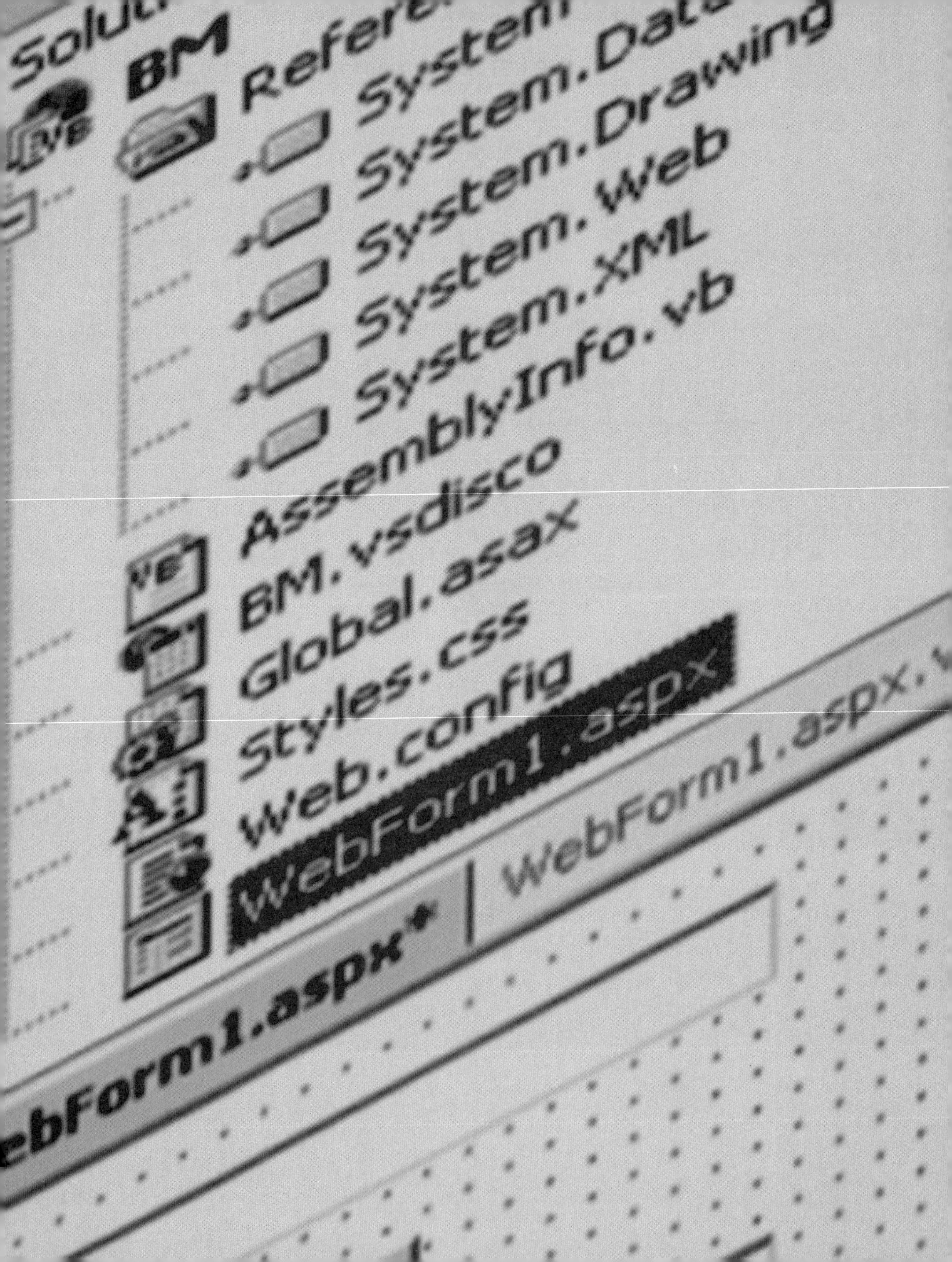

Solut...

BM

Referen...

System.Dat...

System.Data

System.Drawing

System.Web

System.XML

AssemblyInfo.vb

Assembly

BM.vsdisco

Global.asax

Styles.css

Web.config

WebForm1.aspx

WebForm1.aspx.v

ebForm1.aspx*   WebForm1.aspx.v

Performance and Scalability

The title of this chapter alone implies that performance and scalability go hand in hand, and indeed they do. However, it is important to note that while these two topics are often discussed together, they differ greatly in definition. This chapter will set out to give you a brief explanation of what these terms mean, how they differ from each other, and how they work together. Additionally, we'll give you a few tips and tricks to help you measure performance and design scalable web applications.

First, it's important that we understand exactly what we're talking about:

❏ **Performance** refers to how an application responds to requests, and how well it utilizes the resources of the machine the code executes on.

❏ **Scalability** refers to how easily an application can increase its capacity by increasing the resources available to it.

With those simple definitions out of the way, we can see more clearly why these two terms are spoken of together. When performance deteriorates due to increased use of an application, you should be able to improve matters by increasing the resources available. However, it doesn't always work that way: sometimes, scaling an application can adversely affect performance. This happens when the overhead associated with making the application scale is greater than the benefit of adding additional resources.

Scaling in the Real World

Let's put this into more tangible terms by thinking about an example. Imagine that a small local bank has an application that accepts input from a few ATMs spread throughout a city. A diagram of this type of application might look something like this:

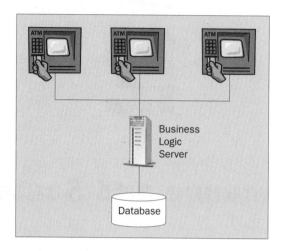

As you can see, the ATMs are connected to a business logic server, and the business logic server is connected to a database. This model is fine, *as long as there are not a large number of transactions being processed simultaneously.* What happens if the bank adds a few more ATMs that connect to the same business logic server? What happens if these ATMs are placed in high-profile areas where transactions take place all the time? Performance may start to deteriorate. Reliability of the responses may start to suffer. If the bank is bombarded with requests and transactions, the application may time-out before a response is received. For a bank, this could clearly be devastating.

So what's the solution? If this application was built to be scalable, we could simply add more resources to the business logic layer – that is to say, an additional server. With that in place, we could configure some of the ATMs to use one server, and the remainder to use the other server, as shown below:

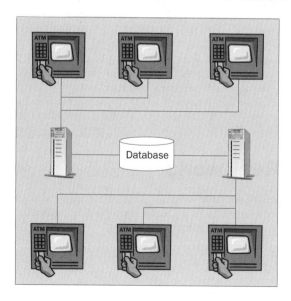

On this occasion, we didn't add another database server – both of the business logic servers now connect to the same database. At some later time, the bank may decide that it needs a second database server, and that should be fine too. The point is that with a truly scalable application, we should be able to add resources to any layer of a tiered system, without necessarily needing to upgrade the other layers at the same time.

Programmers are therefore faced with two imperatives. First, they have to write applications that scale well. However, because scaling implies more resources, it can be expensive – so the second imperative is that applications should perform well in the first place! In the next section, we'll start to look at some ways to find out whether they do.

Measuring Performance

Making our applications perform well means that we first need to *measure* their performance, and then tweak them as necessary. Microsoft has long included a way to track performance in applications through the use of **performance counters**, and this has been continued in the .NET environment. The performance counters can be viewed in the Performance tool in Windows 2000 and Windows XP, which you can see by going to Start | Settings | Control Panel | Administrative Tools | Performance.

The Performance tool allows you to pick and choose what information you want to monitor, the interval at which you want to monitor it, and when you want monitoring to start and stop. The table below describes the performance counter types provided by .NET, and what information they make available:

Counter Type	Description of Statistics Obtained
Exceptions	Exceptions thrown in an application
Interop	Interoperation with COM, COM+ and external libraries
JIT compiling	JIT-compiled code
Loading	Classes, assemblies, application domains, and anything else that's loaded into the CLR
Locks and Threads	Managed locks and threads in use within an application
Memory	Memory in use and garbage collection
Networking	Information sent over a network connection
Remoting	The 'remote' objects in use within an application
Security	Security checks provided by the CLR

Each of these counter types is capable of tracking a different kind of information. For example, the Exceptions type provides data such as the number of exceptions thrown and the number of `finally` blocks reached, while the Networking type provides information such as the number of bytes that have been received and sent over the network.

Be aware of a slight problem with performance counters. The counters themselves carry a small hit on the resources of the server. Each piece of data that you monitor carries just a little more overhead, so your performance counts may be slightly affected by the very act of monitoring them.

Try It Out – Monitoring Performance Counters

Before we go any further, let's take a look at an example of performance monitoring, in which we'll see how to use the Performance tool, and use it to see how many exceptions are taking place in the .NET Framework.

1. Open up the Performance tool, as outlined above. The standard window will then be displayed, with no counters currently active.

2. To add counters, right-click in the System Monitor (that is, the right-hand) pane, and choose Add Counters from the drop-down menu. From the Performance object selection box, chose .NET CLR Exceptions. Next, click on the Select counters from list radio button, and click on the Explain button in the upper right-hand corner.

When you do that, an additional window will appear that describes each of these counters and what they provide. As you click on the different counters, new information appears. Your window should look something like the following screenshot:

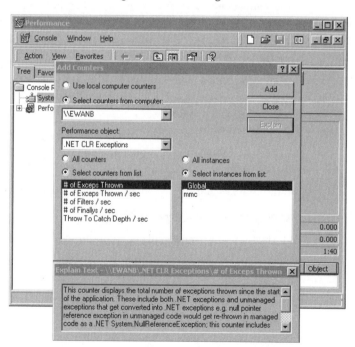

3. When you're ready to continue, choose # of Exceps Thrown, and click the Add button. If you have no applications running in the background that are throwing exceptions, then you should find that the performance counter isn't collecting any data.

4. In order to clearly see the exceptions that we're going to throw, we need to change the scale for the counter that we've just added. Right-click on the counter and choose **Properties** from the resulting menu. On the dialog box that appears, choose the **Graph** tab, change the vertical scale to have a maximum value of 15, and click the **OK** button. We've still got no data to collect, but we're going to fix that next.

5. Create a new ASP.NET Web Application project in Visual Basic .NET called `Chapter12`. In the web form that's added, drag a `Button` web control onto the design surface of the page. Double-click the button to display the code-behind page, and add code to the `Button1_Click()` event handler so that it looks like this:

```
Private Sub Button1_Click(ByVal sender As System.Object, _
                          ByVal e As System.EventArgs) Handles Button1.Click
    Dim num As Integer = 7
    Dim den As Integer = 0
    Dim errorResult As Integer
    errorResult = num / den
End Sub
```

6. Save the page, build the solution, and then browse to the page you created – which will display an error immediately, as we're trying to divide by zero. Switch back to the performance monitor, and you'll notice that the counter has incremented. Try refreshing the errant ASP.NET page a few times, and watch the counter climb. Your console will now resemble this picture:

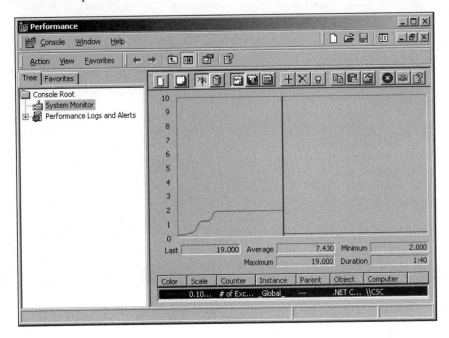

How It Works

This example is really quite simple. The Performance tool is implemented in a file called `perfmon.exe`. At our request it starts sampling the performance counters and displaying the results in the graph. The vertical line that you can see in the screenshot (and on your screen!) moves across the graph horizontally as time elapses and samples are taken.

When you browse to the web application and an exception is thrown, you see the exception reported as an error by the web server. When you switch to view the Performance tool, you'll find that the count of exceptions has increased. Each time you refresh the page, you'll receive the same exception message in your browser, and the performance counter will increase. When the vertical line reaches the far right of the graph, it starts again on the far left and overwrites the displayed values.

Web Application Stress Tool

Despite the flexibility of the Performance tool, and its ability to monitor the behavior of our web applications at run time, it would be almost useless if we were unable to simulate realistic conditions: there aren't many web applications out there that are used by only one user at a time! Microsoft has recognized this problem, and come to the rescue with a stress-testing tool known as the **Web Application Stress tool**, or **WAS** for short, which incorporates the functionality of `perfmon.exe`. The tool is free, but it must be downloaded from http://webtool.rte.microsoft.com.

WAS allows us to simulate the load on a web site, with options for simulating different user numbers, bandwidth, browsers, and authentication mechanisms. It uses test scripts that can be generated by recording browser activity, or even by pointing to an IIS log file. Being able to test a web site's resilience under load with these options gives you a huge advantage, because you can test your application on a staging server before placing it into production, and fix bugs as you go along. The tool also allows you to view your results in a simple report format, which makes it clear what you're seeing.

Installing WAS

Installing WAS is a straightforward process. After downloading the `setup.exe` file, double-click on it and installation will begin, prompting you only for the location of the installation. Despite the simplicity of this procedure, keep in mind that you should *not* install WAS on the server that you wish to stress test against. This application uses its own set of resources, and you'll wind up with false readings if WAS is running on the same machine as IIS. Install it on a workstation instead!

> *Another reason why WAS shouldn't be installed on the same server that you're testing against is that your tests will not include the network latency that your users will experience.*

Try It Out – Using WAS

Using WAS is a sizable subject – too large for this book – but being able to test the performance of your application under stress, and identifying the required resources for your application, is an important skill. As such, we need to cover at least basic use of WAS; so get your mouse ready and open up the WAS tool from the Start menu in Windows.

1. On opening WAS for the first time, a dialog will prompt you for your desired action:

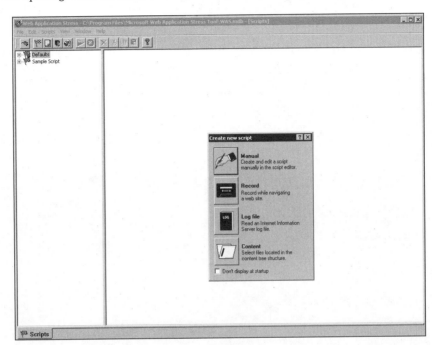

2. Select the option to **Record** a new script. This allows us to navigate through our application as if we were any other user. However, WAS will record our navigation, and create a script to perform the same actions.

3. You will now be prompted with a dialog of choices that allow you customize the behavior of your script:

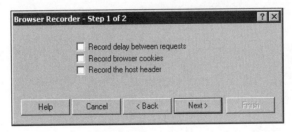

If you wish, you can record the pauses that you make while navigating the application. This gives your test a more realistic result set – after all, your users aren't likely simply to jump from one page to the next as fast as they can. Additionally, this dialog allows you to record any cookies that are sent to the browser – if the application you're testing requires cookies with information such as the currently logged-in user, this may be an important option to check. Lastly, you can also specify whether you want to record the host headers that form a part of the request.

4. Without making any changes on this occasion, we can move on to record the actions you want the script to perform. Click the Next button, and you will be asked to open your browser in preparation for recording. Open your browser, and then return to the dialog and click Finish.

The browser will now be sent to a local page instructing you to start making your requests. Type the address of the first page you wish to navigate to – in other words, the location of the application you want to test. The browser will request the page and return it, as you would normally expect. You are now free to continue typing in additional requests, or to click on links on the pages you've requested.

5. If you look at the WAS application while you're navigating the site, you'll see the script being generated on-the-fly:

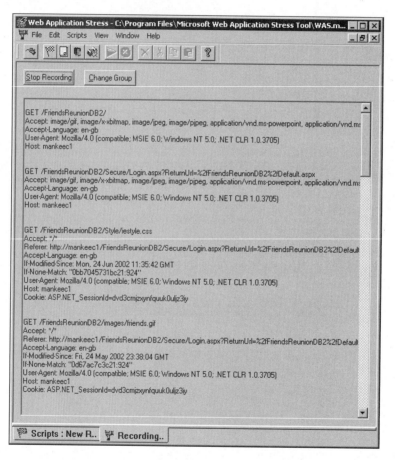

6. Finally, when you're done, click on the Stop Recording button. The application will immediately return to a screen displaying a list of scripts in a tree view on the left, and a summary of the script on the right. This view allows you to create notes describing what the script does, and also allows you to direct the requests to a different server:

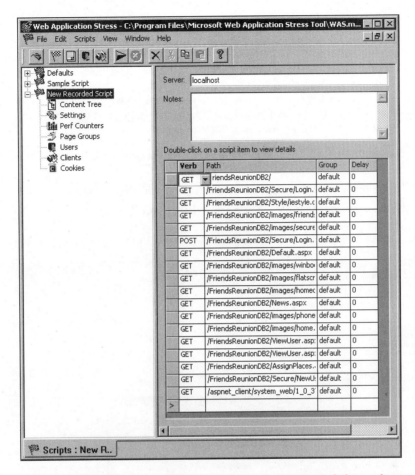

Looking at the screenshot above, you'll notice that each request made by our browser has been recorded. This is a list of every item that the browser requested from the remote server, including the images on the pages, and the initial 'default' request if you didn't specify a full file name.

Try It Out – Configuring your WAS Report

Once you have recorded your test, you'll want to configure it to generate the type of report you're after. WAS allows you to configure your test so that it simulates the number of users you want, for the period of time you desire.

1. Click on the **Settings** tree item under your script. This will provide a list of configurable options for your test. We won't spend a lot of time on this screen, but we do want to set a few things up for our example:

- ❑ **Test Run Time** section – set the period that your test will run for to 5 minutes.
- ❑ **Request Delay** section – check this box to include a delay between requests.

2. The next thing that we want to do is to set up some performance counters that we'll monitor during our test. To do this, click on the **Perf Counters** tree item, and then on the **Add Counter** button at the right-hand side of the WAS interface – at which point things should start to look familiar. (You'll recognize this dialog box from our previous discussion of the Performance tool.)

First of all, you need to set the **Computer** to the server on which the web application will be executing. Obviously, this will be the machine whose pages you were browsing when you created the script. Then, we want to add some items:

❑ Under the **ASP.NET Applications** object, add the **Requests Succeeded** and **Requests Failed** items.

❑ Under the **Memory** object, add the **% Committed Bytes in Use** item.

❑ Under the **Processor** object, add the **% Processor Time**.

Your screen should then look something like the one in the screenshot below:

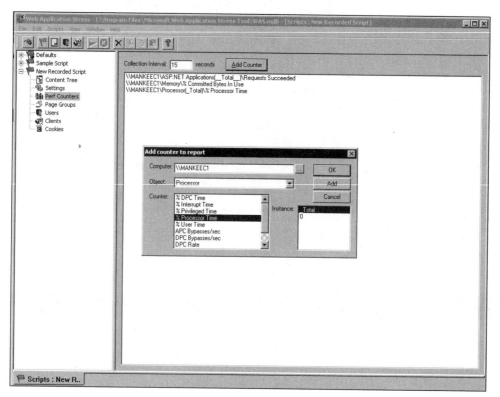

3. Once you've finished adding all of your counters, click the **OK** button on the **Add Counter** dialog. This will return you to the WAS console.

4. We have now recorded the actions we want to perform, we have told the application how long we want to test our application, and we have told WAS what information we want to collect while executing this request. It's time to execute our sample script. To do so, click on the Scripts menu, and choose Run from the options provided. Your script will begin executing, and you'll see a progress bar indicating how much time your test has remaining:

5. Once this script has completed, you can see a report of the results by going to View | Reports in the menu bar. On the reporting screen, WAS displays another tree view of all the scripts that have been run. Under each script name is a list of the dates on which that report was run. In our example, select the report you last ran under the script you last created. Clicking on the script date itself will provide you with a text-based overview report.

6. Expanding the tree, you should find several report views – one of which is the Perf Counters report. This report displays the results of the performance counters as they were collected during execution of the script:

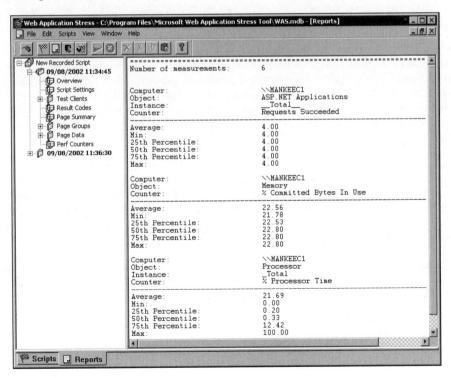

How It Works

In this example, we set up a simple example that demonstrated basic use of WAS. We installed it on a remote workstation, and created a script to make requests against a server on another machine. When it executes a test, WAS does two things. First, of course, it requests the items recorded in the script. Second, it samples the performance counters on the remote machine that we specified in our configuration. WAS compiles the results from these two actions into the report we saw above.

Reading the report can be a bit daunting, but the most important thing to note is that for each performance counter, there is an average, a minimum, and a maximum. These three figures give you the best indication of the resources your application uses, at the level of stress you provided in WAS.

As well as indicating whether your requests have succeeded or failed, the counters we've included will tell you how much memory you have in use, and how taxed your processor is under load. A good rule of thumb is that if either of these counters reaches 80% of its capacity, you should consider making some performance changes to your application, or scaling your application and providing some more resources. However, that's certainly not a hard-and-fast requirement, as we're about to discuss.

Aims of Stress Testing

Once you've decided to subject your application to stress testing, it's not usually a good idea just to jump in and start testing. The point of stress testing is to find weak points and bottlenecks, with the intention that you can take steps to address them, or at least list them as known 'features' of your application. Before you even open WAS, you should determine what results you wish to receive. Different phases of your application's life cycle will require different types of testing. As such, each stage of testing should be planned out ahead of time.

Planning for testing begins when you determine what you want to test for. You may wish to load your application until processor utilization reaches 90 percent. Alternatively, you may wish to see how far you can push your site until memory utilization reaches 85 percent. These percentages are not significant; the point is that you need to set goals, and maximum tolerable utilization levels. Whatever your boundaries are, the ultimate goal is to determine at what point a user's experience with your application is unacceptably degraded due to the load on the system.

There are actually two approaches to testing. The first we have already touched on: testing for maximum possible load within the boundaries that we've determined to be key to maintaining an acceptable user experience. This type of testing can take a long time, and requires many modifications and executions of a test script to obtain the data you need. The second approach to testing is to determine whether your application will support an expected load. This type of testing is usually accomplished when an application is already in use, so the expected load can be determined by monitoring the use of a previous revision of an application.

The first approach is probably the most useful. If you can determine your application's limits, then you can react properly as use of your application grows. If you test for only the current load, you have no idea how well your application will perform if the load increases. Proper decisions regarding additional hardware can only be made if you test your application to its limits.

Microsoft has included an example script on the download site that will continue to create and execute tests until processor usage reaches 90 percent. This script can be modified to include the benchmarks and counters you want.

Caching for Better Performance

The Web was created to solve the problem of sharing information in a manner that didn't require a specific type of computer or a specific type of operating system. As the formatting capabilities of HTML improved, however, and people started adding back-end processing into the mix, the strain on web servers grew exponentially. In particular, one situation in which performance started to suffer is where applications executed the same command over and over again, for frequently viewed pages.

To improve performance, it's possible to store common output from these 'back-end' processes. The data to fulfill subsequent requests can then come from static storage, rather than requiring the processor to crunch the same code again, and again, and again. It's further possible to tailor the frequency with which the back-end processes are run, to account for data that changes hourly, daily, or weekly. The idea of storing results to prevent unnecessary execution is known as **caching**. Proper use of caching in your applications can give an enormous boost to performance and scalability.

Aside from being able to cache data on the web server, caching can also occur in other places: on proxy or caching servers, and in the browser itself. Each of these locations has its own advantages and disadvantages in terms of development, ease of implementation, and controllability of the data.

- ❑ Caching on the browser allows the user to control how often they want a new version of the data to be presented. However, if the developers of a page intend for data to be updated more frequently than that, this is not a wise choice.

- ❑ Caching on a proxy server is simple to implement, but requires more hardware and administration than browser caching, as well as causing a bit more network traffic.

- ❑ Caching on the web server allows the most control over what is cached, and how often you update the data.

Caching Types

Not only are there three places where caching can occur, but also ASP.NET provides three types of caching for a developer's use: output, fragment, and data caching. Having these different types allows precise control over exactly what gets cached, and makes best use of server resources. Instead of simply caching everything, you can intelligently add and remove data from the web server's cache, as you see fit.

Output caching (also known as page caching) is the most basic form of caching available in ASP.NET – it just involves the storage of the results of a dynamically generated page. Each subsequent request for that page will then come from the cache, rather than requiring further processing. For highly data intensive pages, this could be the best alternative to executing numerous data requests every time the same page is requested.

A more specific type of caching is **fragment caching**, which allows the programmer to cache only the portions of a page that do not often require updates. For instance, a page may be dynamically generated for the most part, but have a control or other information that changes on an hourly, daily, weekly, or even monthly basis. For instance, while each page on an e-commerce site may have dynamically generated information about the items in the store's catalog, each page may also have a header with the site's logo and standard menu that never change.

Finally, we can store single pieces of information in a cache, in a way that's very similar to how we stored information in the `Application` and `Session` objects that we saw in Chapter 7. Storing pieces of information in this manner is known as **data caching**.

In the next few sections, we will discuss each of these caching types in detail. You'll see how to configure each of them, and of course how to use them in your applications.

Output Caching

We've already let the cat out of the bag on what output caching *is*, but we certainly haven't told you everything there is to know. At the very least, you need to know how to use output caching, and how to control what triggers a page to be cached again.

Since output caching deals with a whole page at a time, it stands to reason that we should be able to configure each page differently. Similarly to the way that the `<%@ Page %>` directive at the top of your ASPX pages controls some of the pre-compilation information about a page, the `<%@ OutputCache %>` directive allows you to control the caching functionality of that page. *All* caching configuration at the page level will happen within this declaration, which can also be made in ASMX (web services) and ASCX (user controls) files.

Controlling the Output Cache

Of course, adding this directive to the page will do nothing by itself. You must specify how you want the cache to be controlled – and to do that, you must add some attributes. The following attributes work with `@OutputCache`, and we'll consider them all here:

❑   `Location`

❑   `Duration`

❑   `VaryByParam`

❑   `VaryByHeader`

❑   `VaryByCustom`

Location

Do you remember when we said that caching could occur in three places: the client, a proxy, or the web server? It makes sense, then, that you should be able to specify where you want to cache a page. This is done with the `Location` attribute, which allows you to provide one of five possible settings.

Setting	Description
`Client`	This setting tells browsers that they *may* cache the page, if they wish to. This is implemented by sending headers to the client browser according to the setting you choose. It's important to note that the user may have their browser set not to cache your page anyway.

Setting	Description
Downstream	This setting tells proxies that they may cache the page if they are configured to do so. This is also implemented with headers in the response. Again, remember that the caching may not occur if the proxy or caching device is not set to hold this page.
Server	This setting is fairly simple – it saves the output of the page on the server. This setting gives you the largest amount of control over what's cached and what isn't.
Any	With this setting, the output is cached on the server, but headers are also added that allow the page to be cached at either the proxy or the client browser – or both.
None	This setting disables caching for this page. You may want to use this setting if data is constantly changing and you do not want users to see old data. However, any user controls inside the page that have an @OutputCache directive will still be cached according to the settings they have chosen.

This attribute *must* be specified when you use the @OutputCache directive. If it's left out, the page will throw an exception when accessed.

Duration

Another setting that's always required when you use the @OutputCache declaration is the Duration attribute, which specifies the number of seconds that the page should be held in memory. This parameter allows pages that are accessed most frequently to be cached, and those that are not used very often to be removed from the server's cache memory. The page will throw an exception if this attribute is excluded.

The last attribute that's *required* when using @OutputCache is VaryByParam, which we'll examine in the next section. However, it's necessary to introduce it now, so that you can see how to implement caching on a page. The code you'd need to set the cache for a page to be held in memory on the server for ten minutes would be written as follows:

```
<% OutputCache Duration="600" Location="Server" VaryByParam="none" %>
```

VaryByParam

We used this attribute in the previous section without explaining it. Now it's time to describe it properly. Imagine a page whose appearance will vary depending on a value that's passed in a query string, or on a form. (For example, you could have a page for displaying the items from a catalog that accepts an item identifier in the query string.) If you were to cache this page blindly, you'd always display the same item, regardless of the identifier passed. VaryByParam allows you to cache different versions of a page, depending on a given parameter. With our item identifier example, you could use VaryByParam like this:

```
<% OutputCache Duration="600" Location="Server" VaryByParam="itemid" %>
```

397

We can go further. Imagine now that your site hosts several catalogs, with the possibility of different catalogs containing items with the same ID. Now we need to vary the output based on more than one parameter, but that's no problem. We can list as many parameters as we want, separated by semicolons, like this:

```
<% OutputCache Duration="600"
    Location="Server" VaryByParam="itemid;catalogid" %>
```

If you want the cache to store a different page for every possible parameter that can be passed to it, you can use an asterisk as a wildcard character in the VaryByParam list. You might want to do this if your page is generated differently as a result of every parameter that's passed to it:

```
<%@ OutputCache Duration="600" Location="Server" VaryByParam="*" %>
```

Lastly, you may decide that you don't want the page cache to be affected by any parameters passed in. You can accomplish this by using the example we used in the first place:

```
<%@ OutputCache Duration="600" Location="Server" VaryByParam="none" %>
```

VaryByHeader

VaryByHeader is very similar to VaryByParam. With it, you can cache different pages based on one or more of the headers that are sent in a request to a page. For instance, if you wanted to cache different versions of a page based on the language settings of the client browser, you could use the Accept-Language header. The syntax is very similar to VaryByParam:

```
<%@ OutputCache Duration="600"
    Location="Server" VaryByHeader="Accept-Language" %>
```

VaryByCustom

The last change that we can make to output caching is done with the VaryByCustom attribute. With this, you can choose what gets stored in the cache by using custom logic and business rules. This attribute can also take the value "Browser", which will result in different pages being cached based on the client browser's major version and browser name.

The name that you specify as the value for your VaryByCustom attribute will be used in a function in the Global.asax file. But before we take a look at that, here's an example of the syntax for VaryByCustom. It's not very different from what we've seen before:

```
<%@ OutputCache Duration="600"
    Location="Server" VaryByCustom="ClientJavaScript" %>
```

In this snippet, we've given a value of "ClientJavaScript" to our attribute. At this moment, however, that value means nothing at all to ASP.NET, which has no idea what to do about it – except that it should pass it as an argument to a function called GetVaryByCustomString() in the Global.asax file. Such a function might look something like this:

```
Public Overrides Function GetVaryByCustomString( _
                      ByVal context As HttpContext, _
                      ByVal arg As String) As String
   Select Case arg
     Case "ClientJavaScript"
       Return "Client JavaScript = " & context.Request.Browser.JavaScript
     Case "SomeOtherValue"
       Return "Some other value was passed here"
   End Select
End Function
```

GetVaryByCustomString() is a member of the System.Web.HttpApplication class, from which the Global class defined in Global.asax inherits. However, we have to override it in order to provide our own functionality. The value that we placed in the VaryByCustom attribute is passed as the arg parameter to this function, and we can place logic in it to determine what happens after the argument is evaluated. (In our example, we've used a simple Select statement.) The code we've written here simply writes a string to the browser letting us know whether the client supports JavaScript.

Try It Out – Output Caching

Now that we've seen a few code snippets demonstrating different ways to affect the cache, you're probably anxious to see how all of this works together. Let's write some demonstration code that shows the effects of caching.

1. To the ASP.NET application we were experimenting with at the start of the chapter, add a page called CachedTime.aspx, and set it to be the project's start page.

2. Drag a label onto the page, and set its ID to lblTime. Switch to HTML mode and add an @OutputCache directive to the page, as follows:

```
<%@OutputCache Location="Any"
              Duration="600" VaryByParam="itemid;catalogid"%>
```

3. Now switch to the code-behind view for this page, and add the following code to the Page_Load() subroutine:

```
Private Sub Page_Load(ByVal sender As System.Object, _
                      ByVal e As System.EventArgs) Handles MyBase.Load
   ' Put user code to initialize the page here
   lblTime.Text = Now()
End Sub
```

4. Go ahead and rebuild the application, and then browse to this page in your browser of choice. Make a note of the time that's displayed, and refresh the page. You should find that the time does not change.

5. Try modifying the request by passing one of the parameters we specified in our `VaryByParam` attribute. Your new request may look something like one of the following:

```
http://localhost/Chapter12/CachedTime.aspx?itemid=1
http://localhost/Chapter12/CachedTime.aspx?itemid=2
http://localhost/Chapter12/CachedTime.aspx?catalogid=3
http://localhost/ Chapter12/CachedTime.aspx?catalogid=2
```

How It Works

Each request that differs only by the `itemid` or `catalogid` parameter will cause a new version of the page to be cached – each new page generated will contain the current date and time. If you try going back to the first URL you entered, you'll find that the time on this page has not been updated. For each different set of parameters you pass to this page, the output will remain the same for ten minutes (that is, 600 seconds).

Fragment Caching

As you may recall, fragment caching is the ability to cache only certain portions of a page. An additional difference from output caching is that you can't set the location of the cache to be on a proxy, or the client browser – the cached fragments *must* reside on the server. Fragment caching requires us to create pages that are made up of bits of cached code and bits of dynamic code, and only on the server is it possible to put such things together.

When we say that portions of a page may be cached, we're referring to the idea that we can segment a page, and choose which of those segments are cached. This segmentation occurs through the use of user controls, which we covered back in Chapter 3. To tell the server that a user control should be cached, we use the same basic technique that we used to cache an entire page. This time, however, we put the `OutputCache` declaration in the user control itself, rather than the page that contains it.

VaryByControl

When you use the `OutputCache` declaration in user controls, the `VaryByParam` attribute is still supported, as is a new one called `VaryByControl`. This attribute deals with the web form controls of the user control – you might, for example, want to change the output of a user control based on some setting that has been chosen within the user control. This attribute can use a single value, or a list of values separated by semicolons. The strings you use must be the fully qualified names of controls within the user control.

Try It Out – Fragment Caching

The `VaryByControl` attribute can sound a bit confusing until you get your hands on some code. In this example, we'll create an ASP.NET application and add a user control to it. It is in that control that we will implement fragment caching.

1. In Visual Studio .NET, create a new ASP.NET application called `UsesSelector`, and add a user control to the project named `StateSelector.ascx`.

2. Drag a **Label** web control onto your user control, and change its ID to `lblDate`.

3. Next, drag a **DropDownList** onto the user control, giving it an ID of `StateDDL`. Click on the `Items` property in `StateDDL`'s property list, and add a few US state name abbreviations.

4. Switch to HTML view, and you should see something similar to this:

```
<%@ Control Language="vb" AutoEventWireup="false"
                        Codebehind="StateSelector.ascx.vb"
                        Inherits="UsesSelector.StateSelector"%>
<p>
  <asp:Label runat="server" id="lblDate"></asp:Label></p>
<p>
  <asp:DropDownList id="StateDDL" runat="server">
    <asp:ListItem Value="CA">CA</asp:ListItem>
    <asp:ListItem Value="OH">OH</asp:ListItem>
    <asp:ListItem Value="NY">NY</asp:ListItem>
    <asp:ListItem Value="SC">SC</asp:ListItem>
  </asp:DropDownList></p>
```

5. Add the following line to the very top of the HTML file for the user control:

```
<%@OutputCache Duration="600" VaryByControl="StateDDL" %>
```

6. Switch back to the design view for this user control, and double-click anywhere on the form to bring up the `Page_Load()` event handler for the control. Add a line to update the `lblDate` label with the current time, as follows:

```
Private Sub Page_Load(ByVal sender As System.Object, _
                      ByVal e As System.EventArgs) Handles MyBase.Load
  lblDate.Text = Now()
End Sub
```

As you can see, we've created a user control, and set the `VaryByControl` attribute to the name of the drop-down list. In the event handler, we set the time so that we can see that the page is indeed cached, and not just being executed again to return new output.

7. Let's set up a way to test this control out. Rename the usual `WebForm1.aspx` page for this project to `TestFragmentCaching.aspx`, and open it up in the design view.

8. From the Solution Explorer, drag the ASCX file onto our form. Next, drag a **Label** onto the page, and give it a new ID of `lblPageDate`. Lastly, drag an HTML 'Submit' button onto the page.

9. Double-click anywhere on the web form to bring up the code-behind page, and add the following line to the `Page_Load()` event handler:

```
Private Sub Page_Load(ByVal sender As System.Object, _
                     ByVal e As System.EventArgs) Handles MyBase.Load
    ' Put user code to initialize the page here
    lblPageDate.Text = Now()
End Sub
```

10. Now you should be able to test the project, so build it, right-click on the TestFragmentCaching.aspx page, and choose **View in Browser** from the menu. The output should look something like this:

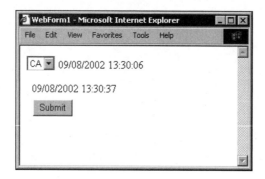

How It Works

The first time this page is executed, the time for the user control and the time for the page are exactly the same. Try refreshing the page a few times, however, and pay close attention to the difference between the user control time and the page time: the user control is being cached, but the page is being executed every time the button is clicked. Next, try changing the state to something other than your first selection. Click the **Submit** button again, and notice that the time for the user control has changed to the current time.

Clearly, the fragment caching we've demonstrated in this example is very basic – we wouldn't really want to cache a user control just to keep from calculating the time over and over again. However, imagine that our application had a database that listed all of the cities for a given state, and that our user control had a data grid that displayed this data depending on the state selected. If we fragment-cached this portion of our page, the query would be executed once, and then the results cached for as long as we specified. This would have significant performance benefits, because a query wouldn't be executed every time the page was hit.

Cached Controls Cannot be Programmable

An important thing to note about cached controls is that they are not programmable from their parent page or parent control. If you attempt to execute code against a cached control, you'll get an error. This restriction exists because cached controls don't have instances of a class to code against. Once a fragment (or a control) has been cached, additional requests for the page do not produce instances of the user control until the duration time has been exceeded. Attempts to bind to properties of the cached control, or otherwise manipulate the control from the parent container, will result in an ASP.NET error.

Data Caching

We've arrived at our final data caching type, and this is one that shouldn't cause us too much further difficulty. Data caching is not very different from what we saw back when we were programming with session and application variables in Chapter 7 – it simply allows us to store anything, from a data grid to a simple string or integer value, into a variable. Using the instance of the `System.Web.Caching.Cache` class that's available to all ASP.NET web applications, the syntax for adding data to the cache is as simple as:

```
Cache.Add("MyVariable") = "This is my cached data string"
```

Or alternatively, you could store an object like this:

```
Cache.Add("MyObjectVariable") = MyDataSetObject
```

Cached data has a significant advantage over session and application variables, in that it allows added functionality including the use of dependencies, expiration, and callback support. We'll go over each of these items in detail in this section.

Dependencies

Dependencies allow you to remove data from the cache based on differences between files, the current time, or keys:

- ❑ File-based dependencies will make an item in the cache invalid when a file or files change. If we were to import data from a flat file or an XML file, for example, we could cache the data retrieved, but force the application to reload the data if the file or files changed.

- ❑ Time-based dependencies expire items at a specified time. This can be set to something like "two hours from now", or you can reset the time every time the page is requested. On the absolute scale, the cached data will become invalid at the time you set, regardless of its usage pattern. On a sliding dependency, the duration of the cache is extended for as long as the page is being requested. This means that if a page is constantly requested, the cached data could remain in the cache indefinitely.

- ❑ A key-based dependency has the same ability as a file-based dependency, and allows us to make the data for one cache variable invalid should another cache variable change. If we were holding two datasets in the cache, for example, we could arrange things so that should one dataset change, the other is forced to refresh too.

> Note that for items to take advantage of *any* of these dependencies, you need to use the **Add()** or **Insert()** methods of the **Cache** object when placing information into it.

Caching Priorities

We mentioned that it's possible to set a time-based dependency for our cached data, and this is quite true, as we'll see in a moment. However, the server has the right, should it need to do so (say, it's running low on memory), to delete cached items before they have 'officially' expired. If you have a strong preference for one item to remain in the cache at the expense of another in this situation, you can give it a higher **priority**.

Now, adding an item to the cache with a given priority has a fairly simple syntax:

```
Public Function Add( _
    ByVal key As String, _
    ByVal value As Object, _
    ByVal dependencies As CacheDependency, _
    ByVal absoluteExpiration As DateTime, _
    ByVal slidingExpiration As TimeSpan, _
    ByVal priority As CacheItemPriority, _
    ByVal onRemoveCallback As CacheItemRemovedCallback) As Object
```

For example, let's say that you wanted to store a dataset in the cache that will expire 30 minutes after the last request for the data. Let's also say you wanted this to be a cached at a very high priority. Your code might look something like this:

```
Cache.Add("UserData", MyDataSet, Nothing, Nothing, _
          TimeSpan.FromMinutes(30), Caching.CacheItemPriority.High, Nothing)
```

Most of the parameters for this method have been passed in as Nothing, *because we don't need them for our purposes here. At this point, we don't want to set a dependency, and nor do we want to set an absolute expiration time.*

The line of code above simply adds a dataset called MyDataSet into a cached variable called UserData. After thirty minutes of inactivity, this data will be removed from the cache. If, in the interim, the server needs to free up some memory, any other items in the cache with lower priorities than this one will be deleted first.

Summary

In this chapter, we have presented you with a few ideas with the aim of whetting your appetite. We discussed how performance and scalability are different, but work together to present a favorable user experience in your web applications. We also discussed the fact that making your applications perform more efficiently can save you money on software as well as hardware, because your need to scale application tiers diminishes with better performing applications.

To achieve better performance, we need to be able to determine the load that our site can handle. We want to determine at what point our user experience has the potential to fall away. Using the Web Application Stress tool and performance counters, we can determine how use of our application affects the server's resources, such as memory and processor utilization.

Lastly, we discussed the various uses of caching to increase performance. By caching the output of parts of our application, we can limit the amount of processing that needs to occur to present pages to the user. We can limit what is cached, and even cache different versions of our application pieces, based on different configuration parameters that are available to us.

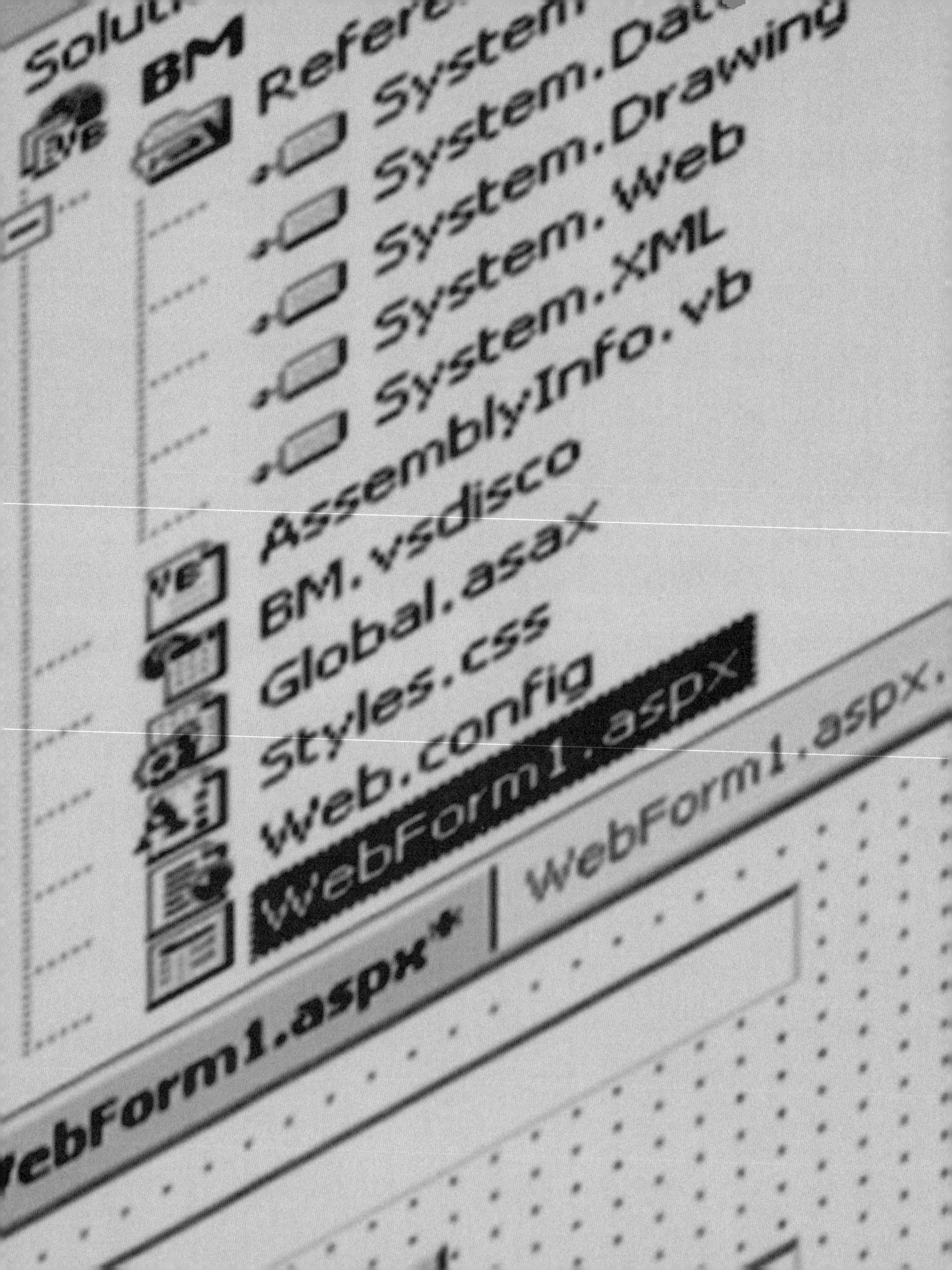

Solut...

BM

Refere...

System.Dat...

System.Drawing

System.Web

System.XML

AssemblyInfo.vb

Assembly

BM.vsdisco

Global.asax

Styles.css

Web.config

WebForm1.aspx

WebForm1.aspx* | WebForm1.aspx.

WebForm1.aspx*

Publishing Web Applications in .NET

Let me paint a picture of an idyllic development department, where that application for an important customer has been completed on time and it does exactly what they asked for. However, there are some final hurdles that must be overcome before the customer gets to see just how good your application is:

❑ It must be installed on their system

❑ A way of updating the application to fix bugs or add new functionality must be devised

❑ Common installation components must be located and made use of

❑ The application must be configured for the customer's system and existing applications

It's all too easy to underestimate these tasks, perhaps partly due to the excitement of finally completing the application successfully. The customer's first sight of the finished application is likely to be during this install phase, so if it goes horribly wrong, as it sometimes can, the customer will start with a bad impression of you and your product. For instance, if you say that it will be installed in 30 minutes and it takes three days, or you get into obvious technical problems, it will not fill the customer with confidence. As a consequence, they may be less inclined to invest the effort required to make use of the features that you've slaved many a weekend perfecting.

This scenario is not uncommon in the computer industry. Within this chapter, we'll provide an insight into the intricacies of the installation process, to give an understanding of the issues concerned with deployment. Our aim is to make deployment familiar and take the mystery out of it, because in programming, familiarity breeds confidence and with confidence comes the ability to experiment. Experimentation brings experience of each system's installation and configuration requirements; experience that is often the best way to make sure any particular installation runs smoothly.

There are a number of techniques and methods for installing .NET client applications, web services, user controls, and so on. In this, the final chapter, we'll examine the following:

❑ The architecture of web applications and web services, as they'll appear on our customers' machines

❑ Creating a Web Setup project with Visual Studio .NET, and assessing the functionality it gives us by default

❑ Customizing a Web Setup project through the addition of dependencies, conditions, and custom actions

By the end of this chapter, you'll have gained a good understanding of how to get the web applications you've developed with the help of this book into the hands of your clients, with the minimum of fuss.

Deployment that Works

Microsoft does not have a great name when it comes to deploying applications. Before .NET, there was the Visual Basic Package and Deployment Wizard, which just about did the job, but left much to be completed by the programmer. So when Microsoft said that it had incorporated a fully featured deployment manager into Visual Studio .NET, many of us took it with a pinch of salt. However, Microsoft's publishing and deployment system has now come of age, and poses a serious threat to the market shares of those third-party installers that have thrived in the absence of a suitable product from Microsoft.

The Multi-Tier Approach

In many places in this book, we've discussed environments in which client processes (such as validation, or mouse/cursor movement between form fields) are separated from application functionality (such as database updates, and business rules). These distinct layers, or tiers, can be encapsulated in separate VB.NET projects, possibly residing within a single solution. This idea of multi-layered development also continues into the design of a satisfactory installation process, and each tier will generally require its own installation project so that each can be installed on a separate machine.

For distribution and version control, things are also much easier if we keep each development tier separate. If we did not, then a web application would have a single entry in the Add/Remove Programs dialog box in the Control Panel. This would mean that when all installation tiers are installed on the same machine, and we later wish to install a newer version of one component of the application, we would be forced to uninstall and reinstall the entire product. If, on the other hand, we can uninstall (say) just the client, other parts of our application, such as the web service, will continue to work. This helps to minimize downtime and disruption for the customer.

The other important benefit of keeping each tier separate is that it allows us to install a project across several machines easily. Each machine could have its own setup program, allowing us to create powerful systems that process the application between them. Each system could be upgraded separately without affecting the others.

ASP.NET Web Service Architecture

Before we look at the Visual Studio .NET web application installer project, we'll run through the process of installing a web service and an ASP.NET application project manually. In this way, we'll gain an understanding of the underlying architecture involved, and make the installation process easier to understand. To do this, we'll create a minimal web service project that uses the 'Hello World' web method that's generated automatically by Visual Studio .NET when a web service project is created.

Create a new ASP.NET web service project, and call it `Hello World`. When the new project has been set up, open the default `Service1.asmx` file, remove the comment marks from the three lines of code highlighted below, and build the project.

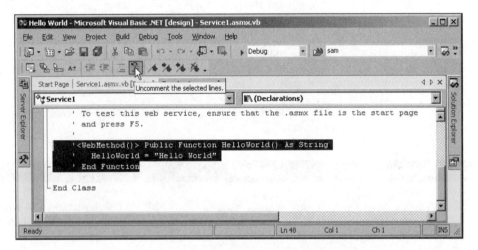

If you choose the **Show All Files** button in the Solution Explorer, you'll see that even this rudimentary project consists of a good many files:

However, a lot of these files are needed simply to maintain the project, and the files listed below are the only ones that are *actually* required to run the application:

❑ `bin\Hello World.dll`
This is the project DLL file, containing the functionality representing the project's classes, methods, declarations, and so on. In this case, there is only one class (`Service1`), with one method (`HelloWorld()`).

❑ `Service1.asmx`
This file represents the application entry point. It contains an HTML link to the VB.NET code for the web service (the code-behind page), and also tells the .NET Framework the name of the class that contains this web service's functionality. However, the VB.NET code in `Service1.asmx.vb` is not needed when the application is running – it has already been compiled into `Hello World.dll`.

❑ `Web.config`
This is the XML file containing ASP.NET configuration information for the web service. It can be changed without recompiling the entire project so that, after installation, it can be altered without affecting the other two files mentioned above.

That's it! It's a pleasant surprise that despite the sophistication of the .NET Framework, projects often do not result in a plethora of files and directories.

Try It Out – Manually Installing a Web Service

Now that we know exactly what files are actually *required* by an ASP.NET web service, let's check out the process of manual installation. We'll assume here that the destination server has IIS installed, but does not yet have the .NET Framework – after all, it could be that your new application is your client's first encounter with .NET.

1. The first step is to install the .NET Framework runtime files, so that IIS can recognize and process ASP.NET file types such as `.asmx`, `.aspx`, and so on. Microsoft provides a freely distributable package that installs the files required to run any .NET application (not just web applications). This file is called `dotnetfx.exe`, and it can be found on the Microsoft Windows Component Files CD that is supplied with Visual Studio. It should be located in a subdirectory named `dotNetFramework`.

Running this file installs all of the essential run-time libraries for VB.NET, C#.NET, and C++.NET, such as `System.dll`, `System.Data.dll`, and so on.

> The version of `dotnetfx.exe` that's run on the target machine *must* be the same as the version of the Framework on the machine that compiled the original project. This is one of the most common causes of installation failure, and something we'll come back to in Step 6.

2. Next, copy the essential web service files that we listed earlier into a new directory somewhere on the target server's hard disk. The convention is to make this a subdirectory of `c:\Inetpub\wwwroot`, although in fact you're free to put it anywhere you fancy. Here are the files to copy again:

```
bin/Hello World.dll
Service1.asmx
Web.config
```

You need to make sure that you place the `Hello World.dll` file in a subdirectory called `bin`, but there's no need to register it. All `.dll` files in the `bin` folder will be registered automatically when `Service1.asmx` is first called.

3. Now we need to create a virtual directory, using the target server's IIS manager. (This utility can be found at **Programs | Admin Tools | Internet Services Manager**.) Right-click on **Default Web Site** in the left-hand pane, and select **New | Virtual Directory**:

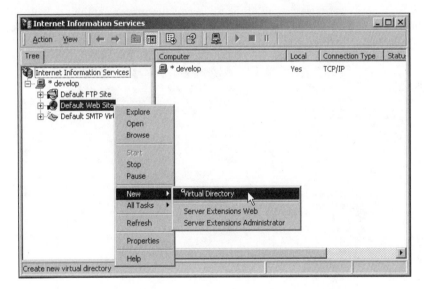

4. The Virtual Directory Creation Wizard will now open. Press the **Next** key on the welcome screen, and then enter the alias for our virtual directory – this will be used in the URL for the web service. Use `wrox_manual` for this example. On the next screen, enter the path to the folder where the web service files were placed in the previous step:

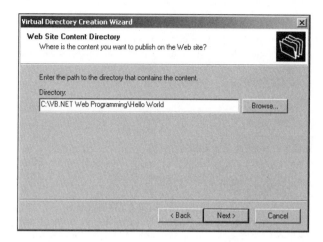

5. Finish off the Wizard, leaving all of the file access permissions at their default settings. The IIS manager should now show our new virtual directory under the **Default Web Site** node, as in the following screenshot:

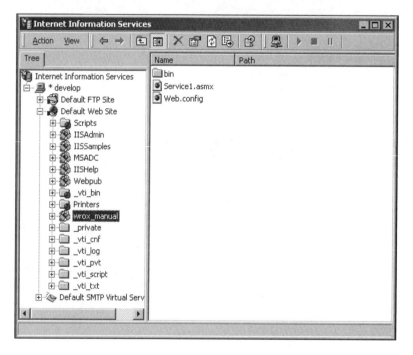

6. Before we verify that the web site is installed properly, we're going to digress a little, and show you a good way to check the version number of the .NET Framework. Right-click on the `wrox_manual` virtual directory, and select **Properties**. Then, press the **Configuration** button that appears in the lower right of the resulting dialog. This brings up another dialog that shows the file type associations for the .NET Framework runtime components.

Scroll down a little to the .asmx and .aspx extensions. Files of this type are run using the aspnet_isapi.dll, which will be located in a directory named after the version of the Framework to which it belongs. Below, we can see that the Framework version is 1.0.3705:

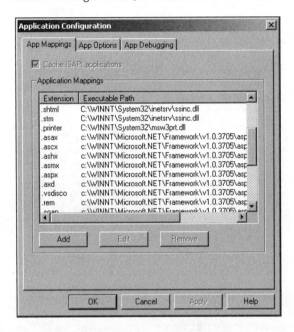

If you're getting problems when you run an application on the server, but it runs fine on the development machine, it's worth checking that both machines use exactly the same version number. If not, then you'll need to upgrade either the target server or the development machine. If you upgrade the development machine, then you'll also have to rebuild the project.

7. Diversions aside, we're now ready to test the installation. Open your web browser, and type in the following URL:

http://localhost/wrox_manual/Service1.asmx

The web service's test page should now appear, allowing us to invoke the HelloWorld() web method. Because Service1.asmx is nothing more than a link to the executable code residing in Hello World.dll, whenever the code changes and the project is rebuilt, all that needs to be done to deploy the latest version is copy the new DLL to the bin directory. Equally, any changes to (say) Web.config will take immediate effect, without our having to reinstall or even restart the web application.

ASP.NET Web Application Architecture

Now that we've covered web service architecture and installation, let's see how ASP.NET web applications differ. You'll be glad to hear that their architecture is equally elegant, and that they follow a similar installation procedure.

For this example, we'll add a new ASP.NET project to the current solution, and deploy it manually to the same `wrox_manual` web site. Right-click on the `Hello World` solution in the Solution Explorer, and choose **Add | New Project**. Create a new web application with the name `HelloClient` – this application will be a client that consumes the `Hello World` web service:

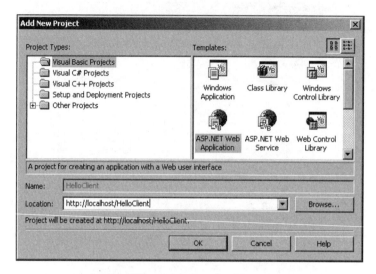

We now need a reference in the client project to allow it to use the web service. Right-click its **References** folder, and select **Add Web Reference**. Type in http://localhost/wrox_manual/service1.asmx, or copy and paste the URL from your web browser, and click **Add Reference**. Your solution should now look like this:

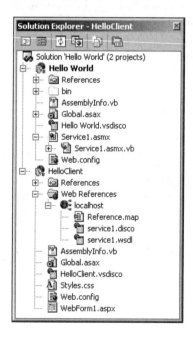

Now let's place some simple functionality in the client application that uses the `Hello World` web service. The `WebForm1.aspx` page should be open in design mode in Visual Studio .NET, so double-click anywhere on the blank form to open the code view at the `Page_Load()` event handler. We just need the following two lines to invoke `Hello World` and display the message it returns:

```
Dim oObj As New localhost.Service1()
Response.Write(oObj.HelloWorld)
```

We're using `localhost` here to qualify the web service class in as straightforward a fashion as possible. We could have chosen a more identifiable name had we wished to do so.

Try It Out – Manually Installing a Web Application

Manually installing an ASP.NET web application is a very similar process to that for a web service. This time, however, we won't need to set up a virtual directory in IIS – we'll just use the `wrox_manual` one that we created earlier.

1. Rebuild the `Hello World` solution to complete our preparation. This time, the essential files for the application are:

❑ `bin\HelloClient.dll`
This is the project DLL that contains the compiled program functionality for the application's classes, methods, declarations, and so on.

❑ `WebForm1.aspx`
This is the server endpoint for the application; it contains any HTML required to render the page. The `Page` directive in this file tells Visual Studio .NET where the VB.NET code-behind page is, and also tells ASP.NET at run time where to find the compiled code. Again, the VB.NET code file (`WebForm1.aspx.vb`) is not required while the application is running, as it has already been compiled into the `HelloClient.dll` file.

❑ `Web.config`
This contains configuration information in XML format for the web application. As with web services, details in this file can be changed using a regular text editor without having to recompile the project.

2. Simply copy these three files to the physical directory that you specified for the `wrox_manual` virtual directory, again placing the DLL in the `bin` subdirectory. This means that the existing `Web.config` file will be overwritten, but this is not a problem – both web projects can use the same `Web.config` file quite happily.

3. All of the files should now be in place to run our very simple web site. Load up Internet Explorer and type in http://localhost/wrox_manual/WebForm1.aspx. When the page finishes loading, the words **Hello World** will appear, indicating that the web service was successfully called, and its output was sent to the `Response` stream by ASP.NET.

How It Works

Looking back at this process, we have taken the minimum files produced by Visual Studio .NET for an ASP.NET web application project (client tier) and a web service project (functionality tier), and copied them to our server directory.

Note that when combining projects into a single web application at installation like this, a compatible naming convention for the projects is essential. In this case, our two projects have distinct names (Hello World and HelloClient), so the two DLLs created by Visual Studio .NET can be placed in the same bin directory without name clashes.

The Visual Studio .NET Web Setup Project

Having looked at the steps required to install the above applications manually, you should now have a good understanding of what any automated installer is going to have to do. With that in mind, let's move on to take a look at the project type Visual Studio .NET provides for installing web applications. This creates a single Windows installer file (with a .msi extension), which offers the user an easy-to-understand GUI for directing installation, including copying files, configuring the environment, and registering components.

A **web setup project** combines the output files from other Visual Studio .NET projects, along with any other necessary files, to create an installation file that can be copied and run on the system that is to host the application. Just for reference, the following table contains descriptions of the other setup project types available in Visual Studio .NET:

Project Type	Description
Setup project	Used to create installers for Windows Forms applications (rather than web applications).
Merge module project	Creates a "merge module" project, which can be reused in several installations. If certain groups of components or files are common to many applications, then instead of copying such files one by one into each setup project, we can create a merge module containing a group of files. We can then use the merge module in our setup project to include the common files it contains automatically.
Setup Wizard	Not really a setup type in its own right, this option simply asks a series of questions in order to determine the setup project type to use. It also sets certain options within the setup configuration.
Cab project	Creates cabinet files that can be downloaded to a legacy web browser. This project lets us package ActiveX components so that they can be downloaded and installed onto a client's machine from a web site with a single click.

In Visual Studio .NET, setting up web setup projects (and indeed any of the other setup project types) is very simple. A series of editors is provided to alter each stage of the installation – they let us specify amendments that should be made to the registry, any extra files that are required, the look of the installation interface, and so on. When a web setup project is selected in Solution Explorer, the mini-toolbar at the top changes to display an icon for each of the editors available for this project. The icons correspond to the setup editors as follows:

Icon	Editor Type	Description
	File System Editor	Allows creating, updating, and property setting for all physical files, assemblies, and folders of the project to be installed.
	Registry Editor	For creating or modifying values in the registry of the machine where the application is being installed.
	File Types Editor	Can create specialist file type commands that assign processes to specific file extensions. Particularly useful if the installed project uses a unique file suffix.
	User Interface Editor	The installation process comprises a series of dialogs that are displayed to the user. This editor allows us to amend or delete any of the default dialogs, or to create new custom dialogs of our own.
	Custom Actions Editor	This editor allows us to specify additional processes that should be performed on a target computer during installation. The process can take the form of a DLL, an executable, a script file, or an `Installer` class file within the solution. For instance, we could create a Visual Basic script that creates a new administrator, or a SQL script that creates a database.
	Launch Conditions Editor	The installer uses conditions specified in this editor to determine whether the installation can proceed, or dependent components need to be installed first.

Try It Out – Creating a Web Setup Project in Visual Studio .NET

We'll now create a Visual Studio .NET web setup project that installs the same projects as we just installed manually.

1. Open the `Hello World` solution we've been using, and add another new project to it. This time, select **Setup and Deployment Projects** in the left-hand pane, and choose **Web Setup Project** in the right-hand pane. Give it the name `HelloSetup`, and click **OK**:

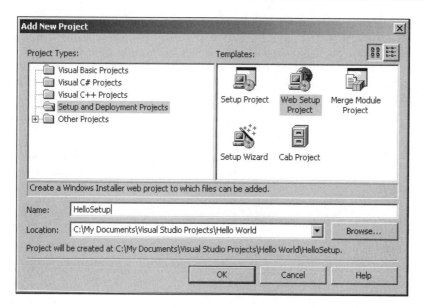

Once the `HelloSetup` project has been created, the solution should look like this:

2. After our investigations in the first part of this chapter, we know that the minimum files needed to run both our example projects are:

```
bin/Hello World.dll
bin/HelloClient.dll
Service1.asmx
WebForm1.aspx
Web.config
```

At this point, we use the file system editor to add these files to the `HelloSetup` project, so that the installation process knows that we want to install these files on the target web server. With the `HelloSetup` project selected in Solution Explorer, click the **File System Editor** icon on the toolbar to open the view shown here:

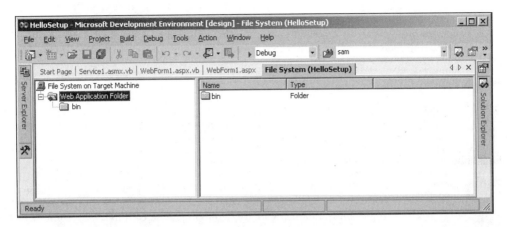

This editor uses a layout similar to Windows Explorer, with a tree view on the left, and a detail pane on the right showing the contents of the item selected. To include a file in the installation process, we just need to place it in the appropriate folder in this editor. By default, the bin folder is already created, ready for us to place our executables and DLLs.

The editor lets us drag any file on our system directly from Windows Explorer and place it in the desired folder. Also, we can specify that we want to use the primary output files created by other Visual Studio .NET projects. For web service projects and web application projects, the primary output is the .dll file that we've already seen.

3. To add the primary output from our two projects (that is, bin/Hello World.dll and bin/HelloClient.dll), right-click **Web Application Folder** in the tree view, and select **Add | Project Output**, bringing up the following dialog:

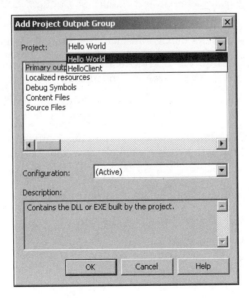

The **Project** drop-down at the top of this dialog selects the project whose output we want to use, from those currently attached to this solution. The list underneath the drop-down shows the different types of project output that we can choose, as described in the table below:

Output Type	Description
Primary output	The compiled executables and libraries (that is, files with a `.exe` or `.dll` extension). This does not include any DLL or EXE files that have simply been copied into the selected project.
Localized resources	The locale- or culture-specific resources for a project.
Debug Symbols	The debugging files produced for the project, with either a `.dbg` or `.pdb` extension. These files are required for debugging the project remotely; they are not required if you are deploying a live commercial system.
Content Files	HTML and other client-facing files, such as `.asmx`, `.aspx`, `.asp`, `.htm`, and images. Also includes files such as `Global.asax` and `Styles.css`.
Source Files	These comprise the code-behind files for `.aspx` and `.asmx` pages, as well as other code files such as modules and classes.

It's also worth noting the **Configuration** dropdown:

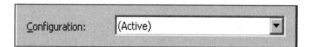

This specifies whether the setup project should use **Debug .NET**, **Release .NET**, or **(Active)** output for the selected project:

❑ **Debug .NET** – Includes debug information, making it slightly less efficient

❑ **Release .NET** – Strips out all code that uses the Debug command (see below), and also omits all debug information from compiled code

❑ **(Active)** – Uses whichever one of the above two configurations has been set as the default configuration for the project you're attaching to this installation

It is also possible to select different code for different configurations at compile time, on a conditional basis. Look at this simple example as an illustration:

```
#If Debug Then
  Response.Redirect ("http://localhost/Kitana.aspx")
#Else
  Response.Redirect ("http://www.dogandmistress.com/Kitana.aspx")
#End If
```

This **compilation directive** (as denoted by a leading hash character, #) is similar to a regular if statement, except that it controls the behavior of the compiler itself, rather than the compiled code. If we were to select Debug .NET in the Configuration box above, in this example the command would redirect to the Kitana.aspx page via localhost. If not, the full URL would be used.

4. So, we want to add the primary output of the Hello World and HelloClient projects, which will include the .dll files in the installation, and we also want to do the same for the content files of both projects. This will include the .asmx and .aspx files, along with their associated Web.config file.

With each project selected in the Project drop down in turn, select both Primary Output and Content Files (by *Ctrl*-clicking on each), and click OK. Leave the Configuration drop down at (Active). Once you've done this for both projects, the HelloSetup project should now look something like the following screenshot:

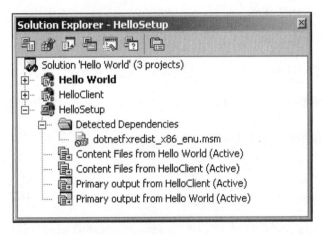

Each of the entries for the content files and primary output are really just shortcuts to the project output files themselves – a sort of list of what files are to be included, rather than duplicates of each individual file. This means that the setup package adjusts itself to use the latest version of the included files at the time the installation project is built, reducing the danger of producing a setup package that installs an out-of-date application.

5. That's all we have to do to create a simple installer for our projects in Visual Studio .NET. To build the setup package, right-click the HelloSetup project in Solution Explorer, and choose Build.

How It Works

When Visual Studio .NET builds a setup project, it creates all of the files that we might need to distribute in order for our users to install our .NET application. We can see what these are by browsing to the directory that we specified when the HelloSetup project was created. This directory will contain two sub-folders called Debug and Release. The compiled code for the installation will be found in one of these folders, depending on your default project configuration – 'debug' by default. The files created are as follows:

❑ `InstMsiA.exe`
This installs the Windows Installer for Windows 9x and Windows ME. This is only needed if installing onto a machine that does not already have Windows Installer, or has a version prior to version 2.0.

❑ `InstMsiW.exe`
This installs the Windows Installer for Windows NT, Windows 2000, and Windows XP. Only needs to be included if installing onto a Windows NT, 2000, or XP machine that does not have the latest version of Windows Installer.

❑ `Setup.exe` and `Setup.ini`
This program will examine the system to determine whether Windows Installer itself needs to be installed. If so, it will run the appropriate file of the two above, depending on the operating system running. It will then install our application, using the next file described. All of the other installation files must be in the same folder for this to work correctly.

❑ `HelloSetup.msi`
This package contains all files for installing our application with Windows Installer. If we are certain that the required version of Windows Installer is already installed on the target machine, this is the only file that we need to distribute.

Windows Installer is the default method of installing any Windows application, and Microsoft and other third-party software vendors throughout the industry use it. We'll come back to `HelloSetup` shortly, and have a go at running it, but there are a couple of things that we need to address first.

Dependencies and Outputs

When the `HelloSetup` build process has finished, you'll find that a couple of warnings have appeared in the Visual Studio .NET Output window. One of these relates to the `dotnetfx.exe` file that we mentioned earlier, and is there because the target machine must have the .NET Framework installed:

> WARNING: This setup does not contain the .NET Framework which must be installed on the target machine by running dotnetfx.exe before this setup will install. You can find dotnetfx.exe on the Visual Studio .NET 'Windows Components Update' media. Dotnetfx.exe can be redistributed with your setup.

This is something that we dealt with when installing manually by copying the `dotnetfx.exe` file to the target machine and running it to install the .NET Framework. Now that we're having Microsoft do the work for us, we can include the `dotnetfx.exe` file in the installation package – but bear in mind that `dotnetfx.exe` is 40Mb in size. As it only needs to be installed once, it's probably better to install it manually on the target machine.

It is, however, extremely easy to include the `dotnetfx.exe` file with your installation. If you were watching closely earlier, you may have seen a file with a similar name, `dotnetfxredest_x86_enu.msm`, under the detected dependencies of our setup project in Solution Explorer. To include this file in all subsequent installation packages, we just right-click this entry, and uncheck Exclude:

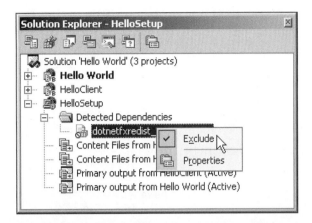

The reason why the file has this name and the `.msm` extension is that it's a **merge module**, which means that it contains one or more files required for a specific and common installation process. If you want to, you can view the files it contains by choosing **Properties** from the context menu shown above, and clicking the ellipsis button for the `Files` property:

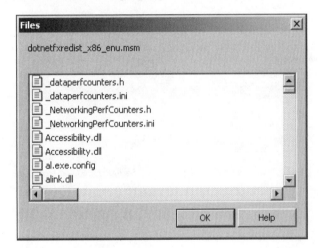

This list includes all files within the merge module, including any that come from merge modules that this module contains. We'll return to look at merge modules in more detail at the end of the chapter.

At this point, you may be wondering how Visual Studio .NET knows that components like `dotnetfx.exe` should be included in the first place. Some files (such as Visual Studio .NET DLLs) need other files to be already installed if they are to work correctly, and these other files are called **dependencies** of the file that requires them. We can view the dependencies for the files in our install list by right-clicking the appropriate file in the right-hand pane of the file system editor and choosing **Dependencies**. The following is the list for the primary output of `HelloClient`:

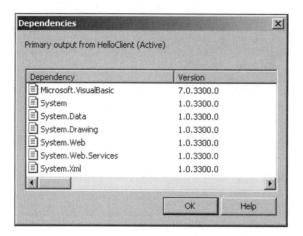

This dialog shows the components (and their versions) this file or package is dependent on, and which must therefore be included in the installation for it to operate correctly. All of the above dependencies are installed with the .NET Framework (by running `dotnetfx.exe`).

Another thing that's often useful to know is exactly what files are actually being included with the installation, especially in the case of these shortcuts to project output. To see the actual files being installed, right-click on an item listed in the right-hand pane of the file system editor, and this time choose Outputs. Here's what we get with this option for the `HelloClient` item:

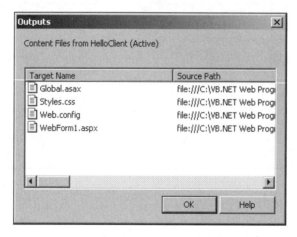

Being able to see the outputs and dependencies for files is invaluable when creating an installation project for a web application.

Using the Setup Project

Having explored the ins and outs of a Visual Studio .NET Web Setup Project, we'd better find out what actually happens when we use the files it creates. Once we've seen that, we'll have a clearer idea of the aspects we might want to change.

Try It Out – Running the Installation Package

This example does exactly what the title suggests: we're going to move the installation files to another folder, and see how they behave.

1. Copy all of the files from the Debug directory to a single folder. (Ideally, this should be on another machine, although you can use a directory on the development machine for testing purposes.) This can be any directory at all – it doesn't have to be where the web application will finally reside. During the manual setup process, we had to set up IIS ourselves, but that won't be necessary this time.

2. Once the files are on the target machine, just double-click Setup.exe to start the install process. If the target machine doesn't already have the correct version of Windows Installer, it will automatically be installed. This process isn't particularly interesting to us, as it's not something we can change, so we'll concentrate on the installation of our Hello World and HelloClient programs.

3. The installation process now follows the standard Wizard format of a sequence of dialogs, asking a series of questions. In our case, all we need to do is confirm the details of the virtual directory for IIS, including the port to use:

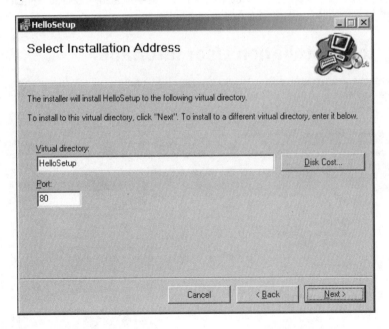

4. Leave these settings at their defaults, and click **Next**, and then **Next** again, to complete the installation process.

5. Now we can test that the installation worked OK. Load up Internet Explorer and enter the following URL:

http://localhost/HelloSetup/WebForm1.aspx

You should see the Hello World message displayed, just as it was for the manual installation.

How It Works

The installation process simply creates the specified virtual directory in IIS, along with a directory with the same name as the setup project in the `Inetpub\wwwroot` directory. If you browse to this directory, you'll see the files that were installed by the installation:

```
bin\Hello World.dll
bin\HelloClient.dll
WebForm1.aspx
Web.config
Global.asax (new)
Styles.css (new)
```

As you can see, these files include the same ones that we installed earlier, manually. In addition, the `Global.asax` and `Styles.css` files that Visual Studio .NET automatically creates for all web applications have also been copied, although our particular application doesn't require them (that's why we didn't need to worry about them during the manual installation we performed earlier).

Amending the Installation User Interface

We've now seen the user interface that Visual Studio .NET creates for the installation process by default, but we can change it to insert new dialogs or delete existing ones by using the user interface editor, shown below:

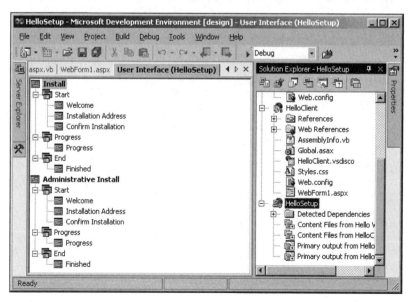

This editor is split into two sections: the upper is for changing the main installation process, and the lower for the "administrative install". The former is used in almost all situations; the latter only for installations onto a network or shared folders:

❑ Install
This section details the user interface for installing from either the `.msi` file, or a network-ready installation. (A network-ready installation is one that has been installed to a network drive using the `msiexe.exe` Microsoft Installer command that we'll look at shortly.)

❑ Administrative Install
This section pertains to the interface to use when a system administrator uses the `msiexe.exe` command to install the application to a network drive, ready for other users to install from later. We can alter the user interface to suit the requirements of the administrator – for example, we may wish to allow the administrator to install to any network location, but to restrict the users' installation to a specific path. In such a case, we would disable the Installation Address dialog in the Install section, but leave it intact under Administrative Install.

Each of these two sections is itself split into three:

❑ Start
Dialogs that appear here will be displayed before installation takes place, and include welcome screens, validation screens, folder browsing, custom actions, and so on.

❑ Progress
This section contains dialogs that will appear during installation, such as a progress bar. Only the Progress dialog may be placed within this section, and it may only feature once.

❑ End
The dialogs here will be shown once the installation has completed, to display things such as a simple completion message, details of documentation, or where to check for updates.

Before you get too enthusiastic about the possibility of adding custom dialogs to various stages of the installation process, you should know that, as with other, third-party installers, the functionality they allow is very limited. In the case of Visual Studio .NET, such dialogs can only perform a specific task, and/or simply pass on user-entered values for use during the installation. These might be used to make crucial decisions related to the installation, or to provide values to place in the registry for retrieval by the application once it's been installed.

There are *fourteen* basic types of dialog that Visual Studio .NET will let us add to the installation sequence, but be aware that you may only have one of each type within a given installation. To reduce the effect that this restriction may have, the dialogs that are used most frequently (namely checkboxes and textboxes) have three dialogs each (A, B, and C), each of these being identical in design. So, if you have already added a Checkboxes A dialog and you want to add another checkbox dialog, you could use Checkboxes B instead.

Dialog Type	Description
Checkboxes (A, B, or C)	Presents up to four choices using checkboxes. Checkboxes can be used to set conditional values that are used throughout the installation process.
Confirm Installation	Allows the user to confirm settings such as installation location before the installation gets under way.
Customer Information	Prompts the user for information that may include name, company, and product serial number. Serial information can be checked immediately against a specified template. The customer information dialog, like many of the dialogs here, is built on a template and therefore offers little in the way of customization.
Finished	Notifies the user when installation is complete.
Installation Address	Allows the user to choose the IIS virtual directory where the application files will be placed.
Installation Folder	Allows the user to choose the folder where application files will be installed.
License Agreement	Presents a license agreement for the user to read and acknowledge. *You* can set the license.
Progress	Updates the user on the progress of the installation. This is the only dialog type that can be used in the Progress section of the installation.
RadioButtons (2, 3, or 4 buttons)	Presents a dialog containing a radio button that allows the user to choose between two, three, or four mutually exclusive options.
Read Me	Displays a file written in rich text format.
Register User	Allows the user to submit registration details by running an executable that you supply. This executable can display a dialog of its own, capture the registration, and save it to disk, registry, or the Internet. This executable will most likely need the .NET runtime in order to work, and therefore it's better to place it at the end of the installation, once the runtime has been installed. Placing it at the end of the installation also lets us pass in values (using arguments) that have been collected from the user by the installer.
Splash	Presents a bitmap to the user generally representing a logo for the company or product.
Textboxes (A, B, or C)	Prompts the user for custom information using one to three textboxes.
Welcome	Presents introductory text and copyright information to the user.

Try It Out – Modifying the Installation User Interface

Let's have a go at creating our own welcome screen that takes some relevant input from the user. If it isn't already open, load up the `Hello World` solution in Visual Studio .NET, and we can make a start.

1. Select the `HelloSetup` project in Solution Explorer, and click the **User Interface Editor** icon on the Solution Explorer toolbar.

2. We're going change the files that get installed, depending on what company department the user works in. This will require a new dialog to accept a departmental name, replacing the default welcome dialog. Right-click the **Welcome** dialog under the **Install** section, and select **Delete** to remove it from the installation sequence.

3. Right-click on **Start** underneath the **Install** section, and select **Add Dialog**. We are now presented with a set of template dialog boxes to choose from. In this example, we'll use a radio button to select between two departments that we'll use later on in the installation process. Select the **RadioButtons (2 buttons)** dialog, and click **OK**.

4. By default, the dialog will be placed at the bottom of the **Start** section, meaning that it would appear last in that sequence. We need this dialog to be the first one that the user sees, so drag and drop it to just below the **Start** section name.

5. We have to change the details shown on a dialog by changing its properties – unfortunately, there's no graphical interface. Change the properties of the new dialog so that they match the ones shown below:

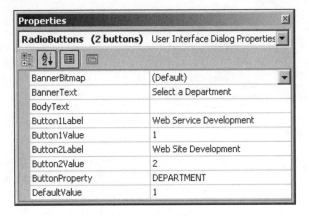

The dialog will now have two options that the user must choose between, depending on whether they are in web service development or web site development. The value returned by this choice (in either `Button1Value` or `Button2Value`) will be placed in the `DEPARTMENT` property, which can then be used like a global variable during installation, and can be read by any item capable of accessing global conditions.

6. Now that we've captured a global condition, let's use it to change the course our installation process will take. Switch back to the file system editor, and select **Content Files from Hello World** in the right-hand pane. Open the **Properties** window, and change the `Condition` property to DEPARTMENT=1:

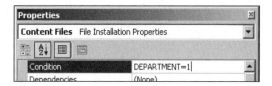

Now, the content files for the `Hello World` project will only be installed if this condition evaluates to `True`. The `Condition` property is available for many different items in the installation process.

7. Next, change the `Condition` property on the content and primary output for `HelloClient` packages to DEPARTMENT=2.

8. Finally, compile the `HelloSetup` project (which also compiles the attached projects), copy the `.msi` file to the target machine, and run it. The first dialog you're presented with will be this one:

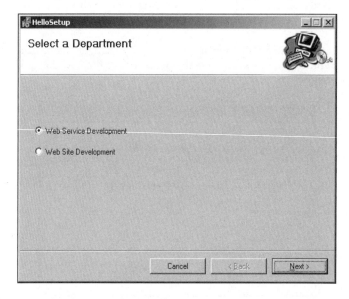

Once this choice has been made, installation continues pretty much as before, except that this time only the files for the selected application are installed.

How It Works

The choice that the user makes on the dialog that we added is used to determine the value of the internal DEPARTMENT condition, which will take the value 1 or 2 accordingly. This value is then used to decide whether to install only components for the `Hello World` web service, or components for the `HelloClient` client web application.

Be aware that the `Condition` property can also contain operands, so that if we had chosen a three-option radio button dialog instead of just two, and the third option were to offer the choice of **Both**, with a value of three, the `Condition` property for `Hello World` content files would be set like so:

```
DEPARTMENT=1 OR DEPARTMENT=3
```

A similar change to the `Condition` property would have to be made for `HelloClient` content files too. In this way, we can create a single installer that can install two different products to two different web sites (even hosted by separate machines), or can combine them into a single site.

This example illustrates how the `Condition` property can reflect choices made in the installation dialogs to decide which components are to be installed. For another, quite different example, if our application had accompanying technical documentation, we could install alternative documentation depending on the department chosen by the user at install time.

Launch Conditions

As described earlier, launch conditions allow us to specify certain environmental conditions that must be satisfied before an installation can continue, or to locate a specific value that can subsequently be used within the installation process. For instance, we could vary the installation procedure according to the value of a particular registry key already set on the destination computer, or we could change the installation process (or stop it altogether) if a certain file is missing.

We can add or modify launch conditions using – you guessed it – the launch conditions editor, shown in the following screenshot:

The launch conditions editor is divided into two sections – **Search Target Machine** and **Launch Conditions** – that work together to ensure a given launch condition is met. The default conditions for web setup projects check for the presence of IIS version 4 or higher, and the .NET runtime.

Search Target Machine

In this section, we can set up a search for a registry entry, a file, or a Windows component. The result of the search can then be used in one of two ways:

❑ As a value to be used elsewhere in the installation, like the DEPARTMENT condition we captured earlier

❑ In a test that must be satisfied before the installation can continue

The screenshot below shows the properties for the **Search for IIS** entry under **Search Target Machine**. The Property property denotes the name of the condition, which will be set to the value of the registry entry specified by the RegKey property. This gives excellent flexibility, but does require a certain amount of knowledge about the organization of the Windows registry.

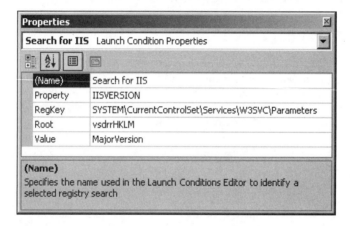

Launch Conditions

Searches for items on the target machine are *always* performed before the processing of the launch conditions in this section, so any properties set by searches can be used here. If you again check the properties of the **IIS Condition** entry, you'll see the IISVERSION property mentioned above in use:

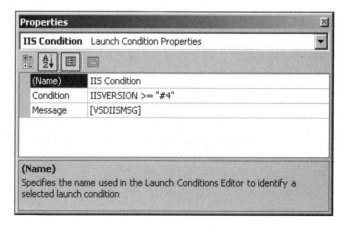

All launch conditions must evaluate to `True` if the installation is to take place, so the #4 above represents the minimum version number of IIS required in order to install the web application.

The `Message` property indicates the message to display if the condition is not met, and is set to the standard IIS error message held in `VSDIISMSG`. This is automatically localized (tailored to the user's location) when creating a localized installer. You can replace this with your own message, but such messages will not be localized automatically.

Try It Out – Setting a Launch Condition to Determine the ASP.NET Version

A perfect example of a launch condition for our example `HelloSetup` project would be to check that the version of ASP.NET installed on the target machine is the same as that used for compiling the project.

1. To begin, open the launch conditions editor using the icon at the top of Solution Explorer.

2. Right-click on Search Target Machine, and select Add Registry Search. Give it the name Search for ASP.NET:

Don't worry about the blue wavy line that will appear underneath it – this indicates that the search is not yet set up properly, and it will disappear after the next step.

3. Open the Properties window for the new search, and set the properties as in the following screenshot:

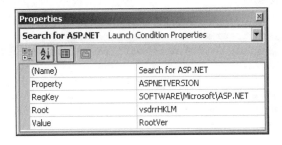

4. We now need to set up a launch condition that checks that the `ASPNETVERSION` property contains the version number of the .NET Framework on the development machine, which in this case is 1.0.3705.0. Right-click on **Launch Conditions** in the editor, and choose **Add Launch Condition**. Give it the name **ASPNET Condition**:

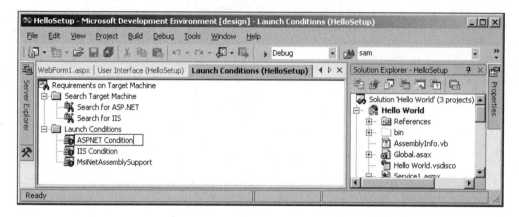

5. Set the `Condition` and `Message` properties of the new condition as shown, using the version number currently running on your development computer:

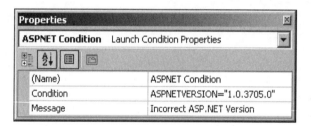

6. That's all that's required. When you now rebuild the setup project, the `.msi` file it creates will not proceed with the installation if a different version of ASP.NET is detected on the host machine.

Custom Actions

A **custom action** is an executable or a DLL that can be attached to an installer to perform a specific task that would not be possible using the standard install project dialogs. Without further ado, let's see when such a thing might be useful.

Try It Out – Creating a Registration Form

For this example, we'll add a step that asks the user for registration details, and then uses a web service to send us an e-mail containing these details. We'll use a freely available web service called `Ccomms`; others can be found at sites such as www.salcentral.com and uddi.microsoft.com – see Chapter 9 for more information on web services.

1. First, we need to create the executable that will collect the user's e-mail address and send it to a designated address using the `Ccomms` web service.

Add a new Visual Basic .NET Windows application project to the `Hello World` solution, and give it the name `RegisterClient`:

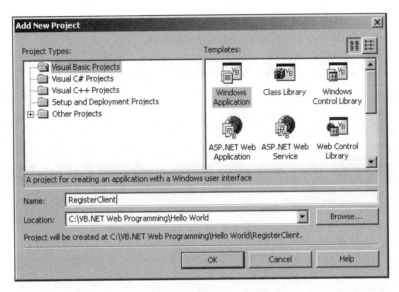

2. To keep this example quick, we'll just use a couple of simple controls on this form, although there's no restriction at all on what the executable can do. Drag a `Label`, a `TextBox`, and a `Button` from the **Toolbox** onto the `Form1.vb` form, and place them as shown. Also for speed, we'll leave the components with their default names.

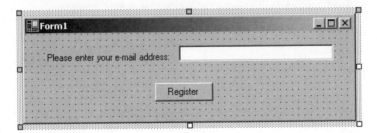

3. Now we need to add the reference to the web service to our project. Right-click on **References** in Solution Explorer, and select **Add Web Reference**. Enter the URL below, and press the **Add Reference** button:

http://www.soapengine.com/lucin/salcentral/ccomms.asmx

4. Now double-click the **Register** button, and type in the following code:

```
Private Sub Button1_Click(ByVal sender As System.Object, _
                    ByVal e As System.EventArgs) Handles Button1.Click
    Dim oEmail As New com.soapengine.www.ccomms()
    oEmail.SendEmail(TextBox1.Text, "Register <register@mycompany.com>", _
                "Automatic Registration", "Hello World Registration", _
                com.soapengine.www.MailFormat.Text)
    End
End Sub
```

> This code will simply take the e-mail address entered, and send it to the address provided. You'll need to substitute your own e-mail address if you want to see the mail that gets sent.

Now test the `RegisterClient` project by setting it as the startup project in Solution Explorer and hitting *F5*. Enter an e-mail address, and click the button. You should shortly receive a mail with the address you supplied in the body of the message.

Try It Out – Adding a Custom Action

Now that we've created the registration form, we can add it to the `HelloSetup` project as a custom action.

1. Select the `HelloSetup` project in the current solution, and click the **Custom Actions** button on the Solution Explorer toolbar.

2. Right-click the **Install** folder appearing under **Custom Actions**. Select **Add Custom Action**, double-click on **Web Application folder** in the dialog, and click the **Add Output** button:

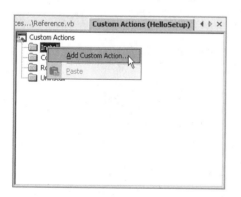
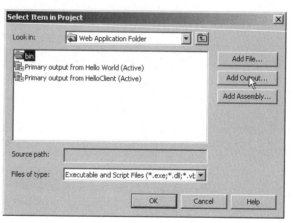

3. This opens the familiar **Add Project Output Group** dialog we used earlier. This time, we need to install the output from `RegisterClient` into our `HelloSetup` project. Select **RegisterClient** from the **Project** drop down, select **Primary output**, and click **OK**:

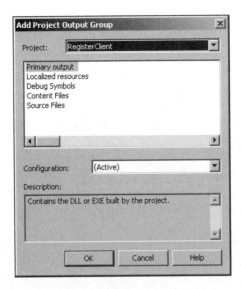

Click **OK** to close the **Select Item** dialog, and we've now added the registration application as a custom action of the installation process:

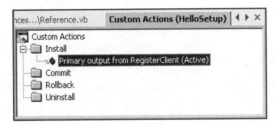

4. Before we're through, we need to set the properties of the custom action so that the installer knows exactly what file is to be run for this step. Even though our current example doesn't do so, a project's primary output can contain multiple executables or DLLs, and Visual Studio .NET needs us to be clear.

Right-click on **Primary Output from RegisterClient (Active)** and select **Properties Window**. We need to do two things: change **InstallerClass** to `False`, and then set **Arguments** to `RegisterClient.exe`:

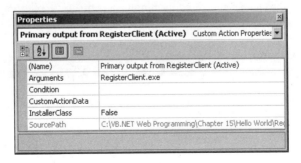

The `InstallerClass` property is used when we need rollback capabilities – that is, if we need to be able to undo any actions performed during installation, such as creating a SQL database. This option is quite advanced, however, and we won't confuse matters by looking at it here.

5. That's it. We can now rebuild the entire solution (Build | Rebuild Solution from the menu bar) and run the new `HelloSetup.msi` file. The installation now proceeds as normal, and once all files have been installed, we are presented with the following form:

Enter an e-mail address, and press the Register button.

6. An e-mail message should soon arrive in your mailbox. If we wanted to, we could create a more sophisticated web service, perhaps to register complete details, or to check for a newer version. Alternatively, we could create a standalone executable (without a web service) if we wished to perform some other action. For now though, we're done.

Merge Modules

The last thing we're going to cover in this chapter is the **merge module**. Merge modules are similar to setup projects in that they are packages that can deploy the set of files required for a given application, and they are created in a similar way. However, there are also a few subtle differences to be aware of, and we'll examine those in the forthcoming example.

One difference is that merge modules *must* be added to another setup project in order to deploy the application they contain – they *cannot* be installed independently. However, merge modules are a recognized standard, and any that we create in Visual Studio .NET can be attached to other installers, such as InstallShield.

Creating merge modules for common tasks is simple, and follows pretty much the same procedure as regular setup projects. Merge modules can also contain other merge modules, allowing us to compose a single module containing all of the elements required for running a particular application. Such modules could include database access components, Wizards, custom Visual Studio .NET project templates, and so on.

Try It Out – A Simple Merge Module

Once completed, merge modules can be added to any relevant setup project – including those of our customers – time and time again. We'll now see how to create a merge module containing the Hello World application.

1. Add a new project to the `Hello World` solution, selecting the **Merge Module Project** template from the **Setup and Deployment Projects** category. Give it the name `HelloModule`:

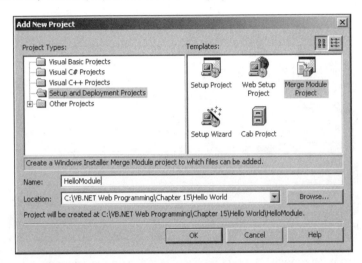

Because merge modules are not complete installations in their own right, they don't have all the editors that are available to regular setup projects. Specifically, they do not offer user interface or launch conditions editors, as these areas will be handled by the setup project that the merge module is imported into.

2. Right-click on `HelloModule` in the Solution Explorer, and select **Add | Project Output**. Add the output of the `Hello World` project using the **Add Project Output Group** dialog, just as before.

3. Build the merge module by right-clicking on `HelloModule` and choosing Build.

4. You can see the `.msm` file that has been created by browsing to the `Debug` folder within the `HelloModule` directory in Windows Explorer.

Merge Module Versioning

When creating a merge module, it is good practice to indicate clearly the version of the application it contains in its name, and also to avoid changing a module's contents unless a new version of the product is released. This is especially true if we intend our merge module to be used by third parties as part of their own installers.

There's no problem creating multiple setup projects, each containing a different version of a merge module. It is this ability that means we should endeavor to create distinct setup projects with alternative merge module versions, rather than simply update a single project. In general, we know which version of the module a setup project is using, so it's easy to notify the relevant customers that they should update their version when that becomes necessary. If we were simply to update individual DLLs in a module without changing the module's name, it'd be much harder to tell exactly what version of each DLL or executable a particular customer has.

We can set the version of a merge module by changing the `Version` property in the **Properties** window for the project. Merge modules have another property called `ModuleSignature` that provides a unique identifier for the project, for use by containing setup projects:

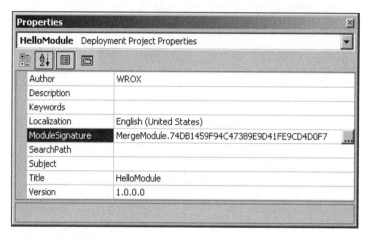

It's good practice to use a unique signature for each version of a merge module, which we can do easily enough with the dialog that appears on pressing the ellipsis button in the `ModuleSignature` property box. With both of these changes in place, the chances of version mismatches are tiny indeed.

Summary

We began this chapter by looking at the barest minimum files that are required to run ASP.NET web applications and web services, and seeing how and where they should be placed on a server that is to host them. We also saw how Visual Studio .NET can easily create self-contained installation packages for our projects that are good enough to distribute to our clients. Although we are somewhat limited in the modifications that we can make to the dialogs that the installer presents, we set up a dialog of our own that caused different files to be installed, according to a choice made by the user.

In practice, the limit on the changes possible does not constitute a problem – in fact, it encourages us to keep our install Wizards streamlined and straightforward. We don't want to bewilder our users with an array of options and choices before they've even started using our programs! The Visual Studio .NET setup project offers an intuitive way to create professional setup programs that meet all but the most exceptional requirements. We can change all the elements of the process that we are likely to want to, and tailor the process without moving too far away from the established sequence with which users will be familiar.

At the end of this chapter, and therefore the end of this book, it seems fitting to present an outline of the process of developing a web application and then preparing it for installation, with an obvious focus on the areas we've been discussing most recently:

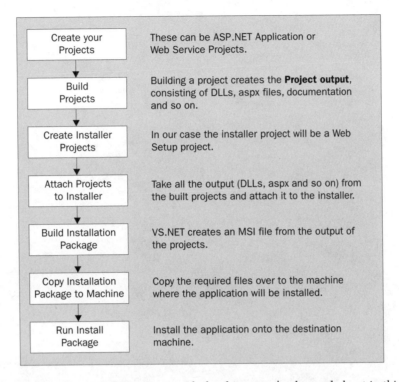

Create your Projects	These can be ASP.NET Application or Web Service Projects.
Build Projects	Building a project creates the **Project output**, consisting of DLLs, aspx files, documentation and so on.
Create Installer Projects	In our case the installer project will be a Web Setup project.
Attach Projects to Installer	Take all the output (DLLs, aspx and so on) from the built projects and attach it to the installer.
Build Installation Package	VS.NET creates an MSI file from the output of the projects.
Copy Installation Package to Machine	Copy the required files over to the machine where the application will be installed.
Run Install Package	Install the application onto the destination machine.

That, for now, really is the end. Experiment with the things you've learned about in this chapter, and of course in the rest of the book, and keep your eyes on the Wrox web site for updates, and on the P2P lists for discussions with people in the same position as you – you never know what you might find. Good luck!

Solut...
BM
Refer...
System.Dat...
System.Drawing
System.Web
System.XML
AssemblyInfo.vb
Assembly
BM.vsdisco
Global.asax
Styles.css
Web.config
WebForm1.aspx
WebForm1.aspx

WebForm1.aspx* | WebForm1.aspx...

ebForm1.aspx*

Index

X